Scenic Art for the Theatre

Scenic Art for the Theatre

HISTORY, TOOLS, AND TECHNIQUES

Susan Crabtree and Peter Beudert

985

Focal Press

Boston   Oxford   Johannesburg   Melbourne   New Delhi   Singapore

Focal Press is an imprint of Butterworth–Heinemann.

Copyright © 1998 by Butterworth–Heinemann

℞ A member of the Reed Elsevier group

∞ Recognizing the importance of preserving what has been written, Butterworth–Heinemann prints its books on acid-free paper whenever possible.

 Butterworth–Heinemann supports the efforts of American Forests and the Global ReLeaf program in its campaign for the betterment of trees, forests, and our environment.

Library of Congress Cataloging-in-Publication Data

Crabtree, Susan, 1959–
    Scenic art for the theatre : history, tools, and techniques /
Susan Crabtree and Peter Beudert.
        p.   cm.
    Includes bibliographical references and index.
    ISBN 0-240-80187-3 (alk. paper)
        1. Scene painting—Technique.   2. Scene painting—History.
3. Artists' tools.   4. Artists' materials.   I. Beudert, Peter.
II. Title.
    ND2885.C73   1998
    751.7'5—dc21   97-34534
                                                                    CIP

British Library Cataloguing-in-Publication Data
A catalogue record for this book is available from the British Library.

The publisher offers special discounts on bulk orders of this book.
For information, please contact:

    Manager of Special Sales
    Butterworth–Heinemann
    225 Wildwood Avenue
    Woburn, MA 01801–2041
    Tel: 781-904-2500
    Fax: 781-904-2620

For information on all Focal Press publications available, contact our World Wide Web
home page at: http://www.bh.com/focalpress

10 9 8 7 6 5 4 3 2

Printed in the United States of America

Cover Credits

Figure 1: Peter Beudert and Susan Crabtree painting a rendition of the drop designed by Leon Bakst for a recreation of Diaghilev's staging of *Afternoon of a Faun*, interpretation by Peter Beudert, painted at the University of Michigan Power Center Shop, photograph by Tom Rogers (courtesy of *Michigan Alumnus*).

Figure 2: Linberg Gun Shop, Grand Rapids, 1890s, Public Museum of Grand Rapids, painted by Crabtree Painting, signage painted by Grand Rapids Museum Staff.

Figure 3: Tomb, 5th Degree (ca. 1920, Don Carlos Dubois, artist) Great Western Stage Equipment Company Collection (courtesy Performing Arts Archives, University of Minnesota Libraries, St. Paul, MN).

Figure 4: Tent Encampment, Sosman and Landis Scenic Studio, Chicago. Holak Collection (courtesy Performing Arts Archives, University of Minnesota Libraries, St. Paul, MN).

Figure 5: Western town, painted by Susan Crabtree, Charlotte Pritchard, and Yasmin Entmadi; designed by Ann Mundall (Courtesy Kenmark, Inc., Las Vegas, NV).

Figure 6: Trompe l'oeil fresco. Museo dell' Accademia, Florence, Italy.

Figure 7: Assorted set pieces, *Butterfingers Angel*, painted by Susan Crabtree at the University of Michigan Power Center Scene Shop, designed by Gary Decker.

Contents

Acknowledgments

Susan Crabtree and Peter Beudert wish to acknowledge the many individuals who have helped us in the preparation of this book. The following individuals aided us in materials acquisition: Terry McClellan, Bonnie Carpenter, and Alex Adducci of Northern Illinois University; C. Lance Brockman, University of Minnesota; Barbara Bezat and Alan K. Lathrop, Performing Arts Archives, University of Minnesota Libraries, St. Paul, Minnesota; Dale Seeds of the College of Wooster in Wooster, Ohio; José Varona, Michael Anania, David Birn, Anne Mundall, Rachel Keebler, John Shack, and James Joy, Cobalt Studios; Sue Barris, *Michigan Alumnus;* Kay A. Zuris, Public Museum of Grand Rapids, Michigan. The following individuals lent valuable commentary in the manuscript preparation: Rachel Keebler and the painters of Cobalt Studios; Howard Jones, Clare Rowe, Gary Decker, Jeffrey Kuras, Anne Mundell, Dick Block, Deb Sheldon Clow, and Monona Rossol of *Arts, Crafts, and Theatre Safety.*

We would like to thank the wonderful and patient members of the Focal Press editorial department who we have worked with over the years including Karen Speerstra, Sharon Falter, Valerie J. Cimino, Tammy F. Harvey, and Jodie Allen.

Susan Crabtree would like to acknowledge the following who lent help in materials acquisition: Van Caplin, Civic Light Opera of Pittsburgh; Mark Short, Kenmark, Inc.; Bill Ebbling and Billy Drefts, Tobins Lake Studios; Bill Abbott; and Toni Auletti. Thanks to Nina Couch and Alan Woods, Lee Lash Institute, Ohio State University; Denny Nelson, Purdy Brush Company; Howard M. Wagman, The Wagman Primus Group; Robert Clack; Dave Clow; Karl and Don Armbruster; the staff of the United Scenic Artists, 829 New York, Miami, and Chicago offices for information. Thanks to Susan A. Lipschutz, Provost, George Williams, and the Center for Research on Learning and Teaching, University of Michigan for support. Thanks to my colleagues at the Departments of University Productions and Theatre and Drama, University of Michigan, for moral support. Thanks to Smudge, DuMar, Fanny, Spike, and Aunt Lou Lou for warming my lap and doing some light typing. Many thanks to Amy, David, Dave, and Deb Clow for putting up with all the disruptions. Special thanks to my father Donald L. Crabtree, I thought, I thought.

My appreciation to every scenic artist, scenic designer, and student of scenic arts I have had the opportunity to work with over the years. You may see parts of yourselves in this book. That is because I have learned everything I know about scenic artistry from you.

Peter Beudert acknowledges several individuals for their help. The following lent assistance in material acquisition: Heather Snow and Linda Hardberger from the Tobin Collection of Theatre Art at The Marion Koogler McNay Art Museum. Thanks to Paul Sypherd, Provost, and Martha Gilliland, Academic Vice President for Information and Human Resources of The University of Arizona for support. Thanks to Wendy Woods, Sandra Berthold, Lorraine Salgado, and Justine Collins of the Department of Theatre Arts, The University of Arizona, for assistance. Special thanks to Donald Beaman and John D. Ezell for their inspiration. Thanks to Clare Rowe for artwork and commentary. Thanks to Hercules and Silo for company while working. Many thanks to Anne W. Beudert for everything.

Introduction

To paint is to decorate and beautify or simply to paint a picture. We all understand that a picture also is a story. One might use the phrase "to paint a picture with words," and we know it means to tell a complete and detailed story. Painting and painted things can carry meaning and emotion from the artist to the viewer. Painting pleases the eye by making plain objects more colorful, delightful, and attractive. Painting also can trick the eye into perceiving something is there when clearly it is not.

Decorative painting has been a significant part of worldwide society since at least the Paleolithic age. We know that early cave dwellers painted their caves. They left paintings of their own existence in plain view, at eye level on the wall. Through line and color they made images describing their lives. The great early civilizations used paint to both decorate and tell stories. The Egyptian, Minoan, Persian, and Babylonian cultures have left records of their thoughts through the way they painted the rooms they lived and died in. The Greek and Roman civilizations, where theatre was a significant artistic element, used decorative painting extensively in domestic buildings as well as the theatre. We know from Vitruvius that painting in the Roman Empire was to recreate the world in a pleasing arrangement, a perfect vision. Painting was done to make believable images.

Scenic art most certainly is an ephemeral art. It rarely is intended to last very long, and few wish to go through the trouble of saving any of it. Although painted decoration has been a presence on the stage since the earliest recorded descriptions of theatre, we have virtually no examples of it until the Renaissance. As to who painted scenery for the ancients, we do not know. Their techniques, tools, thoughts, and experiences are lost to us, so we may only speculate as to their lives. Business records help us understand how the craft operated in the Middle Ages and that individuals were singled out to paint scenic pieces. As theatres were built again during the Renaissance, the process of decoration fell to the architects and painters of the day. From this background, the scenic artist and scenic designer emerged as specialists in their own right by the sixteenth century.

This book is about scenic painting and the scenic artist. Scenic painting is a unique sort of painting. It serves to decorate the large space that is the stage as well as to communicate the thoughts and feelings of the scenic designer to an audience through the work of the scenic artist. Scenic painting is unique in the scale of its work and the finished product. To paint a backdrop a thousand square feet or more in area is "normal" work for a professional scenic artist. One may forget that this sort of painting boggles the mind of almost anyone else. There is a very special quality in a nearly finished backdrop, on the ground or on a paint frame, that never fails to impress the observer and satisfy the artist.

The scenic artist is both laborer and magician. A scenic artist produces miracles of beauty, breathtaking feats of illusion, but does so wearing filthy clothes and toiling twelve hours a day. It is a quirky job, let there be no doubt to that. The hours might be unusually long and the conditions grueling. Every day of work requires extensive set-up and cleanup time. You work totally behind the scenes and rely on skills that few people may even understand. The scenic artist's work is often recognized by the public as the creation of the scenic designer, rarely your own. It is significant to remember that the formal division between scenic artist and scenic designer is a phenomenon of the twentieth century. In the 2,400 years between Aeschylus and our era, the role of the scenic designer was often indistinguishable from the work of the scenic artist.

Modern scenic artistry is a craft that maintains a distinct resemblance to its own past, at least in terms of practice. Painting is painting after all. We use brushes and paint much in the same way as in the Renaissance and Baroque periods, when scenic artistry and scenic design flourished. Scenic painting seems most often to be "handed down" from one generation to the next. The skills that make stage scenery look vibrant under stage light involve a subtle understanding of color, line, and shadow, learned by practice. Some modern scenic artistry easily might be interchanged with nineteenth-century work and vice versa. Few crafts practiced today could make a similar claim. To be a scenic artist is to know these skills and use them daily. To be a scenic artist is to fulfill the dreams of talented dreamers (sometimes, your own) and have the public pay to see them. The scenic artist participates in the business of fantasy—motion picture, theatre, television, and theme park. To those who work in these fields, it may seem like just another job, but for most it is a unique livelihood that rewards the talented and industrious and allows for great individual freedom.

Part One
The Role of the Scenic Artist

Fiorello, city drop, designed by Michael Anania, Pittsburgh Civic Light Opera.

chapter 1

Training and Working as a Scenic Artist

TRAINING THE SCENIC ARTIST

Scenic artistry has been a career choice, vocation, job path, or whatever you wish to call it, for many centuries. As you will read in Part Four of this book, the history chapters, scenic painting had a recorded presence as far back as the Greek and Roman theatre. Scenic artistry went so far as to become a highly visible trade during the eighteenth and nineteenth centuries. The skills of scenic art were not taught, but essentially handed down through families or by apprenticeship. Today the craft and art remains very active. The skills of scenic art are taught at many colleges and universities as well as through the apprentice relationship. United Scenic Artists (U.S.A.) has successfully established nationwide standards of quality through their system of examination; however, not all professional scenic artists belong to U.S.A.

A scenic artist is both a creative artist and a skilled, highly specialized technician. His or her specialty is to execute an image or series of images that make a cohesive part of a stage design. The scope of what those images might be is very broad, ranging from traditional backdrops and two-dimensional architectural detail, painted to look three-dimensional, to sculpture and pronounced aging or texturing of existing materials. Usually, a scenic artist is interpreting the work of a scenic designer from a very small scale into a large size appropriate for the theatre. The key to the craft is the ability to interpret. Most anyone can trace or mechanically reproduce an image. The scenic artist has to interpret drawings not just by their surface appearance but also by their meaning. This interpretive skill, the ability to use many different painting techniques in large scale and usually fairly quickly, allows a scenic artist to work in a variety of other similar situations like film, television, large-scale display, and interior decoration.

This chapter addresses the knowledge and skills a scenic artist ideally should have, how and where to learn these skills, and the working conditions to expect in the United States. The role of unions, the United Scenic Artists and the International Alliance of Theatrical Stage Employees (I.A.T.S.E.), also is discussed here.

What a Scenic Artist Should Know

Successful scenic artists, like many artists in the theatre, need a wide array of skills and interests to serve them in their profession. Of course a scenic artist must draw and paint very well. It is vital that the scenic artist possess knowledge in the areas of drafting, calligraphy, and sign painting. In this profession, where visual images are reproduced on a large scale, such expertise is the foundation. In addition to these skills, the exceptional scenic artist will have acquired a wide base of knowledge to support the visual images and effects that he or she is asked to create. Knowledge in the areas of art and art history, architecture, architectural and theatrical history, photography, printing and mechanical image reproduction, geometry, natural sciences, and cartography are all part of the body of knowledge that contributes to the day-to-day work of the scenic artist. A keen curiosity and good powers of observation will help put this acquired knowledge to work. Travel and experience certainly contribute to the important ability to synthesize one's knowledge of the physical world.

Drawing, drafting, and *geometry* are the framework on which visual images are created. Even the simplest blending of one color to another must have proportion to look correctly balanced. Complex images, like a perspective street scene, may be reproduced only by an artist who has comprehensive drawing and drafting skills as well as an understanding of perspective. Geometry is essential, because it provides a rational, mathematical basis for the visual arts. Classical Greek ideals of proportion and form are based on geometric rationality. These aesthetics of proper proportion and perfect form are the core of many visual images we see today.

The rules of *calligraphy* and *sign painting* govern letters and words, perhaps the most precise set of graphic images in the world. These images are familiar to all viewers. Instinctively we will recognize good or poor lettering. The rules and techniques of calligraphy and sign painting are ones with which the scenic artist must be well acquainted.

Scenic artists are dependent first and foremost on their skills as a painter. These skills must be solidly based in the fundamentals of *drawing* and *color theory,* the knowledge of *tools* and *materials,* and a variety of *painting techniques.* The scenic artist must be well versed in how painting techniques themselves have evolved. Scenic artistry is a profession where the artist might be called on to recapture the soul and substance of art from all eras in history. In one production, a scenic artist may be called on to recreate in a very large scale Rembrandt's *The Night Watch,* whereas in the next production the challenge might be to create wallpaper in the style of Andy Warhol. A scenic artist must understand the methods whereby these works were originally created to recreate them on stage. Furthermore, the scenic artist must be able to recreate these images very quickly. A scenic artist could not reproduce *The Night Watch* with the thickly applied oil-based pigment that Rembrandt used or turn to silk screening a pattern as Warhol did. So a scenic artist will have to rely on his or her knowledge of modern mediums and alternative techniques to recreate the same effect quickly while fulfilling the vision of the scenic designer.

Knowledge and understanding of the *history of art, architecture,* and *theatre* are essential to understanding what a scenic artist is called on to paint. A scenic artist needs to thoroughly know and understand the scenic designer's artistic intent behind a design so the intent comes through clearly in the contemporary artist's execution of it. Theatre is tremendously reliant on history and historical references. We work with four hundred–year-old plays as a matter of course. Although the statement a production makes, obviously, is a contemporary one, the elements of expression often are drawn from history. If relying on phrases to evoke a scenic vision such as "the cool controlled world of Vermeer" or "the vibrant palette of Matisse," all the while describing a design for *The Life and Death of King John,* the scenic artist had better know what these coded words mean. Many scenic designers describe their work in terms of other artists or artistic movements, even if no direct imitation is involved. These references are a way of describing the intangibles of design. Sometimes, the best way to put words to an image is to bring to mind the memory of a well-known image as a vehicle to convey style.

Photography is useful because it forces the photographer to consider light, both natural and artificial, in a very analytical way. Light reveals all visual images. Understanding and reproducing how surface, form, and atmosphere respond to light is the mark of a proficient painter. Interest in photography can help scenic artists look more objectively at the world they encounter. A personal stock of photographs can provide a resource of useful images to scenic artists. For example, a small album of cloud and sky photos will come in handy more often than you think.

Knowledge in the *technology* of related crafts has direct application to scenic art, particularly with computers and mechanical image reproduction. The copy machine and the computer now are irreplaceable tools for most scenic designers and scenic artists. Complex signage is easily cartooned or actually cut into many commonly used materials with the aid of a computer. Stencils of any type can be made in the same way, and a computer will aid the registration process. Digital image manipulation can aid a scenic artist in adapting paint elevations to odd sizes or creating more mechanical "looks," like dot screening. Scenic designers have used xerography and digital imaging extensively, particularly with collaged images. For the scenic artist, the copy machine provides a source for finished, or nearly finished, color images for the stage. Poster-size printers make 36"-wide color prints affordable and a reasonable replacement for hand painting, particularly when photo-realistic effects are sought.

Natural sciences such as *geology, taxonomy,* and *geography* are a means of defining our world. Geology, taxonomy, anthropology, and cartography certainly are removed from the study of painting and theatre; but for an artist responsible for painting representations and aspects of the world we live in, there is no area of knowledge that will not at one time or another prove invaluable. For instance, how often will you as a scenic artist be called on to paint stonework? Painting marble, limestone, and fieldstone are all part of the scenic artist's repertory. Understanding the science of the structure of the earth will help you in creating a faux drift marble finish as much as geometry will help you to understand architectural shapes. The same can be said of taxonomy, the classification of all organisms; anthropology, the study of the cultural development of humankind; and geography, the study of the earth's features—all areas of knowledge that will be of great value to you throughout your career as a scenic artist. Surely no one person can be expert in all these areas of study, but a general knowledge of these areas of studies, a personal library of books on various topics, and knowledge of any area of interest and study will add accuracy and depth to your understanding of the scenes that you will be called on to paint.

The experience of *travel* certainly is an obvious asset for any scenic artist, as it is an important means for understanding the world one lives in, firsthand. It is shocking the first time one goes to Italy and sees the blue sky there contrasted with the red tile roofs. Then and only then do the colors Italian blue and Venetian red make any sense at all. It is as much a part of their world as the "purple mountained majesty" is a part of the Americas. So many aspects of the world cannot be fully captured in a photograph, such as the diminutive size of an old European village or the massive quality of Manhattan building details. Travel is not just leisure time for the scenic artist; observing the variety of the world builds integrity into his or her work. Time and time again, a scenic artist is called on to fill in the blanks, make up a detail, or flesh out a piece of trim. Having a personal reserve of experience will make that work all the more interesting and authentic.

umber or a thin glaze of pthalo green. These touches are what mark the difference between adequate and excellent painting.

Formal Training

Until the twentieth century, training in the art of scenic painting was available only to the sons of established scenic artists or young men willing to work under a long apprenticeship. As in many other professions, the twentieth century has been witness to the inclusion and proliferation of women in the ranks of scenic artistry. In this same time period, scenic painting has come to be taught at many American universities and colleges, making a comprehensive exposure to the craft available to many students.

University Programs

The population boom in the United States during the twentieth century created a large university network, making postsecondary schooling available to millions of students. Many universities in the United States have adopted practical training for theatre trades into their curriculums. The growth of this system has taken place at roughly the same time as the growth of unions representing the theatrical trades. Some of the first influential American scenic designers, all U.S.A. members, established theatrical training programs at universities. Yale University established the first training program for scenic designers in the 1920s under the direction of Donald Oenslager. Yale Drama School continues as one of the finest training programs in the country, particularly in the design fields. The basic format of that program has been widely imitated throughout the

250 American universities,
ate, offer advanced training in
. Many of these offer degrees spe-
rical production at the graduate and
e level.

niversity setting may be the most logical
begin training as a scenic artist. In these pro-
, classes are available in the many disciplines
theatre, such as acting, directing, design, stage
management, and technical theatre, which will help
students understand the work done by all the contributors to a theatrical production. Most programs
include theatrical history and critical studies, which
will help create an understanding of dramatic literature. The student of scenic artistry will find that
classes in design, technical drawing, and rendering
will have a direct application to their craft.

Also, the university provides other classes that
are equally important to the scenic artist. The topics
of art, art and architectural history, painting, photography, natural sciences, and many other useful
fields of study will be available to the student in this
setting. As well as providing an excellent means to
explore many topics related to scenic painting, a university program will give the student the opportunity
to gain practical experience while working on well-
organized productions with a professional staff. Universities are a sound environment in which to enter
into the practice of scenic artistry.

Only comprehensive theatre programs offer
classes specifically in scenic artistry. Many university programs have only one class in scenic painting; some have two. Beyond these courses in the
curriculum, students with keen interest may enroll
in independent studies to continue the study of scenic painting. Students with an interest in scenic artistry often obtain a Bachelor of Fine Arts degree in
theatre or theatre production. Many students opt to
go on and obtain a Master of Fine Arts degree in
scenic design. As of the publication of this book,
only the North Carolina School for the Arts offers a
degree that includes scenic artistry and properties
painting.

Any student interested in studying scenic art
should pay a visit to the college or university
before choosing to attend classes there. Look
through the curriculum and inquire about scenic
art classes and practicums. Meet with the professor
teaching the scenic art classes and any staff scenic
artists. Tour the facilities to determine if the equipment and space available are conducive to good

painting. Gather information on some of the following points:

- Is there a paint frame or wooden deck space
  large enough to handle a full-stage drop? If not,
  chances are that drops are not done there very
  often.
- Are the working conditions comfortable and
  safe? Is there adequate light and ventilation?
- Are materials handled and stored properly? This
  will be an insight to the general working conditions and attitudes.
- Is there enough space to conduct a scene painting class?
- Is there enough time in the production schedule
  to allow for scene painting instruction, or is it
  taught only by working on productions?
- Are there good opportunities to work on productions with professional supervision? Ask to
  see photos of past productions where the design
  incorporated advanced scenic art technique.
- See a production if you can, or at least look at
  the scenery in the shop. See if the painting looks
  professional to you.
- Try to get a sense of the production schedule in
  terms of how the painting is considered in the
  construction period. If the scenic artist or technical director maintains that most of the painting
  for a production is done in a weekend, look elsewhere.

Specialized Schools or Programs

Because ongoing and intensive training in the area of
scenic art is difficult to find in college and university
settings, some students of scenic artistry opt to obtain
training in specialized schools or studios.

From the 1950s until 1988, the Studio and
Forum of Stage Design, operated by Lester Polakov,
trained scores of scenic artists and designers. But
when the studio closed its doors it left New York
City, the traditional center of scenic studios in North
America, without a place to study scenic art. As of
the publication of this book, Cobalt Studios in
White Lake, New York, is the only school currently
operating that offers training exclusively in scenic
artistry.

Cobalt Studios maintains an ongoing offering of
courses. Students can attend intensive two- to four-
day sessions, two-year programs, three-week short
courses, and frequent weekend seminars. Cobalt also

is a working scenic studio, which provides a unique opportunity for its students to work on high-profile scenic productions with well-known professional designers. The studio also serves the professional community as a hub for information about the profession, methods, materials, and techniques.

The scenic artists' union, United Scenic Artists, has sponsored painting workshops featuring the "old masters" of New York from time to time. These generally are available only to union members and are not a regular occurrence. The United States Institute for Theatre Technology (U.S.I.T.T.) annual conference often includes some scenic art demonstrations of a very high caliber. However, these tend to be not more than a half-day in length, at best.

Many European countries have followed the system, begun during the eighteenth century, of establishing a large centralized art school such as L'Académie des Beaux Arts in France. Many branches of painting, sculpture, and architecture are taught in these art schools, including scenic artistry and decorative painting. This is a much more intensive system of specialization than is found in United States universities. These schools are few in number and highly competitive.

Apprenticeships

Some form of apprenticeship, either formal or informal, is essential to learning the profession of scenic artistry. The experience and training students gain in a university situation does not fully prepare them to work in or run a professional shop. The skills and knowledge expected of a scenic artist are too vast; the confidence the scenic artist must have to perform the job with alacrity generally comes only with seasoned experience. Nearly every scenic artist has had a master-apprentice experience in his or her own training, one or two individuals who "showed the artist the ropes," or buckets in this case. No better training can be obtained than the one-on-one instruction of working with a master scenic artist for an extended period of time. The student of scenic artistry also will find that every work experience and every scenic artist encountered through the course of a career will have something of value to offer, perhaps a new technique, a different source of supplies, or even something as simple as a certain way to snap lines. Every scenic artist encountered will have knowledge to share. As one advances through one's career, this will include students as well as the old pros.

Formal apprenticeships are not common, so most scenic artists find that their first few jobs are more or less informal apprenticeships. United Scenic Artists does not have a specific apprenticeship program in scenic painting, as it does in lighting design. Cobalt Studios devotes approximately half of its curriculum for long-term students to work with actual productions in its studio. In this way, it can offer an apprenticeship in tandem with the scenic art course work. Many professional scenic artists are happy to informally instruct assistants. Most seasoned professionals are pleased to share what they know with a novice, because they themselves got their start in much the same way. Compensation may be problematic, but as the scenic artist fresh to the professional world acquires and displays skill and confidence, the pay will improve.

The three types of training of a scenic artist listed here—university schooling, specialized training, and apprenticeship—together form an excellent path to becoming a scenic artist.

WORKING AS A SCENIC ARTIST

Getting and keeping work as a scenic artist requires considerable time and effort, particularly at the beginning of your career. In the profession of scenic artistry, very few regular full-time jobs are available. When starting a career, much of the work available is on a short-term freelance basis, which means that, at first, you cannot turn down many job offers. If your work is good, one job inevitably will lead to another. Most practitioners of the theatrical trades will know someone you may have worked with; scenic artistry is no exception. Once you have worked well for one company, the word of your performance will precede you to the next job. Employers want to hire known quantities, so get known for the right reasons. If your work is good, on schedule, and within budget, you will be sought out by producers, designers, and colleagues.

When you are contracted to do a job, work a season, or are contracted to deliver a product, the company that hired you is your client. Before you work that first job, take a few moments to consider what a good scenic artist is and what an effective employee or contractor is. One of the best ways to do this is to imagine yourself in the client's place. The client hires a scenic artist with the expectation that the artist will fulfill a function or perform a task. This means a high-quality job done on time with no unnecessary problems or holdups by a person with a professional attitude. A professional attitude is very important. "I have no complaints about the work that person did but I don't have time for the hassles" paraphrases the reason often given by clients for not rehiring talented and skilled individuals. It is not enough to paint beautifully; the work should be well managed and performed with cordiality. If problems do arise, and they often do, the scenic artist should always try to find a solution on his or her own before making demands on the client. If the problem needs to be brought to the attention of the client it should be presented along with one or two suggested solutions. If your engagement has made the client's job easier or made the contract run more smoothly, there is a strong chance that you will be asked back.

The employer also must have a professional attitude. If you are working as an employee, it is the employer's responsibility to provide you with an adequate work space. The work space must be large enough to accommodate the project, have adequate lighting, a mixing area, a water source, heat in the winter, and be safe and secure. If you are working in a bad part of town, you should not have to worry about your personal safety or the safety of your vehicle. If you are working in a warehouse, you should not have to be concerned about working in a toxic environment. Chapter Four discusses the work space at length. The employer also must provide adequate materials to work with and a reasonable time frame for all the painting to be completed. If time is short, the employer must provide means to hire additional assistants. If one of these work conditions is constrained—not enough time, space, or assistants—the employer must be willing to compensate you for the extra effort you will have to make to get the project done on time. There is a saying in theatre, "We can do it fast, cheap, or good. Pick any two." Obviously, if there is plenty of time and money, the product will be beautiful. If quality is important but there is very little time, then the product will be very costly. If the employer insists the product be done quickly and cheaply then the quality will suffer.

Many scenic designers, when starting their careers, find that they also must fulfill the function of the scenic artist on the project. This is very common in educational, community, and small regional the-

atres. For this reason, many scene designers have discovered that scenic artistry is a useful skill in developing their careers.

Freelance Work for Theatre

Freelance means that you do not work full-time for one specific company; rather, you take jobs whenever and wherever they arise. This is the most common format for work in the early careers of scenic artists. One of the reasons for this is that many theatres operate on a seasonal basis and are "dark" for several months of the year. The most common seasons span the summer months, as in a summer festival or musical season, or the seven to eight months from fall to spring. This is common for many regional repertory companies or universities. Because of these split seasons, beginning scenic artists often have difficulty finding a year-round engagement. Many scenic artists fall into a pattern of working for the same companies season after season and having to move their households back and forth between the cities where the companies are based. Some scenic artists enjoy this "theatre gypsy" lifestyle, because it gives them the opportunity to see different parts of the country and to work with and learn from other professionals. Even some professional scenic artists with a permanent position at a scenic studio still work extensively on a freelance basis.

As a freelance scenic artist, you may wish to base your location in a major metropolitan area, where work is plentiful and there is enough demand for scenic artists to keep you employed year-round. Freelance scenic artists work on call for production companies, shops, or individual projects. These jobs can be for long or short periods of time. In New York City, Chicago, or Los Angeles, theatrical and movie production is an ongoing business, although there are other major metropolitan areas like Seattle and Miami, to name just a few, that can keep scenic artists very busy. Once established in such an area, you will get work continually as your reputation as an efficient and talented painter spreads. If you have poor work habits or are unreliable, your reputation will precede you and keep you from getting calls.

It deserves mention that scenic artists often are the most highly paid and sought-after of the skilled professionals in the technical theatre. A huge amount of painting is done in theatre, television, movies, and industrials, not to mention commercial display, advertising, museum display, interior decoration, and so on. Scenic artists are in demand for many reasons. Painting is faster than building, and the results are spectacular. Producers find painting very cost effective. Certainly advertisers and filmmakers find painting a background less expensive then going on location. Skilled painters have been a source for decorative work since the classic Greek theatre. It is unlikely that this demand will change in the near future.

Employment at Scenic Studios

A far simpler life than freelancing is to get a permanent job at a scenic studio. The advantages to this are tremendous. One of the most obvious advantages is that you will have a steady paycheck and, in most cases, health insurance. Because you are in a consistent work environment, you can store your tools in the shop. You can drive or take public transportation on the same route to work every morning and choose to live in a place convenient to the job site. You can use your favorite coffee mug at work and not lose it when you forget to bring it home.

The artistic advantage of working in a studio is that you will have more control over projects in development, rather than being called in the last two weeks of job in progress. The work site can be set up and maintained for the convenience of the people that work there. Your materials and tools can be arranged and installed in an orderly fashion rather than stored in cardboard boxes piled up around makeshift mixing tables. A stock of mediums, paints, and finishes can be maintained rather than sending someone out to the store every time you need something or having to scrounge around in an unfamiliar shop.

The hard part is getting such a job. Perhaps 150 full-time theatrical scenic studios are operating in the United States today. There are more theatre companies than scenic studios; however, not all of these need a scenic artist on a year-round basis. Many such theatres generally use scenic artists only on a job-by-job basis. The large theatrical scenic studios, common in the early part of this century, staffed with dozens of scenic artists, are a thing of the past. Many modern-day scenic studios have only one or two full-time scenic artists on staff, and hire extra scenic artists as needed. There are some scenic studios that maintain staffs of several scenic artists, but that job market is rather small.

As your career takes off, you may find yourself being offered more work than you can handle. This may happen particularly if you have a full-time position with a scene shop and your first responsibility is to your permanent employer or because you have a steady flow of freelance work coming in. You may be able to squeeze in a weekend job here and there, but the call for a profitable two-month-long opera job would be out of reach to you due to previous commitments. Another code of professionalism comes into play when you find yourself having to turn down work. You should assist, if you can, the client who contacted you in finding someone who is available for the job. There are two reasons for doing this. First, when you have assisted the client in locating a scenic artist that client will be more inclined to call you on another project in the future. Second, once you have attained some measure of success you should give a hand to other scenic artists just starting out in the business or in a dry spell. These scenic artists will then be more inclined to help you out at some point in the future when you are making the calls, looking for assistance on a project.

Movies and Television

Film work is one of the most lucrative options for the scenic artist in the United States. The movie industry is based primarily in Los Angeles and New York City. As in the theatre industry, employment is found through a scene shop (either on the studio lot or in an independent scene shop that caters to films) or on a freelance basis through film production companies. Work in the scene shops tends to be more steady, although many shops operate by laying off staff and then rehiring them on a recurring basis. The compensation in the shops is good, but working on a freelance basis directly for a film company or contractor to a film company usually will pay better. Film production companies are formed for the production of a specific film. Once the film is completed, the company is dissolved. One reason the pay is so high in film work is that the work week is predicated on overtime just to stay on schedule. A typical work week in feature film runs sixty to seventy-two hours. After the initial forty hours the crew makes one and a half times their regular rate. The cost of performers, directors, production staff, and studio time is so high that it is less expensive for producers to pay overtime to the film crew or the extra expense to the scene shop rather than to keep the primary people on contract longer or rent the studio for an extended period of time.

The downside to working on films is that the jobs are not steady or even predictable. Most films hire their crew very quickly with little notice. If you happen to have taken a long weekend to go to a family function you might miss a call that would have resulted in several weeks or even months of work. Frequently, there will be a call for another film in a week or so, but there might not. Toward the completion of shooting, or the wrap of a film, layoffs begin, usually with little or no warning. The general rule of layoffs is that the last person hired is the first person laid off. So most painters are aware that their employment could be coming to an end, but other than networking with other painters on the job site, there is little or no time to look for the next job. Because of the lack of warning about when the next job will start, it is difficult to plan anything during the time off.

Some painters have developed a reputation for working as a *charge painter* on films. The charge painter is the person responsible for organizing and managing the painting on the production. In most cases, the charge painter also rents a kit of tools back to the production company. The charge painter usually is contracted in advance of the production, so people in this position have the luxury of knowing where their next job is going to be at least a few weeks in advance of everyone else. Most charge painters call on a group of people who work with them on a fairly regular basis. Because of this alliance, such people also may have a few weeks' notice on where their next job is going to be. If they are good, they can feel fairly confident about gainful employment for most of the year.

The major television networks also support permanent staffs of scenic artists. As with films, Los Angeles and New York City are the largest metropolitan bases for this industry. Television series and soap operas keep many scene designers and scenic artists employed. Soap operas rely on nearly round-the-clock calls to keep up the shooting schedule necessary to produce a new segment five days a week. Many weekly television series are budgeted for one new set per segment, in addition to maintaining the standard sets for the series. Each daytime drama and television series has a small army of set painters, set dressers, buyers, property artisans, grips, and designers to keep up with the shooting schedule.

The explosive growth of cable television also has provided work for many designers and scenic artists. Scenic support for cable network feature films, dramas, talk shows, and comedy series has become as extensive as that for network television.

Freelance Work Outside of Theatre and Film

A good scenic artist will soon discover that his or her training and skill has in great measure been preparation for work in other fields. Beyond the world of entertainment lies a wealth of challenging work for the scenic artist. Commercial display, interior decoration, museum display, and restoration all call for highly skilled painters. For some, scenic artistry may be a stepping stone into these professions, and for others these options present an interesting sideline.

Contemporary interior decoration utilizes faux finishes and decorative painting techniques to a large degree. Trained faux finish painters are in high demand in residential and commercial projects. Very skilled painters also may find work as muralists. This may be in addition to services that you can offer as a faux finish and decorative painter or this profession may become your solid stock and trade.

Also very challenging are professions in restorative painting and museum display. In many ways these professions cross over the two fields, because restorers frequently find themselves working on an object or in a building of such priceless beauty that it may as well be in a museum, or they may find themselves having to recreate or touchup a surface originally created in antiquity. Some restorers with the proper expertise are employed by museums to clean and repair damaged or aged paintings. Some of the best training to be had in this profession can be obtained in Europe, where restoration studios accept apprentices. Once when visiting a small cathedral in Orvieto, Italy, I looked into the aisle where a canvas was under restoration. With elaborate care a huge canvas had been taken off its frame and laid down on a deck where it was being restored by the artists who were walking on it, their feet wrapped in cotton booties, using bamboo extensions with their brushes just as scenic artists do when they paint a drop on a paint deck.

In the profession of museum display there are a great many varied challenges. In the last few decades, museum displays have moved out of their display cases and into interactive, walk-through exhibits. Diorama painting for displays has become even more challenging as greater levels of realism are expected by museum goers. The scenic artist who is searching for a challenge might find that work in the profession of museum display with its high standards of excellence and longevity can be very satisfying.

In all of these professions there are standards and levels of expertise. The artist may start out working on small jobs or as an assistant learning the trade. The profession of restoration is not something that should be entered into without specialized training. Work in all of these areas can be very fulfilling because of the high level of quality and polish necessary for work that is to be closely scrutinized. It is satisfying to work on a project that will last for years or even decades rather than the run of a show.

Contracting Skills

Regardless of what direction your career may take, you may find yourself in the position of working as a contractor. Many of the responsibilities of the employer to the freelance employee mentioned earlier are the duties of the contractor. A contractor is the person or company that has agreed to execute the work and take care of every aspect of the project from locating the working space and hiring the staff to delivering the finished work to the client. There may be some variations in the specifics of a contract. For instance, as frequently happens in the case of scenic art contracts, the client may agree to deliver the raw materials, in this case the scenery or drops, to you. The space might be on site or it might be the space of the contractor who is building the scenery. The contract might be structured so that the scenic artist is a subcontractor and the primary contractor is building the set. However the contract is structured, you must be very clear on what are the terms.

The first step to working out a contract is to talk through the scope of work with the client. This discussion should be accompanied by information related to you on blueline plans of the project, color copies of the paint elevations, and written descriptions from the client outlining what your responsibilities will be. Then you will need to submit a bid to the client, in other words what your price will be to do the job. When you are formulating the bid for a job you must consider the following terms.

- *Space*—Who will provide the space in which the work will be done? If you provide the space, how much will the rent cost? If you are the owner of the space, what are your costs?
- *Materials*—What will be the cost of your materials? Who is responsible for purchasing and delivering these materials?
- *Labor*—Who will contract the labor? If you, what will you pay the employees? Are you paying them on an IRS Form 1099-MISC, as contract labor, or will you have to withhold and file payments for social security, state and federal income taxes, and Medicare, as well as making the employer's contribution for social security and state and federal unemployment insurance? If your employees are union members, and you have signed a contract with a union, what percentage of the labor cost do you have to pay to the union's health and welfare plan? Ethically, if your employees are long-term or permanent you should set up a health care and pension plan if they are not otherwise covered by a union.
- *Kit Fees*—What fee should you charge for the use of your tools on the job? If your crew members are bringing their own tools to the job, should you give them a kit fee? Do you have to rent or buy any tools or equipment for this job?
- *Out-of-Town Expenses*—If the work is out of town, have you looked into what your expenses will be for housing, food per diems, and transportation for yourself and your crew? Do you have to ship or rent a truck to transport tools and materials?
- *Insurance*—If you contract work on a regular basis, your may need to start carrying general liability insurance. What will this cost?
- *Accounting*—If you do contract work on a regular basis, your tax returns can be very complex. If you are withholding taxes for your employees, you also have to file quarterly statements. What are these costs?
- *Extra Costs*—Just figuring out a bid can consume a great deal of time. It also takes time and is costly to compose and send faxes, talk on the telephone, handle the billing, and enter costs in a register. Time is involved in collecting the materials and supplies for the job. If the job is not at your regular work site, time is involved in packing up and transferring materials to the work site and bringing them back again. Did you include time for clean-up after the job has been completed?

If this all sounds a little overwhelming keep in mind that, when you first begin to contract work, it will probably be on a small scale. You and an associate may decide to contract a job that you can do in someone's garage or you might accept a small contract that you can do over the weekend. Working up to large-scale, lengthy contracts can and should be gradual, so that you can learn the business. Some scenic artists find that they would rather be employed than be the employer, so that they have time to do the actual painting and do not get bogged down in business details. Contracting your own jobs will give you an appreciation for what your employers have to deal with on a day-to-day basis.

THE UNIONS—U.S.A. AND I.A.T.S.E.

Membership in the United Scenic Artists union, Local 829, is considered by many scenic artists to be one of the gateways into a successful career. The U.S.A. began in 1896 as a union for scenic artists. In 1922, the union subdivided to recognize scenic artists and scenic designers separately. Since then, the union has branched out to represent costume designers, mural artists, diorama and display artists, makeup artists, lighting designers, and many more artistic disciplines. The national representation of the U.S.A. is in the New York City office, and leadership of the union is elected from the ranks of its members. U.S.A. also maintains offices in Chicago, Los Angeles, and Miami. The International Alliance of Theatrical Stage Employees (I.A.T.S.E.) also represents scenic artists in some regions of North America for the film industry as well as theatre. I.A.T.S.E.'s primary membership consists of stagehands, projectionists, and other support trades involved in the entertainment industry.

How to Become a Member of U.S.A.

Members are admitted to the union through an examination process created and judged by union members. The examination process ensures that the members will be made up of high-quality artisans and, for that reason, always be in demand. The U.S.A. admits members by two types of examinations: Track A and Track B.

Track A is a relatively new attempt to streamline the entry process for more experienced scenic artists. The applicants' resumes are screened before they are accepted into the Track A examination. This examination consists of an extensive interview, portfolio review, and three letters of recommendation from current U.S.A. members. Applicants are interviewed by a panel of union member judges who review each applicant's work and resume. Based on these interviews, the panel decides which applicants should be recommended for entry into the union. Track A exams can be taken in New York City, Chicago, and Miami. Information concerning this examination is also available through the office in Los Angeles.

The Track B examination is the traditional path of entry into the union. This lengthy practical examination is offered in New York City and Chicago. All examination applicants are kept anonymous, known to the judges only by number, until the names of those who pass the examination and join the union are published in the U.S.A. newsletter. The exam is in two parts: one spans six weeks of preparation, the other is the on-site, weekend-long practical exam.

The first part is called the home project. Applicants are sent a packet of one to five separate projects that are to be completed and brought to the exam site. These home projects are designed not only to test each applicant's scenic art skills but their knowledge of art and architecture and their capacity to follow instructions.

The second part is the on-site practical exam, which, until recently, took place over the course of two seven-hour days. It now has been abbreviated to one seven-hour day. In this section of the examination, applicants are provided with instructions and a paint elevation to execute on a 5' × 5' flat or small muslin, drop, paint, buckets, and a mixing area, nothing else. The applicants are responsible for bringing with them any tools that they will need during the examination. At the beginning of the day the applicants are given instructions on what is to be painted on the flats or drops during the course of the day. The applicants' works are judged after completion by a panel of union members on drawing accuracy, color accuracy, technique, rendering of light and shadow, and overall ability as a scenic artist. Until recently a portfolio review was also included in the examination. Applicants also submit to the judging panel three letters of recommendation from union members. The applicants will be notified of having either passed or failed. This test is not perfunctory. Many applicants do not pass it the first time. But the test may be taken as many times as desired in subsequent years. The exam requires a nonrefundable examination fee and a refundable deposit of one-half the initiation fee.

The Benefits and Advantages of U.S.A. Membership

Once admitted, the new member pays a one-time initiation fee and then quarterly dues. In return, the union negotiates wage scales and terms with scenic studios and producers to standardize and maintain wage scales in the industry. The union also establishes basic working conditions and monitors scenic studios and producers to ensure adherence to the union agreement. The union represents its members in cases of unfair labor practices. It also monitors the activities of nonunion studios and theatres that employ union scenic artists by individual letters of agreement.

Because so many theatre artisans work on a freelance basis, the union also collects health and welfare contributions from employers hiring union members, which are invested in health insurance and pensions for the members. These benefits are available to union members who have made or have employers who have made contributions to the fund during the course of their careers. The union also provides a small death benefit to the member's survivors.

Gaining membership in the union is an accomplishment and an affirmation of one's talents and skills. The sheer fact of membership allows scenic artists to expect good compensation for their work, good working conditions, and a partnership in a very unique labor union. When seeking work, your membership will serve as a recommendation of your skills and professionalism to prospective employers. Your union membership allows you to raise your standard of compensation for work. By reporting into the union office and keeping the union appraised of your whereabouts and work situation, it can call you and alert you to calls for jobs in your area. In busy metropolitan areas, such as New York City and Chicago, union calls may be a main source of employment for union members. The union maintains an availability list of scenic artists throughout the country.

The Disadvantages of U.S.A. Membership

The primary disadvantage to union membership is the onerous cost of joining. The initiation fee, at the time of this publication, is $3,000 for Track A applicants and half that for Track B. In addition, nearly $300 is required upon entry into the union for the first six months of dues and processing fees. Membership dues cost $350 to $400 a year plus 2 percent of the gross wage earned on employment covered by union contracts. Another drawback is that the union is not fully represented across the country. In several "right-to-work" states, collective bargaining is not allowed; in these states the United Scenic Artists may only sign contracts for the individual scenic artist on a case-by-case basis. These states include Arizona, North Carolina, and Tennessee among others.

Some union representation may be available for scenic artists in these right-to-work states through I.A.T.S.E., which normally represents stagehands, electricians, projectionists, and many film technicians. However, I.A.T.S.E. does not guarantee as high a base wage standard as the United Scenic Artists.

Union membership is not a guarantee of employment. Individual members must not expect the union to find them work. If you do not happen to live in New York or Chicago but in a city where the union has no strong foothold, the union office may not be able to send you out on many work calls. You must be prepared to continue the task of finding and keeping work on your own.

The International Alliance of Theatrical Stage Employees

I.A.T.S.E. provides representation primarily for stagehands, grips, electricians, technicians, and engineers in theatres and the film industry throughout the United States and Canada. Recently, this representation has been extended to professionals from many different walks of life that are associated with the theatre and film industries. Professionals in management, promotion, first aid, teaching, and many others have been accepted into I.A.T.S.E. Members of other trades commonly associated with scenic arts skills, such as sculpting, plastering, painting, designing, animation, and sign painting, also are represented by I.A.T.S.E. locals. Local 816, Painters and Scenic Artists, located in Sherman Oaks, California, specifically represents scenic artists in the theatre, broadcast, and film industries. This local has jurisdiction in thirteen states. In addition to scenic artists and painters, members in this local also include those in professions as varied as courtroom artists and computer graphic artists.

The initiation fees, dues, and requirements for membership vary from local to local. All I.A.T.S.E. locals are governed by the International I.A.T.S.E. office located in New York City. The officials and board of the international office are elected from the membership throughout the United States and Canada. These officials are elected at the biennial conventions by delegates representative of all the locals.

chapter 2

The Relationship Between the Scenic Artist and the Scenic Designer

INTRODUCTION

The scenic artist handles much of what is important to the scenic designer's vision. The artist is in fact the primary medium through which the designer's work will ultimately be realized. The color, drawn line, texture, and style are the elements of the scenic design that the scenic artist will execute in full scale in the scenic studio. Some of these elements are tangible, some are not. The success with which these elements come together is aided by a good collaborative relationship between the scenic artist and the scenic designer.

Many scenic designers document their design concepts by painted models, paint elevations, or renderings. Therefore, there is a great deal of empathy between the scenic artist and the scenic designer. Generally, if you were to place a designer in a scenic studio, he or she would feel comfortable painting. Many professional scenic artists are also excellent designers. The easy crossover between the two disciplines might be due to the long tradition of stage design as a painter's art. This commonalty is why the scenic artist will be able, perhaps more than any other vocation in the theatre, to understand fully and interpret the designer's work.

THE COLLABORATIVE RELATIONSHIP BETWEEN THE SCENIC ARTIST AND THE SCENIC DESIGNER

Scenic artistry is only one aspect of a larger production staff who all contribute to the goal of fulfilling the scenic designer's vision. But it is the scenic artist who is the last in the chain of planners, engineers, carpenters, welders, and other artisans who create the scenery. Stage scenery is often painted extensively. It is not unusual to hear a production staff refer to a specific design as a "big paint show." These productions rely predominately on lengthy and complex paint treatments to achieve the stylistic vision of the scenic designer. In most cases it is the scenic artist who finishes the work begun by these contributors.

Although many scenic designers are accomplished scenic artists in their own right, most scenic designers do not practice these skills often enough to efficiently paint large productions. Even if the scenic designer is a very accomplished scenic artist, the constraints of the production schedule will frequently call them away from the paint shop to consult with other departments, designers, and the director of the production. Therefore, it is often the scenic artist who represents the interest of the scenic designer in the scene studio.

As the interpreter, the scenic artist is a chameleonlike artist. His or her goal is to thoroughly capture the spirit and letter of the designer's creation. The scenic artist's skill in painting must be matched by an innate sense of what looks correct in a theatre space for each production. The scenic artist must also have firm grasp of the scenic designer's intentions. The scenic designer may have had a very particular image in mind when painting the model and paint elevations. Or the designer may have created the visual image from a gut reaction to the production, toying with the paint palette and working layers over one another until a satisfactory image emerged. The designer may make several attempts before being content with the results. This is part of the scenic designer's artistic process. When it comes time for the scenic artist to recreate these images his or her efforts must be tight and purposeful.

The scenic artist must ask himself or herself a series of questions: How do I capture the spirit of the designer's work? Is the painting style to be precise and rigid or loose and impressionistic? What materials and tools can I use to emulate the style and effect of the designer's images? The scenic artist can answer these questions only with a full understanding of the scenic designer's work and visual style. This understanding comes from a knowledge of art, artists' styles, architecture, and painting techniques gathered through years of education, experience, and observation.

Working Together

Many scenic designers prefer to have a close collaborative relationship with the scenic artists they work with. This collaborative approach may even result in the scenic artist becoming an important part of the designing process. Occasionally, when a scenic designer is working with a scenic artist whose skills and talents are well known, he or she may elaborate or expand the design to cater to the scenic artist's abilities.

It is important to recognize that the scenic artist is much more than a person who enlarges the designer's paint elevations. Their relationship is true artistic collaboration. Like two good cooks creating a complex meal, their sensibilities and tastes complement one another. Comments like "a slash of red" or "just let it run" need not be defined or measured. On the other hand, finding a common vocabulary is very important. If the scenic designer asks for a "fine mist

of raw umber" the scenic artist should be certain that he or she understands the meaning of that phrase. It may be necessary to do a sample for the scenic designer's approval.

It is essential that the scenic artist and the scenic designer communicate frequently, from the initial stages until opening night of the production. This contact may take the form of formal or informal meetings, phone calls, e-mails, or whatever it takes to exchange information. Many scenic designers like to be around the shop while their designs are being painted. This is particularly true when working with a scenic artist for the first time. Many scenic artists prefer to have the scenic designer drop by the shop regularly so that they can be confident that the quality of the work is as the scenic designer had envisioned. Both the scenic artist and the designer have a responsibility to communicate with one another. A routine should be set up to ensure that this happens. It may be difficult if the scenic designer is out of town while a show is being painted, but it is not uncommon by any means. Frequent phone calls, shipping paint samples, even Polaroid photos sent via overnight mail are efforts that may seem excessive but will probably save time in the production process.

Visual Materials from the Scenic Designer

The materials the scenic designer uses to communicate information to the scenic artist are paint elevations, a painted model, draftings, samples, and references or research. The scenic designer may, but seldom needs to, provide the scenic artist with all of these. These are simply the tools and means of communication available to the scenic designer. It is the responsibility of the scenic designer to provide enough visual information to communicate completely his or her intentions to the scenic artist.

Draftings and White Models

The scenic designer expresses his or her ideas to the technical director and the construction staff through draftings and a scale model. The model may be a white model, which means that it is not painted and may only be a guide to the three-dimensional structure of the design. The draftings consist of ground plans, sections, front elevations, and detail drawings. From these the technical director and construction staff can determine the size, shape, placement, and materials of the scenery to be constructed.

The scenic artist must always be provided with a blueline set of copies of the draftings for even the simplest scenic designs. The scenic artist must have the drafting skills necessary to read plan views of the scenery. The scenic artist will use these bluelines as the guide for creating estimates of materials needed for the production, patterning the contours of profile units, determining the correct size of soft goods, drafting out the position of trim and details on hard units, and understanding the overall shape and materials used on any two- or three-dimensional scenic unit. The scenic artist also uses the ground plan and white model to assist his or her understanding of relative placement of the scenic units on stage. It is important to understand which units "play" together in the same scenes and which units need to take "focus" in the scene.

Paint Elevations and Models

The scenic designer's paint elevations or painted model, which may serve as the paint elevations, are the primary medium by which the scenic designer expresses the scenic vision to the scenic artist. These scale drawings, paintings, and three-dimensional pieces must accurately reflect the line, color, and texture of the painting as well as the style, mood, and subtlety that the designer seeks in the finished scenery. They can be very beautiful examples of painting in themselves. Some scenic designers pride themselves on their meticulous and finely detailed elevations. Sometimes, however, the elevations can be last-minute scribbles of line and color delivered to the scenic artist with references and a lengthy explanation. Usually, the finesse of the paint elevations lays somewhere between these two extremes. Scenic designers often create the paint elevations on bluelines or photocopies of the draftings that have been mounted to illustration board.

There are no specific standards for paint elevations, but some standard guidelines reflect the norm. Paint elevations must be rendered in an accurate and measurable scale so that they can be read and interpreted and measurements can be transferred. The scale of the paint elevations usually ranges from one-half inch to one inch per foot. The paint elevations should be clearly labeled. It should be noted on the elevation if the scenery is to be finished with a sheen of satin or gloss. The color, line work, and technique choices should be clear so that they can be read by the scenic artist. The elevations should be a convenient size for the scenic artist to hold and carry while working.

For complex figurative work, such as a full stage backdrop of a street scene in perspective, the scenic designer also should supply the scenic artist with a line drawing, called a *cartoon*. This cartoon is a copy of the line work on the paint elevation just before the scenic artist paints it. Normally the painting process tends to obscure the line work of an elevation, making it difficult for the scenic artist to determine how the cartoon should be laid out on the scenery. In some cases the designer may draw the cartoon on the front elevations. However, usually the front elevations are primarily for the construction crew's benefit, and the cartoon of two-dimensional images is left off to avoid confusion.

When color models are intended to be used as paint elevations for a production, the model must be designed to come apart. This way the scenic artist may use individual pieces of it while working on a specific unit of scenery. Because most scenery is painted by crews of scenic artists rather than one individual, pieces of the model will be needed at the same time in separate areas of the shop or even separate buildings. Also, it is difficult to take measurements from an assembled model, carry it around, and protect it from damage while mixing colors. I have seen many carefully assembled and glued-together models disassembled (as carefully as possible) by the scenic artists. But in spite of the care taken to repair these models, they were returned to the designer somewhat worse for wear. If a model also is the working elevation for a production, it must be clear to other departments that, once the scenery goes into the shop, the model must reside there as well.

Samples

If some of the scenery or an entire set has a specific paint treatment, finish, or texture the designer may provide the scenic artist with a full-scale sample rather than a paint elevation. Sometimes, these samples are actual pieces of wood, marble, or other material that the scenic designer would like the scenic artist to reproduce as closely as possible. Other times, the scenic designer generates the samples and passes them on to the scenic artist with an explanation of how they were produced. The scenic designer may also request or assist the scenic artist to generate paint samples so the two can confer about the paint treatment. The sample may be shown to the director for approval.

References and Research

Another effective means of visual communication the scenic designer might use is references and research. These are the visual sources that the scenic designer used for inspiration: a small brassy area on an elevation might be further enhanced by a picture of a well-aged goblet in a reference book; a picture of a deep green forest glade in a magazine might clarify how the designer intends a translucent backdrop to look when light shines through it. Or, as discussed in Chapter One, a reference might be made to the work of a specific artist that is to serve as the stylistic touchstone for a stage picture or painting technique. These references can come in the form of pictures in books and magazines, photographs, photocopies, lithographs, and as many different forms as there are reproduced visual images.

UNDERSTANDING THE SCENIC DESIGNER'S INTENT

In any case, it is unusual if a scenic designer's paint elevations and related visual information given to the scenic artist are so complete that they fully describe every detail of the finished scenery. Designers often will work in a kind of shorthand to eliminate repetitive parts of the job or, realizing that the scenic artist will grasp their intent, take shortcuts in the completion of the paint elevations. The scenic designer's work frequently is done in a reduced scale, which in itself forces the image to be somewhat simplified. Also, when working through the paint elevations or painting a model, the scenic designer may be more concerned with the overall appearance of the scenery rather than specific paint details. Part of the scenic artist's responsibility is to fill in the artistic gaps in the elevations and flesh out the details so that the painting is effective for the full-scale scenery.

Studying and Preparing the Paint Elevations

The scenic artist needs to "read" and fully understand the paint elevation and all related visual material in preparation for painting. If a crew of several scenic artists is working on a production, one of the crew is the charge painter. The charge painter studies the packet of bluelines, paint elevations, and other material from the scenic designer to ensure that he or she understands how the set is put together. Next, the charge painter should go through the paint elevations and make sure that he or she understands how the paint elevations relate to the bluelines. Often a designer will make notes in the margins of elevations or attach notes to references or samples. The charge painter should read all these notes. All reference material that relates to a specific elevation also should be attached to that elevation for later use by the paint crew. Later, when the elevations are covered with a protective coating of acetate or clear vinyl, these references, along with any notes concerning those elevations, can be mounted on a board. While looking through the packet, the charge painter will compile a list of questions to ask the scenic designer. Next, the charge painter will discuss this material and related questions with the designer.

Light and Paint

When studying paint elevations, it is important to view them in appropriate light since some lighting may cause the appearance of color variance. Color is seen as the result of light reflecting from a surface. The type of light used when viewing an elevation has a big influence over the color one will see. It is important that the scenic artist view the paint elevations in a light that is as close as possible to stage light. This is particularly important in the paint mixing area, where colors are matched to the paint elevation. It is crucial that the scenic artist be able to clearly view and match color, so that the elevation may be reproduced with the same degree of subtlety. It is essential that the scenic artist understand how scenery appears when it is under stage lighting. Furthermore, it may also be useful for the scenic artist to know if the scenery for a specific scene is seen under specific lighting moods such as moonlight or a blazing Arizona sun. These variations of lighting intensity will affect the painting techniques.

Many scene shops are lit in a completely different manner than the stage where the final painted work is to be seen. Incandescent lighting is very close in characteristics to stage lighting, but not commonly used in scenic studios for economic reasons. Standard fluorescent, "daylight" fluorescent, low-voltage fixtures, mercury vapor, high-pressure sodium, HMI, and even sunlight have color temperatures very different from stage light and will change the apparent color of a model or paint elevation (see Chapter Six for further discussion of color temperature). Often economic lighting is used throughout the shop, and the paint mixing area is the only area where incandescent light fixtures have been installed.

Interviewing the Scenic Designer

Talking with the scenic designer is important to get answers to the questions that the paint elevations themselves do not and cannot answer. Simply talking allows the scenic artist to grasp the paint process the designer used making the paint elevations or envisioned being used on the scenery. It also establishes how various samples and references sent with paint elevations fit in. This interview may entail asking questions as simple as "What did you use as a base color?" "Do you want the overall paint treatment to be opaque or layers of glazes?" or "What process did you use to obtain these results?" It is common sense to try to emulate the designer's painting process, which sometimes is not clear at first glance, to obtain the same results. Many variables are involved in any painting process. During this interview the charge painter should take detailed notes. If notes are specific to a particular paint elevation, they should be attached to that particular elevation.

Beyond understanding the painting processes, this interview with the scenic designer is very important in terms of understanding the designer's overall scenic vision. Is it a dark and dreary dungeon in the spirit of Piranesi's prison etchings? Perhaps the entire scene is to have the filmy depths of a Watteau painting. Some scenic designers may communicate ideas at a more pragmatic level. For instance, the designer may simply say, "I first underpainted everything with red." The charge painter should use this interview as the best chance to get the designer's overall impression of how he or she envisions the painting of the design. Because many designers must work on two or three designs at the same time, a personal interview at the beginning of the paint process may be the last time the charge painter and scenic art staff can speak with the designer face to face until the scenery is nearly ready to leave the shop. Occasionally, because of conflicting schedules, the charge painter must conduct this initial interview with the designer over the phone and exchange pertinent visual information via overnight delivery services.

Reading a Paint Elevation

What the scenic artist must understand from the paint elevations and talking with the scenic designer are the color, technique, texture, style, and intent sought in the scenic design. It is easy enough for the scenic artist to make assumptions and surmises about the designer's paint elevation, but unless the designer has been questioned about the specifics, there is no way of knowing whether these assumptions are correct. In some cases, the designer may have no strong opinion about how the scenery is to be painted; in other instances, the designer may feel strongly that the painting should be approached in a specific manner.

Color is probably the most evident aspect of a paint elevation. Some scenic designers may include their color swatch boards with the paint elevation packet. The swatch board is a scrap of illustration board on which the paints have been paletted that can give the scenic artist useful clues to how the colors were mixed. In terms of color, the scenic artist should ask very specific questions, such as "Does this shadow have a purple tint?" or "Was this gray mixed with blue and burnt sienna?" More importantly, the scenic artist may want to ask some broader questions about the palette of the elevation. The designer may have chosen a palette that is cool or that is primarily warm. That palette may be based on complementary colors, opposing hues, such as reds and greens or yellows and purples. The palette may be primarily monochromatic, using one color varying only in value and neutrality. Or, the palette may be based on two colors, dichromatic, perhaps based on blue and umbers.

Technique refers to how the paint or texture should be applied. This may not be entirely clear by looking at the paint elevation. For instance, if parts of the paint elevation have been rendered in colored pencil, does this mean that the designer wants colored pencil–like lines in the painting or was the pencil used just for the sake of accuracy in the reduced scale of the elevation? In terms of the painting technique the scenic artist must discuss with the scenic designer the medium itself. Is the paint to be opaque color or is it applied in transparent layers creating variation and depth? A paint elevation that, to the eye, appears to be made up of a multitude of subtle variations may actually have been painted with only five separate hues of transparent colors. These are the questions that the scenic artist must put to the designer.

The technique may also affect the way the scenery is to be approached in the paint shop. If the scenic designer has rendered the paint elevations with transparent pools of color and wants this effect to be replicated in the painting of the scenery, then the scenic artist needs to bear in mind that painting of this sort is done most easily in the continental style, horizontally rather than vertically. The paint will need to be thin and of the right intensity. Obviously, this will involve considerable floor space and drying time. Both of these factors will need to be addressed when the scenic artist is planning time and space. It is crucial for the designer to be aware of what the shop can provide in the time budgeted. The scenic artist should have an understanding of the shop's potential. If the scene shop lacks sufficient floor space or time to leave flats down for a prolonged period, other techniques may have to be considered and discussed with the designer. Some very elegant solutions can come from the necessity of working within time, space, and budgetary limitations.

Texture and finishes are issues that must be decided from the onset of a project. Every building material has an inherent texture, and if the scenic designer desires that texture to be altered so that it is either smoother or rougher, the scenic artist must be aware of it from the start. If the texture is something that must be applied before the painting starts, as in the case of a rough-cut wood or fieldstone, then the scenic artist will have to apply the texture before the color. The texture could be just a matter of finish such as a glossy wood paneling or smooth marble. In this case, extra finish work, sanding, and spackling may need to be done on the scenery before the painting. Like technique, texture, its application and drying time, must be factored into the time frame of the scene shop. How the texture is applied is important. Many options are available for application, such as hopper guns, brushes, grainers, rollers, trowels, and hand work. These techniques produce different

results, take varying amounts of time, and have different costs involved. The scenic artist and the scenic designer must decide which techniques would best suit the resources of time, budget, and labor to produce the desired results. (Texture tools are discussed in Chapter Five and texturing techniques are discussed in Chapter Nine.)

Every scenic designer brings a quality called *style* to a production. Style is the invisible glue that aesthetically holds together the scenery. It is absolutely crucial that the scenic artist understand the style the designer has chosen. Also important is that the scenic artist understand that this style in part may be the personal style of the designer. In this, the scenic artist must be neutral and objective enough to conceal his or her own personal style and, for that production, adopt the style of the designer. The chosen style for the production may be a clear historic reference, such as German expressionism or French art deco. The scenic artist must understand and retain this style for every piece in that production. For the charge painter, this means monitoring the work of the entire paint staff throughout the production.

In addition to technique and style, the scenic designer and the scenic artist need to make sure that they understand one another on the artistic content of the design. This area, *intent*, is a primary area where the art of scenic artistry comes into play. The scenic artist needs to fully understand the designer's stylistic intent and be able to recreate it in full scale. This includes understanding where the designer wants the focus within any given scene or a recognition of the overall effect of the scenery. This, as with style, is where a good scenic artist becomes invaluable to a scenic designer. It is impossible to express a sense of style or theatricality without understanding the intent behind the style.

INTERPRETING THE SCENIC DESIGNER'S WORK

A good scenic artist should be able to work in a variety of styles. A scenic artist must be as flexible stylistically as an actor in a repertory company who has a role in an Anton Chekhov play one night and a Christopher Durang play the next. Within the spirit of that style the scenic artist needs to improvise a little on sections of the scenery that are not fully described by the paint elevations, rather than infuse the painting process with his or her own style.

Checking Elevations and Draftings with the Scenery

The charge painter is responsible for checking all the scenery as it is received from the construction staff against the designer's elevations. This is very important since painting scenery twice is a very costly exercise. Here is an instance where the scenic artist represents the interest of the designer in the paint shop. If possible the charge artist should monitor the construction of the scenery so that he or she may be aware of construction techniques or materials that will require extra attention once the scenery reaches the paint shop. Remember: forewarned is forearmed. Usually at the beginning of a build the charge painter and the technical director will meet to discuss schedule and construction techniques that will have a bearing on the painting of the scenery. For example, will the units need to be spackled and sanded; will the units need to be painted on the floor or assembled and vertical; should the stiffeners be removed before the scenery can be painted? During the building process the technical director may ask the scenic artist, "Can you paint on this material?" or "Do we need to build a bridge so that you can reach into the center of this unit?" Once the scenery comes into the shop there may still be some differences in the way the scenic artist understands the scenic units' design function and the way they have been built. The charge painter may need to consult the designer or technical director before proceeding. Issues such as reveals on doors and windows or floor treatment through doorways are not often clear on the paint elevations. In some cases the construction staff may need to do some additional work on a particular unit. In other cases, the charge painter may need to call the designer, explain the differences, and ask how he or she would like to deal with discrepancy.

Enlarging the Design to Full Scale

One skill important to scenic painting is the process of enlarging small drawings and paintings to full scale for the stage. This is an interpretive skill, calling on artistic judgment and a sense of what is theatrical. This skill is intuitive and takes time to develop.

Scale

The fact that paint elevations and cartoons are drawn in small scale is an important consideration. The scenic artist enlarges these drawings on the scenery. However, simply enlarging the original work like a copy machine won't result in a complete description of the scenic designer's vision. This transition requires interpretation of the designer's work and some significant decisions on the part of the scenic artist. These may include the clarification of small details or of a light source suggested by the painted highlights and shadows. Perhaps the scenic designer made part of the paint elevation fade off into expressive and indistinct blobs of paint. But the scenic artist, working in full scale with large brushes, may need to know exactly what those blobs of paint are. Is the blob a house or a tree? Will the contours of that blob have a sense of the organic or the architectural? The scenic artist may need to complete the picture.

Understanding how the scale of the painting will read in the theatre where the scenery is to be installed is important. In a large house, highly detailed objects can be painted in broad paint strokes. The observer will complete the image and believe it to be detailed. Paradoxically, in this situation highly detailed painting may actually appear to flatten the image. On the other hand, forms created with broad paint stokes may appear overly simplified in smaller theatres. Color is not the same close up as at a distance. As demonstrated by the methods of Seurat and Pissarro, the eye will mix separate colors at a distance. So the surface of a gray stone wall that responds so beautifully to any color of stage light actually, on close inspection, may be a combination of peach, ocher, and Italian blue sprays.

Technique

Selecting the proper paint techniques for a design is a major aspect of the preparation process. The scenic artist must determine how to recreate techniques of the paint elevations made with the small brushes and art tools of the designer. The obvious answer, with larger brushes, is only part of the solution. Brooms, sponges, garden sprayers, feather dusters, and all manner of implements can become paint tools as long as they achieve the desired effect (see Chapters Five and Nine). At this point, the scenic artist combines a knowledge of the field of scenic artistry, the designer's advice, experience, and imagination to devise a solution. As you gain experience, you will find that more and more frequently the answer to interesting problems already will be at hand. However, even the most experienced scenic artist will encounter a new challenge that requires a fresh approach and experimentation with conventional and unconventional tools before finding the right solution.

Character

The key to good interpretive skills is identifying the essential elements and character of a scenic designer's work. These elements could be the line of the drawing or perhaps the sense of the color itself. A scenic artist may have faithfully and laboriously copied every line and mark from the scenic designer's paint elevation, yet the essence of the drawing is missing. Strict adherence to every detail may obscure the spirit of the work. Vladimir Polunin described this phenomenon in his 1927 book, *The Continental Method of Scene Painting:* "Carefully examine it from several points of view to ascertain if the drawing on the canvas represents the same characteristic lines contained in the tracing. If it fails to do so, it is proof that you have allowed the detail to break up the important lines. Correct, always bearing in mind that in scenery it is the general effect that is essential." Remember that the scenic artist is an artist and interpreter of the design, not a mimic. Without the interpretive skills of a scenic artist, a simple sky drop will lose the dramatic quality of style that makes it theatrical.

Making Samples

Sometimes traditional painter's elevations are not enough to describe the paint treatment. Scenic samples often are an indispensable part of the preparation of painting and may be done by the scenic designer or the scenic artist. Heavily textured or layered surfaces or work with nontraditional unprocessed materials are some instances where it is better to work from a sample. This part of the preparation is best done by collaboration between the scenic artist and the scenic designer.

A sample is a full-scale swatch of the finished scenery. This swatch may be a small test flat, a 4' ×

8' piece of sheet stock, or a piece of the material out of which the scenery is to be constructed. In some cases, the construction staff may have to build a small mock-up of scenery for the sample work. On a sample, you can experiment with different materials, application techniques, distressing techniques, media mix, and finishing techniques. The time taken to work up a sample will save time in the long run by answering questions about the process.

There are no rules about how samples are done or who does them, but some commonsense guidelines may help. The scenic designer always should provide some sort of visual image as a starting point and reference to the visual image he or she envisions. This reference may be a photograph, a piece of finished wood, a piece of stone, or even references out of books or magazines. In some cases, the designer may refer to some common visual image easily identifiable to the scenic artist such as "concrete" or "brownstone." The scenic artist will then create a sample for the designer's approval.

The sample usually is created in the scenic studio. The scenic designer who has presented the scenic artist with a completed sample must be able to thoroughly explain the recipe and techniques used to produce that sample, so that the scenic artist can replicate it, explain the process to others, and budget time and materials for the scenery. One of the great benefits of working up a sample are the questions that knowing the process and materials can answer, such as "What materials were used?" "How many distinct steps were involved?" "What was the order of these steps?" "What was the drying time between steps?" "In all, how long did the process take and what was the cost per square foot?" The sample allows the scenic artist to determine the feasibility of a process for a given production. Is there enough time and space? Is the process durable to withstand moving and trucking? Will extra labor be required? Can the materials fit into the budget for the production?

In some situations, a sample makes a lot more sense than a paint elevation. Situations that call for a simple paint treatment on specific material are a perfect example of where a sample may be all the information a scenic artist needs. However, it is important not to overlook the need for some sort of elevation or rendering to give an overview of the scenery. Even a simple treatment of wood may vary from light to dark applications depending on where it plays on stage. In many cases the scenic designer may give the scenic artist a paint elevation describing the value and color variation over the surface of the scenery that is to be used in conjunction with a paint sample. In some instances the lighting designer may request a sample of one or more paint techniques for their own design process.

Using the Scenic Designer's Research

Concepts and ideas are difficult to express in words. There is never any guarantee that one person's comprehension of an idea or concept is the same as that of the person endeavoring to express it. But the scenic artist's need to know and understand the scenic designer's meaning is crucial. Communication and comprehension are at the core of their collaborative relationship. The designer needs to express an overall concept to many different people. Those of us who share in the responsibility of executing the separate pieces of scenery that make a design need to share in the rationale behind it. We all know that a picture is worth a thousand words. Looking at the same image can be wonderfully objective. The designer, by providing the scenic artist with a few key images that epitomize the design concept, a specific texture, or paint treatment, instantly can clarify his or her intent. In some cases, the designer may want the scenic artist to focus on a specific area of reference. All that may be needed in some cases is a color photocopy that has one corner circled in red with a note that reads "These are the type of rocks I want!"

If the paint elevations are not enough information or the scenic designer is not able to fully convey his or her intent through them, then research and specific references may have to fill the gap. Generally, the designer will supply the scenic artist with copies of these sources or, if the reference is well known, tell the scenic artist what it is. For instance, the designer might say, "This is a Roman ionic column and capital" or "I want the painting style to be reminiscent of a Renoir oil painting." Most scenic artists are bibliophiles and may well have the reference material in their own libraries. A well-equipped paint shop will have a small library of architecture and ornamentation reference books. The scenic artist who needs more information can ask the designer to supply it, or in some cases, it may be just as easy for the scenic artist to go to the local library and collect the sources.

When Research Takes the Place of an Elevation

In some cases, the scenic designer's references for a production may supersede the paint elevations in part or completely. The designer may give the scenic artist a color elevation of a city street that is descriptive of the line work but is accompanied by a page from *Architectural Digest* and a note that says, "Here, use these colors and shading." The designer may send a photo of birch trees with an elevation of a foliage drop and indicate that these are specifically how the trees are to be rendered on the drop. In some instances, the designer may lay a color wash over a black and white photocopy or collage by way of a paint elevation. In instances like these, it will be up to the scenic artist to merge these visual images. The musical *Sunday in the Park with George*, which revolves around the painting of *Sunday Afternoon on the Island of La Grande Jatte* by Georges Seurat, is a perfect example. Here, a natural progression takes place from the reference, the work of art itself, to the designer's elevations, and how the scenic artist integrates the two in the painting of the scenery.

In other cases, there is no need for the scenic designer to do a paint elevation of a particular scenic unit. Photographic imagery often is used by designers as a style as well as for content. The scenic designer may present the scenic artist with an actual photograph or picture from a book or magazine to be rendered on the scenery. In the future, as the cost of full-scale color reproduction becomes more affordable, making this technology more accessible and economically viable for theatre productions of varying budgets, full-scale color reproductions will be more commonplace, and will replace complex painting. Then, the challenge for the scenic artist may be to seamlessly merge conventionally painted scenery with the color reproductions in a given scene.

In even more demanding situations, the scenic designer actually may ask the scenic artist to complete the painting in the style or spirit of the reference material. I once got a piece of stationery from a designer that had been printed with a cloud motif. The designer's instructions were to "Paint clouds like these on the drop." This is where the scenic artist–scenic designer relationship can be a little fast and loose. The designer has provided a broad concept for the scenic artist to follow, but it is up to the scenic artist to fill in the detail and create the actual image. A designer may have a very elegant sense of design, but painting may not be his or her forte. Designers such as this rely on the scenic artist to understand and carry out the intent of the design, filling in what the designer can imagine but not execute.

Copying Works of Art

The research that the scenic designer has done may appear in a very literal way in the design. It is not unusual to see outright copies of other artists' work on stage. Copying a work of art opens up a new set of challenges. The designer will have to determine if the work must be reformatted to fit into the design. Also, there are amazing variations in the quality of color reproductions in secondary sources. In the case of *Sunday in the Park with George*, the designer was obliged to send to the Art Institute in Chicago for a color-correct print. Because one of the main themes of the production is Georges Seurat's preoccupation with color, it was inconceivable that the designer and the scenic artist should reference anything other than an accurate reproduction of that painting.

Another consideration in copying a work of art is that often the overall impression of a work of art is different from the real thing. Many people are surprised and occasionally a little disappointed when viewing a famous work of art for the first time. The *Mona Lisa* may seem surprisingly small and dark when viewed in the Louvre for the first time. Ultimately, the scenic artist may need to do some interpretation to adapt the reproduction of a work for stage. What is the vision that motivated the designer or director to select this image? What is the context of this viewing? The concept behind the selection of a particular piece will be revealing.

As the designer for a restaging of Diaghilev's *L'Après-Midi d'Une Faune*, I had to reconstruct the design by Leon Bakst. In reproducing the original backdrop, I was struck by the tremendous variations available in book reproductions. Which one was correct? The key to reproducing the drop was first to choose the version that best represented the vision I had of the music. Then I worked a palette of colors from several different versions

that appeared to harmonize with each other. I used palettes from different versions because the printing qualities varied from book to book. Some versions had beautiful, subtle greens where others turned the greens to brown. The versions with the good green tones rendered the background nearly black, others had it rather bright blue. Finally, the description of Leon Bakst's work in Polunin's *The Continental Method of Scene Painting* (pp. 37–82) led me to understand the spirit of the work I had undertaken.

Understanding the Limitations of a Paint Elevation

A scenic artist should be aware that scenic designers use a shorthand in making paint elevations, and some details or portions of the built scenery may not be included. Keep in mind some simple facts:

1. The scenic designer's elevations usually must describe three-dimensional units in two dimensions, which could mean that something is not shown!
2. The elevation may overlook corners or reveals, the areas within openings and under overhangs. The scenic artist will have to decide or ask the designer what to do around the corners of a unit.
3. The designer may have drawn the objects to be painted in a different size or shape than what the scenic artist is asked to paint.
4. The change in media from high-quality artists' color on paper to scene paint on the real scenery can present problems. The paint elevation often is done on smooth illustration board. It may not reflect the actual texture of the surface on which the scenery is to be painted or how the scene paint will behave.
5. The change in texture from the elevation or model to the scenery can have a tremendous effect. Paint will react very differently from one material to another. The scenic designer has the freedom to work on a smooth surface. The scenic artist, however, needs to get the same effect from multiple surfaces with varying textures. The scenic artist should pay close attention from the beginning to how the units of scenery are built and particularly to what materials are being used. In some cases, the scenic artist can have influence on how the scenery is built and how surfaces are treated. Careful attention to

construction techniques will save the scenic artist from having to deal with materials that will not accept paint evenly.

6. Repeating patterns, wallpaper patterns, molding, bricks, and lettering may not register the same on the scenery as in the elevations. The smallest change in the dimension of the pattern or the scenery may throw off the repetitions. Also, the designer may have simply painted a section of a repeating pattern in the paint elevation and then noted that it should continue. However, when the pattern turns a corner or descends a stairwell it may not make sense. It may be up to the scenic artist to make the necessary adjustments so that the placement of the pattern looks logical. The scenic artist should be certain of the registration, or alignment, of a pattern on the scenery in its entirety before paint is applied.

WORKING WITH THE SCENIC DESIGNER IN THE SHOP AND ON STAGE

As a production enters the painting phase, collaboration and communication with the scenic designer is essential. Most scenic artists prefer to have the scenic designer in the paint shop as much as possible for feedback in a timely manner, to ensure that the painting is as the scenic designer has envisioned. Before backdrops are folded and scenic units are stacked and stored away it is best if the scenic designer has had a chance to approve the scenic artistry. As the set moves into the theatre, the scenic artist and the scenic designer will collaborate on fine tuning the painting of the design.

Communicating with the Scenic Designer During the Painting

On-Site Designers

Having the scenic designer onsite is a great luxury for the scenic artist. Generally, the designer will visit the paint shop every day while the set is in production, to keep track of the progress or even, if allowed by the union, pick up a brush and paint. In some cases, the designer simply will want to perform as one of the paint crew, asking the charge painter what he or she wants the designer to do. In other cases, the designer will volunteer to paint a particular unit such as a portrait or a particularly complex piece of scenery. It is preferable in almost all cases to have the scenic designer as close at hand as possible to monitor the progress.

Off-Site Scenic Designers

When the scenic designer is out of town while the design is in the paint shop, the designer and the scenic artist should check in with one another at least once every business day. This serves two purposes. It gives the scenic artist a chance to ask the designer questions that arise on a day-to-day basis concerning the painting of the production. Daily check-ins also keep the designer up to date on the progress of the production. The scenic designer must inform the scenic artist of where he or she can be reached on any given day. It may be best to have a preset time of day to check in by telephone. The alternative, trying to find a designer who is shopping or in a rehearsal, can be difficult.

Communicating with the Scenic Designer to Finish the Painting

Just because the separate units of scenery are painted does not necessarily mean the painting has been completed. As the set pieces near completion, the scenic designer or scenic artist (or both) should take the time to study the paint elevation or model and look at the scenery in the context of the whole design. Do the set pieces join together visually in an appropriate way? Does the painting technique flow well through one scene and from one scene to another? If changes or additional painting are anticipated, this is the time to do it, not when the set has already been delivered to the theatre.

Finally, the set is delivered and set up on stage, more or less finished. Some touch-up painting will have to be done at this time and a list of notes from the scenic designer may include repainting or adjusting some pieces. Bear in mind that some of these notes may come from the producer, director, costume designer, or lighting designer and are filtered through the scenic designer. For this reason, it is a very good idea for the scenic artist to go to the theatre and examine the set under rehearsal conditions. How can a scenic designer's note truly explain the contrast problem between a gray suit and a gray drop? As a scenic artist, your insight into color may provide the objective eye that a scenic designer needs to decide what to do. The scenic artist can make a significant contribution to a production even after the scenery has left the paint shop.

Finishing Work on Stage

The final phase of finishing a set is a very important time for the designer. As the load-in date looms closer, time will be very tight, particularly if an off-site designer has not had the opportunity to see all elements of the set until it is on stage. Once all the elements are assembled and seen under stage light, the designer may request that some additional work is done to "gel" it together.

This work is done at the scenic artist's *touch-up* on stage. The touch-up is scheduled after the scenery has been fully unloaded on stage and assembled, usually after the stage carpenters have completed most of their work and the scenic designer has had a chance to see the set under stage lights. Ideally, the touch-up should be scheduled at a time when the work lights can be on and the stage is relatively quiet. All too often, this is not the case. Stage time during the technical rehearsal week is very precious. The scenic artist and the scenic designer often have to share the stage with the properties department, stage carpenters, electricians, the lighting designer, and sometimes the performers.

Most of the notes that the scenic designer will give to the scenic artist are very standard: "Paint the edge of the flat that is still raw wood." "Spray the wrinkles out of the drops." "There are bolt heads visible on the step facings." Some designers do not even give obvious notes such as these, assuming that the scenic artist will see the problems and take care of them as a matter of course. The notes that the designer is apt to be the most concerned with are those involving the aesthetics of the design. These notes may be more along the lines of, "The distant landscape of the ground row is too sharp. Could you spray it down with some blue gray so that it is more atmospheric?" or "The rocks are flattening out. Work more highlights and shadows into them."

Planning and Doing the Touch-Up

It is time to start planning the touch-up when the painting of the set nears completion. If the paint shop and the performance space are in separate facil-

ities this usually begins with the charge painter conferring with shop assistants about what paints, tools, and materials will be needed in the touch-up kit (the touch-up kit is discussed in Chapter Four). The color and paint most integral to the painting on the scenery will need to be included in the touch-up kit. For instance, if the majority of the set is painted with a wood grain technique, then these paints and finishes will need to be included in the kit; or if there are three major elements in the set—a house, a deck, and a garden wall—then the primary colors used in these set pieces should be packed. In some cases specialized colors that combine color and finish in one bucket may need to be mixed for catching edges and scratches on the scenery. If the designer has seen the set under stage lights and given a list of notes to the charge painter the day before touch-up, then some specific paint and materials may be packed for dealing with certain notes. For instance, the designer may have asked that a sign be painted on the side of a building. If this note is given in time, the charge painter may have been able to prepare a pounced pattern, a perforated drawing, ahead of time.

During the touch-up, the charge painter will assign notes to the members of the scenic art staff. The scenic designer usually is present during the touch-up and even though his or her energy may be divided between many different departments and individuals, the designer will be available for consultation. At some point, either right at the beginning of touch-up or at a technical rehearsal the day before the touch-up, the charge painter should meet with the designer and go through the list of notes together to ensure the charge painter completely understands the designer's notes.

Changes in the Theatre

Typically, changes in the theatre are minor, but occasionally the notes that are given for touch-up include major changes, rather than finessing and fine tuning. Extra units of scenery may be added at the last minute, or the color of the entire set may need to be changed. A simple note to tone down all the walls of the set can result in hours of work on ladders or scaffolding. On the set of a production of *Fool for Love,* I was given a note that the actress would be thrown against the walls of the set repeatedly and the texture of the walls was too harsh. The entire set had to be given a smooth texture skim coat, after which the walls had to be repainted and aged down again. The stage schedule had to be adjusted to accommodate this change. The charge painter may have to adjust the touch-up schedule and possibly the paint schedule of the next production to accommodate major changes. This may involve scheduling an additional touch-up, hiring extra crew members, bringing a piece of scenery back to the shop for repainting, or building and painting additional pieces of scenery to be sent to the theatre as soon as possible. At this stage in the production schedule, such changes always are problematic. When asked to do major changes in such a tight time frame, the charge painter should consider realistically how the change can be done. If more time in the schedule, overtime, or extra crew members are needed, then the charge painter should make sure that these needs are clearly stated to everyone concerned.

If the scenic designer has requested a major change in the painting of the set after it has gone to the theatre then it must be very important to him or her, the director, and the management or it would not be requested. However, the scenic art staff must not be expected to carry out this work without more time, personnel, or compensation.

POSSIBLE PROBLEMS IN THE SCENIC DESIGNER–SCENIC ARTIST RELATIONSHIP

The so-called bottom line during the production process is that scenery must be built and painted on time so technical rehearsals may take place and a show can open as planned. Neither the scenic artist nor the scenic designer has the authority to alter the deadline, unless that person also serves as producer. This may place undue pressure on a scenic artist for several reasons. As said before, the scenic artist usually is the last one to work on scenery before a load-in, which means the scenic artist will be vulnerable to glitches in the design or construction process. The scenic designer may not have presented the paint shop with enough information, or provided it in a timely fashion. Perhaps construction started late because of poor management or problems on a previous production. A scenic designer may want to make substantial changes in the painting, whereas the producers and technical director are pressuring the scenic arts staff to finish the set and move on to the next production. Part of being a professional sce-

nic artist is learning how to balance the needs and demands of the scenic designer with the reality of the production schedule and resources.

Late Design and Lack of Design Information

The scenic artist needs to know the entire scope of a project before time and costs can be planned. Frequently, a design is priced out and approved, based on the bluelines and a color model. Then, later in the production schedule, the scenic designer may be late in submitting paint elevations or may omit information that the scenic artist needs to stay on schedule. When this happens, it frequently is because the designer is overextended. Often the scenic artist can readjust the schedule after getting assurances from the designer that a necessary piece of information or paint elevation will arrive by a given hour on a given day. If the problems with late work continue, the scenic artist should alert the production management so the problems can be resolved. It should not be the responsibility of the scenic artist to police the designer.

Tinkering

Occasionally, the scenic designer will be insecure or unhappy with the design after seeing it on stage. One of the easiest ways to change a design once it is on stage is to resort to paint. So, in the course of the touch-up notes, the designer will give the scenic artist notes designed to solve these problems. However, if, once these notes are done and the official touch-up day has come and gone, the designer continues to give the scenic artist complex notes contrived to solve design issues, it can be problematic for several reasons. The prolonged touch-up may cut into the production schedule of the next production. If the production comes at the end of a season or is on a single contract, the scenic artist will have committed to letting the paint staff go by a certain day, usually the day after touch-up. So the scenic artist may not have adequate staff to take care of the extra notes. If this is the case, then the scenic artist may need to inform the production management of the problems. If the designer can talk over his or her concerns with the production manager, artistic director, director, or producer, perhaps these concerns can be addressed without belaboring the touch-up.

Replacement of a Scenic Designer

In very rare situations, a scenic designer who has failed to perform to the producer's satisfaction may be let go. This situation will have an impact on every department. The scenic art department, being the last to deal with the scenery, will be set behind the farthest. When the designer is let go, one of two things may happen. If it is early enough in the process, the producers may decide to hire another designer to submit a design or complete the design in progress. If the dismissal is too close to the opening, then the producers may ask a member of the production staff to serve as designer and usher the original design to completion. The scenic artist is an obvious choice to replace the designer, because the scenic artist is one of the people best equipped to understand what the design is to look like, based on the preliminary information. However, if this extra responsibility falls to the scenic artist, extra compensation must be made. Having to make the final decisions in the design process is a great responsibility and cannot be shouldered lightly.

CONCLUSION

The scenic designer always will benefit from a healthy collaborative relationship with the scenic artist and vice versa. This is true throughout the entire production and rehearsal process. The scenic artist's role may seem less important after the set leaves the shop, but the scenic artist's intimate knowledge of the technique and color of the painting can prove to be a tremendous asset to the production. The scenic designer sat in a studio choosing chrome green over emerald green for some oddball bounce-light color. Since that time, perhaps no one person could ever begin to realize the unique aesthetic qualities of that set nearly as well as the scenic artist. He or she knows every detail of the set's surface, because this person actually made the image appear. The scenic artist knows how much ultramarine blue really is in that gray color everyone else is upset about—and probably just how to fix it. No other person in the entire production staff actually emulated the designer's hand at work to such a degree. The scenic artist needs to be an extension of the artist that is the scenic designer.

chapter 3

The Scenic Artist and the Scenic Studio

INTRODUCTION

Theatrical scenery is fabricated in scenic studios, where many diverse artisans work together. The trades working in a scenic studio include carpentry, drafting, welding, electrical and mechanical engineering, sculpting, scenic artistry, and properties crafts. This diversity is necessary because building scenery demands many different types of skilled professionals. Successful shops are made up of very talented craftspeople whose dedication to and enjoyment of the unusual demands of theatre is evident. It is very gratifying to make your living in a profession that you enjoy. A scenic studio is an interesting and rewarding workplace, because the work itself always is changing and presents constant challenges to the artisans. Few days seem "just like the last."

Many of the trades in theatre are backed by labor unions that influence and regulate basic working conditions. Scenic studios are either union, non-union, or a combination of the two. Because different unions may represent different departments some shops may not be represented uniformly.

TYPES OF SCENIC STUDIOS

There are many different kinds of scenic studios in the United States. Some are commercial scenic studios that are well outfitted, working year-round. Others are associated with nonprofit theatres and work less regularly in smaller studios. Some scenic studios come to life seasonally, sprouting up in the summer occupying pole barns or other alternative spaces. Some shops are assembled for one or two productions. They may have a staff of three or seventy. One element common to them all is that they need scenic artists in some form or another.

The common types of scenic studios that build scenery and employ scenic artists in the United States are:

1. *College- or university-affiliated scenic studios.* These scenic shops are usually noncommercial. In some shops, professional scenic artists are hired on a permanent, seasonal, or temporary basis to paint productions. These scenic artists generally work with student assistants. Professional scenic artists in these shops may also teach classes or seminars. In other university-level scenic studios, the scenic artists are drawn from students studying for a degree in technical theatre or theatrical design.

2. *Semi-professional theatre scenic studios* (equity waiver). These organizations may be commercial or nonprofit and may employ one nonunion individual, chiefly to paint and possibly work on other tasks. Often in these situations volunteers, interns, and the scenic designer may all take part in the painting process. These studios may be active for only part of the year.

3. *Professional theatre scenic studios* (equity theatres, League of Resident Theatres [LORT], large-scale civic associations). These studios serve professional theatrical associations and

regional theatres. They may be commercial or nonprofit. These organizations may have a contract with I.A.S.T.E. or U.S.A., or hire U.S.A. scenic artists on individual contracts. They may employ one or several scenic artists full-time or on a seasonal basis. The painting staff may be augmented with temporary overhire or relocation of staff members from other areas.

4. *Independent, professional, commercial studios* (for-profit scenic shops). These are commercial scenic studios. This type of studio may be either union or nonunion. The shop may not have a union contract but hire U.S.A. scenic artists on individual contracts. If the studio uses U.S.A. individuals on a regular basis it may be approached by U.S.A. to sign a blanket contract. Generally the construction staff in these studios are covered by an I.A.S.T.E. contract. Union shops have carefully regulated wage scales based on union standards and make contributions to the union health and welfare plans. Nonunion shops may have similar wage scales and company benefits, but the grievance processes and union benefit plans available to employees of a studio under a union contract will not be available to them. These studios can be of any size; some of the largest scenic studios in the country are independent commercial studios that build and/or paint for a variety of clients in venues including theatre, opera, musical theatre, industrial displays and presentations, industrial film work, commercial films, and television. These shops work primarily on a contractual basis with individual clients.

5. *Film and television scenic studios.* Many of these studios operate in major media centers such as New York City and Los Angeles. They are usually covered by I.A.S.T.E. contracts since U.S.A. contracts are not common outside of New York City. These shops may be year-round operations that work on a contractual basis with individual clients, or they may be temporary or seasonal, serving as the production company for a specific feature film or television series. The affiliations of these studios may be complex. The lines between profit and nonprofit organizations may be blurry; for instance, a nonprofit civic theatrical organization may operate a commercial scene studio to subsidize its operation.

THE STAFF IN A SCENIC STUDIO

Scenic studios are intricate workplaces where differently skilled people are working towards a common goal. The artisans and craftspeople working in these shops are valued for their speed as well as overall skill and artistic ability. Theatrical productions often work on compact time schedules. Little room is left over for last-minute changes. Overages and production changes do happen, of course, and some artisans may have to work overtime to get caught up. Overtime is regulated in shops covered by a union contract, so that members are compensated for any time worked beyond an eight-hour day and a forty-hour week.

In the scenic studio there are individuals who are department heads of specific areas of scenic fabrication and support. These departments must collaborate with one another since their responsibilities are frequently interdependent and intertwined. The organization of individual effort, space, time, and finances is the key to a smoothly running shop, so there are individuals who serve as managers and liaisons among these departments and the designers.

The primary individuals and departments involved in the fabrication of scenery for a theatrical production are:

- *Scenic designer.* This person is responsible for creating the vision for the scenery for a given production and communicating it to the staff of the scenic studio.
- *Production management.* This department is responsible for setting and supervising the budget and the schedule of a production.
- *Technical director.* This individual coordinates the efforts of the individual departments involved in the fabrication of the set for a production.
- *Construction department.* This department builds the set and is managed by the construction shop manager, who is also called the head carpenter.
- *Paint department.* This department is responsible for all the texture and paint treatments on the set and is managed by the charge painter.
- *Properties department.* This department is responsible for the fabrication, acquisition, organization, and installation of all the hand properties and set dressings. This department is headed by the properties manager.

There are no rigid rules concerning the hierarchy of managers and individual departments in a theatrical production or their responsibilities. Frequently one individual will function in two or more capacities, particularly in the case of smaller organizations. The technical director may also be the production manager or the designer. One person may be responsible for building and painting the set. There are also many other individual positions and departments in a production company that, because they are far removed from the fabrication of the scenery, have little or no direct impact on the scenic art department.

The Scenic Designer in the Scenic Studio

The *scenic designer* is an outside contractor in many professional scenic studios. Some studios and theatrical companies hire staff scenic designers; this may be the case in regional and university-affiliated theatre companies. Only very rarely is the scenic designer also in charge of the of the scenic studio. Usually this occurs only in the case of small production companies, some university theatres, and when the scenic designer actually owns a scenic studio. In most shops, the scenic designer does not decide who, when, where, and how many people paint the design. That is the job of the charge painter, technical director, and production manager. But it is the responsibility of the scenic designer to provide the production company or scenic studio with all the information they need, on schedule, so that the design can be costed out and executed according to the production's timetable.

The Technical Director and the Production Manager

The *production manager* is an important part of a theatrical production. This person is responsible for the entire organization of a theatrical production, from contracting to scheduling, and final construction to shipping. Production managers are most common in large theatre organizations, with multiple productions, contracts, or stages. Smaller theatres or independent commercial scenic studios may not have a production manager at all. When present, their role can change drastically from shop to shop. In large operations they manage the theatre production as a whole, including scheduling production

meetings and communication between producers, designers, directors, cast, and crew. In most organizations the production manager will assign the overall budgets to the departments and supervise the budgetary flow of a production through the organization. Time management is a large factor in the operation and long-range planning of a scenic studio. Labor is generally the greatest cost. If problems arise the production manager will assist in troubleshooting and reallocation of finances. But it is up to the technical director and production shop heads to handle the details of day-to-day affairs.

In commercial scenic studios, the production manager may have an even larger responsibility, that of bidding on potential contracts. The production manager must manipulate the internal costs of the scenic fabrication while bidding against competitors. He or she may also be owner or part owner of the scenic studio. Large-scale commercial scenic studios generally have a much more narrow focus than a performance-oriented organization. A commercial studio generally will only deal with the technical aspects of a production, working as a contractor or among the contractors to the performance company. The performance company may have their own production manager who will consult with the management of the scenic studio.

Production managers may or may not be specialists in construction. In both commercial and noncommercial studios, the production manager may be involved in the actual construction decisions, depending on that person's area of expertise. A production manager may be an expert in metal work or hydraulics and contribute to the planning and execution of scenery. However, it is rare that the production manager would actually work on a regular basis on the shop floor. The production manager's responsibilities will always pull that person back to the phone or some crisis. The technical director and the production shop heads will normally do the nuts-and-bolts decision making.

The *technical director* is primarily responsible for the traditional scenic areas of scenic construction and painting of scenery. In smaller and noncommercial studios the technical director also may oversee the costumes and lighting. The technical director's primary functions are to control the financial aspects of construction, draft or oversee the drafting of construction drawings for the construction staff, and coordinate the three scenic departments: construction, art, and properties. Before a design is sent to the department heads the technical director will cost out the construction of the design for the production manager to determine its financial feasibility. In costing out a design the technical director may only be concerned with construction, or he or she may be responsible for coordinating the cost of the design in other departments such as paint and properties. Once a design has been sent to the shops the technical director will supervise finances in the construction shop, and, in some cases, the paint and property shops as well. Financial control translates into two broad categories: money spent on materials and money spent on labor. The technical director's duty will be to see that these two commodities are used efficiently and wisely in the departments. He or she is responsible for the production schedule in each department and for assisting these departments in coordinating their efforts.

Scenic construction and scenic painting probably are the most closely interdependent shop areas, because they both handle the same physical elements. The scenic artist cannot start work until some of the scenery is constructed. The need for cooperation is paramount in these areas. The technical director should decide the most effective way for these two areas to assist each other. This may mean shifting labor resources to build the bulk of the scenery as early as possible, which would let the scenic artist have as much time as possible to paint the scenery. This logical conclusion is not as easy as it sounds and it requires careful planning.

Production Shop Heads

The six primary departments of theatrical production are costumes, lighting, paint, properties, scenery, and sound. An individual runs each of these shops. These are the costume shop manager, master electrician, charge painter, properties master, head carpenter, and sound technician. Some areas may have need for further subdivision depending on a production. Armor, sculpture, drapery, special effects, and various other specialties may demand that another department be added, with its own staff and staff head. They may be attached to one of the six departments listed previously. The shop managers spend a great deal of their time organizing their own areas. However, they also are experts of their areas and are a significant part of the skilled labor in their department. The job of a shop manager is to decide how

jobs are to be executed, in what order, and to assign staff members to the job. The shop head is responsible for keeping the shop on schedule and within budget. If there is a specific problem concerning the management of these areas, then the shop head will need to ask the technical director or production manager for assistance in resolving the problem.

Paint, Props, and Scenery—A Team of Three Departments

Scenery production encompasses three departments: scenic art, scenic construction, and properties. These three areas are run by separate individuals but work toward the common goal of having high-quality scenery completed and installed by the first technical rehearsal. It is absolutely critical that these areas be well organized and in accord, so that the scenery is finished in a rational and efficient manner. The department head for each of these areas (charge painter, properties manager, and head carpenter) work together to sort out day-to-day planning issues. The technical director will be involved in many of the decisions of larger issues among these three areas, regarding questions of resource management. For example, the technical director must ensure that the paint department receives the soft goods for painting early in the construction process, when space is available in the paint shop. Early in the construction process the technical director will have the head carpenter build or contract the building of all the soft goods. Then the technical director, scenic artist, and head carpenter will allot space and time for painting. The scenic artist can work on the soft goods while the head carpenter and the construction staff get started on the other scenery.

THE PAINT DEPARTMENT STAFF
The Charge Painter or Charge Person

The working relationship between painters is fairly common to any shop situation where two or more painters work together. When painters work together, generally one painter will serve as a liaison between the painters and the designer, organize the studio schedule with the technical director, and coordinate between all painters. If there is no one painter who is the organizational and artistic leader of the crew, the paint shop is apt to be chaotic and the scenery inconsistently painted. United Scenic Artists calls this manager the *charge person*.

Lead Painter

The charge painter may assign a *lead painter* to be in charge of a particular aspect of a project. The scope of a project may be just too large for one person to supervise effectively, so the lead painter will be given a portion of the project to supervise. For example, the charge painter may lead on all the soft goods, while the lead painter supervises the painting of the hard scenery. The lead painter may be the individual who paints all the foliage for a show or is in charge of all lettering. The lead painter may or may not be assigned assistants by the charge painter based on the production's needs. Several lead painters may work on a particular production or project, depending on the scope of the show and the skills needed. In a large studio, more than one production may be in the shop at one time. The charge painter may decide to assign a lead painter to one of those productions.

Assistant Scenic Artist

The assistant scenic artists work directly with the charge and lead painters. They are the part of the staff that does much of the painting under the supervision of the charge painter and the lead painters. United Scenic Artists calls a scenic artist at this level a *journey person*. The size of the paint crew depends on the size of the production in the studio. Some productions require a staff of only one or two people. Other productions may require a score of painters. The painters on a crew may have various skill levels, specialties, and experience. The charge painter's job is to coordinate and orchestrate the expertise of these individuals on the production.

Shop Assistants

The shop assistants maintain the shop and function as a support system for the scenic artists. In a large paint shop the tasks of preparing scenery to be painted, ordering stocks of paint and materials, running errands, maintaining tools, and simply keeping the shop clean and organized can be immense. The shop

assistants accomplish these duties so that the scenic artists can spend more time painting. In some shops the shop assistant functions as a managerial assistant to the charge painter. In very large operations there may even need to be a shop manager to supervise the shop assistants. The position of shop assistant is a valuable one. Good shop assistants make a huge contribution to a smoothly running shop.

Apprentices or Interns

Apprentices serve as assistants on a production. Depending on their experience, they may work as painting assistants or as shop assistants. Although apprentices are in the studio primarily to learn the trade of scenic artistry, this education involves a lot of hard work, and they are usually paid for their efforts. The charge painter and more experienced scenic artists in the shop will work with the apprentices in the course of production to help them advance and improve their skills. Not all shops have apprenticeship or intern programs. In many situations, even though there is no formalized apprenticeship program, the more expert scenic artists are always mindful of mentoring the inexperienced members of the crew.

PAINT DEPARTMENT MANAGEMENT

Management is a large part of the job of a charge painter. It requires constant attention and considerable skill. A charge painter can no more ignore the management part of work than walk away from a half-primed seamless drop to take a lunch break. A charge painter needs to do the following:

1. Coordinate the sequence of construction with the technical director and production manager;
2. Maintain adequate supplies of paint and other materials;
3. Supervise the output of the crew of painters and shop assistants;
4. Coordinate the interaction with other departments of the scenic shop that require paint or a painter;
5. Oversee all time, space, and personnel scheduling;
6. Oversee all purchasing within the area;
7. Serve as liaison between the scenic designer and the scene studio (see Chapter Two).

The job is even more complicated if a scenic artist is working as a freelance contractor and hiring assistants. Freelance scenic artists are expected to be totally self-sufficient. Issues of budget, finance, painting space, and equipment become much more complex.

Problems That May Occur in the Painting Schedule

The scenery should be finished by the date for *load-in* to the theatre. This means that, by the load-in date, the drops should be in their bins, the flatage should be stacked against the wall of the shop near the loading doors, the deck should be on a roll or sheet cart, and the touch-up kit should be packed up and ready to go. The reality of the expression "time is money" is obvious when a crew of stagehands is assembled to load-in the set and the scenery still is scattered around the paint shop or a drop still is stapled to the paint deck. In most productions, no leniency can be shown to the paint shop concerning the load-in date. In one of the most out-of-control productions I have ever been involved in, I saw scenery that had yet to be touched by the painters loaded on the truck. Nothing could be done—the truck was rented, the load-in crew had been called. The scenery had to be finished as well as possible in the theatre at touch-up. The main factor in this debacle was that the charge painter had realized from the beginning that the production was overdesigned and behind schedule. She had tried to explain these circumstances to the production management. But her warnings had gone unheeded. Naturally, the hours we put in during the week before the set loaded in were extensive. This unfortunate situation cannot be laid at the feet of the designer either. She was doing her job. She presented the shop with a design that had been approved by the director and production management. The design was sent straight into the shop without having been costed-out by the scenic artist and the technical director.

Costing Out a Design

Fortunately, most production management personnel are not so shortsighted. Out-of-control productions can result in a small fortune being paid in overtime wages. Inadequate preparation of a production is the number one reason for emergency situations. In most productions, the technical director and the scenic artist will be asked to cost out the design before it is released to the shops. When costing out a design, the scenic artist will need to consider three separate issues: time, materials, and space.

Costing out *time* will involve totaling the projected figures for hours of work, the time of the charge painter, scenic artists, and shop assistants. Once these hours have been totaled, they must be divided by the number of weeks and the number of regular work hours available in those weeks. If not enough work hours are available to paint the set, then the production management will have to be alerted that overhire or overtime will be necessary.

The cost of *materials* is the total cost of paint, finishes, texture, consumables, kit fees, and rental of special equipment that will be needed to paint the design. Also added to this figure should be a shop budget to cover the wear and tear on the shop equipment that has to be replaced and repaired on a regular basis.

The scenic artist inexperienced in costing out a production should carefully match the square-foot coverage information listed in the directions on cans of paint and finishes with the square footage of the scenery. When costing out labor and materials a contingency of 15% over the estimate should be added into both projected budgets to cover unforeseen expenditures.

Budgeting *space* is more involved. Painting scenery takes up a great deal of square footage. The amount of scenery that can be laid out in the space or that can occupy the paint frame, if there is one, at any one time is critical. No number of extra painters will help get the scenery painted any faster if there is not enough space for them to work in. The amount of scenery that can be laid out at the same time and the length of time it will take to paint and dry must be projected into the time available. If this figure comes up short, then more space will have to be rented, which will be an extra expense.

When budgeting time and materials on a design, the scenic artist works with the designer and the production staff to see if the design is feasible. If limitations are discovered, it does not necessarily mean major cuts are needed or that a redesign is necessary. Many times creative solutions are found that make it possible to realize the design. This is just another phase of collaboration.

Preproduction Planning

The charge painter normally begins a project before any of the other paint staff. Initially, the charge painter will study the bluelines, paint elevations, and additional material from the scene designer, outlining the scope of scenic art on that production. Then, the charge painter will talk with the designer concerning questions he or she may have about the scenic art in the design. This interview also will be instrumental in clarifying, for the charge painter, the designer's vision for the scenery (see Chapter Two). The charge painter's next task will be to evaluate the project for materials and labor needs as they fit into the schedule and the space available. The charge painter will submit the paint budget to the technical director or production manager for approval. Once the budget is approved, the charge painter usually will hire shop assistants to begin preparing the scenery and placing orders for the paints, special materials, and equipment for that production. Commitments will be made to other members of the crew based on the projected schedule for the production. The charge painter will do sample work needed at this point. Lead painters may be brought in to do samples and begin work on cartooning. The rest of the crew will be hired as soon as the scenery is loaded into the paint shop and ready for painting.

Frequently, the start-up for the paint crew at the beginning of a production is not as leisurely as this sounds. Only a few days' time may be available between the hiring of a charge painter and the first full day of painting. Skilled personnel may be difficult to locate. The shop space may not be adequate for the scale of the production. The time frame already may be compressed. It is not uncommon for the charge painter to find that problems like these must be resolved from the very start of a production. However, most producers and production companies are aware that committing to a charge painter and crew early and getting the design information to the charge painter long before the scenery comes into the paint shop are good business. Building and painting scenery in a crisis time frame will simply make the project more expensive and compromise the quality.

The Balance of Time, Space, and Labor

At the beginning of the production, the charge painter must weigh the staff requirements against the time and space available for painting. If the design requires twelve 60' × 27' drops, there will be

very specific space demands to execute them. If two drops can be painted side by side, then two teams of scenic artists will need to be hired. If the space is limited to painting one drop at a time, then the time frame for the project will need to be longer and the staff relatively small. Working vertically or horizontally also may have an effect on the time frame of a project. If a paint frame is available to paint drops on while the hard scenery is being painted on the floor, the production may be able to move through the shop very swiftly. All these factors will be part of what determines how many painters are needed for the project and the amount of time required for the job.

Before deciding on the number of people on the paint crew, the charge painter must look at the volume of scenery to be painted and determine if it can be painted in the space available in the given amount of time. It is a great luxury if there is such a vast amount of floor space in the paint shop that all the scenery for a given production can be laid down all at once. However, this very rarely is the case. Usually, the charge painter will have to decide how much scenery can be laid out at a given time and in what configuration. Then, the charge painter can begin to plan out how many teams of scenic artists are necessary, how many scenic artists on each team, and how long these teams, if working standard days, will need to finish the production.

When planning how to use the available space, it is crucial to take into account whether the paint area is shared with other shops. When space is configured so that the painters and construction crews are in the same space, the head carpenter and the charge painter must plan together the use of the space. Early in the production, the charge painter may need a lot of square footage for painting soft goods, ground cloths, or masonite decking. All these space-hungry units typically are painted early in the production, because they can be built quickly, painted while more space is available, and do not take up much room in storage. Later in the build, the construction shop may need the greater share of space for assembling and rigging large scenic units. It is imperative that these two departments schedule the use of space early on, to determine if extra shop space must be secured. Storage is another important issue to be discussed by the charge painter and the head carpenter ahead of time. Scenery stored in the paint area will slowly encroach on that space as the units are completed.

When scheduling which scenic units are painted and at what point in the time schedule, the charge painter should first divide the scenery into similar groups and then divide those groups among the teams of scenic artists working on the production. For instance, suppose there are two different scenes, each consisting of a backdrop and hard scenery, one scene primarily painted as marble and the other primarily painted as wood paneling. Given enough space, the charge painter may decide to have two teams of scenic artists working on the scenes simultaneously. To begin, the first team will paint the drop for the marble scene on the paint deck while the second team paints the hard units for the wood paneling scene elsewhere in the shop. Then these two teams will switch locations in the shop. The first team will move on to the hard scenery for the marble while the second team moves to the paint deck to paint the backdrop for the wood paneling scene. This way the painting within each setting is consistent and the space in the paint shop is efficiently used.

On a day-to-day basis, the charge painter must judge if the work is proceeding according to schedule. This is one of the most important aspects of a charge painter's work. Estimating the time needed to paint a piece of scenery is a skill that comes with experience. A charge painter needs to envision every step of the painting process and how long each of these steps might take. Keep in mind that oil-based paints and finishes take more time to dry than water-based mediums, so the space involved will be tied up longer. Also, when dealing with toxic materials more space and time might be necessary so that these processes can be isolated from other people working in the shop. If unsure, always estimate conservatively. Do not overlook color mixing, preparation, priming, layout, drying, handling the scenery, and clean-up. All of these nonpainting activities take quite a lot of time. For instance, stretching and priming a drop can take two people several hours. Usually, a full day of preparation and drying will be needed before cartooning and painting a drop can begin.

The charge painter must have a firm idea of how much time is required to paint a production. A production may require more painters than currently are allotted by the production company or more hours than are in the standard workday. The load-in day is the finite point in time by which the scenery must be completed and generally is not a negotiable item. If additional staff or shop time will be required, it is important to advise the technical director or produc-

tion manager of this well in advance. It always is much more difficult to add staff at the end of a project. Asking for more painters at the end can be a sign of poor planning and money may not be available for overtime. A well-prepared and experienced charge painter can predict well in advance whether resources are adequate to meet the demands of the project.

Independent Contracting

A scenic artist working as an independent contractor has a larger job. After learning the time frame and the design particulars from the client production company, the independent contractor will need to prepare a bid for the job. Included in the bid will be the costs for:

- An appropriate space for painting.
- The cost of crew members, including base pay, social security, workers compensation insurance, unemployment insurance, food and housing per diem for employees, tool or kit fees, and travel expenses.
- All standard equipment normally found in the scene shop; this list may include air compressors, airless sprayers, fans, and maybe even a paint deck.
- Any special equipment necessary for this production that may have to be rented or purchased.
- Beyond the obvious physical needs are the additional business overhead needs and expenses that others rarely need to consider; items such as insurance, shipping, office expenses, accounting expenses, and the time it takes to deal with contracts, payroll, quarterly withholding and tax payments, workers comp, and other complex financial considerations are a necessary part of independent contracting on a large scale.

Working with the Other Painters

Scenic artists work in physically demanding conditions for long hours, creating large, complex, two- and three-dimensional works of art based on the visual information from the scenic designer. The charge painter must carefully blend the combined efforts of these many hands as seamlessly as possible and be able to recognize the strengths of each painter and put those strengths to good use to ensure that the whole project has a stylistic continuity.

To synthesize the efforts of the scenic art crew, the charge painter will break down a project into stylistic units. For example, one might mentally put all the wood graining into one slot, the foliage into another, and the lettering into a third. Each of these types of painting is going to use different tools, colors, and skills. The charge painter who assigns a scenic artist or teams of scenic artists to different elements of the scenery will carefully match the skills and experience of crew members to the projects at hand. Lead painters may be asked to create samples of specific treatments. After approval by the designer, these samples and techniques will serve as guides for other members of the crew. As more people are added to the crew or team, they can refer to the sample work for stylistic continuity. When assigning scenic artists to execute freehand or loose techniques like foliage or marble, the charge painter should select artists that can see the project through until the end, for the sake of continuity. Some painters may never "click into" the style needed, and the charge painter may need to reassign them or put another painter on the project. It must be added that one of the greatest pleasures of charging a production is watching other experienced artists masterfully paint the units they are assigned. By giving other artists enough psychological space to do their work in their own way, the charge painter stands to increase his or her knowledge.

Working with the Technical Director

What to Build and Paint First

Ideally, the charge painter and the technical director will cooperate on a construction schedule that will emphasize completing units in the order that they most logically should be painted. It is important to paint like units and units common to the same scene together, in order to use the paint time and space in the most efficient means possible. The technical director and charge painter also must take into account that texturing processes and sculpting can require enormous amounts of time to execute, seal, and thoroughly dry. These should be addressed at the very beginning of the construction and paint process. In some scenic designs, the properties place great demands on the production schedule and are considered an important part of the scenic construction. It may be necessary to include the properties manager in preliminary discussions. Much of this communication will take place in production meetings, where information is exchanged between departments.

Special Construction Requirements for the Scenic Artist

Scenery needs to be built to allow efficient painting, and thought should be given to how the scenery needs to be handled by the scenic artist. Proper construction technique includes allowing the scenic artist to paint all the scenery in the shop as thoroughly as possible. This may seem obvious, but it is a critical part of the construction process. Also important is that the scenic artist oversee the construction process to catch potential problems before the scenery reaches the paint shop. Building even simple scenic units involves many, many variables. The placement of seams on and between units greatly influences the final outcome. Some designers are extremely precise as to where seams should fall, while others may pay less attention to these small details that can potentially interfere with appearance of the scenic art. For instance, if there is a predominantly vertical pattern on the walls from a wallpaper pattern, the seams of the walls themselves should be incorporated into that pattern whenever possible. The scenic artist should pay close attention to how units are built, whether or not the scenic designer does. The scenic artist should pay close attention to what scenic materials the scenic designer has specified for scenic units. Unorthodox materials may require special attention or sampling to search for compatible mediums. During the construction of the scenery, the designer may notify either the technical director or the charge painter about changes in specified materials or treatments. The technical director and the charge painter always should check with one another when any changes occur in construction specifications.

Other issues that the scenic artist and the technical director may need to discuss are application of hardware, window and door thicknesses or reveals, and decorative moldings to the scenery. Reveals in doors and windows may need to be detached from the units so that they can be laid out separately for the painters. These reveals can be painted and attached to the units later. Some hardware may be put right in the middle of where the painter needs to make a careful blend. Better that the hardware is fitted, then removed for the painting. The same can be true of decorative moldings. It may also be simpler to paint them separately if they take a different color or paint treatment. Better to fit moldings first, carefully label them, and attach them to the unit after both have been painted. This approach has pitfalls, too. The scenic artist must be prepared for touch-ups over nail and bolt heads.

The scenery should be ready to paint when transferred to the paint shop. Ready means no unfilled holes, edges sanded as needed, no hardware in the way, and so forth. The scenery also must be structurally sound enough to be handled, painted, and in most cases, carefully walked on by the scenic artists. The scenery must be accessible to the scenic artist, which may require building custom supports for heavy scenic units or scaffolds for the scenic artists. Often, a technical director and scenic artist will need to coordinate the schedule of their crews just to allow for handling scenery in the paint process. If a unit weighs 1,000 pounds and needs to be moved, who moves it? That is not the job of the painters alone. Some shops prefer that scenic artists do not shift or stack the scenery.

Working with Other Production Departments

Theatrical production departments are interdependent because the production itself is the product of all the departments working together. So it should not be a surprise to the scenic artist when the stage director, stage manager, or publicity manger shows up in the paint shop. Usually, the paint area gets a visit from other departments simply because painters do best what nearly every other area needs sometime or another. The publicity department may need a sign painted and lack the means to get it done. Perhaps an electrician needs footlights painted gold. In theatre, people generally help each other out with the little things. (Do not forget to ask for extra tickets or an extra light by the mixing table!)

Other departments may be expected to paint their work for a production. Costume and properties generally have sizable paint areas. But scenic artists should be aware that these departments still may rely in part on the paint shop, because the paint shop is probably the best equipped area in which to paint.

Working with the Costume Shop

A well-equipped costume shop will usually have a subdepartment, the crafts department, where hats and accessories are made or altered and where materials and costume items are dyed. The crafts department will usually have a dye vat for mixing and heating large volumes of dye. The dye vat is very useful to the paint department, because scenic artists frequently are called on to dye soft goods to a specific color for the scenic designer. In the case of such a request, the charge painter will have to make arrangements with the crafts departments or costume manager to use the dye vat, based on shop demand and schedule. The paint shop may be able to return the favor when the costume shop needs floor space to distress a large quantity of costumes or use the large-volume spray booth in the paint shop.

Working with the Properties Shop

The properties shop has a lot of crossover work with the paint area. Unlike the scenic construction area, the properties shop generally paints the units that it builds. This custom is true particularly with furniture pieces and small hand props. There are exceptions; some property shops may be understaffed or set up only for acquisition and construction. Generally, a good props shop will keep its own supply of paint, stains, solvents, and brushes for their own needs. It is unlikely, however, that the props area will have everything needed for more complex paint jobs. Frequently, members of the properties shop will visit the paint shop to borrow a cup of this or that, a particular tool, or to ask the favor of having a scenic artist mix up a specific color.

Occasionally the scenic designer will design the properties to be painted in an abstract or stylized manner that matches the scenery. Perhaps a large property has been designed that is the focus of a scene or production. In this case, the charge painter and properties manager will need to plan props painting together. Occasionally, a production will come along that is particularly extensive in terms of the volume of properties or the amount of properties that have to be built. In such a situation, the paint department, if not likewise overwhelmed, may assist the properties shop by taking over all or a large percentage of the properties painting for that production. When a charge painter comes into a new organization, it is important to meet with the properties manager, technical director, and production manager to discuss how the painting of properties is handled in that organization. Otherwise, after working hard to get the scenery done, the charge painter may be surprised by the pile of properties that appears in the paint shop the day before load-in.

CONCLUSION

The key to staying current with the developments in other departments is communication and cooperation. A scenic artist needs to keep in mind that he or she does not work in a vacuum, and that, in theatre, this occupation is very heavily intertwined in the complex world of scenic production. In addition to the weekly or monthly production meetings scheduled by the production manager, the charge painter should make it a habit to check in with the technical director, head carpenter, and properties manager on a regular basis. Different organizations have different methods for keeping the lines of communication open. These methods may depend on the preferences of the individual department heads. In some organizations, the shop heads make a point of having lunch together the same day every week. When working as the staff charge painter for the University of Michigan, the technical director and I informally conferred when we went out for coffee during afternoon breaks. This ten to fifteen minutes three or four times a week was very valuable in terms of a smoothly running shop.

chapter 4

The Scenic Artist's Working Space

with contributions by Monona Rossol

INTRODUCTION

The primary purpose of the scenic artist's working space is to quickly and efficiently complete a production as designed. Producers and technical directors as well as scenic artists should be aware that speed and efficiency can only be attained if the scene shop has sufficient space, adequate lighting and electrical outlets, running water, the right tools for the job, and adequate safety precautions (nothing can halt production like accidents).

Scene shops are hazardous workplaces. Toxic paints, electrical equipment, scaffolds and ladders, and other hazards are present. For this reason, the materials, equipment, and even the design of the shop itself must meet the regulations of the Occupational Safety and Health Administration (OSHA).

Other rules that must be considered are local fire and building codes, environmental protection rules, and toxic waste disposal regulations. Some of the local rules and the OSHA regulations will be covered in this chapter when relevant. However, no text can cover all these regulations. Instead, OSHA requires employers to determine which regulations are applicable to their particular workplaces and to train and protect their workers. Employers in scene shops rarely meet these obligations. As a result, scenic artists usually must educate themselves about safety and health.

THE PAINTING SPACE

For safety and efficiency, scene shop painting areas should be located apart from construction areas. Construction areas have different lighting and space demands and usually produce wood dust and other dusts that will settle on painting. Wood dusts and welding fumes are also hazardous for painters to breathe.

On the other hand, painting can be hazardous to construction workers. Solvent vapors, spray mists, and other flammable materials are toxic for construction workers to breathe. In addition, some materials can be fire and explosion hazards around welding or some types of woodworking machinery.

Unlike construction areas, paint areas do not necessarily need a lot of expensive equipment. In fact, for most productions, a paint staff can operate well with only good brushes, paint, and water. Painting areas also need even lighting throughout, some areas where light can be focused, running water and sinks, plenty of electrical outlets, counter areas for mixing, handy storage areas for paints, good equipment for applying and mixing paints, and good ventilation.

But most of all, paint areas must have space—and plenty of it. Scenic artists must spread out their work. Many individual pieces should be worked on in sequence and left to dry without being moved. Although rarely possible, the aim should be to have enough space on the floor and paint frame areas to lay out an entire show at once.

High ceilings are also necessary. It is not unusual for scenic artists to be expected to paint fully constructed units that are eighteen- to twenty-four-feet tall.

THE LAYOUT OF THE SCENIC STUDIO

The production process has a flow that we have discussed in the first chapters of this book. Timing, sequencing, and cooperation are critical to the fabrication process, and this interdependence is reflected in the physical layout of the scenic studios. The fairly simple pattern of the flow of materials in a scene shop affects how the paint area works in relation to the other shops. Generally speaking, large pieces of raw materials come into the shop through a loading door. These raw materials of muslin, wood, and metal are crafted into smaller pieces and assembled into units of scenery. The scenery then is passed on to the scenic artists for painting, texturing, and finishing. Once painting is completed, the scenery is stored until it is time to move it on stage or onto a truck for shipping.

To accommodate this pattern easily, a scene shop should have three elements:

1. Enough space to move scenery around easily;
2. Separate spaces for the construction and paint shops so that the staffs of both shops can work simultaneously;
3. Areas in the shop where raw materials and finished scenery can be stored.

Many shops have severe space limitations. Some productions will even press the limitations of the most spacious shop, forcing the construction and painting to be done in a specific sequence. This is why it is very important for the technical director, the construction shop head, and the charge painter to work together scheduling the movement of scenery through the shop.

THE SCENIC PAINTING AREA

Painters need two basic kinds of work area: a painting area and a preparation area. The painting area can be very simple. Any large interior with a flat floor, high ceiling, and good light is a fine painting area. The space can become more flexible and sophisticated with paint frames, specialized flooring, specific lighting, even a viewing gallery. The preparation area must have a sink with running water, a mixing table or bench, and storage, and good quality lighting is particularly important in this area. There also may be a spray booth, customized storage areas, flammable cabinets, and a separate drafting area for complex drawing projects.

Managing the Painting Area

Minimally, a paint shop needs enough space to lay out a full stage drop or a stageful of hard scenery with room enough to walk around the units. Any space beyond this minimum will increase the efficiency of a paint shop. The paint process often starts with the dance of moving scenery around; the scenery must be choreographed carefully through the shops.

If the construction shop and the paint shop space are combined in one room, the space must be flexible enough to accommodate either the construction staff, painters, or both, as necessary. The size, shape, and amount of the scenery certainly will dictate this. The efficiency of a paint shop is related directly to the amount of space available. Time, space, and labor are interconnected. If a production design includes fourteen large wall units, all of them textured and colored similarly, the most efficient way for the scenic artists to work would be to address all of these units at the same time. In this way, each step in the painting process is completely finished on all the units. After the wall units have been stored away, the next phase of the design can be laid out for painting. This phase may be the stage deck or the backing units. But, if space is limited and only half of the wall units can be painted at a time, the painting schedule will take longer and special care will have to be taken to ensure consistency between the two groups of scenery. With less space, it may be necessary to hire extra painters to finish the scenery on time, however, due to the spatial limitations, these painters will not be able to work as efficiently.

Enough space to paint a full stage backdrop is critical in a paint shop. Without adequate drop layout space, either up or down as described next, a paint area is hampered. Drops should be laid out fully to be painted efficiently. A rented space may turn out to be cheaper and more efficient in the long run. If no space is available for a full stage drop in the studio, consider the stage itself. Otherwise, the option is to paint the drop in *two bites*. A drop can also be divided into smaller sections by the designer to fit in the shop space and later used on stage as a single unit or a group of units.

Shop Configuration and Painting Techniques

A paint shop basically consists of a floor and walls, both of which are important as potential work surfaces. These surfaces also represent the two choices a scenic artist has in methods of working: vertically or horizontally. An extensive scene shop will be configured so the scenic artists have the choice of painting in either method.

The Eastern or Vertical Style

Painting *vertically*, also called *working up*, *painting up*, or the *eastern style*, is a common method and one of the oldest methods of painting scenery. Until the beginning of the twentieth century, scenery, for the most part, was two-dimensional. Much of the scenery made by production companies in the nineteenth century was painted on a frame hung on the back wall of a theatre's stage. Painting in this style requires that either the drop must move up and down in front of the painters, or the painters must move up and down in front of the drop. This technique requires one or two important pieces of equipment. The first is a large wooden frame to mount the drop on. The frame either moves (called a *floating frame*) or is fixed (a *static frame*). A static frame requires a second piece of equipment called a flying bridge or scaffolding that a painter can use to reach the entire drop on the frame.

Painting up still is particularly useful and space-efficient for painting soft goods. The frame provides one large work area, while other pieces of scenery can be worked on the paint deck. Painting up is convenient as painting tools are at hand at all times, and it is easy for the painter to view the work in progress. Painting work directly in front of you is easier on your back as well, but painting up makes the paint and any washy or wet techniques difficult to control.

The Continental Style

The alternative is to work with the scenery laying on the floor, also called *working down* or the *continental style* (Figure 4.1). Working down is fine for nearly all styles of scenic painting, but it requires more caution to avoid spills and walking on wet areas of the scenery. Painting scenery on the floor requires that painters use long-handled brushes or brushes in bamboo or dowel extensions. Working with extensions is necessary because it is brutally hard on one's back and knees to bend over and down all day. The brush extensions take a little time to adapt to, but the skill is developed rather easily and will stay with you. Once accustomed to painting down, it is as comfortable as painting up.

How These Styles Developed

At the turn of the century, American commercial scenic studios and production company scene shops tended to work vertically (Figure 4.2). Vertical painting once the frames are installed makes good business sense. A scenic studio based on the eastern style, churning out backdrops, needs much less floor space. The technique of working down adapted well to studio spaces where height is limited. This sort of low studio was common in continental Europe where this style evolved. Continental style permits the painting to be looser and wetter, more like actual watercolor technique. The Austrian designer Joseph Urban brought this technique to the United States in 1911. He brought an atelier of scenic artists with him from Vienna to Boston when he became artistic director of the Boston Opera, and the continental style came with them (Larson, 1989). The style was sporadically imitated at first, as most American scenic studios relied on the eastern method and older scenic artists resisted the change. However, scenic designers of the early twentieth century sought new techniques, and such designers as Urban, Robert Edmond Jones, Lee Simonson, and Norman Bel Geddes designed scenery that relied on continental style. The Adler brothers, who came over with Urban, founded Triangle Studios in New York City and popularized the style. Robert W. Bergman, of Lee Lash Studios, New York, developed many innovative painting techniques for these designers in the 1920s that relied on the continental technique (ibid.).

Most students of scenic art today probably will start to learn the trade by painting down, now the most common system of painting scenery. This method of work allows for greater freedom in painting technique. A scenic artist can apply paint much more freely and rapidly working down. The drop or

Figure 4.1 Scenic artist Kat Sharp painting with extensions at Cobalt Studios (scrim designed by José Varona for Miami Ballet Company production of "Nutcracker").

the scenic unit can be soaked, sprayed, scumbled, or whatever without fear of paint running and streaking. Almost all blending techniques are easier on the floor, and it is as comfortable as painting up. Working down is more convenient because painters can access all areas of the drop at the same time. One painter can be finessing the sky while another painter is working on foliage at the bottom of the backdrop.

Working in the Eastern Style

Working up generally is limited to two-dimensional scenery, such as drops and flats. One of the hardest aspects of working up is to achieve techniques such as glazes and spatter without drips and running paint. Paint may have to be thickened, blends may need to be sprayed with paint guns. It can be neater,

because the scenery is not walked on and there is less chance of spillage. However, a paint drip can run for several feet. Many paint frames are hung to tilt out four to six inches at the top so that most drips fall harmlessly to the floor.

Working vertically with efficiency requires certain large pieces of equipment to move either the painter or the work up and down. Paint bridges, on which the painter stands while working, are expensive permanent pieces of shop equipment, but they allow the painter access to the full width of the drop at once. Bridges themselves also can move up and down, or the frame can move in front of the bridge. Alternately, a drop or unit of scenery can be stapled or nailed to a wall or paint frame and reached by ladders, scaffolding, a lift, or a specialized paint scaffold called a paint *boomerang*. In the case of these

Figure 4.2 Twin City Scenic's studio interior. Painters worked on narrow, static paint bridges between floating frames, St. Paul, Minnesota (courtesy of C. Lance Brockman).

last few methods, the painters have to move themselves side to side and climb or raise the lift to the levels where they need to work. To paint a house by these methods is fine; but for the complexities of scenic art, these methods of working up are inefficient and can be exhausting for the scenic artist.

Paint Bridges and Static Frames

If the painters move, they require a floating *paint bridge* wide enough to span a frame large enough to accommodate a full stage drop. Standing on the paint bridge, scenic artists can move themselves up and down to work on whatever section of the drop they need access to and can walk back and forth in front of the drop. The bridge is counterweighted for ease of movement. The bridge should be moved by a motorized winch, with limit switches at the upper

and lower limits of travel for safety. The controls for the winch should be located on the paint bridge with a remote switch. The front of the bridge, facing the work, should be as open as the OSHA regulations regarding fall protection will allow. The bridge must be railed and gaited all the way around with toe boards at the edges. Whenever workers are ten feet above the floor, they must be harnessed and tied off. The back of the bridge should have a shelf to hold paint and brushes that also are tied off so they cannot fall and hit someone below. The bridge also may be outfitted with pneumatic air chucks for working with spray equipment.

The flying bridge (Figure 4.3) gives the painters access to the scenery, drops, or flats that are attached to a *static frame*. Static frames are either wood trusses or free-span frame. In the case of a trussed

Figure 4.3 Susan Crabtree painting on a freespan frame and flying paint bridge at Tobins Lake Studios, Brighton, Michigan.

frames, wood battens are added to the frame to match the shape of the soft goods in order to provide a complete nailing surface all the way around the perimeter of the drop (Figure 4.4). This feature allows any size soft goods to be painted on the frame. Wooden truss frames easily can leave an imprint on a drop, as the fabric of the drop presses on the truss regularly while being painted. After working on the truss frame for a time, a painter will adapt his or her technique and lighten brushstrokes to avoid picking up the pattern of the truss.

Free-span frames have no internal supports to leave an imprint from brushstrokes. The drop is hung off a traveler track, then piped and clamped at the bottom so that it pulls taut. The sides are attached to long boards moved back and forth on tracks behind the soft goods, which can be moved into position at the sides of the drop (Figure 4.5). These boards can be locked into place and sometimes stiffened to withstand the pull of the drop when it shrinks during priming. Flatage can be painted from a free-span frame system by setting the scenery on the floor or a ledge at the bottom of the frame.

Floating Frames

Floating frames are trussed wooden frames rigged to a head block or pulleys that move up and down on steel tracks bolted to the wall or steel beams. The frame is counterweighted and may be controlled by an electric winch. The floating frame is used like a static frame, but it moves up and down instead of the scenic artist. There are two ways scenery on a floating frame can be reached by the scenic artists.

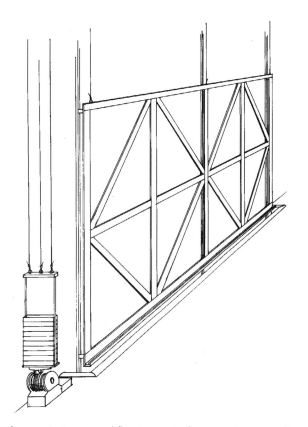

Figure 4.4 Trussed floating paint frame and paint well.

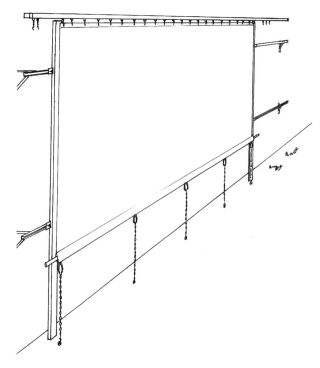

Figure 4.5 A free-span paint frame.

Most common is the floating frame that sinks into a slit in the floor, called the *paint well*, until only the last five feet or so at the top of the frame are exposed. The frame rises up out of the well until the bottom truss of the frame is exposed. This system requires a well about fifty feet wide by fifteen feet to twenty feet high and a few feet deep. The top of the well narrows to a thin slot, only a few inches wider than the frame, for safety reasons. Generally, these wells have a curb in front to keep errant brushes and buckets topside. This curb also acts as a toe stop for the scenic artists. As tools are occasionally dropped into the paint well, there should be an access door on the floor below for retrieving snap lines, brushes, and Frisbees.

Not so common, because it requires nearly fifty feet of ceiling height, is the frame that moves up and down in front of a fixed paint bridge (see Figure 4.2). The painter works on a static bridge or catwalk positioned at mid-height of the room and the frame is raised or lowered so that the painter can

reach any part of the drop. This arrangement is much more efficient if there is access to water, storage, and a lift for paint, so the scenic artist need not spend too much of the day hauling buckets and tools up and down stairs. In all situations, the frame must be controlled conveniently by the painter. This type of frame also may be operated manually or, more conveniently, by a motorized winch with a remote switch.

In all cases, working up always keeps the work at eye level and within arm's reach. The paint buckets are easy to reach from the cart you keep at hand or on a shelf at the back of the catwalk or paint bridge. The paint frame is very useful for working on two-dimensional flatage as well. The limit generally is in the width of the paint well that the frame slips into or the space between the frame and the bridge. Usually, this distance is no more than six inches, so that the painter can stay as close as possible to the work. Painting up like this generally is as fast as painting down. Parts of the preparation and layout can be considerably simpler for one person to do when working vertically.

Working in the Continental Style

Some pieces of scenery can be painted only on a floor. Large three-dimensional units cannot be mounted on a frame at all. In most scene shops, the *paint deck* is the primary painting space. A paint deck should be made of wood, so that drops can be stapled onto it and other scenic units nailed down. Wooden flooring is expensive, however, and new scenic shops may not be able to afford the cost of installing a wooden floor. A full wood deck basically is needed only for soft goods, and there are reasonable alternatives. A wood frame can quickly be assembled to the size of the drop to be painted. This frame can be set down temporarily to accommodate the painting. However, if the soft goods to be painted are very large, the frame may bow or warp while the drop is stretching during priming. A temporary wooden surface of plywood can easily be assembled for use as a paint deck. Even soft fiber boards, like Homasote or Celotex, can be used for a temporary paint deck. These temporary solutions all have some drawbacks. Floors of a sheeting material will shift if they are not anchored down. Temporary sheet stock floors may warp due to humidity, wet paint techniques, or spillage. Uneven surfaces prevent proper stretching of the soft goods and inhibit even brushstrokes. A drop will take on the texture of whatever it is lying over as it is painted, which makes smooth, even flooring surfaces very important. If soft goods are painted in the shop on a regular basis, then invest in a proper three-quarter-inch plywood-covered paint deck. The deck should be securely attached to a subframe, or for greater versatility it may be joined together with coffin locks.

Painting down is flexible and convenient. It requires only space, a bucket, and a brush. Laying out scenery on the floor is much simpler because nothing needs to be nailed to a frame, and no counterweights or winches must be dealt with. Two pieces of equipment are useful when painting down: the paint cart and the bucket basket, or paint carrier (Figures 4.6 and 4.7). Buckets are never set directly on the scenery or soft goods, because paint may run down the side of the bucket and leave a ring on the scenery. And, once working with extensions, it makes no sense for the scenic artist to continually retrieve and move buckets. Paint carts are paint trays on wheels. At one end of the paint cart is a set of upright supports with a bar between them at hip

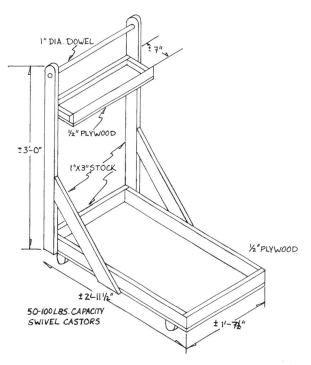

Figure 4.6 A paint cart (design by Mary Ellen Kennedy).

height, so the scenic artist can wheel the paint across a drop or around scenery like pushing a shopping cart. Below the push bar may be a tray for smaller items, such as cartooning tools, or to prop up the paint elevation. The lower tray of these carts should be large enough to accommodate at least two five-gallon buckets or half a dozen one-gallon buckets. Bucket baskets are trays large enough for only one or two one-gallon buckets. These have an upright handle at hip height as well but no castors. They are carried from place to place. For certain tasks, where just one or two buckets are needed, the bucket basket can be more convenient to use than the paint cart.

Working on a Stage Floor

Most theatres come equipped with a large wooden deck that is extremely well suited for painting. This is the stage floor, and it can become a valuable part of the scenic artist's workplace. Yet, important considerations may render the stage floor impractical. Producers and managers make their money from

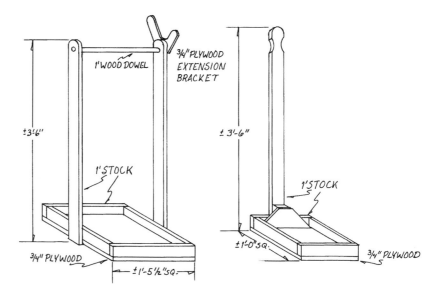

Figure 4.7
Bucket baskets.

performances. Obviously, if a stage is in use as a paint area, the theatre is unavailable as a performance house. An empty theatre loses money, so a producer may elect to put the painting area in a warehouse instead of tying up the stage for the scenic artist. The alternative is carefully planning the stage availability between productions. This returns to the issue of scheduling, which is covered in Chapter Three. If available, the stage floor is very good for painting drops. The floor is usually wooden, very level, and free of any supporting columns. When planning to work on a stage floor, do not overlook having lighting installed, as most stages do not keep a complex system of work lights available. All tools and water will have to be brought to the stage. The stage deck and walls should be protected from paint with drop cloths or plastic sheeting.

Lighting and Other Utilities in the Scenic Painting Area

The lighting in a paint studio is very important. A scenic artist must have considerable light in which to work. It has to be bright enough to see the work clearly and of a very particular quality for theatrical work. A scenic artist must be aware of light intensity and color temperature in the studio.

The Effects of Color Temperature

Stage lighting has a very specific *color temperature*. Color temperature is the relative whiteness of light measured in degrees Kelvin. A heat lamp has a very low color temperature, around 2,200 K, and it casts an orange glow. In the real world, color temperatures of light can vary widely from the average home incandescent light (low color temperature, 2,700 K) to noontime sunlight (high color temperature, 6,500 K) and even much higher natural light conditions. This variance can change the apparent color of paint. The scenic artist must be aware of the lighting conditions for the finished scenery, which for the theatre is around 2,800 K to 3,200 K. A stage set to be viewed under theatrical lighting needs to be prepared differently than a corporate logo meant to be seen in an outdoor setting. This consideration should be addressed in the painting studio. Ideally, a theatrical paint studio will have a bank of stage lights over the paint and mixing areas to complement the existing light. Although fluorescent light is an economical choice for scene shops, it is a very poor choice for the critical work of color mixing. Fluorescent lighting will affect color perception because of its color temperature. Fluorescent fixtures can be corrected to the same Kelvin range as incandescent fixtures with color-corrective filters. Some people can still perceive a shift in color when moving between areas lit with incandescent and fluorescent lights, even when color-corrective filters are used on the fluorescent fixtures.

Sunlight, although aesthetically pleasing, is problematic in a scenic studio. As pleasant as it is to have natural light pouring through the windows, the effect on perception of color is unwanted. Sunlight makes subtle shifts of color hard to detect, bleaches out bright colors, and reflects into the eyes of the painter. The warmth of sunlight can cause patchy and uneven drying. Cover windows with translucent shutters or curtains for any complex painting situation so the sunlight is diffused.

Light Intensity

Light in a scenic studio should be bright and even. Evenly placed lights will illuminate every corner of the paint shop from several different directions and sources. Ideally the lighting should be consistent from the mixing area to the paint area so the colors do not appear altered in different areas in response to color temperature. The lighting should be placed high enough above the scenic artist so that it does not shine in his or her eyes. Many shops are moving toward interior/exterior tungsten halogen fixtures. These put out a good source of light, are much longer-lasting than incandescent sources, resemble stage lighting in color temperature, and are reasonably priced.

Compressed Air

A source of compressed air is very useful for the scenic artist, and ideally, it should be available in several locations throughout the paint shop as well as the mixing area. There also should be a supply of 10', 20', and 30' air hoses for working with pneumatic tools, such as power compressed-air paint guns and pressurized garden sprayers (see Chapter Five). These guns can be primary tools in the painting process of a particular production. Compressed air also can be used to power staplers and air nozzles for blowing off charcoal and pounce dust. Many shops have a compressed air system throughout the complex. In large shops, the source of compressed air is a large reservoir compressor, ideally hidden somewhere out of earshot. If a pneumatic system has not been installed in the shop, a portable compressor will provide plenty of power for most painting jobs; however, portable compressors are noisy and not pleasant company.

The compressed air available to carpenters may have a device in the system know as an *oiler*. Oilers mix small amounts of light oil into the compressed air, which is good for pneumatic nailers and staplers. An oiler is not good for any device that sprays paint or sprays onto a painted surface. The oil will mix with the paint and leave small discolored spots on the painted surface. Scenic shops should run a separate air line without oilers for the paint area.

Either the air lines or the spray tools in the paint shop need regulators to control air pressure. Most pneumatic tools in the construction shop are operated at pressures far too high for paint tools. A regulator in the paint shop can be set to reduce the pressure to 55 psi for spray guns and 30 psi for garden sprayers to avoid overpressurizing these tools, possibly causing a messy rupture in the hose or tank of the tool.

Using Fans

Fans are important tools. They can be used for drying or floating drops as well as for drying paint and texture. Drops stapled to the stage deck must be floated by forcing air under them for proper priming. (Drop preparation is discussed in Chapter Seven.) Fans can shorten drying time and help keep production on schedule. In some climates and during the rainy seasons in others, they are indispensable. Vladimir Polunin ([1927] 1980) refers to the need for fans in 1916: "In England, drying takes much longer than on the Continent owing to the moisture in the air and the fireproofing in the canvas. In Paris, a primed cloth will dry thoroughly in half a day in the summer; in Monte Carlo in even less time. In England, during the periods of winter fogs, a primed cloth may not dry for several days, hence heating and drying arrangements are necessary."

> Standing fans are more efficient than window fans to speed drying time. Box fans, used by carpet cleaners to speed carpet drying, force out air close to the floor surface. They are terrific for drying drops.

Electric outlets for fans should be convenient and easy to reach. Nothing can slow work more than having to look for an open outlet to plug in a fan (see Safety and Health Regulations in this chapter).

Other Work Areas in the Paint Shop

Layout and Pounce Area

A separate work area for cartooning, pouncing (see Chapter Eight), and other drawing projects is very useful in the paint area. Much of the cartooning on the scenery and pounces will be done on the paint deck; however, it is very useful for the scenic artist to have a drawing board where complex images and designs can be drafted. It is efficient and comfortable if a permanent 4' × 8' pounce table is set up in the shop for this sort of work. (Pouncing and cartooning are discussed in Chapter Eight.)

The Office

Every paint shop should have an office area where the business of the shop is conducted. Reference books, catalogues, computers, fax machines, copiers, and other business equipment are kept in this area. This is also where the charge painter manages the paperwork involved in running the shop. The designer's model, paint elevations, and bluelines should be stored in the office in flat storage files. Storage is especially important in shops where more than one design is in production at a time. These materials must be kept sorted out, so they do not get mixed up or lost.

Unless a separate room is available, the safety materials belong here as well, including first aid kits, the "Right to Know" handbook including material safety data sheets and the written Right to Know program, and the telephone with emergency numbers posted prominently near it. The presence of these materials also means that this office must not be locked during any hours where work is on-going.

The Break Area

The employees of scene shops have a right to a break every two hours and one meal break after every four hours worked. OSHA requires that a clean hazard-free environment be provided for breaks and meals. This rule means that the area must not be contaminated with the same dusts and air contaminants as the work areas. The alternatives are: 1) a separate lunch room in which chemical products are not used or stored, 2) designating a part of the office, or 3) allowing workers to eat off site.

THE SCENIC ARTIST'S PREPARATION AREA

The preparation area is where paint is mixed for projects and stored. Painting tools are also stored in this area. This important work area has special requirements and needs good organization and maintenance.

Paint Mixing

Paint mixing, testing, and sample making needs to take place away from the scenery, in a space set up for it. When working in this area, the scenic artists will have specific needs, and the preparation work space should be designed for convenience and efficiency (Figure 4.8).

> I like to compare the layout of the mixing area to a well-designed kitchen. The scenic artist should be able to move between the mixing bench or table, water source, raw color stock, and buckets with few steps, in the same manner that a kitchen is designed for efficient movement between the sink, refrigerator, stove, and countertops.

Mixing paint requires a table or bench, mixing tools, paint, water, and good light. The mixing bench should be at a height that allows the scenic artist to easily see into buckets on the bench, about thirty-six inches. The mixing bench should be at least 4' × 8', which allows two people to work at the same time and spread out as many colors as needed. If several painters work in the paint shop at the same time on multiple projects, then additional mixing benches may be necessary. Mixing colors for a drop easily can require a dozen different scenic paints. The only way to work is with every can of color at hand at all times. Often the individual colors mixed for a drop have very close relationships to each other, as the person mixing them tends to develop them together. In painting a foliage drop, all the green paints will be out: chrome green, emerald, dark green, green shade blue, and so on.

There are different configurations for the mixing bench. The mixing bench often is designed around the available space adjacent to the paint sink. In some cases, the mixing stock used to mix the paint is kept on shelf adjacent to the mixing bench. Even more convenient is for the mixing stock to be stored

Figure 4.8
A paint mixing area.

on shelf units at the back of the mixing bench or in the center of the bench so that two scenic artists can work simultaneously (Figure 4.9). A five-gallon bucket of white latex or acrylic paint, common to scenic painting, should be kept under or adjacent to the mixing bench with a large stainless steel ladle to make it easy to scoop out paint. To keep the paint from drying out, the lid of the five-gallon bucket can be notched out around the handle of the ladle. If the mixing bench cannot be located near the paint sink, then several five-gallon buckets, or a trash can, of fresh water and a ladle should be kept at the mixing table as well.

The mixing bench should have a bucket of a dozen or so large stainless steel spoons for scooping paint out of the mixing stock. Concentrated paint is very thick; many a plastic spoon has broken off in the bucket. Metal rice spoons and ladles work very well. There also should be several rubber bowl scrapers to squeegee the thick paint off of spoons and ladles. With the bucket of spoons and scrapers, there also may be a bucket of water for dirty utensils, so the paint does not dry up on them.

Stir sticks and kitchen whisks have been used to mix paint for decades, but modern paint shops rely on drills with a paint stirring attachment for mixing paint. The paint drills should be kept adjacent to the mixing table with the attachment in a bucket of water to keep it clean, or stored in holders connected to the edge of the mixing table. The drum-style paint stirring attachments work best because they direct

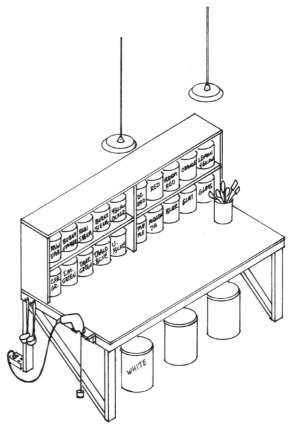

Figure 4.9   A mixing table with shelves for mixing stock.

the paint down into the bucket and not out onto your face or onto your shoes. Some shops keep two paint drills by the mixing bench: one each for one- and five-gallon quantities. A bucket of water for cleaning the drill should be kept there as well. The drills relegated to the mixing bench should be of very good quality and powerful. A one-half horsepower variable-speed drill is needed to mix large quantities of paint and texture. A weaker drill will burn out the first time a heavily textured production comes up.

Containers for mixing paint should be located as close to the mixing bench as possible. A paint shop needs a plentiful stock of one- and five-gallon containers. Crates of one- and five-gallon lids should be stored near the buckets. Also keep a crate of small containers, such as used yogurt containers and baby food jars, for the jobs that require small quantities of paint.

Also at the mixing bench should be a handheld blow-dryer for drying paint samples on small pieces of muslin, scrim, or bristol board. A rack

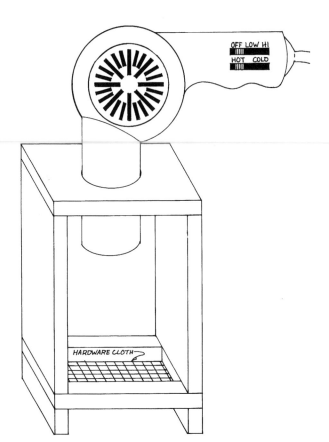

Figure 4.10 A blow-dryer rack.

should be made, nine inches or so tall, that holds the dryer so that it dries the paint chip from above (Figure 4.10) while the scenic artist moves on to mixing the next color. This way the scenic artist does not have to stop and stand at the mixing bench drying a paint chip.

Good light of the proper color temperature is absolutely critical at the mixing bench, so it may be necessary to have additional lighting. It is desirable that the work area has the same light as the mixing bench, but this is not always the case. The scenic artist must be aware that the colors mixed are correct, even if they appear different in the actual painting area.

Water and the Sink Area

A supply of water is essential to a scenic artist; one could not work without it. Water makes up much of what scenic paint is, and painters use water throughout the day to wash brushes and thin paint. Water should be available at a large sink at a comfortable working height. A supply of hot water should be available for cleaning buckets and tools. Dried paint softens considerably in hot water. Also, because scenic artists have to have their hands in and out of water all day long, hot water is essential for their comfort. In a shop where several painters are working at the same time, a large sink should be partitioned into multiple basins with two or more faucets. Multiple basins and faucets mean that the shop assistants need not be interrupted constantly while cleaning buckets by painters needing to thin paint or clean tools. If only one basin is available in the shop, then water can be kept in a bucket at the bench for mixing.

Counter space on either side of the paint sink for soap, cleaning tools, a strainer, and the like is very useful. Dirty buckets often are the bane of the paint sink and should not be stored in the sink or on the counters. Theoretically, dirty buckets will be cleaned regularly so they will not stack up all over the mixing area. If they are not, however, soaking buckets should be stored under the paint sink where they are out of the way.

The paint sink requires maintenance. The sink must be cleaned regularly to avoid clogging. It is a very good idea to build framed wire screen inserts to fit in the bottom of the sink. These should be made of brass or aluminum screen so they do not rust. These inserts can be cleaned regularly, as they will keep paint chips and other annoying blobs from swirling into the abyss and creating a nightmare for a plumber. Ideally, a sink should be fitted with an industrial paint trap, installed at the base of the drain pipe. These traps contain a stainless steel box-shaped basket or screens that can be removed and cleaned. The basket or screens trap paint chips and should be cleaned regularly. The drain pipes should be fitted with removable plugs, so that the drain pipe can be cleaned out with a snake. These precautions will delay the inevitable clogging of the sink.

Paint Storage

Two sorts of paints must be stored in the preparation area: open and unopened raw scenic colors, also called *stock colors* or *mixing stock*, and the colors mixed for shows, called *show colors*. Both need to be stored in a way that allows easy access. The opened stock color should be located adjacent to or on shelves on the mixing bench. The unopened buckets of stock colors can be stored elsewhere. In some paint shops, because of the expense of scenic paint, the stock colors are stored in lockable cabinets or in a paint pantry, much like locking tools up in a tool room in the construction department. Paint always should be stored with all labels visible, so that the contents are obvious. When a paint shipment comes into the shop, the new paint should be rotated to the back of the shelves. Stock color should be arranged in a predictable order, like earth colors to warm colors to cool colors. This makes finding a color and checking stock considerably easier.

Each show color needs to be labeled immediately and clearly on the bucket, not on the lid, as lids can get mixed up. The scenic artist must be able to find a color mixed last month in a few seconds. Show colors should be stored separately from stock colors. Each production will need its own storage or shelving area. Buckets should be stored off the floor because they can be a hazard to staff and scenery if left in the work area. The show colors should be grouped together by scene or technique. All paint that has been mixed needs to be stored in as small a container as possible for the quantity. Five gallon buckets with small amounts of paint in them are inefficient, because the paint will evaporate more quickly. If a painter needs a larger bucket for working, the paint can be put into a working-size bucket. Often paint is mixed to a high concentra-

tion and diluted for actual use, so two buckets are required anyway. It is crucial to save paint in a very organized manner, particularly when working on more than one production at a time. It is very irritating to lose a mixed color while working on a show. This always happens near the end of a long workday, when there is no time to go back and remix. It can be difficult to match a color that has completely disappeared.

Until a production has opened, none of the essential show colors should be thrown away. Always save base colors for touch-ups. If a show is going on the road, the scenic artist should make a touch-up kit (Figure 4.11) to send out with the production. Touch-ups always are needed, no matter how carefully the load-in was handled. For very long-run productions or scenery intended for storage and eventual rental, the scenic artist should make a swatch sheet of the important colors, so that replacement color can be matched to the swatches in the future.

Many other materials are used for paint, finishes, and textures in the paint shop with enough frequency that they must be kept in stock:

- Mediums like water-based finishes, urethanes, clear latex binder, and clear acrylics;
- Fabric dyes and synthetic dyes; specialized powdered mediums, such as bronzing powders and powdered graphite;
- Foam coatings and heavy duty primers;
- Glues and adhesives, such as water-based contact cement, rubber latex, fabric glues, and flexible glues;

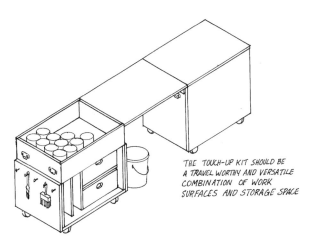

THE TOUCH-UP KIT SHOULD BE A TRAVEL WORTHY AND VERSATILE COMBINATION OF WORK SURFACES AND STORAGE SPACE

Figure 4.11 A touch-up kit.

- Texture mediums such as plaster, drywall compounds, either premixed or in dry form, and bags of quick texture spray medium;
- Texture fillers such as silicate sand, vermiculite, perlite, cocoa mulch, and clay.

All of these materials should have permanent storage places.

There are some common sense rules for storing these mediums. All like material should be stored together, if possible. Easily reached areas should be used to store five-gallon quantities of stock mediums and bags of dry mediums. Heavy items such as five-gallon buckets and bags of heavy materials should not be stored where access is only by ladder. Hazardous mediums, such as bronzing powders, which are a health hazard if inhaled or ingested and an explosive hazard in the presence of a spark or open flame, should be stored in tightly sealed containers in a closed cabinet. Powdered fabric and synthetic dyes also are hazardous if inhaled or ingested and should be stored in tightly sealed containers and in a cabinet.

Shelves and bins in the storage areas should be thoughtfully designed to handle all the stock materials apt to be used in the paint shop. The storage areas for these materials should be designed not just for convenience and easy access, but with concern for the safety of the staff.

The Touch-Up Kit

The touch-up kit is taken to the theatre to be used for a mini storage area and mixing bench. If the theatre is adjacent to the paint shop it may not be necessary to have a touch-up kit. However, if the theatre and the shop are on different floors or in separate buildings then a touch-up kit is a necessity. Having to organize a touch-up kit by bringing over everything the paint department needs in cardboard boxes can be very inefficient. If the tools for a touch-up kit have to be repackaged for each show something important will inevitably be forgotten. By having and maintaining a touch-up kit stocked with the tools and commonly used mediums and paints you may be more certain of having the materials you will need at the theatre. After the touch-up has been finished for a production the kit should be returned to the paint shop so that it can be prepared for the touch-up call of the next production. In the touch-up kit you should keep an inventory list of the tools and materials that it should be stocked with. Check this

inventory list each time you are preparing the kit to go to the theatre. Before each touch-up the kit is also stocked with careful selections of the paint and mediums that have been mixed for that production.

The touch-up kit should be designed so that it can be transported to the theatre by truck. It should be a self-contained road box when it is closed. All the doors and lids on the kit should have hasps that can be secured during shipping. If the side door of a touch-up kit filled with buckets of paint opens during shipping, the results could be disastrous. If all the areas of the kit that will have liquids in them are designed so that they are loaded from the top there will be less chance of spillage during shipping. Also, if a bucket of paint is spilled in the crate during shipping it will be contained inside the crate instead of seeping out underneath a side door. The kit should sit on castors so that it can be rolled to and from the loading docks. The sides of the kit need handles so that it can be lifted on and off loading docks. Since the kit will be filled primarily with buckets of paint it can get very heavy. For this reason the kit should not be too large or it will be impossible to lift. By designing the touch-up kit in two sections that fit together when opened, there will be two manageable road boxes instead of one huge impractical one. Once the kit is opened the lids should be braced so that they serve as counter spaces for color mixing.

The touch-up kit should always be stocked with the following tools and materials:

- A selection of brushes, including 1", 2", 3", and 4" flat-ferrule brushes. These should not be the shop's favorite brushes, since brushes at touch-ups receive some serious abuse. Because these brushes should stay with the kit they will have been removed from the stock of brushes available to the shop. Include a selection of small scenic liners for detail work; a plentiful selection of sash brushes ranging in size from 1/2" to 3"; and a plentiful selection of foam brushes ranging in size from 1" to 3". Many painters also prefer to bring some of their own brushes to the touch-up so they may be assured of having the right brush if a job comes along that requires some finesse.
- Sponges, including both natural sea sponges and cellotex sponges. There is a job at nearly every touch-up that requires the use of a sponge. Sponges are useful for toning down areas of scenery, particularly on stage, because use of a

sprayer may be impossible due to the fact that overspray may damage other parts of the scenery or properties. Sponges will also be needed for cleaning up.

- Sprayers, including one or two small one- or two-quart garden sprayers for small spray jobs; large two- or three-gallon garden sprayers for spraying the back of drops with cool water to smooth out wrinkles or to handle large touch-up notes; small aerosol sprayers are especially important and useful for any number of jobs at a touch-up requiring the control afforded by these sprayers.
- Extensions for brushes, for painting on the deck as well as those jobs where you may need to dab paint on a surface high up that cannot be reached with a ladder.
- Rags.
- Bristol board, to use for edgers or for making stencils.
- Mat and X-Acto knives.
- Markers and laundry markers.
- Pencils and a pad of paper.
- Vine charcoal.
- Twenty-five–foot measuring tapes, assorted rulers, and scale rulers.
- Short handheld lining stick; larger lining sticks may be brought to the theatre if there is a specific job they will be needed for.
- A framing square; 45° and 30° triangles.
- Visquene, rolls of long sections of brown paper, and drop cloths; the visquene should be spread out and taped down over the stage deck where the touch-up kit is located to protect the floor.
- Masking tape; a fresh roll of one-inch and two-inch, for masking paint projects and taping down visquene.
- White and black gaffer's tape; these strong cloth tapes are always useful and can be used for odd projects where it is easier or necessary to tape over a surface rather than paint it.
- A fan; a small one would be best to save room.
- Clip lights; frequently the touch-up day is shared with the lighting department. This means that from time to time the lights will go out. If the touch-up kit is set up on stage then the paint crew will need light for working on the projects that are painted near the kit and for color mixing.
- A paint drill.
- Extension cords.

- Black latex; there are almost always jobs at touch-ups that involve painting surfaces and edges black so that they will not be noticeable.
- White latex; at least one or two gallons for mixing colors, depending on the size of the production.
- Small containers of nearly all the stock mixing colors; unexpected projects, such as decorative painting on props, or a quick portrait frequently pop up at touch-ups. You will need a selection of mixing colors for these jobs. Some hues that can be easily mixed with other stock colors such as chrome green and golden yellow can be left off.
- Dull and gloss water-based urethanes or clear acrylics; satin sheen can be mixed with a combination of gloss and dull.
- The show colors needed at the touch-up.
- A selection of one-gallon buckets, small containers, and three or four five-gallon buckets; for mixing paint in and for water storage by the touch-up kit.
- Black, gold, and silver spray paint; glass frosting for mirrors and windows; brown wood tone sprays; these are some of the most frequently needed spray paints called for at touch-ups.
- Clear and white pigmented spray shellac; a small can of clear shellac; for prime coating surfaces that do not readily accept paint.
- All the crew members should bring their respirators to the touch-up.
- Rubber gloves.
- Hand soap and vegetable oil soap for brushes.
- Wire or nylon brushes for cleaning paint brushes.
- Scrub pads for cleaning buckets.
- Any stencils or pounces that will be needed for specific jobs.
- The designer's elevations that are related to specific tasks anticipated at the touch-up, for instance, painting the stage deck or toning a unit of scenery.

When you get to the theatre for a touch-up the first person the scenic artist should contact is the head stage carpenter. This person will tell you where on stage you can set up the touch-up kit. Because scenery is shifted around on stage, this spot may be a different place than where the kit was set up in the last production. If you do not ask, you may find that after having unpacked the kit and set up the paint area in some corner of the stage, you have to move everything because that is where a large stage wagon is stored for the shift into the next scene. Next locate the water source; if it is far away from the area where the kit is set up, bring over a couple of five-gallon buckets of water for thinning paint and for rinsing dirty brushes, stir sticks, spoons, and the paint drill. Frequently the charge painter will consult with the designer and the head stage carpenter while the rest of the crew unpacks and sets up the kit. The charge painter will need to ask the head stage carpenter what ladders the scenic artist can use. In some union theatres, scenic artists are not allowed to use ladders and lifts without a stage carpenter in attendance. In this case the charge painter will need to work out the schedule of the day's tasks that involve the use of a ladder or lift with the head stage carpenter. Flying in drops is another job that scenic artists may be prohibited from doing, so a schedule for access will need to be worked out ahead of time. In any event, drops should not be flown in without first consulting the head stage carpenter, who will be aware of the schedules of other departments, such as those of the stage carpentry department and the lighting department, as well as stage hazards.

If the scenic designer has not yet given the charge painter a list of the day's tasks, then the charge painter will need to seek out the designer right away. The charge painter may want to get the crew started on some obvious touch-up notes to keep them occupied while he or she is consulting with the scenic designer. As mentioned before it is preferable for the charge painter and the scenic designer to discuss the touch-up notes before the day the actual touch-up arrives. These notes can then be arranged in order of priority and scenery availability. Touch-up can be a very busy and hectic time for all the departments. The charge painter should also consult with the properties manager to see if they have received any notes from the scenic designer that will require the assistance of the paint department. For the scenic designer the touch-up is the last chance to adjust the set. At the beginning of the day, the list of notes may seem like an impossible amount of work, but if this list is approached systematically, it may be surprising how much can be done in one day.

Storage of Brushes and Other Tools

Painters' brushes are their most important tools. The discussion of tools in Chapter Five describes proper maintenance of brushes. Having a storage area for brushes is part of good maintenance. Many painters own their brushes and may take them back and forth to work. Brushes stored in a shop need to be stored away clean and in a rack, so the bristles dry in a usable form. Brushes should be stored where air can circulate around them. Locking away damp brushes will cause both the bristles and wood handle to mildew and rot. Because brushes are so costly, it may be best to store the more expensive brushes in a lockable cabinet. This precaution is not to protect the brushes from being stolen as much as it is to protect them from misadventure, such as a three-inch fitch being used to spread contact cement by mistake.

All brushes must be stored lying flat or hanging up so that the bristles do not set badly. Flat-ferrule brushes can be hung from nails, since most have holes in the handles. A fitch or liner handle is too narrow to accommodate a hole but can be hung by gluing Velcro to the handle and attaching the brush to strips of Velcro arranged in a well-ventilated cabinet or on the wall. However, when these brushes are used with extensions, the Velcro may get ripped off the end of the brush. A favorite storage method, because nothing needs to be done to the handles, is to drill a series of three-quarter-inch holes into a piece of plywood or stock lumber, to be assembled into a shelf or storage ledge. Cover the top of the wood with a heavy rubber pad. Staple the rubber firmly in place all around the holes, and cut one straight slit through the center of each hole. The end of the brush can be inserted through the hole and slit from underneath and the rubber pad will hold the end of the brush firmly until it is needed again (Figure 4.12). Brushes may also be stored flat on open mesh-covered shelves.

If you need to carry brushes back and forth from a job site, use a canvas brush bag, which allows your tools to breathe and dry out between uses. If you have a tool box or road box, drill some holes in the compartments where the brushes are stored. If you must carry your brushes back and forth, store the flat-ferrule brushes in the cardboard cartons they came in to keep the bristles from setting in odd positions. For liners and fitches, you can fashion a pocket-lined cloth roll that ties up around the outside, which, when the brushes are wrapped up inside, will protect the bristles and allow the brushes to breathe. Always be very careful about storing wet brushes in vehicles or sheds where they run the risk of freezing overnight.

Many other tools in the paint shop must have permanent, convenient, and secure storage areas. A lockable cabinet for storing costly spray equipment, such as garden sprayers, spray guns, and airbrushes is necessary. Hooks are needed for storing reels of pneumatic air lines and extension cords. Air lines and cords should not be left on the floor when not in use, as they are a hazard. Lining sticks pose a similar hazard and can be stored in racks or on pegs hanging on a wall. Lining sticks too long to be stored in this fashion should be stored in a specific place in the paint shop, next to a wall where they are out of the way. When fans are not in use, they need a storage area as well. Bamboo and dowel brush extensions should be stored upright in a bin. Large pieces of equipment, such as an airless sprayer, should be stored in specific places. If there is a concern about theft, an airless sprayer can be stored in the paint pantry or chained to a bolt in a wall. Delicate equipment, such as an overhead projector, should have a storage place out of harm's way and under a dust-cover when not in use. Cartooning tools, measuring tapes, charcoal, snap line, measuring sticks, and so forth should be stored together on a cart or in a cabinet. There should be a cabinet for the tools essential to a paint shop, such as staplers, hammers, tack and staple pullers, and pliers, as well as the wrenches and screwdrivers necessary for tool maintenance. Paint bridges (see Chapter Seven) should be stored on a rack or shelves. Even brooms and dustpans should have a specific storage place, if for no other reason than the convenience of always knowing where to find one when it is needed.

Storage of Flammable Products

Flammable paints, shellacs, and other solvent-containing products must be stored in a safe place. Every shop that uses flammable products should have a flammable storage cabinet that meets the standards of the National Fire Protection Association. These bright yellow or red metal cabinets are designed for solvent storage; they have containment trays in the bottom so a spill will not leak all over the shop. They are required by OSHA and by local fire laws.

The cabinets are required because they will delay an explosion should the room be involved in a fire. This delay provides protection for firefighters. It is also the reason the cabinets must be located far from exits or entrances to the room. Place a diagram of the location of the cabinet at entrances with an inventory

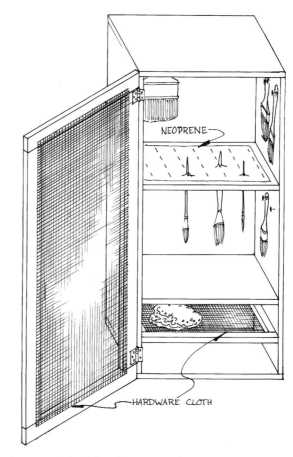

Figure 4.12 A brush storage cabinet.

of its contents. If information on the location of hazardous chemicals is not available, firefighters have the option to "contain" the fire and let the room burn rather than enter it and risk their lives.

Contrary to common opinion, flammable storage cabinets do not contain toxic vapors. They are not airtight. But they will contain vapors enough to be dangerous if leaking or open solvent containers are left in the cabinet. This creates a potential "bomb" by enclosing an explosive mixture of solvent vapor and air. Be sure solvent containers are closed and dry before putting them in the cabinet.

Never store anything in the cabinet that is not labeled "flammable," "extremely flammable," or that is a "combustible liquid." Substances such as acids, corrosives, caustic, or solid materials must be stored elsewhere. In fact, some of these materials will react chemically with solvents. Storing them together also creates a potential "bomb."

In certain cases, such as when there are spigotted containers in the flammable storage cabinet from which solvents are dispensed, the cabinets can be vented. There are closed bungs at the top and the bottom that can be fitted with duct work and exhaust fans. Never open these bungs unless the cabinet is vented with professionally designed ductwork and a fan.

SAFETY AND HEALTH REGULATIONS

Scenic shops come under regulations of the Occupational Safety and Health Administration (OSHA). Most scenic shop rules can be found in the OSHA General Industry Standards (29 CFR 1900–1910). In certain instances, however, scenic work is regulated under the Construction Industry Standards (29 CFR 1926). OSHA's definition of construction work is broad and includes any "alterations or repair, including painting and decorating." Any large construction work in shops or on stage is regulated by both standards.

A copy of both sets of rules should be kept in the shop. Call your local department of labor and find out whether you come under a federal or state OSHA agency and ask how to order a copy of the appropriate regulations. (See Reading and Resources chapter.)

OSHA requires a formal approach to health and safety. Examples of laws found in OSHA's part of the Code of Federal Regulations (20 CFR) that apply directly to scenic work include the following:

- Hazard communication (1926.59, 1910.1200)
- Respiratory protection (1926.103, 1910.134)
- Personal protective equipment (1926.28, 1910.132)
- Emergency plans and fire prevention (1910.38, 1926.150)
- Fire extinguisher use and training (1910.157, 1926.150)
- Ladders (1910.25–26, 1926.1053)
- Fall protection (1926.500–503)
- Scaffold regulations (1910.28 and 1926.451)
- Occupational noise exposure (1910.95 or 1926.52)
- Flammable and combustible liquids (1910.106 or 1926.152)
- Electrical safety (1926.401–405, 1910.301–304)
- Medical services and first aid (1910.151, 1926.50)
- Bloodborne pathogens standard (1910.1030)
- Sanitation (1910.141, 1926.51)

Many of the regulations have formal written programs and training programs. The problem is that many scenic artists and their employers are not familiar with these laws. Compliance and training are rare in shops and studios. This noncompliance not only puts the artists at risk from accidents and occupational illnesses, but it puts employers at great risk of OSHA citations and fines or even lawsuits if accidents do occur.

Hazard Communication Laws

Of all the OSHA regulations, the "Right-to-Know" law is most important for scenic shops. This law mandates a formal approach to chemical health and safety. It is the cornerstone of good health and safety programs. Right-to-Know laws require employers to:

1. *Develop a written Hazard Communication Program* that details how all the provisions of this rule will be met. Fill-in-the-blank programs are available (see Reading and Resources chapter).
2. *Compile an inventory of all potentially hazardous products on the premises.*
3. *Obtain Material Safety Data Sheets (MSDSs) on all potentially hazardous materials.* It is easy to obtain these if they are made a condition of payment on purchase orders. Otherwise manufacturers usually are very willing to fax or mail them.
4. *Label all containers of chemicals in accordance with the Hazard Communication Standard rules.* Most products are already properly labeled. What scenic artists must not do is transfer materials into unlabeled containers for use of more than a single shift.
5. *Train all employees who are potentially exposed to toxic chemicals.* It is useless to collect MSDSs if scenic artists cannot read and understand them.

MSDSs are full of technical concepts such as threshold limit values, teratogens, evaporation rates and the like. It is not easy for busy scenic artists to take the time to study concepts or for employers to set aside time for training. Yet this training is required by OSHA. Some suitable training materials can be found in the Reading and Resources Chapter.

Respiratory Protection

Employers of workers wearing masks and respirators are required by OSHA to develop a respiratory protection program. In general, the minimum acceptable program would include:

- A written program explaining how the employer will meet the requirements and how respirators will be selected. Fill-in-the-blank prototype programs are available (see Reading and Resources chapter).
- Formal fit testing of workers by a qualified person using one of the approved methods done at least annually.
- An annual check on employees' medical status to assure that they are physically able to wear a respirator and tolerate the added breathing stress safely.
- Procedures for regular cleaning, disinfecting, and maintaining of all respirators. Respirators that are shared must be disinfected after every use.
- Procedures for formal, documented training of workers.

Air-supplied respiratory protection (e.g., self-contained breathing apparatus) is needed for products that emit toxic substances for which there are no air-purifying cartridges. The most hazardous of these toxic substances are all of the two-component urethane products that outgas chemicals called isocyanates during foaming, casting, or painting. Examples include Great Stuff®, Insta Foam®, Insta Pak®, Imron® paints, and RHH Versi Foam®. These are among the most hazardous products used in scenic arts.

Protective Equipment

The use of goggles and safety glasses, face shields, gloves, protective clothing, steel-toed shoes, hard hats, and all types of protective equipment are regulated by OSHA. The rules also require documented training of workers. Training is necessary because it is common to see scenic artists using the wrong equipment. For example, "impact" goggles can be mistakenly used for "chemical splash" protection and vice versa, or using rubber gloves for protection against all products without realizing that many solvents will penetrate rubber gloves without changing their appearance.

Fall Protection

All situations in which workers could fall a significant distance to the floor (four or six feet depending on the situation) are regulated by OSHA. This includes the use of ladders. One ladder rule frequently broken is standing or sitting on the top section or the top step.

Scaffolds or paint bridges that place a person ten feet or more above the floor come under the new OSHA scaffold rules. The scaffold must be railed and toe boarded and a person needs to be tied off. The new rules that will be in effect in 1998 no longer allow belts—full harnesses must be used.

It is important to keep up with the new rules on fall protection because theatres and shops are full of old scaffolds, paint bridges, stationary ladders, and other equipment that is noncomplying. There is no "grandfather" clause on fall protection rules. The old equipment must be modified or discarded. If there is an accident, the employer or supervisor will be found responsible for not meeting the new regulations—even if they didn't know about them.

Studio Building Hazards

Look at scenic studios and shops. Most are located in old warehouses, piers, basements, factories, and other low rent facilities. You need to be certain that they provide minimum requirements for your personal safety.

Fire Safety

If there is an overhead sprinkler system, find out if it is in working order and if it is a dry or wet pipe system. Dry pipe systems allow a short time to turn the system off if a head is accidentally damaged during construction, thus avoiding water damage.

If there are no sprinklers look for hand-held, ABC-type extinguishers located at least every seventy-five feet. The tags on the extinguishers should show they have been recently inspected. OSHA requires that individuals be trained to use the extinguishers. But if this is unlikely, at least read the directions on the particular extinguishers in your facility.

Emergency Exits and Escape Routes

OSHA rules require employers to hold a formal meeting to explain the workspace hazards and emergency procedures whenever new employees arrive on site. If employers do not follow these laws, employees need to protect themselves. Look around you; there must be at least two escape routes from all areas. Exits or exit signs should be visible from all locations. Fire doors and panic bolts must be in good repair and must *never* be chained or locked while the building is occupied.

Changes in Elevation

Any elevated platforms, storage areas, shafts, or holes where people could fall more than six feet must be guarded. Standard railings (either permanent or temporary) and covers over holes must be installed. Stairs having four or more risers or that rise more than thirty inches must be equipped with at least one handrail and one stairway system along each unprotected side or edge.

Electrical Safety

Outlets should be available in many areas in the painting area. If the paint shop has a large expanse of floor space, then overhead reels with multiple outlets should be installed at regular intervals through the center of the shop. OSHA now requires outlets used for power tools on construction sites and outlets within ten feet of a source of water to be ground-fault-circuit interrupted (GFCI). Extension cords must be equipped with GFCI devices.

It is an OSHA violation to break off a ground prong or fit a two-prong plug into a three-prong outlet or vice versa. Using an adapter is not permitted. Purchase good ground-wired, double-insulated tools. Get rid of cheap hair dryers, drills, fans, and other equipment that is substandard.

Do not ignore flickering or dimming lights, frequently interrupted power, damaged wiring, service panels or conduit junctions without metal covers, or other electrical defects.

As you work, always be aware of extension cords lying in areas where people walk. Such cords must be run through hard rubber covers or at least duct-taped to the floor.

Ventilation

The building's ventilation will be the deciding factor in choice of materials. If there is no spray booth, spraying should not occur except when everyone is wearing respiratory protection. If there is no good general movement of air, solvent products should be severely restricted. (See Reading and Resources chapter.)

Bathroom Facilities

Clean bathroom facilities must be present in sufficient numbers to accommodate the size of the workforce. If not, portable toilets must be rented until bathrooms can be installed. Portable facilities alone are not adequate. A water supply for washing hands and cleaning up must be available.

Drinking Water

In older cities and buildings, service pipes and plumbing pipes often are made of lead. Lead also may be found in solder used on potable water pipes (lead was banned for this use in 1986), faucets, and floor model water coolers. The only way to know if water is safe to drink is to have it tested. If the water has not been tested, or if the test shows the water is above the accepted limit, drink bottled water.

Lead Paint

Buildings built before 1978 should be assumed to contain lead paint unless actual testing shows otherwise. Even well-maintained older buildings may contain painted-over or encapsulated lead paint that can be made airborne if renovation of any painted surface is planned.

The OSHA Lead in Construction Standard forbids sanding, resurfacing, removal, or demolition of any painted surface unless the paint has been professionally tested and shown to be lead free. If lead is found, only trained lead abatement contractors can do the work. Scenic artists must never do this work.

Even undisturbed old paint can be hazardous. Testing of the dust in the shop should be done if there is obvious paint dust, chips, or powder near friction surfaces (e.g., places where window frames create dust when drawn over each other).

Asbestos

Watch for sources of old asbestos in the shop. Common sources of asbestos include:

- insulation around pipes and furnaces;
- composition ceiling tiles;
- acoustic board and tile;
- Transite® and other asbestos boards;
- old wall board and plaster;
- vinyl floor tiles;
- roofing felts, tar paper, and caulks;
- spackle plaster repair compounds;
- wiring (e.g., fuzzy white wires on old lighting instruments); and
- old textured scenery or papier-mâché props.

Garbage and Toxic Chemicals

Only professional waste handlers can safely remove refuse that contains animal and human waste. Only *toxic* waste disposal contractors can legally remove old chemical products and containers, unidentified or unlabeled substances, asbestos and lead paint waste, and other chemicals.

Summary

These are just a few of the many laws and regulations that apply to scenic work. But even if every rule is followed, accidents still will not be reduced if scenic artists work without sleep, when they are faint with hunger, or when they are ill. The first and most important of all safety rules is to take good care of yourself both on and off the job.

Please consult the Reading and Resources for information about texts and newsletters on safety in the workplace. It behooves all who are working with toxic materials to educate themselves about the hazards associated with their trade. Anyone in the teaching profession has a duty to teach both through lecture and good example the proper and safe handling of toxic materials.

Part Two
The Tools of the Trade

Oleo drop (courtesy of the Twin City Scenic's Collection, Performing Arts Archives,
University of Minnesota, St. Paul).

chapter 5

The Painting Tools of Scenic Artistry

INTRODUCTION

The fundamental skills of scenic painting are obtained in part through thorough knowledge of the tools of a scenic artist. As in the fine arts, faux painting, and related fields, knowing a tool and its uses is the first step toward mastery of a skill. Tools are the link between the scenic artist and the paint. Although it may be a cliché, tools are an extension of the scenic artist. Tools are to the scenic artist what language is to the writer. The wider familiarity and skill the scenic artist has with the tools of the trade, the broader will be his or her range of skills.

Nearly anything used to spread, spray, stipple, smear, or sprinkle paint qualifies as a tool. Even though many of the tools discussed in this chapter traditionally are used in the visual arts, many others are far less conventional, but common in scenic painting. The creative application of tools often is what an inventive scenic painting technique is all about. Because the skills involved in scenic painting revolve primarily around painting, most of the tools discussed in this chapter are used for the application and manipulation of paints and finishes.

BRUSHES

Brushes are the age-old and obvious tool for applying paint. A paintbrush is one of the oldest tools of humankind, and skillful handling of it is one of the oldest crafts we know. This skill is as useful and vital today as in the past.

You might remember, in the third grade, when you were painting your art project of the week, the teacher said, "Now remember, class, your brush is your friend!" Brushes are the most important asset in a painter's kit of tools. A scenic artist's ability to handle them with alacrity is one of his or her primary skills.

The Anatomy of a Brush

A brush has three parts: bristles, ferrule, and handle (Figure 5.1). The bristles are the working part of the brush. They absorb, hold, and spread paint. The ferrule is a band of metal, leather, or string used to hold the bristles to the handle. The handle is simply a material carved or molded into a shape that gives the user something to hold and manipulate the bristles.

Within this simplicity lies a great deal of variation in the shape and style of brushes: different styles for different painting applications and actual paint mediums. The shape and style of a brush may depend on a traditional use for a brush or a regional preference. For instance, a European sash brush, used for painting crisp lines and trim, has a round ferrule with tapered bristles so that the bristles at the center of the brush are the longest, while a common sash brush purchased in the United States has a flat ferrule and bristles tapered toward one side of the brush.

Scenic painting for the theater has created its own distinct class of brushes. These brushes reflect the basic shapes and styles of fine-arts brushes but are larger and more appropriate to the scale of scenic

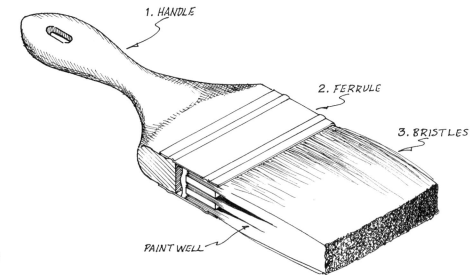

1. HANDLE

2. FERRULE

3. BRISTLES

PAINT WELL

Figure 5.1
The three parts of a paint brush.

painting. For example, fitches in fine arts are oval-tipped, oval-ferrule brushes up to three-quarters of an inch wide. However, fitches may be as wide as three inches in scenic painting. The term *fitch* describes an entire group of high-quality brushes used mostly for detail work. Theatrical liners are part of this group of brushes, particular to scenic painting and used for painting lines. These are very much like oversized versions of brushes common to the fine arts.

Bristles

Animal hair and fur traditionally have been the most common choice for paintbrush bristles, because they handle paint with good control and ease. Paintbrush bristles have been made with vegetable matter like pulped palm, bamboo, and yucca. Today, bristles made of synthetic materials such as nylon and polyester are common. Synthetic bristles have become refined in recent years, leading to the introduction of brushes that serve a scenic artist as well as or, in some cases, better than natural bristle brushes. However, the finest brushes available today still are made from animal hair or fur, much as they have been for centuries.

China bristle is a very common bristle for house and scenic painting brushes. It is valued because of the length, taper, stiffness, and the snap of the bristles. The snap is a bristle's tendency to return to its

original shape after it has been bent. Taper refers to the shape of the bristle at the tip. In the first growth of animal hair, individual strands of hair end in a finely pointed taper. When many tapered bristle strands are combined into a brush, their taper naturally encourages the flow of paint to the tip of the brush. The finely tapered ends of the bristle also clump together when the brush is *charged* (loaded with paint), keeping the paint in the brush until the ends of the bristles are laid on a surface.

Common white, black, and tan china bristles are all hog bristle. The black bristles tend to be finer than the white or the tan. Until the outbreak of World War II, regions of Russia were the main producers of bristle. Peasants in the wooded areas of northern Russia raised herds of semiwild swine that were prized for their long stiff bristle (Wagman, 1952). Traditionally, these bristles came from China, which is why they are called *china bristle*. Hogs are raised in many regions in China; each region produces hogs bristles with different characteristics. Some of the softest bristles come from the regions of Tientsin and Tsingtao. The hogs in Shanghai and Hankow are bred to produce a medium-stiff bristle. The province of Yunnan and the area around the city of Chongqing lead in the husbandry of stiff-bristled hogs (Wagman, 1952). Now, if a scenic artist goes to the paint store and inquires if the bristles of a particular brush are Tsingtao or Chongqing, chances are all he or she will get will be a quizzical look. But as one works with various types of china bristle brushes one may begin to notice some differences in the performance of bristles.

Other less common types of bristles that a scenic artist may encounter are those from the hair of the ox, badger, squirrel, and horse. Ox and badger hair produce very soft, fine bristles, best used as lettering, sign-painting, and varnishing brushes. Ox-hair bristle is obtained from the ox's ear. Squirrel hair produces a soft, fine bristle, frequently used in gilding brushes made for the application of metallic leaf and paints. Horsehair bristle is obtained from the horse's tail. This long gray bristle is used in brushes where an extra-long bristle is required, such as in some varieties of graining brushes used for faux finish work.

After bristles are harvested from the animal hide, they must be cleaned by boiling once, twice, and occasionally three times. This is done to satisfy health restrictions for export. It also stabilizes the bristles, so later on when the bristles are set into a brush they will not warp. Generally, a brush is constructed by setting the bristles into a ferrule and pouring epoxy onto the base of the bristles, which binds them to the ferrule as well as to one another. This is done before the handle is connected to the ferrule so the epoxy can be poured in from the back of the ferrule. The epoxy must be timed so that it sets up before it has run down the length of the bristles but not before it has saturated the base of the bristles inside the ferrule. Otherwise, the bristles will fall out of the brush.

Brushes made from secondary bristle cuttings, coarse bristles, or synthetic bristles may have bristles that were *flagged* or *exploded* on the tip, meaning that the ends of the bristles were intentionally split into several strands so that they behave more like tapered bristles. Bristles cut from animal hair are best laid out in the orientation in which they grew, because animal hair has a growth pattern that causes it to curve slightly in one direction when damp. If the orientation of the bristles is changed when laid into a brush, the bristles may splay in different directions. The finest brushes are built so that the curvature of the bristles is aligned, a consideration that is reflected in the high price these brushes demand. Yet, this does not explain why some costly brushes are poorly made and unreliable.

In most brushes, only one type of bristle is used; other brushes are a combination of bristle. A wide-ferrule brush, called a *Dutch brush* or *priming brush*, is intended for use in covering large areas with paint. One variety of this style brush combines black, white, and tan china bristles into the same brush. Some brushes designed for enameling and varnish work combine the softer ox hair with china bristles. Badger hair also is combined with china bristles in some varieties of brushes.

Stiff bristles that do not hold their shape well are best used for larger brushes, where control and cutting an edge are not a factor. Finer bristles that "bunch" together when the brush is wet are best used for brushes intended for controlled techniques, such as lettering, liners, and sash brushes.

Brush Construction

A clump of bristles may fall out of the ferrule, usually while painting a drop, giving you the opportunity to see the way they are bound. Some brushes have in them what is called a *paint well*. This is a plug or bar separating the rows or sections of bristles. When the brush is dipped in the paint or "charged," the paint well fills with paint. When the brush is pulled out of the bucket of paint the bristles bunch together and hold a paint reserve in the paint well for a time. As the brush is put to a surface, the paint is pulled out from the ends of the bristles onto that surface. Sometimes the paint falls out of the well before the brush hits its mark. A painter will develop a rhythm, gently rotating the brush until it is over the target, between the bucket and the surface, skirting that moment when gravity will pull the paint out of a brush, whether it is over its mark or not. This technique seems simple, so why take so long to explain it? Because as a colleague once pointed out, the paint comes out of the end of the bristles. This elegant observation is the first step in mastering any kind of brushwork.

Brush Handles

The handle of the brush needs little more explanation than the handle of a coffee mug. It is designed simply to give a person something to hold onto when using a brush to spread paint or barbecue sauce. Brush handles commonly are made from wood or plastic. Certainly brush handles have been fashioned out of just about anything imaginable, from bamboo to ivory to precious metals. Large, heavy brushes designed to spread quantities of paint quickly have short, thick handles, so the artist can get a good grip on the tool. Brushes designed for detail work that requires more finesse need to be held and controlled in the same manner as a pencil and, so, they have long, narrow handles similar to the handles found on fine-arts brushes.

Brush Ferrule

The *ferrule* is the part of the brush that connects the bristles to the handle. The type of ferrule often dictates the name of the brush, such as a three-inch flat-ferrule or an oval-ferrule sash. The shape of the ferrule often is determined by the specific application the brush is designed for, so some brushes are also named for specific tasks, like a priming brush or a liner.

The ferrule is attached to the handle with small nails (brads) or by crimping the ferrule around the handle. The ferrule usually is made of a corrosive-resistant metal, such as brass, copper, stainless steel, or nickel-plated steel. Leather ferrules were common until the early decades of the twentieth century. They were flexible and a replacement easily could be cut and assembled when the old one cracked and fell apart.

The Names of Brushes

There are no hard and fast rules for naming brushes. Some brushes are classified by the shape of the ferrule, for example a flat-ferrule brush or oval-ferrule brush. Some brushes are further described by size, such as a four-inch flat-ferrule brush or a two-inch oval-ferrule brush. Brushes may also be described by the job they perform, such as a priming brush, foliage brush, or a liner. A brush may even be described by what it is designed to paint, such as a truck-lettering brush or a sash brush.

Procuring Brushes

Most scenic artists collect a great variety of brushes in the course of their careers. The techniques in scenic painting are so varied that nearly every type of brush available will be put to use sooner or later. Standard house-painting brushes and flat-ferrule and sash brushes can be procured at hardware stores, lumberyards, and paint stores. Specialty brushes, such as liners or fitches, can be purchased at theatrical supply companies and through catalogues (refer to the Reading and Resources chapter for a list of supply companies for brushes and scenic art tools).

Lettering brushes and sign-painting brushes can be purchased or ordered at sign-painting supply shops, some art supply stores, or supply catalogues.

Maintenance of Brushes

As with any tool, proper maintenance will increase the life of a brush. Bristles are most likely to break down first. They should be thoroughly cleaned after each use, and paint should never be allowed to dry in the brush. If a painting technique requires the brush to be laid aside for long stretches of time between uses, the brush should be left in a bucket of water so it will not dry out. However a brush never should be left in a bucket of water overnight, because the bristles and handle will swell with water and may split the ferrule. The bristles of a brush will become permanently curved when the brush is stored or left overly long resting on the bristles.

There is a theory that, if you want a brush to last as long as possible, never dip it into the paint bucket past the ferrule. Since I am a complete failure in this regimen, I always begin cleaning my brush by using a wire or stiff nylon brush to comb the dried or sticky paint off the ferrule and the base of the bristles. Always comb the bristles in their natural direction. Do not scrub across them, which encourages the bristles to separate. Lye-based soaps, designed to remove oils, dry out natural bristle brushes. It is preferable to clean and condition natural bristle brushes with a vegetable oil–based soap, like Murphy's Oil Soap®. To be sure that the brush is clean and no residual paint is hiding in the base of the bristles, wash it out with soap at least three times or until clear water seeps out from the base of the bristles when you gently bend them over.

Repairing Brushes

The ferrules of some brushes, particularly fitches and the larger liners, frequently splits when the bristles first swell with water. Fitches are among the most expensive brushes, the cost varying between $25 to $75 each depending on the brand. Once the ferrule has split the base, the bristles will become misshapen, which diminishes the usefulness of the brush. If this happens you can send the brush back to the manufacturer and exchange it for a new one. However, I have found that the ferrules on the two- and three-inch scenic brushes are so prone to splitting that I decided to fix the problem myself. A copper wire or band can be soldered around the ferrule near the base of the bristles before it splits. To add this band, wrap a cold, damp towel around the bristles to avoid singeing them. Then use a propane torch to solder the copper wire around the ferrule, using 50/50 solder and a lot of flux (see Chapter Four, Safety and Health Regulations). Keep a bucket of cold water nearby to cool the solder when you are done and for emergencies. Wrap the wire around the ferrule so about a three-eighths-inch band of copper reinforces the ferrule. Practice this procedure on an old brush before messing around with a new three-inch fitch.

Most decent brushes cost at least $15. Very large, specialized, exotic, rare-bristle, or just high-quality brushes can cost $50 or more. A scenic artist may have $500 or more worth of brushes in his or her kit. A shop may have $1,000 or more invested in brushes. They are an investment worth maintaining and safeguarding.

Types of Brushes

Knowledge of the various types of brushes, their uses, and applications is essential for a scenic artist. Most scenic artists gradually build up a brush kit that they bring from job to job. They find that a particular brush will work very well for a specific technique. Sometimes brushes are acquired to meet the needs of specific jobs as they arise. I find that I often buy a brush on impulse because it looks interesting. I have yet to buy a brush that did not turn out to be the find of the day on one project or another.

A great variety of brushes and variations are available. Yet, the basic structure of a brush is still much the same as when used in prehistoric times. The following are the brushes you are most likely to encounter in a career as a scenic artist.

Common Brushes

Flat-Ferrule Brushes

The shapes of ferrules have evolved from years of use in particular tasks, like painting crisp lines or smoothly blending colors. The *flat-ferrule* is the most common shape for brushes, and the basic flat-ferrule house-painting brush is the workhorse of the scenic artist trade. The alignment and length of the bristles facilitates both maximum coverage, using the flat of the brush, and razor sharp lining, using the tips of the bristles. These brushes may have rows of bristles separated by a plug of wood or plastic, which forms

the paint well. Flat-ferrule brushes may have only one row of bristles with no paint well, or they may have two, three, or four rows of bristles. The widths of flat-ferrule brushes commonly available range from one-half inch to eight inches; however, some specialty brushes may be wider. Generally speaking, the wider the brush, the more rows of bristles and paint wells it has (Figure 5.2).

Keep in mind as you read this chapter that most brushes can be used two ways. Generally, a brush is held so the side, or flat, of the brush gives the most coverage. The edge of the brush is best for narrow, even lines.

Lay-in Brushes, Dutch, and Priming Brushes

All of these are types of flat-ferrule brushes. The term *lay-in* refers to filling in basic areas of color on scenery. Common sizes for lay-in brushes are one to four inches wide. The tips of the bristles on most flat-ferrule brushes are aligned parallel to the ferrule. These brushes are designed to be held flat for maximum surface contact and coverage. Flat-ferrule brushes are used for a variety of other tasks and techniques, such as lay-in, base coating, wet blending, dry brushing, scumbling, spattering, and glazing (these techniques are discussed at length in Chapter Nine).

A wider lay-in brush, with three or more rows of bristles, was, in earlier times, commonly called a *Dutch brush* because it was used to spread dutchman (wheat paste and scenic dope). Scenic dope, used for priming flats, was a concoction of whiting (a chalk-based pigment), water, and animal glue. Currently, these larger brushes, six to nine inches wide, are often called *base coating* or *priming brushes,* after the tasks for which they are used most frequently.

Sash Brushes

A *sash brush* has bristles trimmed at an angle from one side of the brush to the other. This brush is used on edge, so the brush is parallel to the direction of the stroke. Paint is applied in a narrow, sharp line, also called a *cut line*. Sash brushes are named after what they do in the house-painting industry, trimming the paint on sash windows and trim. In scenic painting, these brushes are very useful for lining with

Figure 5.2
Flat-ferrule brushes: clockwise, from top left, 4" and 3" black bristle lay-in brushes; 4", 3", 2", and 1" white bristle lay-in brushes; 3" and 2" soft black bristle brushes; an assortment of lay-in and sash brushes; priming brushes.

a lining stick. They hold more paint than a standard scenic liner so they pull into a longer line. They also create a more consistent line than scenic liners.

Scenic Brushes

Scenic Fitch or Foliage Brushes

Scenic brushes have developed over the centuries specifically for the scenic art and mural painting professions. The *fitch-style brush* is the basic form for many scenic brushes. The fitch is much like an oversized canvas art brush. Fitches are the scenic artist's brush of choice for detail, freehand, and trompe l'oeil painting. The fitch has a long, slender wooden handle and a ferrule that widens into an oval opening. The bristles most commonly are white china bristles, which hold their shape and have enough spring to keep from flattening out. The scenic fitch has no paint well.

Fitches are available most often in two-inch and three-inch sizes. Long bristles of one length are used in these bristles, usually three inches long. The ferrule generally is elliptical, but some have a flatter ferrule. These brushes are particularly useful for painting organic shapes. Fitches are sold at scenic supply houses and through scenic supply catalogues (Figure 5.3).

The Scenic Liner

Scenic liners are a type of *scenic fitch*. The main difference between a liner and fitch is that the ferrule of the liner is usually gently crimped, so the ellipse of the ferrule flattens out. Some manufacturers set the bristles so that they are tapered, called chiseling or cupping the bristles, so that from the side the bristles appear to be set in a V shape. Bristles in scenic liners set this way will cut a sharper line. Scenic liners range in sizes from one-eighth inch to two inches. The length of the bristles increases as the brushes increase in size. A set of liners is a standard item in the kit of every scenic artist.

The term *lining* refers specifically to the technique of painting a line, either by using a lining tool as a guide to draw the brush along for straightedge work or creating any kind of line freehand. A good liner will hold its shape when charged with paint and will not splay, so that the edges of the line become ragged or feathery.

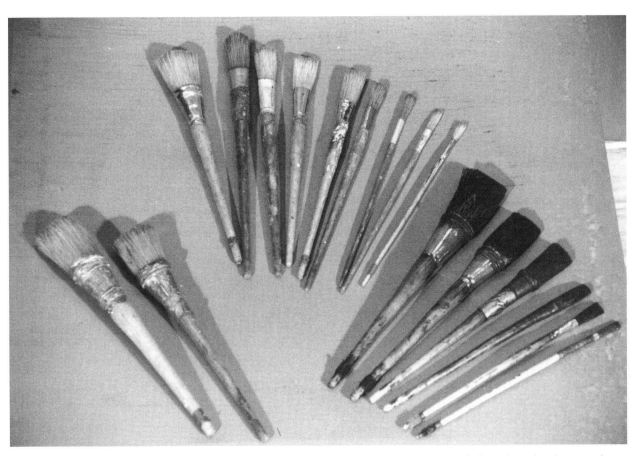

Figure 5.3   Scenic brushes: from left to right, foliage brushes or fitches and a selection of white china–bristle scenic liners (the liners on the right appear black because they are only used with aniline dyes).

Liners also can be used for nearly every kind of detail work: cutting in edges for base coating, base coating in tight areas, tight wet blends, foliage, and chiaroscuro work. Liners should not be used for spattering, drybrushing, or painting on textured surfaces until the brushes are a little gray in the muzzle, because these techniques are hard on brushes and will splay the bristles or wear them down. If you use a brush on a textured surface all day, you can actually see that the bristles are shorter at the end of the day.

Various styles of liners are available to the scenic artist. Depending on the brand, some liners have ferrules that are crimped more tightly than others. Some scenic artists may develop an affinity for a certain brand of liner. Liners come in different styles of bristle as well. Some brands of liners are made with black china bristles. The *deer-foot fitch* or *angular liner* has bristles set in an angle, like a sash brush. Naturally, these brushes are very useful for straight

lining with a line stick. The deer-foot fitch is also great for foliage. The *filbert fitches* have bristles set in an oval shape at the tip of the brush.

Bristles have a natural curve, which is desirable in all brushes, but the bristles in scenic liners should be laid in the ferrule so their curve goes in the same direction. If the curve of the bristles has not been laid properly, it will be apparent as soon as the brush gets wet. Bristles swell in the ferrule when wet and might splay apart if not properly set. Sometimes, the bristles of a brush can be retrained by plastering them together with a vegetable oil-based soap or hair conditioner and then wrapping them together with string. Set the brush aside and let it sit that way for about a week. This actually sets the bristles in much the same way one sets hair. Unfortunately, it is a temporary solution. As the brush gets older, it usually will start to splay apart as it did originally. If a new brush turns out to be unacceptable, return it to the manufacturer for a replacement. Most brush suppliers and manufacturers will stand behind the products they sell.

Once a scenic artist acquires a set of liners, he or she becomes familiar with the personality of each liner. A good set of liners, properly maintained, will serve for many years.

Oval-Ferrule Brushes

Oval-ferrule brushes, also called *oval sash brushes*, sometimes can be obtained at better paint stores and through scenic art supply catalogues. These brushes may be made from black or white china bristles. Their bristles might be flat across the ends or sharpen to a chisel tip, meaning that the bristles at the center of the brush are the longest and the sides are shorter. The ferrules on these brushes are usually copper or nickel-plated steel. The brushes are generally one, two, and three inches in size (Figure 5.4).

Oval-ferrule brushes are excellent for laying in color, wet blends, and broad detail work, because the bristles in these brushes maintain a tight edge.

Round-Ferrule Brushes or Ring Liners

Another variety of sash brush is the *round-ferrule brush*. This style of sash brush, also called a ring liner, is used most commonly in Europe and generally has white china bristles, although some brands of round-ferrule brushes have black china bristles. The ferrule of these brushes may be either copper or nickel-plated steel. To keep the bristles from splaying, the bristles sometimes are wrapped with string at their base. The bristles usually are chiseled at the ends, come in lengths ranging from one-half inch to two inches, and can be used for lining and detail work. When that rare pointillism project comes your way, these brushes will become indispensable (Figure 5.4).

Stippling Brushes

One type of round-ferrule brush that is very specialized is the *stippling brush,* typically an odd, short, squat little brush. The bristles, ferrule, and handle all are short. This tool is not intended for brushing paint but rather dabbing paint on a surface or texturing it

Figure 5.4
Round and oval sash brushes: clockwise from top left, fitch art brushes, deer-foot fitches, round stippling brush, ring liners, oval-ferrule sash brushes.

once it has been applied, a technique called *stippling*. The stippling brush may also be used to gently dry-brush paint through a stencil. Because the bristles are short and trimmed flat, the pattern this brush creates is lacy and grainy.

The stippling brush is not a commonly used brush and can be tricky to master. It is most difficult to work with over a large area, because stippling does not cover square footage quickly. Larger, square-shaped stippling brushes are available through supply catalogues. These brushes come in sizes up to one foot square for covering areas faster; however, controlling the density of paint with these larger brushes is more difficult (Figure 5.4).

Lettering Brushes

Lettering brushes are essential for the good-quality lettering common in scenic painting. They require practice; but once mastered, lettering projects will go much faster and look better. Very specific rules govern the appearance of lettering or signage. That is why doing signage with the right tools is an important skill for the scenic artist to master. (Refer to Chapter Eight for information on lettering and signage techniques.)

Lettering brushes are sold primarily through sign-painting supply shops, found in most larger cities, as well as many art supply stores and theatrical brush dealers. Lettering brushes also can be purchased through supply catalogues but may be expensive. Lettering brushes are made to be used with either water-based or oil-based paint. Lettering brushes made for water-based paint are the most common and useful for scenic painting.

Lettering brushes are available in a great many styles, sizes, and bristle types. Some of these can be extremely expensive. I once selected what I thought was a very fine-looking brush in a sign painting shop—I was right, it was a very fine brush; it cost $140. I am sure it was worth every penny, but I put it back in the rack and made another selection, knowing that theatre life was too hard on fine sign painting brushes. I made two selections from the more economical lines of sign-painting brushes, and they have served me very well.

Lettering brushes are made with the finest quality bristles, such as sable, squirrel, and badger. The ferrules are made from brass, copper, stainless steel, or nickel-plated steel. The ferrule shape also defines the brush: flats have crimped ferrules, and rounds,

also called quills, ferrules that are not crimped. The bristles are often set into the ferrule so that the ends are squared off so the user can cut into the corner of the letter. Lettering brushes run from one-eighth inch up to as much as two inches, depending on the intended use of the brush. It is not necessary for a scenic artist to own a lettering brush much larger than one inch wide. Lettering jobs that require a brush larger than that can easily be handled by scenic brushes. Signage brushes are useful for work on Plexiglas or other slick surfaces, where its softer bristles will not leave "scratch" marks in the paint.

Because a specific lettering brush often is required for a particular job, it is advisable to purchase them on an as-needed basis. I have found that one-quarter-inch and one-half-inch round-ferrule square-end and three-quarter-inch flat-ferrule lettering brushes usually are enough to cover most stray signage jobs that come along.

Other Specialized Brushes

Gilding Brushes

Gilding brushes are divided into three categories: the gilder's tip, the mop or duster, and bronzing brushes.

The *gilder's tip* brush is not designed to get wet. These are made of badger- or squirrel-hair bristles with ferrules made of cardboard or wood. They have no handles but are held by the ferrule. These brushes are used to pick up sheets of very delicate gold and silver leaf. The leaf will lightly cling to the end of the bristles through static electricity, so that it can be moved from the book of metallic leaves to the object being gilded. They are used because the leaves of gold and silver are too delicate to be touched by human hands.

The gilder's tip is used in conjunction with a *gilder's block,* which is the palette used to hold and cut the sheets of metallic leaf. This block is covered with chamois so that the leaf will cling to the surface. The *gilder's knife* is a tool used to move the leaf around on the block and cut the leaf. *Burnishing tools* are used to work metallic leaf into the nooks and crannies of an object being gilded. They are used to make sure the leaf is worked onto and adheres to the medium. These tools also burnish, or polish, the surface as they adhere the material.

Another type of gilding brush is the *gilder's mop* or *duster,* used to smooth the leaf onto the surface of the object being gilded. These brushes are not designed to get wet. They are made of soft squirrel, badger, or ox hair. These soft bristles will not tear or scratch the metallic leaf. The ferrules are made of brass, copper, or copper wire and the handles usually are made of wood.

Bronzing brushes are another kind of gilding brush; however, these are designed to get wet. Bronzing brushes are used to apply bronzing powder mixed with medium. These brushes are made with very soft bristle, such as squirrel, so that they leave no scratch marks in the paint when it is applied. They sometimes have split quills with separate groups of bristles set into copper wire ferrules placed side by side in a wooden handle. These brushes can be used for glazing and graining in some faux techniques because of their very soft bristles.

Generally, real gold or silver leaf is not used on stage scenery. First of all, the expense of real gold leaf is prohibitive. Second, working with genuine gold leaf requires time and a undisturbed environment, which are in short supply in a scenic studio. However, the knowledge of these tools is helpful to the scenic artist.

Pipers

Finger liners, or *pipers*, are unique brushes that have several small ferrules or pipes lined up on a flat ferrule and handle that form a soldierly row. They are made of three to eight liners or pipes set into the same ferrule. These brushes are used for graining and pattern work. They do not hold a very large charge of paint, and they are expensive. This brush would be best purchased on an as-needed basis. These brushes can be purchased through scenic and decorative painting supply catalogues and companies.

Grainers

Some brushes are marketed as *grainers,* specifically for wood-graining techniques. However, this classification can include a wide range of brushes, many of which already have been discussed, such as pipers and flat-ferrule brushes. *Overgrainers* have intervals of the bristle removed, so someone already has cut up the brush for you. Blending and mottling brushes have very short bristles and are made for blending and working areas of glaze medium in faux finish work. Some graining brushes have extra-long bristles; these brushes are used for some specific overgraining techniques, such as flogging or a wavering grain stroke. A scenic artist could spend a fortune buying these specialty brushes. A scenic artist sould

begin by acquiring basic brushes and collect specialty brushes when they are needed.

Other Useful Brushes

In addition to the specialized brushes just discussed, a scenic artist is likely to have a wide selection of cheap yet useful brushes. These are the common brushes found at paint, hardware, and discount stores. Scenic artists and scene shops always need a stock of cheap brushes on hand to handle the jobs for which one would never use fine scenic brushes, such as work with glue, shellac, alkyd paints, or textured surfaces. The surprising thing about cheap brushes is that, once in a while, they turn out to be the very brush for a particular job. For example, while once working on a scrim of the Declaration of Independence, the charge painter I was working with found that a 59¢ one-half-inch white china bristle brush, also called a *chip brush*, was the very brush for doing all the tight lettering on this project. Chip brushes come in a range of sizes from one-half inch to three inches.

Foam brushes are very useful for sharp-edged work and detail and for tasks where a throwaway brush is needed. The marvelous thing about foam brushes is that the tips of them can be cut or notched for a variety of patterns. Foam brushes range in size from one inch to three inches.

Where to Buy Brushes

As mentioned throughout this chapter, some of the best sources for purchasing brushes are hardware stores and household paint suppliers. Theatrical suppliers are the place to go for the specific theatrical paintbrushes listed here (see Reading and Resources chapter). Art stores are an excellent source of brushes used for tight detail work. There are other interesting sources of brushes that you might explore. For instance, you may find that local restaurant supply stores sell pastry brushes that make terrific scenic glazing brushes. If you travel abroad, take the time to investigate the brushes available at the local hardware stores and art supply stores in foreign cities. Odd brushes sometimes materialize from time to time at the local hardware and paint stores and may surprise you. Buyers for these stores sometimes pick up lines of very interesting and useful brushes. For example, in a hardware store in a small midwestern town I happened to pick up two round-ferrule horsehair brushes that are excellent for glazing. Unlike other round-ferrule brushes I have encountered, these had paint wells instead of solid bristle and hold a tremendous charge of paint that can glaze a line for many feet. These brushes were being sold as glue brushes. I am still very pleased with this find.

Brooms, Extensions, Rollers, and Other Painting Accessories

In addition to brushes, every imaginable paint tool can be found in the scenic paint shop. Anything that can be used for spraying, dripping, squirting, or smearing any kind of fluid potentially can be used with paint.

Brooms

Brooms are essential paint tools and not just for sweeping floors. Push brooms are used in scenic art shops to smooth laundry starch, which is used as a primer on some drops. Soft plastic-bristled brooms are the best for starching drops, because natural straw brooms are too coarse and horsehair brooms tend to shed. (For a complete explanation of starching drops, see Chapter Seven.) Brooms and sponge mops can also be used for broad paint techniques and blends of color.

Extensions

As discussed in Chapter Four, the two primary ways to paint flat scenery and soft goods are in the eastern and continental styles. Painting on a paint frame, or up, is eastern-style scenic painting. Painting scenery laying on the floor or drops that have been stretched on a deck is continental scenic painting, or painting down.

The scenic artist actually walks on the scenery while painting in the continental style. Brushes and other paint tools are attached to *extensions,* so the scenic artist need not bend over or squat while working. Extensions also give the scenic artist a free range of motion while working on the scenery. Some brands of scenic brushes have very long handles, specifically for working down. Some scenic artists prefer these. I find that, because my scenic work seems to be divided between painting up and painting down, the more expensive long-handled brushes are useful only half the time but a short-handled brush always can be put into an extension. Some

brands of brushes have handles mounted into screw bases, so that the short handle can be replaced by an extension. Telescoping extensions are sold at paint stores and through scenic suppliers for an adjustable extension.

Bamboo sticks, or rods, make excellent extensions and are widely used in the scenic art industry. Most scenic shops and scenic artists have a wide selection of bamboo for extensions, including bamboo rods of varying diameters and lengths. Generally, the wider is the diameter of the bamboo, the longer it will need to be. Wide-diameter bamboo accommodates larger brushes and gives the painter greater leverage.

> To make a bamboo extension, cut the rod to the desired length. If the cut is made on an angle it will be easier to insert brushes into the extension. Split the bamboo into quarters by tapping the end of the rod with a chisel once and then again, perpendicular to the first split. Split it down only to the first joint. After it is split lightly sand the ends, as freshly cut bamboo is full of nasty splinters. Next, wrap one or two large rubber bands around the splits so the bamboo will grip the handle of a brush. Do not use tape with a bamboo rod to grip a brush—it is messy and it is a hassle to deal with.

Wooden dowel extensions in which screw threads simply are carved into the wood at the end of the handle wear out quickly. You may be starching a drop, and the broom head will suddenly drop off. A wooden dowel extension that has a threaded metal cap on the end will last much longer. If the metal cap comes off, do not despair. Simply fill the cap with a good epoxy and hammer it back on. It will not happen a second time.

Edgers

The house-painting industry has many tools to make painting faster, easier, and cleaner. A scenic artist can benefit from the use of these tools, because painting some kinds of hard scenery is essentially the same as house painting. When painting a trim color, you can use *edgers* to guide your brush and mask unpainted areas. A piece of bristol board, or any other rigid card stock, makes a crude edger but can be custom shaped. After two or three uses, the edge of the bristol board will become gummed up with paint and begin to leave marks. Manufactured edgers have a steel or plastic guide that can be wiped off between uses. These edgers come in lengths from a few inches to three feet.

Another tool also used as an edger is a *paint pad*. This is a foam rubber pad about the size of an index card with a fibrous surface. It leaves a smooth trail of paint with a crisp edge when charged with paint and drawn along a surface. Paint pads hold little paint and must be recharged frequently.

Rollers

Paint rollers are very common and widely available. Rollers are made for use with water-based paints, alkyd paints, or shellacs. Roller units consist of the roller frame and cover and a pan to hold the paint. Roller frames come in various widths: standard sizes are three inch, four inch, and nine inch; industrial-size roller frames are eighteen inches wide and larger.

Roller covers once were made primarily from lamb and sheep fleece, because nappy fur soaks up a good charge of paint and rolls on smoothly. Fleece roller covers still are available, but they are rather expensive. Polyester roller covers paint as well as fleece at a fraction of the cost. Roller covers have a stiff core that slips over the frame. The core may be made of water-resistant cardboard or plastic. Cardboard roller covers are less expensive and fall apart faster. I prefer to use the cheaper roller covers to work with alkyd paint or shellac, because the cost of solvent to clean them is not worth the price of reusing a cover. I use better quality covers with water-based paint and clean them out after each use.

Roller trays hold the paint and allow the roller to be evenly charged, which means to ink the roller with paint. *Roller screens* fit into five-gallon paint cans and serve to squeeze off excess paint after the roller is dipped into the bucket. Standard roller trays are designed to accommodate nine-inch-wide rollers. Standard roller trays have a grill pattern in them. This grill pattern can leave an impression on the roller cover that is transferred to the scenery; cafeteria trays, condiment trays, and homemade trays fashioned out of visquene can be used to avoid imprinting the roller cover. Roller tray liners are useful when any paint other than water-based paint is used. The liner can be thrown away, saving the cost of the solvents it would require to clean the tray.

Large roller trays are available to accommodate the eighteen-inch-wide rollers as well as industrial three-foot-wide rollers.

Cleaning roller covers can be done a few different ways. To clean the covers by hand, without the benefit of some handy device, takes a while. Roller covers hold paint; that is their job. Excess paint can be squeezed out of the roller cover with a cup-shaped paint scraper.

One cleaning tool available in most paint stores is a *spinner-style brush and roller cleaner*. It cleans the paint out of the cover with centrifugal force. The cover slips over the end of the spinner. When the handle of the spinner is pumped, the cover will twirl and the paint will fly off. If you hold the spinner up in the air in front of your face the first time you give it an experimental twirl, you will get covered in paint. If you spin the cover under running water or in a bucket of water, it will come clean very quickly. Spinners are marketed as roller and brush cleaners. I do not recommend using them for brush cleaning, because it is very hard on the brush.

Another type of roller cleaner is a tube that the roller cover fits into. The tube is capped at both ends. One cap has a hole in it, and the other cap has water hose connector imbedded in it. Once the roller cover is inside, a hose is connected to the tube and the roller cover is rinsed. Another cleaner resembles an inverted lawn sprinkler with a hood. It attaches to a standard sink nozzle, and water flows out of the dozens of tiny holes. Insert the roller, and it will spin and rinse clean in seconds.

Roller cover nap refers to the length of the fleece, whatever its composition. Standard lengths of nap are one-quarter inch, one-half inch, three-quarters inch, and one inch. The longer the nap, the more paint the roller will hold. However, one aspect of working with rollers is that they generate spatter as the roller whips back and forth across a surface. The longer is the nap, the more the roller is apt to generate this annoying spatter. The fine spatter can work itself into all sorts of surprising nooks and crannies if you are not careful. Therefore, it is best to use a shorter nap if you are doing work where spatter could be a problem. The shorter nap also is better for clear finishes. A longer nap roller cover mixes more air bubbles into varnish while it is being rolled on, which might create a milky haze in the finish when it dries.

Roller covers can be made with many products other than natural fleece or polyester fleece, such as foam or carpet loop, for specific jobs like texturing and gluing. *Foam roller covers* come in a range of thicknesses but one-quarter inch and one-half inch are the most common. *Foam-texture roller covers* are covered with one-half inch of serrated foam rubber. These covers do not hold a long-lasting charge of paint, so they are best used with thicker paints and mediums. Foam or fleece can be carved away or taped to create your own texture or pattern. Foam rollers designed to paint rough surfaces have a three-quarter-inch foam covering with slits cut into it. These roller covers can be cut or torn up for some varieties of painted texture.

Texture roller covers are not designed to hold any paint at all. Their surface is densely covered with short rubber loops about three-eighths inch long. They create a pebbled texture when rolled across a surface that has a texture coat brushed, rolled, or sprayed on it. The thicker is the texture medium, the sharper the peaks of the texture will be. If the texture is thin, the surface will settle down to a uniform pebbly surface after it has been passed over with the texture roller. Scenic suppliers also market a texture roller cover made with loops of leather. These covers may be used with paint or texture mediums. You may also make your own texture roller by wrapping rags, plastic, rope, or most anything, around the roller cover.

Glue roller covers are covered with shallow looped carpet. These rollers are helpful in spreading wood glue, laminate adhesive, foam adhesive, contact cement, and other similar substances. Fleece rollers are not very effective in pushing sticky substances around; hence, the usefulness of the glue roller covers. These covers make an interesting pattern, but they do not hold a charge of paint for very long and it is difficult to control how heavily the paint is applied to the surface. These roller covers may also be used with a texture compound.

Pattern rollers are available from scenic suppliers with wallpaper-like patterns molded directly on the roller cover. These are sold as units with the carriage and cover sold together and are available in an array of patterns. They have a registration notch so that designs can be lined up. The roller is charged with thick paint and prints in much the same way a rubber stamp prints a pattern. A steady hand is needed to work with these tools and keep the repetition of the pattern flawless. These rollers are not easy to work with on units that have had three-dimensional molding applied to them.

Radiator rollers are narrow in diameter and sold as a complete unit, cover and frame together. They are used to paint behind radiators (hence, the name), refrigerators, and other appliances where the space is too tight to accommodate a full-diameter roller. A scenic artist might find them useful for reaching into tight spaces where a normal roller would not fit.

Power rollers feed paint directly to the roller cover, eliminating the need to charge the roller. Paint is poured into a reservoir connected to the roller by a hose. The reservoir provides a steady and smooth flow of paint. For large projects requiring painting with a roller, a power roller may be a consideration. The power roller will not work for jobs that need to be done on the floor, because the handle has no screw base for use with an extension.

OTHER TOOLS AND ACCESSORIES FOR THE SCENIC ARTIST

A huge variety of other tools is used by the scenic artist to apply paint. Many of these can be made or modified for each job at hand. Keep in mind that many jobs you take on will require the fabrication of some new tool to make the work faster and better. Some of these are discussed here.

Stencils and Stamps

Stencils are used to make repetitive designs and patterns. Stencils can be more intricate than paint stamps and can be registered (that is, precisely aligned) to create very complex designs in layers. A stencil is cut from flat, durable, water-resistant materials. Paint is sprayed, rolled, or stippled across the stencil, which serves as mask for the negative areas of the design.

One important trick to creating designs for stencils is that no design can have any negative areas that are completely surrounded by positive areas or the stencil will fall apart. Negative areas in stencils must be tied together. These ties are often incorporated into the design. If the negative areas are absolutely integral to the design and ties cannot be worked into the design, there are alternatives. The negative areas are cut out with ties left in to link the negative areas together. After the scenery has been stenciled and dried, the print left by the ties can be painted out with the appropriate color. If this approach is not feasible, the stencil can be netted so the negative areas stay in without ties.

Here is how to net a stencil. After the stencil is cut, assemble all of the pieces in their proper place on something flat and rigid, like sheet stock or bristol board. Use rubber cement or tape to hold the pieces in their proper places. Stretch a piece of polyester bobbinet across the top of the stencil. Use solvent-based contact cement over the top of the bobbinet to firmly attach the bobbinet to the top of the stencil (see Chapter Four, Safety and Health Regulations). Cover the top of the stencil and the bobbinet on it completely with the contact cement, being careful not to stick the stencil to the surface underneath. Once the contact cement is completely dry, the stencil is ready for use. This method also will work to reinforce stencils that are fragile and may fall apart through repeated use. The paint will print through the bobbinet. When using stencils reinforced this way, make sure to clean the stencil frequently and carefully. Let the stencil dry out thoroughly if it begins to get soggy. In other words, be patient. Stenciling is a laborious process; take your time and be meticulous. Done well, the effect will be very gratifying.

Several materials are good for making stencils, such as stencil paper, Upson® board, lithography or tin plate, polystyrene sheet plastic, filled fiberglass window screening, and plastic laminate. *Stencil paper*, the traditional choice for stencils, is paper or a hot pressed board treated with wax to make it water resistant. Stencil paper does not hold up well to repeated use with wet techniques, such as spraying, and is not a good choice for repeated use. *Upson® board*, or easy-curve, commonly is used in scene shops. This material comes in one-eighth-inch and one-quarter-inch thicknesses and is used in the same way as stencil paper. The disadvantage to using Upson® board with some stenciling techniques is that it is thicker and will not leave as clean a print as stencil paper or some other products. After a stencil

has been cut out of any paper product, several coats of clear shellac or oil-based enamel should be applied to both the front and back of the stencil to waterproof it, give it a washable surface, and prevent warping (see Chapter Four, Safety and Health Regulations).

Lithography plate, or litho plate, or tin sheeting makes a terrific stencil material. It is impervious to water, very sturdy, and easy to cut. Litho plate can be purchased at printing supply houses. Used litho plate also can be obtained directly from printers. After it has been used, it is of no further use to the print shop. Plates the print shop does not need to keep on file are thrown away. Newspaper printing departments also use litho plate for the inserts. The only disadvantage in obtaining the plates from this source is that they generally will be only as large as the size of the newspaper inserts. Occasionally in a scenic design, there will be a call for a very large repetitive pattern.

Polystyrene sheet plastic is commonly used for thermoplastic molding. It is sold as large as 4' x 8' sheets and comes in a very wide range of thicknesses, from one millimeter to one-quarter inch. Fairly thin three- or five-millimeter polystyrene is suitable for most stenciling. Like litho plate, polystyrene is very easy to cut and waterproof. *Plastic laminates*, or Formica®, make suitable stencils, although they are more difficult to cut. Plastic laminates can be purchased in sheets ten feet in length and five feet wide.

Cutting stencils is labor-intensive work. Stencils made out of card stock can be cut out with an X-Acto or Mat knife blade. Change blades often to keep the job going smoothly. A cut awl is a highly

---

When preparing to cut a stencil, bear in mind that multiple copies should be cut. Repetitive application of paint will build up on the stencil. Eventually, this paint will drip or run under the stencil and ruin the work. Usually, only two to three applications can be done before a stencil will have to be sponged off and dried. Drying the stencil on the side that comes in contact with the scenery is particularly important. Paint will flow to any wet area. With multiple copies of stencils, work will not be interrupted as often for cleaning. The stencils not in use can be put in front of a fan to dry.

mobile power saw used to cut thin material such as Upson® board, litho plate, tin sheet, and plastic sheeting. The cut awl works like a miniature skill saw and has a rotating cuff; the blade can swivel a full 360°, so it can be maneuvered around tight curves and details. The cut awl can cut through Plexiglas, stiff plastics, thin wood sheet stock, and litho plate. For cutting the materials discussed here, the best cut awl blade to use is a #12 blade, which is a sawtooth chisel-tip blade. Pilot holes must be predrilled when cutting plastic laminate or it will shatter. When cutting other materials discussed here, a cut awl can be set right down in the area to be cut away and the blade will puncture the material. Be sure to clamp your material firmly and work on a soft surface like Homasote. The cut awl is a power tool, so when using it be sure to wear safety glasses.

After the stencils are cut out and reinforced, it may be obvious that they are too fragile to last through the job ahead. In this case, attach the stencil to a frame. Make a frame of one-inch to two-inch wood stock, depending on the size of the stencil and the support it needs. Try to keep the frame as lightweight as possible. Always leave a border of at least six inches on every side of the design when making a stencil. This border will serve as a built-in mask and leave something to attach to a frame if needed. The stencil can be nailed or stapled to the frame from underneath. After the stencil has been attached to the frame, seal the inside edges with silicone or latex caulk so that the paint cannot seep between the layers (see Figure 5.5).

Depending on the desired appearance of the design, thick or thin paint can be used with a stencil. Thin paint is more prone to seepage under the stencil. The viscosity of the paint may determine the way paint is applied: thicker paint for stippling and rolling, thinner paint for spraying.

Stencils made for use with dyes are more effective if they are somewhat absorbent rather than waterproof. Dye is dissolved rather than suspended in water, and it is very thin. The viscosity can be increased by adding a gum thickener or starch. When stenciling, it may not be necessary to add thickeners if the dye is sprayed through a stencil made of unsealed Upson® board. The Upson® board will hang on to the thin dye so it does not drip on the project at hand. Multiple copies of the stencils will be necessary, so that they can be wiped off and dried for several minutes between uses (Figure 5.6).

Figure 5.5 Standard stencil construction.

Texture stencils are used to create a textured pattern or design. The stencil serves as the negative area around a mass of thick texture compound. Brick making is the perfect example of a good application for a texture stencil. One-eighth-inch to one-quarter-inch polyethylene or three-, five-, or seven-millimeter-thick polystyrene sheets work very well for making texture stencils. The polystyrene already might be at many scene shops because it is commonly used for vacu-forming. Most polystyrene comes in 4' x 8' sheet sizes. Once the design is cut out, the stencil is ready to use. The texture mixture can be spread over the stencil, and the excess squeegeed off. When the stencil is lifted straight up the textured pattern will remain.

Paint Stamps

Paint stamps are tools for making repeating designs or patterns, such as wallpaper or ornamental tile, and for making repetitive textures and patterns, such as marble tiles, foliage, or terrazzo. They are made of foam rubber cut into a pattern or design and adhered to a plywood base. The stamp is charged with paint in much the same way an ink stamp is charged with ink, and the pattern or design can be stamped on the scenery repeatedly (see Figure 5.7).

The foam rubber for a paint stamp should be at least one-half to one inch thick, so that the plywood backing does not make an impression when the stamp is pressed onto the scenery. The smaller is the stamp, the thinner the foam rubber can be. Some foam rubber has a plastic coating on one side, so be careful that the coated side is the side glued to the

Figure 5.6
Typical stencils: left, wallpaper patterns made to be used together; upper right, a brick texture stencil; lower right, a foliage stencil.

backing. The foam rubber should be cut out as evenly as possible, clean through with an X-Acto knife. Change the blade often so the cutting goes smoothly.

The base of the paint stamp should be cut out to approximately the same shape as the design or pattern. Attach an upright handle of one-inch stock lumber or a wooden dowel to the base before adhering the foam rubber if you are painting in the continental style. Also, a short dowel handle may be attached to the stamp for easy storage; then the stamp can be used with a bamboo extension. The handle should be

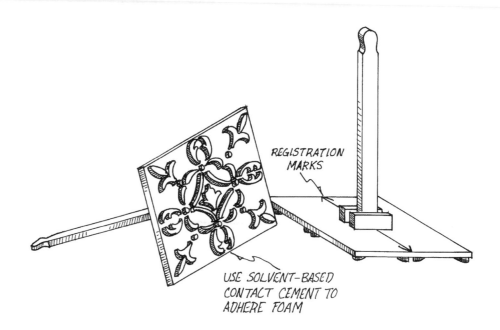

Figure 5.7
Paint stamps and their construction.

REGISTRATION MARKS

USE SOLVENT-BASED CONTACT CEMENT TO ADHERE FOAM

firmly attached so that the stamp can be rocked back and forth ever so slightly to make sure of a good print. Large stamps can get fairly heavy, more so after the stamp is charged with paint. When constructing the base and handles for a stamp, care should be taken to keep the materials as light as possible. Use half-inch plywood instead of three-quarter inch; make the handle out of two-inch stock.

Registration of the paint stamp is critical for multiple layers of color, repeating patterns, or both. Complex stamp designs should be drawn out full-scale on paper first and transferred by a pounce onto the foam rubber stamp as well as the plywood base. Pounces are large tracings made on paper with a pounce wheel (see Chapter Eight). If color separations are needed, each of them should be drawn out on the pounce as well. *Multicolor designs* are done with multiple paint stamps. Separate each color section of the design and create a separate stamp for each color. Each stamp must be the same size and have alignment marks, called *registration marks*, so all stamps will align properly with each other. If a multicolored stamp design is made up of nonconnecting elements, the stamp may be carefully charged by hand, using brushes to "paint" the color onto the foam rubber. This way, only one paint stamp has to be built.

Single-color, *repeating designs* need registration marks as well. The registration marks must correspond to gridlines or guides on the scenery itself. The design should be placed on a square or rectangular base. The top side of the base should have marks at the edges that will relate to lines and marks cartooned on the scenery, so that the design can be placed with accuracy.

After the design has been cartooned and the foam rubber pieces have been cut out, they are ready to be adhered to plywood bases. First, draw and ink the design on the bottom of the plywood base. Cover the base and the back of the foam rubber pieces with contact cement, using solvent-based rather than water-based cement (see Chapter Four, Safety and Health Regulations). Water-based contact cement will come apart after the stamp has been in use for a while. After the contact cement is dry, carefully place the pieces of foam on the base and press them firmly in place. Be absolutely certain of your placement of the two layers. Contact cement does not allow for shifting. Hot melt glue may also be used to adhere the foam rubber. In some cases it may be easier to cover the entire area of the design first with the foam rubber and then cut and carve the design out with an X-Acto knife.

Safe disposal of used blades is very important when using X-Acto knife blades or any other razor-sharp blades. Always tape over the blade before it is thrown away. Often, rubbish gets stuck in the garbage pail and someone must reach in to pull it out. Place tape over the razor edge of the spent blade to avoid a serious accident.

Paint used for stamps should be water based. Shellac or alkyd paint will ruin a stamp. The paint must be fairly thick or it will drip and run to one end of the stamp. The paint to charge the stamp can be poured onto a cafeteria tray. If the tray is not large enough to accommodate the stamp in use, a piece of heavy visquene plastic can be draped in the bottom of a paint cart or stapled to a wooden frame made to fit the stamp.

Texture Tools

Texture-applying tools have been more recently used in theatrical painting and have been taken mostly from other crafts. The techniques of texturing are discussed in Chapter Nine.

Sponges

Sponges of all varieties are essential in a scenic studio. Both natural and synthetic sponges create interesting grain patterns with paint and make soft blends.

A natural *sea sponge* serves as a fine paint tool. These sponges grow in warm ocean climates, where they are harvested by divers. The softer sponges with a consistent pattern are sold for the bath, as janitorial supplies, and to paint suppliers. Coarser sponges with random patterns also are available at janitorial supply and paint stores. Cosmetic sponges, which are very small and have a very fine pattern, generally are much more expensive and not as useful for scenic painting. If you find yourself in a tropical climate where sponge diving is one of the local industries, stock up on sponges as the selection always is better close to the source.

An advantage of a natural sponge in scenic painting is that the imprint that it leaves is organic. Every natural sponge has its own unique pattern. Most paint shops and scenic artists that have a stock of tools will collect a good variety of natural sponges.

> The natural sponge is indispensable in a paint shop for cleaning paint spills. Spills on scenery are very difficult to clean, especially when the scenery has many complex layers of painting on it. A soft natural sponge is the best tool for carefully cleaning the paint spill. Cleaning is a skill, too! Always blot or soak the spilled paint, never scrub or wipe it. Any scrubbing will pull up lower layers and probably work in more of the spilled color.

Synthetic sponges come in geometric shapes by virtue of manufacturing. In addition to everyday cleanup chores, they are useful for certain painting techniques. Synthetic sponges can be cut up or carved into shapes and patterns for creating texture on surfaces like brick or tile. Most synthetic sponges are either cellulose or foam rubber and best used for even-grained stamping. However, foam rubber sponges do not hold a charge of paint as well as cellulose ones. Cellulose sponges have reasonably good organic texture. They are very useful for distressing and smoothing out painted patinas, grime, and dirt. Cellulose sponges can be torn apart along their length. This way a grain emerges that works very well for bricks and some varieties of stone and marbles. Much like a texture stamp, sponges can be used with stencils for uneven, textured patterning, as with a stipple brush.

Rags

Rags, just scraps of cloth, have a great many functions in the scene shop. Every shop should be well stocked with rags for cleaning. Rags can be purchased by the pound at most paint supply stores, and well-stocked stores will have a choice of rags, including lintless rags for staining. Almost every kind or grain of cloth, from flannel and linen to burlap and erosion cloth, is useful for a scenic artist.

Rags also can be used as texture tools. Rag rolling is a common technique. Here, the rag is crumpled up and immersed in paint, then wrung out and rolled around on any surface to be textured. This method can be done with nearly any kind of material. Different types of material create different textures. Finer weave rags sometimes are fringed on the edges to add to the texture. The coarser fabrics, such as burlap and erosion cloth, used in landscaping, can be purchased through landscape material suppliers. Rags are very useful for wiping down and smoothing patinas and aging glazes on scenery. Softer, more absorbent rags will be more helpful in this application.

Floggers

The paint *flogger* is a texture tool made from strips of rag attached to the end of a stick, resembling a mop of sorts. Floggers can be used to create texture by dipping the rag end in paint, wringing it out, and striking the surface (called *flogging*) or gently twirling and dabbing (called *schlepitchka*) (Burris-Meyer and Cole, 1938). These simple techniques produce very attractive random texture patterns. Clean muslin floggers also are used to clean dirt and charcoal off scenery after the cartoon is made. Clean floggers are a staple of every paint shop.

Feathers

Feather dusters may be used in the same manner as floggers to create texture. They are the traditional tools used for the technique of schlepitchka. They may be dragged lightly across a painted surface to create a grain. Feather dusters are sold at discount, grocery, and cleaning supply stores. At cleaning suppliers, a selection of different varieties of feather dusters may be found. The most common feathers to be found are chicken, pheasant, turkey, and ostrich. Of course, different varieties will create different textures or grains. Feathers by themselves sometimes are used for graining faux marbles in extremely fine detail.

Offbeat Tools

All sorts of interesting objects serve as paint tools. When you confront a new texture project or treatment, just consider what kind of object may be useful to obtain the desired effect and then give it a test. For example, for a Jackson Pollock style painting technique, creating long, fat strings of paint, a turkey baster was used to good effect. A stage deck made of several plates of one-quarter-inch steel set one-eighth of an inch apart had raw wood visible in the seams. An oversized hypodermic needle obtained from a research lab squirted paint into the cracks. Trying to recreate the pointillist style of Georges Seurat leads to all manner of rapid dot-painting, including clusters of ethafoam rod, foam bottle brushes, and orthopedic mattresses!

Sprayers

Sprayers are a tool of scenic painting so important and varied that they are second only to brushes themselves. The practice of using paint in garden sprayers was introduced by the scenic designer Joseph Urban and his team of scenic artists from Vienna, all of whom came to the United States in the early 1900s. His scenic artists began one of the largest scenic studios in New York and used sprayers as a painting tool (Figure 5.8).

Sprayers work in one of three ways:

1. Garden sprayers work by pressurizing the air in a reservoir tank, which forces the fluid paint out of the tank through a fluid tube into the hose, wand, and nozzle of the sprayer. Pressure pots and high-volume, low-pressure sprayers work with compressed air in this way as well.

2. Pneumatic spray guns work by sending compressed air through the spray gun, creating a vacuum that pulls the fluid paint up through a suction tube in the paint cup below the gun.

3. Airless sprayers work by pressurizing the fluid paint itself, which is sent through a pressurized hose and spray gun. The paint is sucked out of a reservoir of paint, which is kept in a bucket under the airless. (See Chapter Four, Safety and Health Regulations.)

Garden sprayers are available in many sizes and varieties and are made to spray insecticides and weed killers. They consist of a fluid tank, a pump to pressurize the tank, a nozzle on a wand that aerates fluid as it is sprayed, and a hose connecting the wand to the tank. These tools are meant to be portable, self-contained units.

Garden sprayers are purchased at discount, hardware, and garden-supply stores. They are more easily found during the gardening season than in the dead of winter. Local greenhouses or garden suppliers can order them for you off-season, or they can be ordered from the manufacturer. Garden sprayers come in a wide range of quality, material, reliability, and price. Low- to mid-quality sprayers are sold most widely. If you wish to purchase a better-quality sprayer, most hardware and garden supply stores can

Figure 5.8
Paint spraying tools for scenic artists: left to right, a garden sprayer, a plant mister pump sprayer, spray bottle, one-quart and half-pint pneumatic spray guns; front, respirator for protection.

order one for you. If you are after only top-of-the-line sprayers, place an order with the manufacturer (see the Reading and Resources chapter). You may also obtain the name and telephone number of commercial dealers or manufacturers of sprayers from a large greenhouse or extermination company. This source may be out of state. Call the order department and ask for a catalogue.

A garden sprayer with a tank holding one and a half gallons or more has a wand and hose between the nozzle and the tank. The tank of the sprayer is carried at your side while the spray is aimed in any direction. Three gallons usually is the maximum tank size, as that amount is about as much paint as a person comfortably can carry around.

Inexpensive plastic sprayers have all plastic parts. They are the most commonly available and break down regularly. When they start malfunctioning, they are not very easy to fix. Once clogged or unreliable, it is best to replace them. Repair kits are available for some of these sprayers, so you may replace the parts of a broken sprayer; however, the models of inexpensive sprayers usually are changed yearly and soon repair kits are no longer available. The next step up are sprayers with galvanized steel tanks. It is easier to get repair kits for name-brand sprayers of this quality. Repair kits can be ordered from the store where they were purchased. Stainless steel tank sprayers are the top of the line. They are expensive but very dependable. Repair kits for these sprayers can be ordered from a commercial dealer or the manufacturer for many years beyond the purchase of the sprayer.

Plant misters have fluid capacity of usually about one-half gallon. They have no wand or hose but a spray nozzle attached directly to the unit. These sprayers are made of plastic, and the range of quality is not too vast. Replacement sprayers generally need to be purchased yearly, when they appear on the shelves in the spring, as there seems to be a percentage of failure every year. These smaller sprayers are very useful for working on smaller, tighter projects or smaller-volume jobs. They are as much a staple of the shop as their larger counterparts.

One variety of sprayer not often used in the theatre is a sprayer designed to be carried like a backpack. This type of sprayer would be more useful to a gardener or exterminator, who would not be filling the apparatus with hot starch or having to refill it six times an hour.

Care needs to be taken to keep the nozzle and fluid tubes from stopping up, because they are not made to spray paint. Paint used in any sprayer needs to be fairly thin and strained through mesh or netting to keep the coarser particles of pigment from stopping up the sprayer. Polyester net strainers are sold at most household paint stores. Whenever a sprayer is done with one job the hose should be emptied by holding it above the unpressurized tank. All excess paint should be poured out. The tank will need to be rinsed with water and sloshed out several times until the water is clear. After rinsing, the tank should be filled with water one last time and the sprayer pumped up again so the nozzle, hose, and wand can be sprayed clean.

Here are a few notes on how to make your sprayers more convenient. Pumping a sprayer can be the bane of your existence, especially if you have an all-day spray project. The tank of a metal sprayer can be fitted with a pneumatic coupling so it can be pressurized from an air line. Be very cautious with this system because a tank can be quickly overpressurized and spring a leak or blow off a hose. The tank should be fitted with an air valve so that you can read the air pressure. However, never use a compressor to fill sprayers that have hot starch in them; just use the pump. The heat from the starch compounds the pressure, so the tank can spring a leak, the hose pop off, or the pump of the sprayer in the tank can implode. The hot starch can scald anyone who happens to be in the way.

If disaster strikes and a sprayer begins to spray starch or paint all over a drop, do not panic. If it is hot starch, your first thoughts should be of safety and directing the fountain of starch away from people. Immediately move the sprayer away from the scenery. Turn the tank upside-down in the slop sink or a five-gallon bucket, thus stopping the flow of fluid by getting it away from the end of the supply tube. Then, you can turn your attention to any damage to the scenery.

You will find that each sprayer seems to have its own characteristics—its own personality, if you will. When doing a spray job, you well may find a particular sprayer in the shop that performs just right. If you are in a shop that has four identical sprayers, you can lose track of your favorite. If you name and label these four sprayers John, Paul, George, and Ringo, for instance, or any other names you may be fond of, you can always be sure to find your favorite sprayer again. Also, it is a lot more interesting than naming them sprayers one, two, three, and four.

Aerosol Sprayers

Two-part aerosol sprayers you can put your own paint are useful for toning, props painting, tight detail jobs, and touch-up. The two parts of these *aerosol sprayers* are canisters that screw onto a glass or plastic jar. Additional aerosol canisters can be purchased as replacements. The painter fills the jar with a very thin paint or dye, which can be sprayed in the same manner as a can of spray paint. Paint for these sprayers must be strained. Once the aerosol can is depleted, save the spray tip before throwing away the unit. Later, if a tip on another sprayer becomes clogged, you will have a replacement. These sprayers are somewhat pressure sensitive, so by using a light touch you can control the amount of spray to a certain extent. The companies that manufacture these have recently changed their aerosol formulas to be ozone safe.

Pneumatic Sprayers

Pneumatic sprayers work by mixing paint with compressed air (see Chapter Four, Safety and Health Regulations). The paint to be sprayed is strained into a reservoir cup that can be attached to the base of the spray gun. There will be a pneumatic fitting at the back of the gun so the sprayer may be connected directly to a compressed air hose. The spray gun is sold in two units: the spray gun and the fluid cup. Fluid cups usually are not interchangeable between brands of guns.

The one-quart gun is the most common and versatile spray gun. These guns are good for sophisticated spray work and broad airbrush techniques. For more tricky work, the half-pint size, also called a touch-up gun, is very useful. This gun can do everything the one-quart gun can do and handle tighter detail. The disadvantage is that this gun holds so little paint.

The spray can be controlled in three ways. First, the shape of the spray can be widened from a narrow cone shape to a fan. On the back of the gun is an airflow valve that controls the mix of air coming out of the spray tip; the spray will be flattened into a fan shape by mixing air in from the side or not to keep a cone-shaped spray. The direction of the fan pattern can be changed by rotating the spray tip at the front of the gun to orient the fan vertically or horizontally. Second, the proportional mix of air and fluid can be changed by adjusting the fluid valve, the knob for which usually is located on the back of the spray gun below the air flow valve. Most spray guns are not sold with air regulators to adjust the pressure of the spray. However, any supplier of spray guns will have regulators for compressed air equipment. These attach at the air hose connector at the rear of the gun. I recommend getting an air valve attachment for every spray gun in your shop, as most pneumatic construction tools operate at a higher psi than pneumatic sprayers. Having a valve precludes the need for a regulated air line or separate compressor. It also gives you greater control over the variables of your spray right at the gun.

Purchase a name-brand sprayer from a reputable dealer (see Reading and Resources chapter). Be careful of purchasing seldom heard of brands of spray guns, as replacement parts may be hard to come by. Spray equipment is one of the more expensive investments in the painter's kit. When you invest in spray equipment, learn not only how to use it but how to service it yourself. When the gun begins to act up, you will want to know how to take it apart and fix the problem rather than stopping work in the middle of a project. When you buy your equipment, technical information should be included in the packaging, explaining how to take the sprayer apart and replace parts. Hang on to this information: put it in a safe place and keep it with your kit. It is common sense that your equipment will break down only when you are using it, so learn how to take care of problems.

Paint used in spray guns will need to be about the viscosity of whole milk and carefully strained into the spray cup. If you always strain paint thoroughly so the gun does not plug up, and clean the gun completely between uses, the gun will be more reliable. If the gun has problems you cannot resolve, look for an automotive paint supplier or call the manufacturer for the closest service center. These places will be able to service your gun or refer you to someone who can.

Spray guns are designed to be used with the solvent-based paints of the auto industry. The water-based paints commonly used in scenic painting tend to rust and corrode some parts of the gun. After cleaning, spray a little solvent alcohol through the gun and lift the gun out of the cup and spray air through it to dry out the interior parts. If, despite all your efforts, the spray tip begins to rust, you can replace it with a stainless steel tip. You may want to ask, when purchasing the spray gun, if it is possible to purchase it with a stainless steel spray tip. In the last decade, plastic parts have been appearing more and more in high-quality sprayers, making corrosion less of a problem.

Scenic painting is different than auto painting in that scenic artists often are after speedy coverage and not as concerned about sagging paint. When purchasing a paint gun, inquire if you can get it with a larger-diameter spray tip than the standard one with which the gun is sold. This will accommodate a greater volume of fluid. Spray tips and spray needles must fit together, so a matching spray needle will be necessary as well.

Be aware that some scenic shops have oiled air lines to help lubricate nail guns but, naturally, your latex paint cannot be mixed with oil. If a shop has oiled air lines, you need to set up a clean air line that is convenient to the painters and have air hoses set aside that are used only for spray guns.

High-pressure pneumatic sprayers work by drawing paint out of a container and mixing it with high volumes of air in the gun, which atomizes the paint as it is released from the spray tip. The cup serves only as a vessel for the paint being sprayed and must draw in air to replace the volume of fluid being sucked up the fluid tube. When a high-pressure pneumatic gun is not working, the first check for problems is to see if the air hole in the fluid cup cap is plugged, which will make it impossible for the gun to draw fluid from the cup.

High-Volume, Low-Pressure Sprayers

High-volume, low-pressure (HVLP) sprayers became commercially available only recently (see Chapter Four, Safety and Health Regulations). These sprayers are quickly replacing the high-pressure pneumatic sprayers in the workplace, as development of these sprayers was hastened by concerns over the environment as well as personal safety.

HVLP sprayers are designed to spray a larger amount of fluid than conventional spray guns with much lower air pressure emitted from the tip of the gun itself. The benefits of this design are a much greater control over the spray pattern and significantly reduced paint mist dispersed while spraying.

Typical pneumatic sprayers and airless sprayers release considerable amounts of particulates which simply scatter in the air in normal operation.

The spray patterns achieved with an HVLP sprayer range from a very fine spray, similar to the controlled spray from a high-pressure half-pint touch-up spray gun, to a broad coarse pattern that resembles a fine spatter. This means an HVLP may serve many more of the needs of scenic artists, replacing currently used equipment. Because so much less air pressure is being released from the tip of the gun, usually about five psi, and because the fluid being released at the spray tip is not atomized to the same extent as with high-pressure spray guns, the user has greater control over the amount and direction of fluid being released. HVLP sprayers are safer to use, because less atomized fluid or paint mist is being released into the work environment and directly in front of the user's face. This does not mean that HVLP sprayers can be used without the safety protection of a respirator and proper ventilation. (See Chapter Four, Safety and Health Regulations.)

The HVLP sprayer works by pressurizing the fluid cup, which forces the paint up the fluid tube and into the gun. This process increases the volume of fluid that can be released at the tip and makes only as much pressure as is necessary to atomize the paint, rather than the thirty or more psi that high-pressure guns need to create the vacuum and draw fluid up through the tube.

The low pressure in the term *high-volume, low-pressure* refers only to the psi released at the spray tip. HVLP sprayers need to be operated with a minimum of 60 to 80 psi from the compressor. Most of these sprayers are available from the manufacturer in units with portable compressors that generate a steady psi for the operation of the sprayer. HVLP sprayers are already equipped with an air valve and gauge that will give the user control and a reading of what psi is at the spray tip. The other components of the HVLP sprayer—the spray tip, spray nozzle, spray needle, fluid valve, and airflow valve—work on the same principle and usually are arranged in the same manner as on high-pressure spray guns. However, most HVLP sprayer guns are being designed with plastic bodies, spray needles, spray nozzles, and spray tips. Larger gauge spray needles and nozzles may be purchased for these sprayers. Even the superior-quality HVLP sprayers are made with plastic parts, which are easier to clean and not subject to corrosion.

HVLP sprayers and compressor sprayer units are an expensive investment in shop equipment. However, few shops can afford to be without this very useful and versatile tool. Although the price varies among brands of sprayers, you may expect to pay between $400 and $500 for a good-quality spray gun and an additional $150 to $250 if you are buying a sprayer compressor unit. If your shop has yet to invest in pneumatic equipment of any sort, it is recommended you only consider investing in an HVLP sprayer.

Airbrushes

Airbrushes work the same way as pneumatic sprayers but on a much smaller and finer scale. Airbrushes are useful for very tight spray work. I had gone a long time without owning one, because the need had never arisen. When, at last, I needed to purchase one, I was counseled to get a top-of-the-line tool that had dual control. This good advice means that I can control the amount of fluid and the shape of the spray. The spray can be shaped to a very narrow pinpoint or widened to a cone shape.

Airbrushes are designed to work at an air pressure of around thirty psi or less, much lower than normal shop air pressure. Valves, gauges, hoses, and fittings can be purchased that connect to a regular air line so the airbrush can be used at the lower psi. Special airbrush compressors can be purchased or ordered from any fine-art supply store that sells airbrushes. You will want an extra-long air hose of at least twelve feet, so that you are free to move around the scenery with the airbrush. Aerosol cans can be purchased that will give you about thirty minutes of use with an airbrush.

Most airbrushes are sold with small cups for holding paint, which are designed for tabletop studio work. Paint can be spilled out of them easily, and for scenic work you will need more volume anyway. You can buy spray jars that are covered and hold a larger quantity of paint. The paint you will use in the airbrush will need to be much, much thinner than the paint you use for spray guns. Do not store the paint in the spray jars overnight, because it will settle and you will have to clean out the jar the next day.

Airbrushes are designed for use with fine-arts quality paint, usually watercolors and acrylics. Because the pigments for paints used in scenic painting are not as finely ground, they tend to clog the spray tip more often, so the paint must be carefully strained. The spray tip and the needle that fits it should be purchased in a larger size than the standard one. The standard spray tip for an airbrush has a three-millimeter opening. A five-millimeter spray tip would be a better size for scenic painting.

Always use the finest paint available for an airbrush. High-quality scenic acrylics are fine, but some lower-quality scenic paints are simply too coarse to be compatible with the fine tolerances of an airbrush system.

Pressure Pot Sprayers

Pressure pots are designed differently than spray guns. The fluid pot is not carried around with the gun (see Chapter Four, Safety and Health Regulations). One hose, usually around twenty feet in length, carries the fluid to the spray gun, and a second hose delivers air to the pressurized paint pot. The pressure pot usually holds about two gallons of paint. True to its name, the compressed air is connected to the pressure pot so that the fluid is under pressure. The pressure pot has a gauge on top, so that the painter can read the pressure.

Pressure pots can be a good solution to the problem of having to refill the spray gun every few minutes, particularly on large volume jobs. They also are an arm saver, because you need not hold the paint supply out at arm's length, which can be a strain after a while. However, they take longer to clean and the long hose is harder to clean and it cannot be dragged through wet paint if you are working on the paint deck.

Airless Sprayers

An *airless sprayer* works without compressed air by pressurizing paint as it passes through the sprayer body (see Chapter Four, Safety and Health Regulations). The body of an airless sprayer sits directly over a paint bucket; it has no internal reservoir. The airless sprayer is good for one thing only—speed. The paint comes out so fast and at such high pressure that it will cover almost any surface with paint or starch very fast. It is an excellent tool to have if you or your shop can afford one. Backpainting and applying a base coat over many square feet of hard scenery becomes a small task for one person armed with an airless sprayer rather than an all-day chore for the entire crew. Airless sprayers use a tremendous quantity of paint very quickly and, unlike other types of sprayers, can handle almost any viscosity of paint, even very thick ones. Their ability to pump a lot of paint quickly means you may use about fifty percent more paint as normal when spraying with an airless sprayer.

The airless sprayer consists of a suction tube that is immersed in a bucket of paint, a motor that pressurizes the fluid and is contained in the airless sprayer body, and a fluid hose with a gun, generally about twenty feet to twenty-five feet long, so that a fair amount of surface area can be reached without having to move the machine. The spray gun has little pressure control and only two speeds: on and off. The fan of the spray and the orientation of the fan can be controlled at the gun. The pressure can be controlled to some extent at the motor of the airless sprayer, if there is a high to low setting. Even so, for the gun to work it will generate at least a very powerful 100 psi at the lowest setting.

CAUTION: never point the nozzle of an airless at yourself or anyone else. The fluid is under enough pressure that it can pierce or be injected under the skin. This can result in an embolism or serious infection. Make sure that any injury caused by an airless spray gun is seen by a physician, no matter how slight, even if it is just water, as there is always a high probability of infection.

Airless sprayers are the most expensive of all sprayers. I recommend buying a name-brand sprayer from a nearby reputable dealer, as it will need service from time to time. It is best to have major repairs done by a professional, as a high-pressure sprayer can be dangerous if serviced improperly. Service is expensive because it is not deemed safe to use rebuilt parts, which leaves only replacement of worn or damaged parts.

All paint or starch used in an airless sprayer first must be strained so it will not plug the spray gun. Make sure to pour all the paint or starch through a metal strainer covered with a nylon paint strainer that rests on the reservoir bucket of the sprayer, or simply wrap a nylon paint strainer around the suction tube and tie it off at the top. This will strain all paint automatically as it passes into the sprayer.

If any air is in the system of the airless sprayer, it will not build up pressure. The machine must be primed first, so that all the air can be drawn off. A priming valve and drain tube usually are located at the back of most machines. Sometimes, the drain tube is positioned so that it will discharge back into the reservoir bucket. Once the suction tube is immersed in a full reservoir bucket, the machine should be turned on and allowed to run in the priming mode, located on a dial near the on/off switch, for one or two minutes, or until it has completely stopped burping air out of the drain tube. Oftentimes, the machine will not spray initially because it has not been allowed to finish priming. Once primed, turn the pressure dial from prime to the desired pressure and begin spraying.

Most airless spray guns have reversible spray tips. The spray nozzle has a knob on the side of the gun so that if, while spraying, a piece of dried residue comes loose somewhere in the machine or fluid tube and blocks the spray gun, you can turn the spray tip around and blast away the offending material. Turn the spray tip back, and you will be ready to spray again.

Cleaning out an airless sprayer takes some time. The fluid hose alone will have a fair volume of paint in it. Many gallons of clean water will need to pass through the sprayer to flush out all the paint or starch from the body hose and spray gun. If the airless sprayer is used only occasionally throughout the day, the spray gun can be left immersed in a bucket of water between uses rather than cleaning the machine between each use. After the machine is clean, squirt a little baby oil or mineral oil into the last rinse. The airless sprayer may be flushed with paint thinner if it is going into storage for many weeks or more. This will help keep the parts in the interior of the machine from sticking during long spells between uses. If there is oil or paint thinner in the airless sprayer, make sure to flush it out thoroughly with warm water before the next use.

Pattern Pistols and Hopper Guns

The *pattern pistol* is a pneumatic sprayer designed to spray extremely thick texturing pastes (see Chapter Four, Safety and Health Regulations). The spray gun has a wheel at the spray tip with different-sized openings to accommodate different fluids and various-sized chunks of texture, rather like a multipurpose pencil sharpener. On the top of the gun is the *hopper,* a cone-shaped container that holds the texture and funnels it into the gun. The hopper holds about two gallons of goop, so the gun is rather heavy when full and can be tiring to work with. There is no air valve on a hopper gun; once it is hooked up to the air, it is on. The trigger pulls back the spray tip, which allows the fluid to drop down between it and the spray wheel, where it is blasted out though the selected hole in the spray wheel.

Hopper guns can be purchased or rented at contractor supply houses quite inexpensively. They are designed to be easy to take apart and maintain because all manner of goop is forced through these guns. Often, the best way to thoroughly clean them at the end of the day is to take them completely apart.

This rather simple tool is very useful for covering surfaces with all manner of water-based textures very quickly. They work well with joint compound and plaster-based textures, even those mixed with vermiculite and perlite, cellotex-based papier mâché textures, and Quick Texture (QT) mix, which is manufactured specifically for use with hopper guns.

CONCLUSION

A professional scenic artist will acquire a considerable stock of tools in his or her career. Brushes will be the bulk and backbone of that stock. Remember to take the best care possible with these tools. Brushes can last many years with thorough cleaning and proper storage. A scenic artist will need to use a wide variety of other tools and should know how to maintain them. Garden sprayers are an excellent example of this. Almost every job will call for a sprayer at one point or another, so it is essential to have at least one reliable and somewhat predictable unit in your tool kit. Take the time to learn how they work and what is needed for cleaning, safe handling, and maintaining.

chapter 6

Color and Paint

INTRODUCTION

Color is a key ingredient in all visual images. Colors inform us, provoke us, soothe us, and stimulate us—they elicit a myriad of responses in us. The simple presence or absence of color significantly alters the mood of anything we look at. Many in society have come to associate the black and white imagery of photographs and film as serious or nostalgic. A modern movie made in black and white wordlessly communicates a certain dramatic sensibility as does the somber palette of colors of the paintings of El Greco and the warm pastels of Degas. A message is given through the color and its context.

Color, and the pleasing color of things, also are familiar and easily recognized by almost anyone who sees them. It does not take a trained geologist to appreciate a well-colored piece of marble. Nor do we need a meteorologist to know the sky is a crystal-clear blue. On instinct and experience, people will recognize correct and incorrect colors. Few people could actually identify or reproduce the color of the food they eat, but everyone knows when it is wrong. It takes an artist to create pleasing colors or manipulate them with meaning, such as a disturbing landscape, a menacing urban environment, or a perfectly tranquil sky. But as easy as a good or bad color choice is to recognize, color also is quite difficult to understand and manipulate. Knowing a color is wrong is one thing; knowing how to fix it is entirely another.

Color, in painting mediums, is a raw material for the scenic artist. Colors in paint, dye, metallic finishes, and other products almost always need to be prepared before being applied to scenery. Few colors come right out of a can onto the canvas. Paints are blended together or layered one on another to achieve the correct color. The range, or palette, of colors available to a scenic artist is surprisingly small, yet the potential colors that can be mixed from this palette are virtually limitless. It is important for the scenic artist to understand the colors themselves, so they can be combined, by mixing or layering, into the precise color desired by the scenic designer.

This chapter describes color and the chief medium in which it is used: paint. Color is defined by scientific theory and described through commonly accepted terminology. Paint is a combination of organic and synthetic components with a variety of behaviors, all of which must be known to the scenic artist.

COLOR THEORY

The Physics of Color

The perception of color is a physical phenomenon, the result of correct functioning of the eyes, optic nerves, and the brain. Color is possible only because of light. Light can be of a color, like an amber sunset, or light can reveal color in an object. Through the presence of light, we see the blue sky or a green field. Color is transmitted in light waves, the visible part of the overall spectrum of electromagnetic radiation. The *color spectrum* of visible light ranges from violet to red. In 1676, Isaac Newton observed the relationship of color and white light. He discovered that white sunlight passing through a triangular piece of glass, a prism, "Bent the light waves and broke them up into a color spectrum of red, orange, yellow, green, blue and violet." When this spectrum again passed through the prism, it reformed into white light. A rainbow is an excellent example of the spectrum of visible light and clearly shows the six colors of the spectrum Newton observed.

Visible light is a very narrow band of the electromagnetic spectrum, which ranges overall from the relatively long radio waves to very short gamma waves. In the visible section of the band of light, each color has a specific wavelength. The red wavelength is the longest, at 6,000 microns, and violet is the shortest, at 8,000 microns. Sunlight and white light contain all the colors of the visible spectrum.

We perceive all colors through our eyes, which distinguish light waves through two types of photoreceptors in the retina: rods and cones. These rods and cones are sensitive to visible light in two different ways. The cones respond to color and daylight, and the rods are sensitive to low-intensity light. The cones are centrally located in the retina; the rods are on the edge. That is why dim stars are perceived out of the corner of your eye by the rods. The same stars are invisible to the cones when you look at them directly. This also explains why color is more difficult to perceive under dim light; the cones are unable to function fully. The cone photoreceptors also are color specific, much like the pixels of a television screen. A cone can sense only red or blue or green. The brain combines the various levels of red and green transmitted through the cone to make yellow. The cones and brain ultimately combine the observable light wavelengths into the color one perceives.

The color we see is based on how objects reflect and absorb white light. An object that does not reflect light appears to have no color, to be black. Conversely, an object that reflects all light waves will appear white. If light waves pass through a material uninterrupted, or partially interrupted, that material appears to be transparent, like air, glass, or water. Objects may reflect some of the spectrum and absorb others. Simply put, a red ball absorbs most light waves and reflects only the red wavelength. This narrow band of light is distinguished by the red cones in the retina and the brain discerns the color as red. A blue-green object reflects some of both blue and green wavelengths. The retina's cones responding to blue and those responding to green send their responses to the brain, where the two colors are mixed together into blue-green.

This process of reflection is altered significantly if the light striking an object is not white but a color. A colored light is only a small part of the overall spectrum of light. A blue object seen under primary red light appears black, because there is no blue in the red light to be reflected back to the viewer. Understanding how color results from an object's reflection and absorption of visible light is the key to understanding how colors mix with each other. Essentially, two processes are involved in mixing colors. The two processes can be confusing; they both involve the way we perceive color. One process involves color as pigment or paint, the other involves color as light. Pigment and light mix colors differently. If the six colors of the spectrum are mixed together in equal amounts as paint, they theoretically combine into black through the process called *subtractive color mixing*. Subtractive mixing is the process a scenic artist uses to mix paint. It is important to know that an opposite effect occurs when mixing color in light, as lighting designers do. All colors of the spectrum mixed in equal amounts as light beams will combine to make white. That is called *additive color mixing*. Bear in mind that these two processes do not operate exclusive of each other. Scenic artists work in the subtractive mode but will see the effect of additive mixing on their work on stage. The references earlier in this book to how colors appear under different light sources is an example of the additive mixing process.

The Terminology of Color

Knowledge of the terms used for describing color is necessary for an accurate discussion of color. Color (as pigment) itself has three fundamental properties: *hue*, *chroma*, and *value*. It is essential to analyze a color in regard to these three properties during the mixing process. Actually discussing color would be nearly impossible without terms to further define the properties. These terms define what makes a color, how colors relate to each other and are classified, and how colors are perceived. The following terms are defined in regard to paint and pigment.

Terms That Define Color

Hue is the property of color itself or the perceived color of something. The hue of a clear sky is blue.

Chroma, intensity, and *saturation* describe the vividness of a hue. The three terms are synonymous. Bright red, blue, or yellow has high intensity. If a color is mixed with white, black, or an opposing hue then its intensity will be diminished, its chroma will be lowered.

Value specifies the relative lightness or darkness of a color. Primary red has low-moderate value. A higher value red, with white added to it, becomes pink. Purple is naturally a low-value color; whereas yellow is a high-value color. A value scale of one to ten can be used to define the value of a color. On a gray scale white is assigned a value of ten and black is assigned a value of one. In these terms a value can be discussed in terms of being high or low.

Color wheel and *color model.* Twelve colors are displayed on a color wheel. It is a graphic means to show all twelve hues divided into three groups: primary, secondary, and tertiary colors. The color wheel also shows the relationship between these colors. In a color wheel, the colors are arranged in a circle in the same order as they appear in the rainbow: red, orange, yellow, green, blue and violet. Those six colors are the primaries and secondaries. The six other colors are the tertiary (Colorplate 1). The color model extrudes the wheel into a third dimension and introduces amounts of black or white added to a color. In other words, the color model expresses the value and intensity. High value colors are high in the color model and move closer to center as they approach white. Low value colors are represented low in the color model. They move closer to center as they become neutral hues (Colorplate 2).

The *primary colors* of pigment are red, yellow, and blue. These are considered primary because they cannot be mixed from any other color. In theory, all other colors can be made from the primaries, with black or white added.

There are other primary color groups: light primaries (red, green, and blue) and psychological primaries (red, yellow, green, and blue with black and white), for example. Modern printing systems operate on a system of secondary colors: cyan, magenta, yellow, and black. Remember, the primary colors of pigment are the primary colors in a subtractive mixing system.

The *secondary colors* are the three colors made by relatively equal proportions of any two primaries: red and yellow make orange, yellow and blue make green, and blue and red make purple.

The six *tertiary colors* are mixed from equal proportions of their adjacent primary and secondary colors. For example, the primary blue and secondary green make the tertiary blue-green or aquamarine, yellow and orange make yellow-orange or amber.

Complementary colors lie opposite each other on a color wheel. Every color has a complement. Green is the complement of red; yellow is the complement of purple. The complement of a color involves value and intensity as well as hue. A low-value, high-intensity red has a high-value, low-intensity green as a complement.

A *neutral hue* is a color mixed with its complement. The perfect neutral would be the color that lies at the center of the color wheel, which is gray. Theoretically, each color mixed in the right proportion with its complement will mix to the same neutrality as any other pair of complements. Neutralizing a color is an important phase of color mixing. Bright scenic paint colors often are neutralized for use on stage, such as when yellow is "grayed out" with its complement, purple, to be less brilliant. One of closest colors we have to the perfect neutral in pigments is raw umber.

A *shade* is the darkened version of a color. Any color mixed with black becomes a shade of itself.

A *tint* is the lightened version of a color. Any color mixed with white becomes a tint of itself. (The terms *shade* and *tint* have other important meanings, too. A shade may also be a shadow or anything shown in shadow. A tint might call for universal tinting colors, a common paint product described later in this chapter.)

A *tone* is the relative lightness or darkness of a color. A shade of gray is also a tone.

Palette describes a group of colors that are related by definition or use in a composition.

Warm palette colors are called *warm* because they are the colors of the sun, fire, and the day. They are related to yellow, orange, and red.

Cool palette colors are called *cool* because they are reminiscent of ice, snow, and the night. They are green, blue, and purple.

Earth colors are those whose origins are organic minerals ground for pigment. They are the raw or burnt siennas, umbers, and ochers. Earth colors also are those associated with common rock, dirt, earthenware, mud, clay, and similar things.

Terms That Define Color Interaction

Colors normally are seen in relation to other colors. The immediate environment around a color can dramatically affect how it is perceived. Factors like lighting and adjacent colors can shift the so-called color of an object or surface into something entirely different. Green surrounded by red will look different to the viewer than green surrounded by raw umber. Scenic artists must train themselves to be as analytical and objective as possible when viewing color, particularly when called on to reproduce a color. The eye must be trained to understand the factors that affect perception of color.

Accidental color is the phantom or ghost image of a complementary color that results from a high-chromatic color leaving an impression on the retina. One perceives a color that is not present.

An *advancing color* is a high-intensity warm color that will appear to advance or lie in front of the picture plane.

A *retreating color* is often a cool color, but it may be any color that appears to recede from the picture plane.

Optical mixing occurs when two or more adjacent colors are mixed by the eye to form another hue when seen at a distance. A field of blue and yellow dots or stripes will appear green when seen at a distance. Pointillism in the painting of Georges Seurat is an excellent example of optical mixing.

Push-pull is the effect that occurs when two high-chroma complementary colors are adjacent to one another. The color fields will appear to vibrate or shimmer.

Retina fatigue is a condition occurring when the retina does not see color accurately after having been exposed to high-chroma colors. Complementary colors may appear much brighter than they are and paler colors may appear even paler. If you look at a very strong color, like magenta, for a long time and then look at green, the green will appear extraordinarily bright. A low-chroma green may seem very bright if viewed next to a red field. So, if a scenic artist attempts to mix this same green by glancing back and forth between the bucket and the color green in the midst of a magenta field on the elevation, the green probably will be mixed at a higher chroma than the sample. Now, if you look at a swatch of pink next to that same intense magenta for a long time and then look at a swatch of pink alone, the pink will appear to be very pale or even gray even though it may be a deep pink.

THE PRACTICE OF COLOR MIXING

Mixing paint, or any painting media, to produce an accurate color match depends largely on three factors: the immediate environment of each color, the lighting in the area where the paint is mixed, and the type of paint being mixed.

The *immediate color environment* refers simply to how you actually see a color. Treat each color you mix objectively. Isolate each color to be mixed as much as possible, at least in your own mind. Mask a color with white paper if you are having trouble isolating it optically due to a high-chroma field surrounding it. Dry the paint samples on swatches of white paper or cloth so you can hold them directly adjacent to the color being matched. In a paint mixing area, it is best if the countertops and workbenches in that area are dull colors, preferably gray so as not to interfere with the perception of colors.

The work area's *lighting environment* will further affect the way you see color. The light available for color mixing must be as near as possible to the kind of light under which the audience will view the color (see Chapter Four, Lighting and Other Utilities in the Scene Painting Area). Stage lighting is primarily from incandescent lamps, and most scenic designers work under incandescent light making paint elevations. Incandescent and tungsten/halogen fixtures are the best choice in the paint shop, but bright incandescent fixtures are strongly recommended for the paint mixing area.

Color mixing is affected by the type of *painting medium*. Mixing color with dyes can be different from mixing color with pigments. Mixing house paint is very different from mixing scene paint. A scenic artist will encounter all these media at one time or another, but the following discussion deals with the most common stage media: scenic paint.

When mixing paint, always choose the most direct route as possible to that color. This approach will help you if that color has to be remixed at any time. If your method was something like, "Start with turquoise, but it will be a little too green so add some purple; now it's a little too blue so add some emerald green; the color is too dark so add some white; but now it's too light so add some black; now it's a little too bright so neutralize it with some red; now it's gone too far so add some dark green," you are in trouble. If this concoction were your base coat and you had to remix paint in the middle of a drop, your chances of matching that color are grim.

To mix a color most directly, first choose a *base color* of paint from the mixing stock, the scenic paint you are working with, that is the closest match to the color you wish to mix. Every maker of scenic paint provides a color chart with paint chips, so you easily can match from this chart. Hold the chart up to the swatch or the area on the elevation that you are trying to match and choose the most closely related color to use as your base. After some experience mixing color and working with scenic paint, choosing a base color for mixing will be automatic.

The second step, after you have established your base color, is to analyze the target color for the three aspects of color itself: hue, value, and intensity.

1. Does this color need to be shifted in hue toward green, red, yellow, or whatever? If you need to alter the hue, do so now.
2. Does the chroma or intensity of the color need to be neutralized by a complementary color or earth color so that it is duller or softer?
3. Is the value of the color too high or low? If so, then adjust it with black or white.

When mixing a color, some of these steps may be combined with careful choices. For instance, a yellow ocher may need to be neutralized and darker. Adding raw umber to the ocher could take care of both steps.

A small mistake when mixing color can translate into an expensive waste of paint. Trying to fix a color that has been overneutralized or overtinted can result in using twice as much paint as needed. In some lines of paint, a mistake like this could be an enormous expense. One way to avoid this expense is to do what is called a *palm test* first. Dab the colors that you think you will mix together in your palm. Mix them together in minute quantities first to see if you are on the right track. If you prefer, you can use a paint lid and keep your hands relatively clean. A palm test can save time and guesswork before committing to a large quantity of paint. You may find by doing a palm test that neutralizing turquoise with burnt sienna will yield the same results as neutralizing it with orange and raw umber. Once you have decided that you are on the right track, dry test swatches of color on pieces of paper or fabric. Once the paint is dry on these swatches you can directly compare them to the hue on the paint elevation.

If you are mixing a pastel color, always introduce the color into the white. It takes much less color to make a pastel shade than you may realize. The rule of thumb is to always add the darker color into the lighter. If a color is overneutralized or overtinted, add the mismixed paint into the modifying colors rather than the other way around. This approach will use less paint to fix the mistake.

THE SCENIC ART PALETTE

Theatrical paint, or scenic paint, and the scenic designer's palette are based on the classic European artist's palette. This palette is based on the availability of pigment dating back to the time of the Roman empire. The names of many pigments have come to us from Italian Renaissance painters. Behind nearly all of these traditional colors is a story of discovery or favor by a renowned artist.

The foundation of the fine-art palette is *earth colors*. Two of the most basic earth colors literally are named for the color of earth in the areas they are found. Umbria is the region in Italy northwest of Rome, centered around Perugia. The soil in this area is a distinctive dull brown color. When the soil is refined and ground into a pigment it is called *raw umber*, which as mentioned, is the closest color we have to a perfect neutral. When the same pigment is baked in a kiln the heat alters its color, as heat will do to many other important minerals. You may have seen examples of this if you fire a clay vessel in a kiln to create pottery. When raw umber is baked the pigment deepens in color and become redder. It becomes the rich warm brown color called *burnt umber*.

The city of Siena, south of Florence in Tuscany, is the source of another important earth color. The color of the earth there is a rich yellow-brown color. This is the color of *raw sienna*. When raw sienna is baked the color deepens and becomes redder, as with raw umber. *Burnt sienna* is a rich, rusty brown color and one of the most important earth colors. *Iron oxide*, which is basically rust, is another source of a rich red-brown color, although it tends to overwhelm other colors when it is mixed. This is why burnt sienna is preferred by most artists. *Yellow ocher*, a deep yellow mineral, is the source of yellow ocher pigment.

Through the centuries, other precious minerals for pigments had to be purchased by the artists for their works at great expense. The ultramarine blue backgrounds of the frescos painted by Giotto in the cathedral at Assisi were ground from lapis lazuli. This was and is such a precious pigment that, in centuries following the completion of these frescos, robbers actually scraped the pigment off of the frescos. It was sold for use in lesser works of art.

Umbers and siennas form the backbone of the earth colors. They also are some of the very few colors still made from actual minerals from the source.

Many colors are sold under the same poetic names as their organic predecessors but come from a synthetic source. Chrome oxides can range from a neutral green shade to a bright green and make up *chrome green*. *Cadmium* is a less common and expensive mineral that can range in color from a bright yellow to orange to red. Many of the warm colors have cadmium as their base pigments, which accounts for their expense. *Calcium carbonate,* which is common chalk, *zinc,* and *titanium* all are used as *white pigments*. They are listed more or less in the order of expense. Calcium carbonate is the most common pigment in white scenic paint. The origin of *turquoise* pigment is self-explanatory, although the name now describes only the color and not the content. Phthalocyanine is a pigment derived from copper and used in blues and greens. In paints, it is often abbreviated to the word *pthalo*. *Purple* and *magenta* scenic paint often are augmented with dyes to help them reach the chroma that is necessary and expected. Familiarize yourself with which brands of paint contain added dyes, as these sometimes can stain or bleed through to the surface when painted over.

THE ELEMENTS OF PAINT

Pigment is the material in paint that constitutes its color. Pigment is a very fine powder suspended in a fluid. That fluid is the second element of paint, called the *medium* or *vehicle* of the paint. The third element of paint is the *binder*. Binder is the glue that adheres pigment to a surface after the vehicle has evaporated.

Pigment

Pigments that maintain their chroma through the centuries must be made of an enduring material. These are usually minerals pulverized into a very fine powder. Other pigments can be based on animal and vegetable matter but are less permanent. They are known as *fugitive* colors, because their hue will fade with time. Apprentices in the past spent arduous hours making paint for their masters by grinding color in a mortar and pestle; machines now do the grinding. The cost of many traditional minerals, particularly bright colors, now is prohibitively expensive for the quantities used in the theatre. Because some of these pigments are so expensive, some colors in scenic paint are augmented with dyes to improve the overall saturation of the color and keep down the cost of the paint. In the world of theatre, the permanency of a pigment is not as important as in fine arts.

Many pigments have personalities, if you allow the allusion. Iron oxide overwhelms other colors when mixed with them. Ultramarine blue is the opposite, very shy and retiring, as the color seems to be more fragile and quickly neutralized with a very small quantity of a complement or earth color. Ultramarine blue also is a very heavy pigment and settles out of paint quickly, forming a viscous sludge in the bottom of a bucket. It must be continually mixed back into the paint, or the color of that paint will alter as the blue drops out. One other characteristic that ultramarine blue possesses is a slightly sulfurous smell. This smell is particularly noticeable when a entire drop is painted with this color; even if from a fresh can of paint, it may smell like rotten eggs. You will become familiar with the quirks of pigments and understand their limitations as you work with them.

Vehicle

The vehicle is the fluid that carries the pigment. Water is the most common vehicle of scenic paints. It has a fast drying time and is easy and economical to clean up. Linseed oil is the vehicle for fine-art oil paints. Alkyd paints are suspended in a petroleum-based vehicle. Alkyd paints have been common in other industries as well as theatre through the centuries because they were so much more durable than water-based paints. This is changing now with the introduction of more durable water-based paints and finishes.

The vehicle often is the *solvent* of a paint. Solvents are used to thin the paint, so the solvent in part becomes the vehicle. Solvents serve to clean the paint off of surfaces where it does not belong, like elbows and fingernails. Water is part of the vehicle and the solvent used to clean up water-based paints. Alcohol is the vehicle and the solvent used to clean up shellacs. Oil is the vehicle for oil-based paints and alkyds, and it can be used to clean pigment out of brushes used with these paints. A different solvent needs to be used to clean the oil out of the brushes as well, so that it does not dry and ruin the brush during long periods of disuse. To thin alkyd paint and clean out paint residue, mineral spirits or paint thinner is used. The thinner for linseed oil–based paints

is turpentine. The solvent used to thin and clean up shellac is denatured alcohol. Lacquer thinner is used to thin and clean up lacquer.

Binder

The *binder* is the substance left behind that bonds pigment to a surface once the vehicle has evaporated. It is usually colorless, so it does not interfere with the color of the pigment. Water-based paints must have water-soluble binders added to them, because water itself has no adhesive properties. Water-based paints are classified by the binder in them. Some examples are latexes, acrylics, urethanes, and two-part epoxies. In oil paints and alkyds, the residue from the oil vehicle left on the surface after the arable content has evaporated serves as the binder.

TYPES OF SCENIC PAINT

In the theatre, specific paints are used because of the vast quantities of quality colors. Scenic paint must be easy to prepare, broadly compatible, and somewhat extendible. To extend paint is to thin it down or extend the quantity.

Dry Pigment

Dry scenic pigments are a good place to start the discussion of scenic paint. Dry pigments formed the primary paint system used in theatrical work worldwide for hundreds of years. Not until premixed scenic paints were first offered in the late twentieth century were dry pigments phased out. Dry pigments are now used in very few theatres, because premixed scenic paint is so much more convenient, generally more reliable, and safer to use. The available palette of dry pigment has also diminished over the last two decades. Many of the rich colors such as solferino, malachite, and Naples yellow are no longer available. Dry pigments can be very quirky and down right testy to mix, more so in years gone by. A large part of a scenic artist's skill in the past was the knowledge and ability to skillfully handle these pigments.

Colors still available in dry pigment include raw and burnt sienna; raw and burnt umber; yellow ocher; Van Dyke brown; vermilion red; orange; chrome yellow; chrome green; ultramarine blue; turquoise; cerulean blue; purple; and magenta, to name a few. The range of dry pigments has been narrowed down to a selection that is fairly similar to other lines of scenic paints.

Dry pigments are made to use water as a vehicle, although not all of them will mix readily into water, particularly the saturated pigments, which have dyes in them to achieve intensity of color. Pigments with dye in them will float in water. You can dump them into a bucket of water, stir them in, then stand back and watch as clumps of pigment rise to the surface perfectly dry and seemingly unaffected by the presence of water. Some aniline and fezan dyes used in dry pigments must be dissolved in alcohol before they will readily dissolve in water. Pigments that have been saturated with dyes must first be *pulped*; that is, mixed into a paste with denatured alcohol before they will readily mix with water. Alcohol reduces the surface tension of the water so dry pigment will mix into it.

When I was just learning how to mix paint in a shop that used dry pigment, I was sent off on a rush job, "Quick go mix some green paint for those Venus's-flytraps; photo call is in one hour!" In minutes I had returned with the paint and the Venus's-flytraps were laid out and painted in front of a fan. An actor costumed in his white bellboy pants climbed a ladder and rigged these Venus's-flytraps from above while they dangled around his legs. I thought that the costume manager was very generous toward me; he honestly seemed more irritated at the actor for doing stage crew work in his costume. But I, after all, had forgotten to put the binder in the paint, which had permanently stained the white pants. The moral of the story is that dry pigments must be mixed with a binder!

Everyone who has worked with dry pigment has a favorite, now humorous, disaster story of scenery that could not be touched, ruined costumes, or scenery that had to be painted all over again. Common binders for dry pigment are vegetable- or animal-based. These same binders have been used for centuries in the manufacture of paint. Only in the later part of this century have plastic polymer binders been refined for common use.

One of the first uses of dry pigment was fresco painting. The paint for fresco is very unique in that it actually requires no binder. Egg whites and yolks sometimes are added to help the paint flow onto the surface more readily. The paint was applied only in a limited area of the fresco, which had received a fresh coat of plaster for the day's work. Because the plaster, although firm, was not yet cured, the paint on it dried very slowly along with the plaster. While it cured, over the next few days, it became permeated with the lime and calcium from the plaster and became part of the plaster finish. True fresco work technically is very difficult. If the plaster was made in the wrong proportions, over the years, it might develop a bloom that obscures the painting. A tragic example is Cimabue's frescos in the Duomo in Assisi. These beautiful frescos have an astringent quality that attracts moisture and is decaying the masterpieces from within.

Dry pigment suffers from a fate similar to Cimabue's fresco. Very little scenery has survived from the past due to the limitations of the pigment but mostly from the limitations of the binder. Have you ever painted a drop and expected it to last hundreds of years? Certainly nobody would. Scenery is handled roughly, stored carelessly, and rarely made to last for very long. The binder to some degree plays a role in limited longevity.

Binders for Dry Pigments

Dry pigments were used daily in shops of yesteryear. One shop assistant would do nothing but maintain a large bucket of size water. *Size water* is glue and water mixed into the right proportions to adhere the dry pigment to a surface once the vehicle has evaporated. If there is not enough glue in the paint, it will naturally smear. Too much glue and the paint will be brittle and crack. It will develop dark spots that show the brushstrokes, and it also may develop networks of very fine crystals that reflect light. So, mixing the dry pigments into premixed size water prepared in the correct proportions is a good way of making sure the binder is consistent. The common proportions for size water are about ten parts water to one part binder. This may vary slightly according to the shop preferences and the type of binder.

Different approaches may be taken to mixing colors with dry pigments. One is to mix the color while the pigment is in its dry form, because the vehicle will deepen the value of the color. If the pigment is mixed dry it will be slightly lighter but closer to the color and value of the dry paint. Another method is to pulp all the color pigments beforehand with water and denatured alcohol as needed and to keep them in sealed containers that are checked every day to make sure that they still are fresh and moist. After the appropriate color is mixed from the pulped pigments, the size water is mixed in until the paint is the right consistency. Working with pulped pigments is similar to working with premixed scenic paint, because most scenic paints are concentrated. Dry pigment dust is very toxic (see Chapter Four, Safety and Health Regulations).

The classic binder for dry pigment is *animal glue*. Animal glue is made of inedible leftover parts of slaughtered animals. Finer-quality glue is made specifically from the pelts and carcasses of rabbits. Animal glues include cartilage, hooves, and parts of hide. These parts are rendered into a protein gravy, similar to but not as refined as gelatin. The gravy then is strained, mixed with preservatives, and dried into sheets. The dried sheets are broken up into granules and sold by the pound. Although this process-sounds a little gritty, remember that for centuries there was nothing else—it was animal glue or you did not paint your scenery. In centuries past, scenic painters (like people in many other walks of life) were closer to the source of the materials they worked with. The artist's introduction to the profession would be the responsibility of grinding the color for pigment and going to the butcher or slaughterhouse to buy the animal glue.

Animal glue granules must be rehydrated over heat to be liquefied. A double boiler is best for this task, so the glue does not burn while heating. Burnt animal glue has a very unpleasant and unforgettable smell. To rehydrate the glue, fill a steel bucket half full of glue granules. Then, fill it to the brim with water and let it sit overnight. The granules will swell to fill most of the bucket. In the morning put the bucket in a double boiler and cook at medium heat for forty minutes to an hour. When the glue is a smooth, thick liquid, it is ready for dilution to a usable strength. If concentrated glue is left to cool, it will thicken and solidify. To soften it again, reheat it in a double boiler.

Colloid is an emulsion animal glue that will not gel. This glue remains in a liquid state and is easily rewetted. Once paint mixed with a colloid binder is applied, it can be rewetted and the binder will easily dissolve. The one advantage in using this binder is that paint can be entirely washed off of a surface after painting. Because this binder dissolves so easily,

any muslin mounted on flats can be salvaged and reused later. The disadvantage in using this binder is that it is nearly impossible to put a glaze color or additional color over an initial layer or technique. Any area that has a base color or painted treatment that must be layered with paint applications, such as marble or wood, will loosen, and the paint already on the surface will dissolve.

Flexible animal glue is sold in slabs. It has additives in it to keep it from getting brittle when it dries. It needs simply to be melted in a double boiler and mixed into size water. This glue should be stored in airtight containers. It is more expensive and usually reserved for projects where a flexible paint finish is necessary.

Dextrine glue is made from processed sugar beets and commonly has been used as a binder for bronzing powders. These pigments flow very well when suspended in a dextrine binder and they do not tarnish in this medium. The glue does not cloud when it dries, so bronzing powders maintain their brilliance. Dextrine must also be dissolved in a double boiler. Fill a steel bucket half full of dextrine glue and top it off with water. It will appear milky until it is properly cooked. Set the bucket in a double boiler and cook the glue slowly until the fluid has clarified. Watch the glue closely while it is cooking, as dextrine glue must never boil or it will foam over the top of the bucket. Burnt dextrine glue has a distinctive and unpleasant odor. Dextrine is ready to use at this stage. Thin the glue only as much as needed for the work. Then add the bronzing powder or special pigments directly to the glue. Unused dextrine glue can be stored in a sealed container for later use. It will not solidify or thicken when cool.

Casein is another common binder. It also is a protein-based binder but its origins are not as grisly as animal glue: it is made from processed cows' milk and soybeans. Some lines of premixed scenic paint use casein as the binder. Casein glue is sold in granules and flakes for use with dry pigment. Casein is a cold-water glue and can be mixed directly with water to make size water. A typical ratio is approximately one part glue to seven to ten parts water, depending on shop preferences. It should be mixed into lukewarm water and allowed to sit for about an hour and mixed again so that all of the granules or flakes dissolve. It then can be used straightaway. Ammonium frequently is added to premixed scene paints as a preservative, because casein-based paints will rot, particularly in warm weather. Rosco now is working on a synthetic casein, designed to have all the attributes of a casein, re-workable flat finish, with none of the drawbacks of a protein binder, such as the smell and rotting paint.

The binders discussed so far are declining in use today. Many other binders used in the past no longer are in use, such as rabbit glue and banana oil. Nearly all organic binders have been replaced by plastic polymers. These new binders perform as well and have many advantages over the binders of past centuries. They are more permanent, do not rot as easily, come ready to use in liquid form, and are a great deal easier to obtain than their historic counterparts.

Sources for Dry Pigment

Gothic Coatings and Janovic/Plaza are the primary sources for dry pigment as well as important manufacturers of other scenic paints (see the Reading and Resources chapter for complete addresses).

Modern Scenic Paint

Modern scenic paint is a relatively new arrival to the theatrical world. Halfway through the twentieth century, many theatres and schools still were relying totally on dry pigments. Now, dry pigments are as common as the horse and buggy. Scenic paints are manufactured and sold in the United States by several different companies (see the Reading and Resources chapter for more information). Many manufacturers offer several "lines" or types of paint in very similar palettes. Economy lines, mid-range, and top-of-the-line paints are available. The differences between them are in the pigment and the binder quality as well as the price. If the paint needed is not available locally, it can be ordered directly from the supplier and shipped to you. The finest scenic paints may also serve as paints used for mural and diorama work. Top-of-the-line paints may be available only directly from the manufacturer, as they are too costly for suppliers to keep in stock.

Premixed scenic paints generally will have certain qualities in common. First, they are manufactured in the traditional European artists' palettes as discussed earlier. Second, they are fairly affordable and available in large quantities. Third, scenic paints must dry with a flat finish, as gloss finish paints can be too reflective for general stage use and flat finishes allow the scenic designer or scenic artist to determine the finish. Scenic paint must be of a consistent hue from batch to batch. Last, scenic paint must be durable enough to stand up to the demands of traveling, folding, and shifting.

Systems and Palettes

The *color spectrum*, or *palette*, of scenic paints varies somewhat from brand to brand. Although the range and selection of colors in all lines of theatrical scene paint is based on the fine-art palette, nearly every line of scenic paint boasts certain colors to be a vast improvement over other lines of scenic paint. Despite these claims, you can expect a palette to perform more or less in traditional patterns. What may vary a great deal from line to line is the quality of color. Good color is very expensive. Remember, these are minerals that are mined, ground, and refined or chemically processed. In a more economical line of paint, an orange actually may be a deep peach. If this is the best you can afford, you may be able to increase the chroma of the color with a colorant from the local paint store (colorants are discussed later in this chapter). Many lines of paint use dyes to improve color saturation. Dyes lower manufacturing costs. The more dyes are in paint, the more problematic that paint is to use. You are either painting with paint or painting with dyes; the approaches to working with these two mediums are very different. If there is dye in a paint and you attempt a gauche (the technique of putting a light tint over a darker field), the results may not be what you anticipated. This situation is very similar to the condition of working with dry pigments earlier in this century. Knowing and understanding the characteristics of the pigments was one of the special skills of the master painters of the last century. Our challenge today is that there are many different lines of paint which are often revised and changed by the paint companies. Most scenic artists become comfortable with two or three lines of scenic paint and continue to work with those for many years.

Scenic paint is sold in concentrated form. A gallon may actually be extended, or thinned down, quite a lot. One general rule when working with scenic paint is to use only as much color as necessary to get the job done. Because the viewer is some distance from the subject, good coverage does not mean the same as when painting a living room. Generally, many techniques will go over the base coat, so a thin patch may well escape all but the closest scrutiny. This is not an invitation to do sloppy work. Any base coat needs to have a creamy texture to provide good coverage, but it need not be so thick that the stir stick stands up in the bucket. A lighter weight is an asset for scenery and even thin paint will help the weight noticeably. Thinner paint is easier to apply and allows you to extend the stock of these fairly expensive paints. Also thinner paint treatments will stand up longer to repeated folding and shipping abuses when used on backdrops.

Water-Based Scenic Paint

Casein

Premixed scenic paints with *casein* binders are widely available. Mostly known by the binder and often called *casein paint*, they are the dominant choice for inexpensive, quality color scenic paint. These lines of scenic paint range from the economic to the mid-range prices. In some cases, the quality of pigment is rather good. Many scenic artists appreciate casein because of its extremely flat finish. Casein binder also is preferred by some scenic artists because it may be rewetted and reworked, or the paint may be completely washed off. This flexibility also is one of its disadvantages. When applying a glaze paint treatment, if overworked, the base underneath can pull up and mix into the glaze. The term *glaze* refers to a thin transparent paint treatment.

One aspect of casein paint that has become problematic over the past couple of decades is how it interacts with modern flame retardants. Many soft goods used in the theatre by law must be treated with flame retardants. Some flame retardants will damage the protein-based binders mixed with paint and cause them to deteriorate. When this happens, the paint will become very fragile and flake off the scenery. It is particularly apparent when painting on pretreated muslin used in a drop. One way around this dilemma is to use a size water made from a polymer binder to thin the paint. The size water will reinforce the casein binder and ensure the longevity of the paint job. Clear polyvinyl acrylic or vinyl latex will work as the added binder. Mix them up in a size water proportioned around one part binder to ten parts water. The size water should be used to thin the casein paints, in much the same way it is used with pulped dry pigment. Synthetic casein binders under development may alleviate many of these problems in the future.

Latex

Latex, once processed from the sap of the rubber tree, was one the first water-based binders to be manufactured in this century. It was unstable at first; but in subsequent years, it was improved and eventually combined with other plastic binders to create very stable and reliable polymers. It now is used commonly in many lines of house paint, some lines of scenic paint, and in clear bases for mixing with tints or dry pigments. The polymer used in scenic paint is vinyl latex, an economical choice for smaller theatrical operations, schools, and community theatres. However, highly saturated colors are difficult to acheive when working with a line of paints designed to be used as house and interior paints.

Acrylics

Acrylic binders were invented in the last century but not until the 1950s was a system discovered whereby acrylics could be used as a binder in water-based paints. Acrylic binders are now used in many brands of theatrical and display paints. It is a very reliable binder and generally used in higher-quality brands of paints. Some acrylic-based paints have a tendency to develop a little bit of a sheen when applied thickly. Acrylic paints generally are of very good quality and can be thinned down so the color can be extended into a transparent glaze.

Vinyl Binder

Vinyl binder is prized for its flexibility and durability. Some lines of paint are based on straight vinyl binders, but often the binder is mixed in polymer combinations with latex and acrylic binders. When mixed with acrylics, it improves the hiding or coverage quality of the paint.

Polymers

Polymers are a mixture of two or more synthetic binders, compounding their benefits. Like acrylics, polymers were invented in the nineteenth century but did not gain wide acceptance until the middle of the twentieth century, because it has taken some time to perfect the technology allowing them to be used in water-based paints. All the binders discussed up to now are solids that are emulsified in water. When that water evaporates, the pigment that had been suspended in the water is trapped by the solids of the binder. They are forced together and bond to the surface. Common polymer combinations are vinyl latex and vinyl acrylic.

Paint Compatibility

All polymer paints can be mixed with other polymer paints. So, if you prefer to use white latex for base coating but your favorite line of scenic paint is a vinyl acrylic polymer, you may confidently mix these paints together. It is possible to mix casein paints with polymers as well. One word of warning, if you have used casein-based white glue or wood glue to reinforce a binder and you tint this with casein-based paint, you will end up with a rubbery unspreadable lump.

Occasionally, despite your best efforts, strange things may happen to your mixtures. Odd blooms develop on the paint surface after it has dried, curds float to the top of the bucket, even when you thought the two mediums you were mixing were harmonious. Sometimes, this may happen with theoretically compatible paints. Always try a sample first, giving the sample enough time to react. Setting it aside overnight is a good idea.

Many scenic shops buy one or two types of scenic paint for the shop's color stock. However, to buy white and black in scenic paint may be very expensive due to the tremendous quantities of them a normal show will need. Many shops choose interior flat finish latex from local paint stores for their stock black and whites.

Some lines of bulk acrylic paint available actually are fine-art quality paints made available in larger quantities. These paints are very expensive and have good quality color. They are worth the price if the production budget warrants the expense. Generally, these paints are only used for very long-term or high-quality productions, murals, or display work. These fine quality colors also are handy when the design involves colors that are so intense that they cannot be made from ordinary scenic paint. Acrylic paints can be used for scenic paint and thinned down to an even greater degree than scenic paint while maintaining a high chroma. For scenery that is intended for long-run productions and must hold up year after year, these high-quality paints may be the most economic choice in the long run. High-quality acrylic paints are available from Golden Artist Colors, Inc. (see Reading and Resources chapter).

Black and White Paint

In every paint shop large amounts of black and white paints are used for color mixing. Most paint shops obtain stock black and white paints from the local paint store. The main reason for local sourcing is that the white and black paints available from scenic paint suppliers are much more expensive than house paints. Vinyl latex and vinyl acrylic are the most common varieties found at house paint distributors. As mentioned before, house paint comes in a range of mixing bases. Only straight white house paint should be used as the stock paint for mixing with scenic colors. Other mixing bases will not have the same quantity and quality of white pigment in them. Much of the black paint that is used in theatre is used to mask out the structure of the scenery so that if by chance it is glimpsed by the audience it will be nearly invisible when seen against black masking or in the darkened backstage area. Black house paint is not the best quality, but it is perfectly acceptable for this use. Many paint shops also stock the black paint from the line of scenic paint that is used for mixing the show colors because of its superior quality. When unmodified white or black paints are used on scenery, the white and black paints available through lines of scenic paints are often a better choice because of their superior quality.

Universal Tinting Colors

Colorants are an essential part of the paint mixing systems used in paint stores. A colorant, also called a *tint*, is pure, highly concentrated pigment pulped into a vehicle that is compatible with most types of oil- and water-based binders. House paint is mixed by adding various amounts of these colorants to a premixed neutral base of medium and binder. The bases are gradated from *white base*, which is mostly white, through *pastel* and *medium* to *deep base*, which contains no white whatsoever. This system is an efficient cost-effective way for a paint store to offer thousands of different consistent colors in many different types of binders and finishes for its customers. Colorants, typically packaged in half- or full-pint squeeze bottles, can be purchased separately from paint stores or ordered from theatrical paint suppliers. The actual colors of the universal tints are quite similar to those of scenic paint. These colorants are very useful in a scenic studio to boost low-saturation color or adjust the hue of a paint mix.

Working with this system for stage may be useful, particularly when only a few colors are required and the paint needs to be mixed for good coverage and an exact match. When painting a set that is to be a consistent and untreated color, such as a realistic apartment interior, working with house paints may be the best approach.

Some solvent-based paints do not readily mix with the colorants from the paint store. Universal Tinting Colors (U.T.C.) and Japan colors are formulated to mix with oil-based paints and lacquers. Japan colors also may be used by themselves as decorative colors, and they may be mixed with oil-based glazing mediums and oil- and lacquer-based finishes. Japan colors, having fallen into disuse in the industry, are still available through Mann Brothers and Janovic/Plaza (see the Reading and Resources chapter). U.T.C.s and Japan colors may be mixed into shellacs, but the color in shellac finishes will be cloudy. Pulp the color in denatured alcohol to help it mix into the shellac. Alcohol-based aniline dyes may be used to tint shellacs. Many scenic aniline dyes are waterborne dyes, so they will not mix into shellac. To determine which dyes will mix with shellac, first pulp the dye with denatured alcohol. Two-part epoxy-based paints and finishes must be tinted with colorants specifically developed for epoxy. These colorants are available from the manufacturers of epoxy paint products. Always use the proper safety precautions when using solvent-based paints and finishes (see Chapter Four, Safety and Health Regulations).

Sources for Modern Scenic Paints

Rosco Laboratories dominates the scenic paint market. It manufactures and distributes Iddings Deep Colors, long a standard of casein-based scenic paint. Rosco also offers Off-Broadway paint, an inexpensive acrylic paint in a palette similar to that of the Iddings. Rosco created supersaturated paint in the late 1970s. It is a highly concentrated acrylic paint sold in smaller quantities. Supersat, as it is called, has remarkable pigment intensity and can be thinned tremendously without loosing its intensity. It is an excellent substitute for dyes and a good choice whenever truly brilliant color is desired. Supersat has a palette similar to Iddings with a few slightly different colors, including a unique green shade blue.

There are other manufacturers of very high-quality casein and acrylic theatrical paint in the United States. The Gothic Color Company, as mentioned previously, Mann Brothers, Wolf, and Cal-Western all manufacture and distribute excellent paint in several levels of affordability (see Reading and Resouces chapter).

Dyes

Dyes commonly are the scenic artist's or the scenic designer's choice for watercolor techniques and transparent effects. Aniline dyes are marketed by several scenic paint suppliers in a color range similar to standard scenic paint. Aniline dyes are the most common choice in dyes for scenic painting because the colors are so vibrant.

Aniline Dyes

Aniline dyes most often are used because brilliant transparent color is needed. Aniline is a benzene derivative created from coal tar in a chemical process. It is a highly toxic colorless substance and must be handled with protective gloves (see Chapter Four, Safety and Health Regulations). Because of hazards in manufacturing associated with benzene, aniline has been replaced by *fezan* in many currently available lines of aniline dye.

Aniline dyes are available through Gothic Coatings, Inc., Mann Brothers, Alcone Co., Inc., Tricone Colors, Inc., and the Aljo Manufacturing Company. The dyes are sold in four-ounce, half-pound and one-pound quantities. Most theatrical supply houses do not keep dye in stock, so it must be shipped from the manufacturer (see Reading and Resources chapter).

Here are some notes on mixing aniline dyes. Aniline dye is available in dry powder or crystal form. Dry dye should be premixed into a concentrate form, from which the actual painting colors are mixed at the strength needed. To mix the concentrates, add three heaping teaspoons of dry dye to approximately one quart of boiling water. Mixed aniline dye is mildly corrosive to metal, so the dye should not be stored or heated in metal containers. Quart-size canning jars work very well for storing concentrated dyes.

Mixing color with dye can be tricky. For instance, Bismark, a rich burnt sienna color, golden brown, and Van Dyke brown do not blend well with the other dyes. When they are mixed with most other dye colors, they will precipitate and drop out of the solution to the bottom of the container, leaving you with dirty water. This reaction occurs because the pH of the dye solution may be too high or too low. Adding vinegar to the dye to raise the pH or baking soda to lower it, may solve the problem. However, changing the acidity of the dye may be a hit or miss unless you get very technical and use a pH meter to balance the acidity of the dyes. For this reason, many scenic artists early on learn to mix variations of brown with crystal black and orange. Orange and red dye have their own quirks. After the concentrated red or orange dye has cooled, it sometimes congeals in the jar. To be workable again, the jars of dye have to be slowly reheated in a double boiler.

Many forms of aniline dyes not used in theatre can be mixed only with oil or alcohol. Some dyes must be pulped first in alcohol and then may be mixed with water, although the manufacturers of dye are constantly reformulating the crystal or powder to make pulping unnecessary. If you are unsure of which dyes need to be pulped, try mixing a small quantity of the dye in hot water.

Hazards of Aniline Dye

Do not drop dry dye into a container of boiling water when it is still on a hot plate or other heat source. Remove the container to a separate area for mixing the dye, because the heat of a burner can ignite powdered dye under some situations. Also, no alcohol or dyes pulped with alcohol must ever be placed close to a heat source, as alcohol is highly flammable. To reduce these hazards, use an electric teakettle rather than an open hot plate to heat the mixing water. Aniline dye is extremely hazardous if ingested or inhaled. Always wear rubber gloves when handling and working with dye, and always wear a respirator when handling powdered dye or spraying the mixed dye (see Chapter Four, Safety and Health Regulations).

Working with Aniline Dyes

The viscosity of mixed dye is that of the medium, which is water, so normally a painter works with dye much like actual watercolor. Occasionally, the dye is used in a situation where it must have enough body to cling to a textured or vertical surface. For these applications, dye can be mixed with some water-based transparent medium, such as clear acrylic, latex, or vinyl. It also may be mixed into cooked laundry starch, wheat paste, vinyl wallpaper paste, or a solution of methacel.

Methocel Gum

Methocel is water-soluble gum that is completely transparent when dry. It is sold by the pound by Gothic Coatings, Inc. and Janovic/Plaza (see the Reading and Resources chapter for further information). It is sold in a fine granular form, which is dissolved in hot water. Mix one part methocel to four parts water for a working concentrate. Once dissolved, the methocel can be used in a fairly thick, concentrated form as a vehicle for aniline dyes that gives considerable body. The concentrate may be thinned for use as a primer for china silk, scrims, and other fabrics where bleeding or wicking of dye or transparent paint is a problem. It may also be mixed directly with the paint or dye. To use as a primer, mix one part concentrated methocel with ten parts water. Spray it on the stretched fabric and let dry. This solution will discourage dye bleeding into the fabric as it is brushed or sprayed. A methocel primer will add some stiffness to the fabric, particularly china silk.

Irish Moss

Irish moss is a seaweed that can be used in much the same way that methocel gum is used. It can actually be found on the beach in some areas of the northeastern United States. Irish moss is also sold as a tea and as a dietary supplement at some health food stores. To prepare Irish moss, first soak it in a bucket of cold water until it becomes jellylike. Then cook the bucket of Irish moss slowly until it dissolves in the water and the solution thickens. Before cooking it may be necessary to add more water to the bucket so that the moss is completely covered. Cooked Irish moss can be used as a vehicle for dye, or if thinned (approximately five parts water to one part cooked Irish moss), it can be used as a primer. It is best used in applications of aniline dye on china silk.

Paint Finishes and Binders

Another quality of paint is the *sheen* or *finish* it has when dry. All wet paint has a glossy reflective sheen. Sheen is determined by the type of solid matter, other than pigment, in the paint. Solids used in most binders will dry to a glossy sheen. Many binders, such as clear acrylic or latex, are also sold as finishes. *Flatteners* may be added to paint to dull the finish. Some flatteners cause the finish to cloud over chemically. Flattening oil may be added to oil-based paints and finishes to reduce the sheen. Other flatteners are solids mixed into the sealer as powder to cloud the finish. Mica dust is a common powdered flattener. Paint manufacturers or distributors may sell powdered or oil flatteners separately, if needed to create a special effect. Scenic paints are formulated to have a flat finish. House paints are formulated and labeled as having varying degrees of finish from flat to gloss.

Finishes are sold and used separately. A typical finish product dries clear and has no color. When applied over a dried flat finish paint, most finishes will deepen the color of the paint to the tone that it was when wet. The range of finishes is as follows: flat, velour, eggshell, satin, semigloss, gloss, and high gloss. Not all lines of paints and finishes are inclusive of all of these finishes, but most product lines have a selection from these.

Water-Based Finishes

Water-based finishes are a fairly recent development, and their technology is continually undergoing refinement. The advantages of water-based finishes are low toxicity, fast drying time, and the convenience of soap-and-water cleanup. The primary disadvantage of these products is that water-based finishes generally are less durable than their solvent-based counterparts. For most theatrical applications, however, the advantages clearly outweigh this disadvantage, as truly long-term durability rarely is needed.

Acrylic

Many lines of acrylic scenic paints also offer *clear acrylic sealers*, to be used as both finishes and supplemental binders. They are available in gloss and flat finishes that can be mixed together to the desired luster. These sealers are milky when first applied, but as they dry they become transparent. Care must be taken when using these sealers so they do not cloud over, particularly the flat sealer. If used incorrectly, water can be trapped in the sealer, which will cause it to remain cloudy. Read all instructions carefully; these sealers are designed to be thinned. Use the clear sealers only in warm environments. Do not dry the sealers with a fan or use on scenery in a drafty area. Be very careful when storing scenery sealed in acrylic. Acrylic sealers have a tendency to adhere when two sealed surfaces are pressed together, particularly under warm, humid conditions.

Latex

Latex sealer may be used as a clear primer when it is necessary to maintain the natural color of a material. Latex sealer/primer is available through house-paint suppliers and manufacturers. It is available only in a gloss finish and must be thinned or mixed with flattener to cut the sheen. It is susceptible to some of the same foibles as the acrylic sealers, so take care to thin it, separate surfaces, and keep the scenery out of drafty areas.

Polyvinyl Acrylic

Polyvinyl acrylic (P.V.A.) is used in the same manner as latex sealer/primer—as a binder in many water-based paints. This product is available through many paint suppliers and manufacturers. P.V.A. is especially susceptible to adhering to itself when surfaces are stacked or pressed together.

Urethane

Urethane is commonly available in an oil-based medium; it has only recently become commonly available in a water-based vehicle. Water-based urethane has the same advantages as other water-based sealers: easy cleanup, nontoxicity, and fast drying time. It is much more durable than the other sealers, although it does not yet stand up very well to floor traffic. Improvements are being made continually in these user-friendly, low-toxic finishes. Once cured, urethane will not adhere to itself when two surfaces are placed together.

Epoxy

Water-based *epoxy finishes* are available in precombined components or two-part kits. The precombined components are based on acrylic binders, and the kits consist of resin and hardener. Once the two are mixed together, they cure to a very hard finish. These finishes are compatible with other water-based mediums. Available from paint suppliers, epoxies are among the most durable and costly of all water-based finishes. One disadvantage of epoxy finishes is that they are available only in a gloss sheen. Water-based epoxy finishes are a recent development, and as research continues, paint chemists will most probably produce satin- and flat-finish versions. Proper safety precautions should be used when working with epoxy paint and finishes since they are toxic (see Chapter Four, Safety and Health Regulations).

Solvent-Based Finishes

This discussion of *solvent-based finishes* focuses on traditional finishes that have been in use for centuries. The technology of finishes has improved vastly in the last part of this century. Until recently finishes, like paint binders, have come from organic sources. These include vegetable oils; linseed oils; mineral oils; alkyd paints and finishes; and dissolved solids such as tree sap, lacquers, insect excretions, and shellac. Proper safety precautions must be used whenever chemical solvent–based paints and finishes are used (see Chapter Four, Safety and Health Regulations).

Most solvent-based finishes can take anywhere from six to twelve hours to dry; however, some lacquers are formulated to dry in thirty minutes. Solvent-based finishes used on a floor can take an additional twenty-four to forty-eight hours to cure properly. *Japan dryer* will accelerate the drying time of the finish by accelerating the dryers in the medium, but it may interfere with the sheen or cause the remainder of the finish to set up in the bucket over the course of a few weeks. Too much Japan dryer can cause the surface of the paint or finish to develop a network of small cracks; this is called *crazing*.

Varnish

Traditional *varnishes* are cellulosic solids (tree sap and resins) dissolved in solvents. Modern varnishes are based in petroleum and lacquer mediums. The use of varnish has been widespread for so many centuries that the term has become analogous with finishes. A problem with the older varnishes was that they were unstable. In humid weather, they had the tendency to get waxy, sticky, or develop a bloom. A bloom is a matte white film that obscures the clear finish of the varnish, usually caused by moisture mixing into the varnish. Solvents for varnishes usually are mineral spirits or paint thinner. Varnishes can be tinted with universal tints or Japan colors.

Shellac

Shellac is made by dissolving the excretions of the lac beetle, found on certain species of trees in India, with denatured alcohol. Its price varies from year to year, because it is dependent on the harvest. Shellac is commonly available in paint supply stores. Shellac has a tendency to crack and darken after several years, but this is rarely a problem in theatrical usage. Its theatrical applications include use as a fast-drying, durable sealer for furniture and properties, as a good primer for steel, and as a vehicle for colored glazes. Shellacs can be tinted for glazing with some aniline dyes.

Oils

Rubbed *oil finishes* have little use in scenic arts because they take so long to cure. For finishes on fine furniture, hand-rubbed oil is unparalleled for luster and durability. *Tung oil*, from the tung tree of China, and *linseed oil* frequently are used for such finishes. The solvent for oil finishes usually is mineral spirits, paint thinner, or turpentine, depending on the vehicle of the varnish. Oils can be tinted with universal tints and japan colors.

Lacquers

Chinese and Japanese lacquers, the sort used to coat Oriental decorative and inlaid lacquerware, is a liquid tapped from varnish trees. Modern lacquers are cellulosic solids dissolved in solvent lacquer. The solvent for these is lacquer thinner or acetone. Lacquers can be tinted with universal tints and japan colors and are excellent coatings for brass and other metals, adding luster and durability.

Epoxy

Solvent-based *epoxy finishes* have been used in industry for some time. These durable finishes currently come only in gloss and high-gloss sheen. When working with solvent-based epoxy finishes, take care to test the finish on the painted or stained surface. These finishes are not compatible with some combinations of mediums and have a tendency to discolor or darken some surfaces to a greater extent than other solvent-based finishes. The solvent for epoxies usually is toluene. Specific tints for these finishes must be purchased from the paint supplier or ordered from the manufacturer. Two-part solvent-based paints and finishes as well as toluene are very toxic. These mediums should be avoided. Use only with extreme safety precautions (see Chapter Four, Safety and Health Regulations).

Solvent-Based Paints

There is a tendency to describe all *solvent-based paints*, particularly those with gloss sheen, as enamels. High-sheen latex and acrylic paints may also be referred to as enamels. This is because the term *enamel* is analogous with the sheen of porcelain enamel finishes. However, most lines of solvent-based paints are available in a variety of sheens. Solvent-based paints are very durable. Proper preparation and priming is particularly important when working with them. The finish of a paint is only as strong as its surface.

Solvent-based paints essentially are solvent-based finishes with pigment in them. The same solvents and tints applicable to a varnish will work with the corresponding paint. As with solvent-based finishes, these paints can take some time to dry and cure. Japan dryer will accelerate the drying time of these paints.

Alkyd

Most paints referred to as *enamels* or oil-based paints share the same medium as varnishes. Modern petroleum-based paints are called *alkyds*. Alkyd primers also are available and work well on woods and metal.

Urethanes

Urethanes, so called because they contain urethane solids, frequently are used in porch and floor paints because they cure to a hard, scuff-resistant, waterproof finish.

Lacquer

Lacquer-based paints are excellent for applications where a rich high gloss finish is desired. A positive advantage is that they are among the fastest drying of the solvent-based paints and finishes. When time

will not permit lengthy drying and curing, lacquers, though costly, can be very useful.

Shellac

Shellac with white pigment added is manufactured chiefly as a primer for wood and metal. Colorants added to shellac will cause it to streak when applied. Use Japan colors or universal tinting colors when tinting shellac.

Stains

Solvent-Based Penetration Stains

Penetration stains are solvent-based stains formulated to soak into wood. They are available in a range of colors that can be intermixed to create a desired hue or intensity. These stains are very easy to work with. The stain is brushed or wiped on, allowed to sit for a few minutes while it soaks in, and then rubbed off. The color can be thinned down if necessary with mineral spirits or with the natural tone in that line of stain. Penetration stains dry to a flat sheen and generally need one or two coats of finish, which deepens the hue and luster of the stain.

Oil-Based Stains

Oil-based stains also penetrate the surface and can be applied in much the same way as the solvent-based stains. The stain can be thinned down with untinted oil or mineral spirits. The color of these stains can be deepened with universal tints. Homemade oil-based stains can be made by mixing universal tints into linseed or soybean oil. Oil-based stains have a dual purpose, in that three or four layers can be applied to a hand-rubbed finish. However, each application of stain will be another application of color.

Water-Based Stains

Acrylic-based stains are designed not to penetrate the surface, but rather to be applied thinly and evenly over the surface, then dry to a transparent finish. Acrylic stains must be worked in and rubbed off before they have a chance to set. If the stain or the edge of the stain is allowed to dry, it will be permanent. Acrylic stains can be made by tinting clear acrylic medium with dye or universal tinting color.

When working with clear acrylic medium, keep in mind that the commercial stains have drying retardants in them, so there will be less working time with the acrylic medium.

Aniline dye can make an effective water-based stain. Aniline dye dissolved into water will penetrate and stain clean woods and veneers. However, aniline dyes will fade in time, particularly if exposed to sunlight. Unsealed aniline dye should never be used where it can come in contact with performers; it can transfer to flesh and costumes.

CONCLUSION

This chapter discusses color and the mostly widely available and common forms of paint. Manufacturers are continuing to make breakthroughs in the development of paint products. Keep an eye on the catalogues of paint manufacturers and take time to roam the aisles of the paint store to become aware of new products. If you encounter an unfamiliar product, or if a product has not performed as anticipated, do not hesitate to call the manufacturer. Chemists working for paint manufacturers often are easily reached and able to answer your queries or address your problems with the products.

The composition of paint is so complex that it is becoming more difficult to determine which products are compatible. Sometimes, paint products react to one another in entirely unexpected ways. This can lead to serendipitous or, sometimes, disastrous results. Whenever you are working with an unfamiliar product or process, make samples ahead of time, being careful to work with the same materials used in the fabrication of the scenery. Always take the time to test materials and paint processes. The time taken to create a sample will always pay off by solving problems before committing to the time and materials used on large-scale scenery.

chapter 7

Preparing for Painting and Texturing Scenery

INTRODUCTION

Stage scenery is pure illusion. Very little of what looks real on stage actually is made from a material anywhere close to its appearance. Wood might appear to be metal and metal may masquerade as bamboo. A flat piece of canvas can be transformed into a vast panoramic vista. A humble and prosaic sheet of Masonite can become glorious Italian marble. This illusion is the heart of scenic painting. A scenic artist is expected to beautifully paint all types of materials, and the painting is expected to withstand stage use. To execute all this you must begin with a thorough knowledge of how to prepare these diverse materials for painting; a preparation that is essential for successful results. It is unwise to cut corners with hasty or marginal surface preparation. This is the first point where serious mistakes can be made. Regardless of the finished paint quality, an improperly prepared surface will never achieve its potential. It may never even make it to the finished stage at all. If the priming, base coat, and layout are done correctly, all the applications that follow certainly will go more smoothly and look better. If the preparatory work is done poorly, the problem will take more time to correct than the proper preparation would have.

WORKING WITH SOFT GOODS

Soft goods is a broad term for unstructured fabric scenery. The backdrop is the most common form of soft goods. This term also refers to portals, roll drops, act curtains, scrims, oleos, translucent drops, floorcloths, drapery, soft masking, and soft sculpture, to name just a few items. For centuries, soft goods have been the main type of scenery used in the theatre. From the seventeenth through the nineteenth centuries, soft goods were just about all that scenery was. Very little change has taken place in the way soft goods are fabricated and prepared. However, some of the materials available for the soft goods themselves, as well as paints and primers, have changed considerably, mostly in the last fifty years.

The actual fabric of soft goods varies from application to application. The cost of goods varies widely, too, and will limit choices due to budget considerations. Drops, for example, can be made of a great variety of fabrics like muslin (the most typical), canvas, linen, burlap, scrim, silk, or velour, based on what the designer intends and what the budget allows. The most common fabrics used in the theatre are these:

Bobbinet—A lightweight, very open-weave cotton cloth used for invisible support in cut drops, diffusion effects, and transparent scrimlike effects; available in white or black;

Burlap—A coarse, heavy-weave fabric used primarily for the texture of the weave;

Canvas—A very heavy, stiff cotton fabric most often used for ground cloths or where durability is a concern;

Canvas duck—A low-thread-count canvas used to construct durable backdrops and pipe pockets;

Cheesecloth—A very lightweight, extremely open-weave fabric used primarily as a covering applied over carved foam;

China silk—A very lightweight glossy silk fabric that floats and moves easily on light air currents;

Cotton scrim—A fabric similar to cheesecloth but smoother in finish;

Duvetyn—A soft, flannellike fabric that is light-absorbent and has many practical applications for custom masking pieces; a common, inexpensive substitute for velour; it has a front and a back;

Erosion cloth—A course fabric woven from hemp strands, with a weave that is about an inch by inch square; used in landscaping to cover steep banks and reduce erosion while new growth can be established; used in theatre to cover scenery or to construct drops that require a very coarse-woven texture;

Linen—Made from plant fiber, linen is like muslin, but regarded as a superior painting surface, a very durable and costly fabric;

Monk's cloth—Frequently used in theatre because it has a coarse, raised square texture that reads very well on stage (the even square texture of the cloth is created by the warp and weft threads being grouped together); because the material is all cotton, it is very absorbent and takes dyes very well; often used for pieces that are intended to look like tapestries or have a certain coarse or handcrafted appearance; when it is used to construct soft goods, the cut edges must be well hemmed because they unravel easily;

Muslin—Common polycotton sheeting available in a wide choice of widths and weights, it is the standard choice for drops and covering hard scenery; available in bleached (white) or unbleached (natural ecru), also sold predyed in blue, gray, or black;

Opera netting—Also called scenery netting; a cotton netting with one-inch square openings; constructed to hang vertically and horizontally; used to reinforce cut openings and contours in soft goods; available in white or black;

Scrim—A lightweight, open-ladder weave fabric very commonly used in theatre for transparent and translucent backdrops and special effects, available in wide widths, black, white, light blue, and neutral colors; it has a front and a back; filled scrim is a useful substitute for muslin, particularly for backdrops in touring shows, as scrim drops will not wrinkle as much as regular muslin when stored;

Theatrical gauze—A lightweight, open-weave fabric, either cotton or linen, heavier than cheesecloth, that can be used like scrim; it is not available in wide widths;

Velour—A heavy cotton, polyester, wool, or cotton-silk fabric, with a much deeper pile than duvetyn, it is used primarily for stage draperies and masking; it has a front and a back; it has a directional nap; it absorbs light well; is available in a wide variety of colors; can be ordered in a custom color; and is somewhat paintable.

Soft Goods Construction

Construction of backdrops is the responsibility of the scenic paint staff in some studios. In others, it is done by the carpentry staff. This varies from company to company, sometimes due to the rules of the labor organizations that represent the artisans working within a scenic studio. In the course of a production, it may be necessary to do a great deal of additional scenic sewing for items like patterned backdrops or soft sculpture. Such pieces usually are executed by the scenic paint staff or a contracted specialist. The scenic artist, in all cases, must have a working knowledge of proper construction techniques for soft goods.

Standard Backdrop and Portal Construction

Regardless of whether staff carpenters, painters, or subcontractors build the soft goods, some standards govern design and construction. The traditional materials used for drops are linen, canvas duck, and muslin. All these natural fiber fabrics share one significant and useful property: the undyed and unbleached fabric shrinks when water is first applied to them. Linen was the standard cloth for backdrops well into the twentieth century. Now, cotton muslin is the most common fabric used for painted drops, because linen is considerably more expensive and difficult to find in widths useful for full-stage drops.

Muslin

Muslin is available in a wide variety of widths and weights. Rosebrand, a popular New York-based supplier of theatrical fabrics, offers no less than seventeen variations of standard scenic muslin with additional choices of very wide widths for large, seamless drops. When buying muslin, order the width most applicable to your particular need. Muslin 120 inches wide is very common and useful for drops as well as hard scenery. Muslin sixty inches wide may be fine for some uses, but it would be a poor choice for a drop of any reasonable size because the drop would have far too many seams. The weight of muslin is quantified by the number of threads per inch. The lightest weights, in the seventy-two threads per inch range, are best suited for covering irregular surfaces, covering rigid walls, and generally in places where muslin need not support its own weight. These lighter weights are not recommended for drops. Drops should be built of a stronger medium (128 threads per inch) or heavy weight (140 threads per inch) to endure the stress of stretching so they hang well on a batten.

Making a Drop

Some drops are made from a single, seamless piece of material and others by piecing together strips of muslin. The seams resulting where the strips of material are joined run horizontally, or parallel to the floor. Horizontal seams are less likely to be visible on a finished drop, once it is hung in the theatre and correctly lighted. A painted drop might be built with vertical seams if an image or pattern painted on it corresponds better to vertical seams. Translucent drops must have very carefully placed seams, for any backlighting will expose the seams instantly. Seam placement often is dictated by a conscientious scenic designer. Other soft goods constructed out of velour, duvetyn, or other drapery materials hang most smoothly with vertical seams.

Standard *horizontally seamed drop construction* is a very straightforward procedure. The fabric is measured out to the width of a drop, with an extra foot or so added to allow for shrinkage, finishing the edges by trimming, or turning back the excess to be either sewn or glued. Bear in mind that the side edges of a drop often are finished after the painting. Several of those panels are cut and assembled to the height of the drop. The bottom and top panels of the drop should end with the selvage of the muslin. Extra fabric may be included in the overall height of

the fabric used for the drop depending on the type of pipe pocket the drop will have. A pipe pocket with a skirt needs only enough extra height to account for the seams—two inches per seam and three-quarters inch turnback on the webbing. A hidden pipe pocket will require an additional six inches of height. (Figure 7.1)

The weakest point of a drop is the thread of the seams. Heavy-duty thread should be used for sewing a drop. Industrial sewing machines handle the heavy-duty thread well with fewer breaks and snags. An industrial walking-foot sewing machine will handle the heavier fabric and jute webbing without jamming.

A *pipe pocket* may be sewn into the bottom panel of the drop simply by sewing a three-inch hem. However, the hem makes a poor pipe pocket, because it is only as sturdy as the muslin itself. If the muslin is torn by inserting a pipe, the painted drop will be damaged. Often, a separate pipe pocket is sewn to the back of the drop or on the inside of the hem. This separate pouch of muslin or canvas is the full length of the drop. The pipe pocket is sewn about four or five inches up from the bottom of the drop so that the face of the drop masks it. If the pipe pocket is damaged, it can be replaced without damaging the front of the drop.

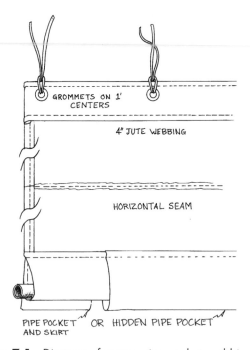

Figure 7.1 Diagram of seams, pipe pocket, webbing, and grommets for a standard drop.

The *webbing* is jute, generally four inches wide, sewn to the back of the drop at the top. The edge of the muslin at the webbing will need to be turned back if it does not end in a selvage; otherwise, it will fray. The webbing is sewn at the top of the drop so that grommets can be placed into the reinforced fabric. If the grommets were set directly in the muslin, the weight of the drop would pull them right out. Spacing grommets one foot apart is standard. They may be installed by hand with a grommet punch or with a foot pedal–operated grommet punch.

The side seams of the drop may be sewn before or after the drop has been painted. When a drop is stretched and primed, the sides normally become scallop shaped unless they have been strengthened. These scallops on the sides give the drop a sloppy appearance. Draw the cut and turnback lines on the unfinished sides of the drop after painting (Figure 7.2). Then the sides can be cut and either sewn or glued back to give the drop a clean finish. Use a flexible or fabric glue to glue back two or three inches of fabric on the side of the drop.

Portals are drops containing large openings, such as doorways, archways, or windows. A portal built so that the center section is left open usually has vertical side panels, or legs. The sides need not have seams in them since they may be a width of muslin as long as the portal leg. When the drop is

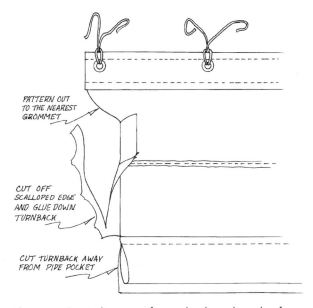

Figure 7.2 A diagram of a turnback on the side of a backdrop.

stretched out the center opening should be drafted out and stapled to the deck or paint frame so that it is square.

Seamless Drops

Translucent backdrops often need to be built from a single, seamless piece of goods. Standard scenic muslin widths are eight, ten, or twelve feet. Wider muslin can be purchased in fourteen feet, twenty feet, twenty-five feet, thirty feet, and forty feet. This fabric is sold by the yard through theatrical soft goods suppliers. These widths of muslin are more expensive by the square foot than standard sizes, because few mills provide such widths of muslin. Obviously, seamless backdrops are used only when necessary because of the expense.

Scrim Construction

Sharkstooth scrim is the standard scrim fabric used for theatrical applications. It is available in widths up to thirty-five feet, in white, off-white, sky blue, and black. Scrim fabric has a grain to it and will hang cleanly if the "teeth" in the weave are vertical. Scrim also has a front side and back side. The back has minute ribbing that make painting more difficult to control. To cut scrim to size, it should be measured along the edge and carefully cut along the grain. The fabric will not rip cleanly on the grain. The fabric has so much give in it that it is impossible to lay it out and snap a straight line on it. Scrim will unravel a bit if it is not hemmed, so all the edges should be turned back and sewn. The edges of scrim cannot be glued back, as with muslin. Glue will stiffen the scrim and cause puckers along the edges. The bottom edge of a scrim drop should have a pipe pocket sewn on the back, or a separate canvas pocket sewn into the hem. Otherwise the open weave of scrim will tear easily when a pipe is inserted at the base to weight the scrim. Sharkstooth scrim has a front and a back. Care should be taken to ensure that the scrim is built so that the horizontal ribs of the fabric are on the back of the drop.

Cotton and linen scrim are open-weave fabrics made of finely woven cotton or linen. Linen scrim, also called theatrical gauze, was the standard for scrim effects until the appearance of sharkstooth scrim. A great advantage of the sharkstooth over linen scrim is its availability in wide widths. Linen scrim drops always had obvious seams, which had to be overlooked. The natural light drab color of linen scrim either may be a drawback or an asset depending on the composition. Cotton scrim is not as transparent as linen scrim when backlit.

Floorcloth Construction

Floorcloths are like drops but made for the demanding wear and tear of foot traffic. Canvas floorcloths should be measured to size and sewn in much the same way as drops, without webbing and pipe pockets of course. Their seams are less noticeable if sewn parallel to the audience, or a majority of the audience. Because canvas stretches so tightly, the floor cloth should be assembled with an extra foot of cloth on all sides, to account for shrinkage, especially if it is large. The edges of the ground cloth may be reinforced with webbing since the canvas will pull on the staples very hard when stretching. Always use pneumatic staples when stretching a floorcloth. The seams of a ground cloth are its weakest point. Only heavy-duty thread should be used. The seams should be flat felt seams, which are doubled over and sewn a second time (like the seams in blue jeans) and constructed to face away from the audience.

Working with Cut Drops and Netting

Painted soft goods include *cut drops, borders, tabs,* and *legs.* Borders are soft goods that do not touch the stage deck, and they may be painted pieces. They play overhead and may serve as masking as well. Legs and tabs fly all the way down to the stage deck, and they may be painted pieces. Legs play on the sides of the stage and may also serve as masking. When legs and borders double as masking they should be backpainted to prevent light leaks from lighting instruments. Tabs play in the center area of the stage as scenic units; for instance, a cut tab may be painted and contoured to look like a tree. These may be irregularly shaped drops, like foliage, for example. The erratic, contoured edges generally are cut after the painting is done and sometimes are reinforced with netting. The contours are drafted and accentuated with an ink marker or paint to serve as guidelines for cutting. The opening should be cut out so that the marker or painted cut lines are cut off. Openings or contours sometimes need to be reinforced, because they receive extra stress. For this, leave about two inches of turnback. After the openings and turnbacks have been cut out, turn the drop on its face and fold and press the turnback. Then brush a diluted flexible fabric glue into the fold and press the two sides of the fabric together. Staple every few feet and at corners so that the turnback does not shrink. If the turnback needs more reinforcement, a length of one-eighth-inch sash cord can be set into the inside edge of the fold with the glue. This works well around windows and door openings cut into a drop that receives a lot of contact with actors and shifting scenery.

Using Netting to Reinforce a Cut Drop

The point of *netting* a drop is to give nearly invisible support to the negative areas of a cut drop that are not self-supporting. These areas may include reinforced openings that may be inclined to sag with repeated use or contours that defy the laws of gravity. Netting is either glued across the entire opening of the drop or only those areas that need to be reinforced. Netting the drop happens after painting. In some companies, it is the responsibility of the construction department, and in others it is the responsibility of the scenic art department.

Types of Netting

Several kinds of netting are available for cut drops. Bobbinet, or tulle, is a small-weave cloth netting with octagonal openings. Bobbinet is sold with openings in assorted sizes and weaves. *Opera netting* is another cloth netting used in the theatre. It is made from cotton cord that has been tied in one-inch squares, giving much larger openings than those in bobbinet. Unlike fishnet, which is tied on the bias, opera netting is tied on the vertical and the horizontal so that it will hang straight.

Netting is sold by theatrical soft goods suppliers. Bobbinet is available by the yard and opera netting by the foot in thirty-foot widths. Bobbinet and opera netting are available in white and black. White net can be dyed to match the background color if needed with aniline dye or a thin acrylic paint of the proper hue. *Nylon garden netting* recently has become common for netting drops. This netting, black nylon extruded into one-inch squares, is available at plant nurseries and garden suppliers. The netting is very strong and very inexpensive; however, it is shiny and available only in clear and black, which cannot be altered or painted over easily. The slippery nylon does not bind well with glue, as discussed earlier. Garden netting is not treated with flame retardant.

Netting Drop

As already discussed, the openings in the drop should be carefully cartooned with a marker or paint, so these areas stand out. Next, the openings and contours are cut out or turned back so that the cartoon lines no longer are visible from the front of the drop. The drop then should be turned over on its face and stapled at the corners of the contour and along its edges before laying down the netting, so that it resists shrinkage, which causes puckering and shifting. The staples are placed approximately one foot apart. The turnbacks, if any, should be folded and glued.

With the drop stapled face down and the turnbacks glued, the openings and contours are ready to be netted. The netting should be stretched across the opening and down to the contours needing support. Take special care to keep the opera netting vertical and horizontal to the center line. Opera netting set on an angle will bias and pucker the drop. Netting that is too taut will disfigure the drop by creating puckers. Netting that is too loose will not support the contours. To ensure that the netting will be straight and of the proper tautness, stretch and size it on netting stretchers when it is laid over the back of the drop. Netting stretchers are pieces of paneling, three inches wide, that have one-inch-square blocks set along one edge with a gap between them for the net. A board with tacks set one inch apart may also be used. The stretchers can be set in position along the edge of the area to be netted and stapled in place with pieces of canvas to prevent shifting. Cut the netting to the approximate size it will need to be for each area to be netted. If the netting is being painted or dyed, dip it in the thin paint or dye. If the color of the netting is not to be altered it should be dipped in size water. Allow most of the size water, paint, or dye to drip off the netting, and blot or wring out the excess. Then the wet netting should be looped over the stretchers and allowed to dry. Glue down the netting along the edges of openings and contours with a full-strength flexible fabric glue. If bobbinet or opera net is being used, merely gluing it down will be sufficient (see the discussion of types of netting). Plastic garden netting, however, will pull free of the glue because it does not actually bind to plastic. If garden netting is used, muslin strips should be glued around the edges of the opening or contours over the netting to hold it in place. Hot melt glue may also be used with plastic garden netting. Keep track of the staples used to hold down the drop while gluing netting onto the back so the drop is not ripped when it is pulled up. Care also should be taken not to glue the drop to the floor or get glue on the face of the drop.

THE ROLE OF FLAME RETARDANTS

Fire codes governing public buildings are strict, particularly in theatres. Tragic fires, such as the Iroquois Theatre fire in Chicago in 1903 and the more recent fire in the MGM Grand Hotel in Las Vegas, have brought great scrutiny to the safety of the patrons from fire in theatres. All materials intended for use in public entertainment and display now are required to be treated with flame retardant.

The terms *flame retardant* and *flameproofing* often are confused. Every substance has a flash point, the temperature at which a given material will support a flame. Cellulosic materials, used often in the theatre, are made up chiefly of plant tissues and fibers. Their flash points are fairly low, and they quickly can catch fire if exposed to an open flame. Total flameproofing is impossible. The realistic goal is to slow down the fire, by making the material flame retardant.

Backpainting as a Flame Retardant

The scenic painting department normally applies the flame retardant to both soft and hard scenery. For hard scenery, a simple coat of water-based paint on wood will provide some protection from fire, by creating a retardant barrier over the wood. Additives can be mixed with paints to make them more flame retardant, and some paints are manufactured specifically as flame retardants, available from most paint suppliers. These paints are very effective in discouraging an open flame. Pretreated fire retardant lumber is another available option but expensive. As the front of the scenery will be painted or sealed in some manner anyway, the back of the scenery will need be painted as well to make the unit flame retardant. *Backpainting* scenery is a standard practice in the theatre. It is best to backpaint the scenery before it has been primed or painted so any of the backpaint that finds its way onto the front of the scenery will not mar the finished work. Many shops save excess paint from past productions for backpaint. Backpainting has other good uses and is standard procedure in the profession. It masks the back of scenery, which may be glimpsed during a scene shift. For this reason, the most popular backpaint color is dark gray. Scenery that has been backpainted looks more professional and it is easier to see any identifying labels.

Drops also can be backpainted to make them flame retardant. But this practice is not useful in many instances for a number of reasons. A translucent drop cannot be painted on the back except where it is opaque. If the drop is going to be recycled, the extra paint on the back may shorten the use and life of the piece. If the drop is going to be shipped on a road show, the backpaint will add unnecessary weight.

Flame Retardants

To protect soft goods, clear flame retardants, available in either liquid or cystal form, are formulated for fabrics. Often these flame retardants already are licensed by the fire marshal in the state where they are marketed. They are available in liquid or ready-to-mix powder forms that can be sprayed on the fabric of the drop. Some flame retardants are concentrated and need to be diluted before being applied to fabric. These fire retardants can be loaded into a garden sprayer for application. Keep in mind that one of the main ingredients of many flame retardants is sodium, which is very corrosive to metals. Do not leave the flame retardant in the sprayer any longer than necessary. If working with flame retardant is a regular occupation in the shop, it would be a good idea to use one particular sprayer, an inexpensive or all-plastic one, for applying flame retardant. The flame retardant should be applied liberally to the scenery. The material being treated should be completely saturated with the fire retardant. Hard scenery should sprayed on the back before the face of the scenery is painted. Drops should be mounted on a frame or the deck first, then completely saturated with the flame retardant. After the flame retardant has dried, the scenery can be primed or starched as usual.

Flame retardants are manufactured by DuPont, Rosco, and Spartan (see the Reading and Resources chapter for their addresses).

Pretreated Fabrics

An alternative to applying the flame retardant to a drop is to construct it out of fabric that already has been treated with flame retardant. It may be more economical to buy the materials pretreated, as labor and space often are a factor in the cost of treating soft goods in-house. Pretreated muslin and other fabrics are commonly available at theatrical soft good suppliers. Bolts of muslin pretreated with flame retardant come with a certificate stating that the fabric has been treated. When ordering a drop or scrim from an outside contractor, a copy of this certificate can be requested.

Fire marshals in most major cities require a flame test be performed on the scenery to determine if the flame retardant meets fire codes. This simple test involves exposing the material to an open flame for ten to fifteen seconds, depending on the requirements of the local fire code. The material treated with flame retardant should not catch fire; rather the carbon buildup from the fire retardant should discourage the flame. If the material catches fire in the time allotted, then it must be retreated to meet the code. To find out the code requirements for your city, call the fire marshal in your district; that office will send you literature on the local code.

A common complaint with pretreated fabric is that, when the flame retardant is rewetted, it dries leaving a ring of salt stains or a white bloom around each brushstroke. This bloom will go away after a number of months, which, of course, is not practical for immediate use of the scenery. One method of treating the scenery with this problem is to spray it with diluted vegetable oil soap after it has been painted. The bloom from flame retardant is caused by the formation of small crystals where the retardant has been rewetted and crystallized when it dried. The soap keeps the crystal from forming while not inhibiting the fire retardant properties. The diluted oil-based soap can be sprayed on with a garden sprayer or pneumatic sprayer. Care should be taken if spraying a drop that has been painted with dyes. The diluted oil soap may cause the dye to blur and sharp lines to run. The surface does not need to be thoroughly saturated with soap to inhibit the bloom.

All flammable scenic elements must be treated with flame retardant. Elements like scenic netting, set dressing foliage, fabric, straw, leaves, and so on can be dipped in liquid flame retardant and laid out to dry. When working with flame retardant, always read the instructions thoroughly and follow directions carefully. Flame retardant is a skin irritant. Care should be taken not to let it come in contact with the skin. Always wear a respirator if applying it with a pneumatic sprayer or airless sprayer.

Synthetic fabrics need to be treated with a flame retardant manufactured specifically for these materials. If you are in doubt about what flame retardant to use on a specific material, call a flame retardant manufacturer. Some theatrical suppliers also manufacture lines of flame retardants and may be able to answer questions that arise about a specific material or methods of application.

STRETCHING AND PRIMING SOFT GOODS

Any new drop has considerable puckers and wrinkles in it when first mounted on a frame or spread on a deck. To prepare a drop for painting it must be shrunk into the final shape. This sizing usually is done with a primer coat that also prepares the surface for painting. The process is similar to preparing a canvas for painting with gesso. A drop that has puckers in it will never hang flat in the theatre.

Soft goods are painted in either the eastern or the continental style, and each technique has some particular requirements for preparing the goods for painting, which we discuss here (refer to Chapter Four for a comparison of these two painting techniques).

No priming is necessary with a drop constructed out of velour or duvetyn. Once it is mounted on a frame or a deck, it is ready to paint. Velour and duvetyn are somewhat resistant to dye, paint, and other water-based products in general. Adding a wetting solution to the paint or dye will help it penetrate the fibers. Leather stores sell wetting solutions as a preparation for dying leather evenly. Wetting solutions are particularly useful with dyes, as they will not interfere with the color. If the fabric still resists paint, any laundry detergent will help paint penetrate the fiber. If suds are a problem, add a defoamer (from the carpet cleaning section of the grocery) to the detergent.

Scenic backdrops must be primed before painting begins, because unprimed fabric does not take paint evenly on the first or second coat. It will not be

A drop constructed of predyed or bleached muslin should be mounted tightly before it is primed because it will have less shrinkage left in it after the dyeing or bleaching process. The starch used to shrink predyed or bleached muslin should be heavy, as the fabric tends to be more absorbent than unbleached muslin. Unbleached muslin will shrink considerably during the first prime coat so it should be mounted on the paint deck or frame so the fabric is loose.

possible to achieve even blends or even solid fields of color when working on unprimed goods. The prime coat seals the fabric from the paint and sets up an even painting surface, much like fine arts canvases primed with gesso.

Mounting Soft Goods for Sizing and Priming

Soft goods must be firmly secured to a frame or a deck before sizing and priming. It is important to use long staples when stretching a drop. Three-eighth-inch staples are the minimum length that will hold, but one-half-inch staples commonly are used, either in handheld or pneumatic staplers. It may be necessary to use pneumatic staples in the webbing of the drop because the handheld staplers may not get enough of a bite into the wood or sheet stock through the thick jute webbing. If a pneumatic stapler is tilted slightly to one side so the staples do not bite all the way into the wood, they will be easier to pull out when the time comes. Handheld staplers should be used with chisel-tipped staples for use with wood and Masonite. Always set the staples about four inches apart for a secure hold.

The most important aspect to stretching a drop on a frame or deck is to keep the bottom and the top edges parallel. Unfinished sides of a drop may not be completely square; that is, perpendicular to the top of the drop and parallel to each other. These can be squared and finished later. If the sides of the drop are finished they should be mounted as straight and square as possible; although there may be wrinkles and puckers, these will stretch out when the drop is primed. It is important to make sure that the drop is not torqued to one side or pulled at an angle, which will cause any verticals on the drop to warp out of square.

Working on a Deck

Follow this sequence when *stretching a drop* on a paint deck for best results. First snap a chalk line the full width of the goods to align the top edge of the drop. Use this line as a guide for the layout of goods and a reference line for the height measurements. Attach the top edge of the drop with staples, working from the center out and smoothing the drop as you go. Then pull the entire drop out until it is relaxed and flat on the floor, smoothing out as many wrinkles as possible. Measure the height of the drop at what looks to be the drop's shortest point. Snap a line parallel to the top to guide the stapling of the bottom of the drop. The top and bottom of a drop must always be parallel. The bottom of the drop should be stapled in the center first and worked out toward the sides. Then the sides should be stapled down, once again starting in the middle and working out toward either end (Figure 7.3). The staples should be kept parallel to the edge. If the edge being stapled is unfinished, a half inch or so of fabric should be turned back so that each staple goes through two layers. This will lessen the chance of the fabric pulling through the staple. The turnbacks on the sides of the drop will be cartooned and trimmed when painting is completed.

If the sides of a drop have been sewn and are finished then they will have to be stapled so they are perpendicular to the top and bottom of the drop. If the drop is to be a specific size, for instance, a twenty-foot by forty-foot drop, then the drop should be stapled into a rectangle cartooned to those dimensions. However, first measure the drop itself to make sure that it is not too narrow or too short. The size of the cartoon may need to be altered to fit the actual size of the soft goods. (Methods for drafting a perpendicular line, so the drop can be squared, can be found in Chapter Eight.) To double check that the square of a cartoon is accurate before the drop is stapled down, measure the cartoon diagonally from corner to corner and then again in the other direction. These measurements should be the same; if they are not the same then the cartoon is not square. When stapling the drop into a cartoon there may be sections that are a little baggy, but once the drop is sized and primed it will shrink into shape.

Working on a Paint Frame

If securing a drop to a paint frame, first staple or hang the drop along the top of the frame. Line up one side of the drop with a vertical frame member to staple to. You may need to nail additional battens to the frame where the other side of the drop falls, to provide a firm support for stapling. Staple the drop to the frame along the bottom as well, adding a batten, a wooden support, as needed. Lastly, staple the sides (Figure 7.4). An advantage of working on a frame is that gravity helps to find true vertical. As you staple the top edge, measure in and find the center of the drop, then mark it for future reference. You will be able to drop a plumb line down from a nail or safety pin at the center to find the center bottom of the drop. You can use this method to establish any vertical on the drop. You also can drop a tape measure from a nail on either side of the drop for measuring heights.

Priming Soft Goods
Floating Soft Goods on a Deck

Gravity will cause a drop to hang slightly out on a frame, so that it does not stick to the frame itself. Stretching and *priming a drop* on the deck is some-

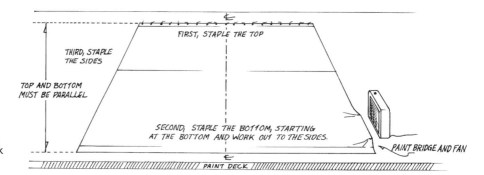

Figure 7.3
Laying out a drop on a deck for stretching and priming.

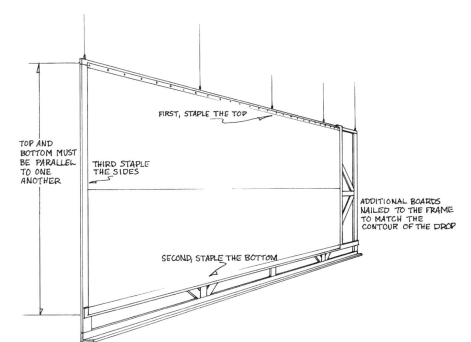

TOP AND BOTTOM MUST BE PARALLEL TO ONE ANOTHER

FIRST, STAPLE THE TOP

THIRD STAPLE THE SIDES

ADDITIONAL BOARDS NAILED TO THE FRAME TO MATCH THE CONTOUR OF THE DROP

SECOND, STAPLE THE BOTTOM

Figure 7.4
Mounting a drop on a paint frame for stretching and priming.

what more problematic than working on the frame. If the drop is allowed to dry while resting on the floor, it will stick to it or whatever is covering the floor, like the bogus paper under it. One alternative is to cover the deck with a visquene sheet. The drawback of priming a drop on visquene is that the primer will go all the way through the fabric and collect in the folds of the plastic. The drop will always have the pattern of the visquene when the primer dries. This pattern will show through all the subsequent layers of paint. The way to defeat these problems is to float the drop. This term *float* means to force air between the drop and the deck so that the drop rises off of the floor while drying. Floating the drop will result in a very clean prime coat and an excellent base for all the layers of paint to follow.

To float a drop while it is being primed, begin by putting a paint bridge under one corner (Figure 7.5). A paint bridge is a structure that holds the edge of a drop about six inches off the floor over a span of about four feet. Air will force the drop up off the floor when a running fan is placed at the gap made by the bridge. A funnel built out of plywood can be set between the fan and the paint bridge to channel more air under the drop. Box fans designed for drying carpets will move a great deal of air under the

drop. They are terrific for getting large drops off the ground, but sometimes these fans move too much air and distort the fabric. A second paint bridge can act as a safety valve to let air escape quickly, but most often, one paint bridge is adequate. If the drop is an irregular shape, for instance, a portal arch, it might be necessary to put a bridge and fan in each leg of the portal to let air pass up and around the arch. When priming a drop that is being floated, start priming on the side that has the paint bridge on it so that the drop starts floating as soon as possible.

The drop should be left floating until it is completely dry. A drop is best primed and floated first thing in the morning, so that it can be watched during the course of the day. If this is not possible then it should be left floating overnight, with the fan on the lowest speed necessary to keep the drop in the air. A drop will stick where it is still wet if lowered to the deck before the back of it is completely dry. If left floating overnight, it may be stretched slightly out of shape. It can be sprayed down with warm water to tighten it up again.

Primers

Soft goods must be primed with something lightweight and fairly flexible. Paint adds weight and

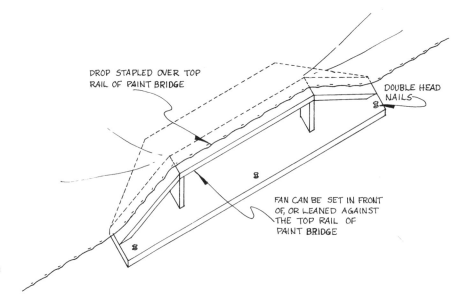

DROP STAPLED OVER TOP
RAIL OF PAINT BRIDGE

DOUBLE HEAD
NAILS

FAN CAN BE SET IN FRONT
OF, OR LEANED AGAINST
THE TOP RAIL OF
PAINT BRIDGE

Figure 7.5
A paint bridge and floating a
drop (designed by Mary Ellen
Kennedy).

inflexibility to a drop. Using a lighter, more supple primer will add to the life of the drop. Some fabrics, such as velour, do not need primer. Scrim may or may not need primer according to the scenic artist's preference.

Thickened *laundry starch* is the standard primer for soft goods. Laundry starch makes an excellent primer because it is inexpensive and very lightweight. It gives the drop an excellent finish that is conducive to painting. The starch basically is regular cornstarch with bluing added, so that white garments treated with laundry starch appear brighter. Regular cornstarch sold for cooking seems to have an astringent quality. Drops primed with straight cornstarch rather than laundry starch become damp in muggy climates.

After the starch has been thinned, it is ready to apply. Starch may be lightly tinted with scenic paint or a small amount of colorant to make it easier to see while being applied to a drop and, as a result, allowing it to be applied more evenly. The tint should relate to the local color of the drop to be painted; for example, use turquoise or ultramarine blue if it is a blue sky drop. The starch must stay clear if the drop is translucent or it will affect all the colors used on top of it.

If the starch is used on muslin or material that has been pretreated with flame retardant, that retardant may break down the starch and subsequent layers of paint. However, starch can be reinforced with

Laundry starch is prepared with hot water. Starch comes in one-pound boxes, so the following proportions are for mixing a full box of starch. Bring a gallon and a half of water to a boil—it must be boiling—in a large steel bucket or two one-gallon buckets. If the buckets are covered they will come to a boil faster. Meanwhile, mix the powdered starch into a half-gallon of cold water. Mixing the powdered starch directly into hot water will cause clumping. Blend the cold water solution with a paint drill to make sure that the solution is smooth. Briskly stir or drill the cold water solution into the boiling water. The solution will thicken and the milky appearance of the cold water solution will disappear. If it does not thicken and clear, the water was not hot enough. Once the starch has been thickened, it should be taken off the hot plate immediately. It then should be transferred to a larger bucket. If several drops are being starched at once, a clean, plastic trash can might be more convenient for the prepared starch. The starch should then be thinned with hot water, about one to one and a half gallons of hot water per box of cooked starch. The point is to have the starch thick enough to seal the fabric but not so thick that it cracks or leaves brush or spray marks as it dries. Each box of powdered starch will yield about two and a half to three gallons of cooked starch. This will be enough starch for approximately 300 to 350 square feet.

a binder such as P.V.A. or latex so that it will stand up to the corrosive nature of the flameproofing. Approximately one cup of liquid binder per gallon of starch is adequate to strengthen the starch.

Old-fashioned laundry starch is getting difficult to find, as there is little demand for it anymore. Starched collars have passed out of fashion. Some markets in old-fashioned neighborhoods may still carry boxes of laundry starch, but this is becoming rare. Argo Gloss Starch is the most commonly found brand in America. Look for the blue box. Most grocery stores stock Argo cornstarch for cooking, so they will be able to special order the laundry starch by the case from their suppliers. The cost of laundry starch is not much over a dollar a box, so ordering it by the case is not too costly. It also is available by the case from the Mann Brothers and Rose Brand catalogues (see the Reading and Resources chapter).

Instant starch is an alternative to corn-based laundry starch. It can be obtained from commercial laundry suppliers. Instant starch need not be cooked, as it mixes in cold water. Instant starch can be mixed in much the same way that wheat paste is mixed, by sifting it into cold water while blending it. Starch should be sifted in and blended until it begins to thicken. If blended with a paint drill, the starch will be smoother. After the starch is blended, it should sit for about thirty minutes to finish thickening. After sitting, it should be blended with a drill again until it is smooth; this will thin it if it has thickened too much while standing. Another alternative to laundry starch is clear vinyl or acrylic finish. These can be thinned down and applied in the same manner as starch. The disadvantage with these mediums is that the finish will not take aniline dyes.

Some shops prime drops with *animal glue*. Animal glue is a flexible and effective primer and was the standard primer as well as paint binder in the years before premixed casein paints became available. The results are excellent. Cooked animal glue is mixed one part glue to five parts water for a priming solution. It is applied in the same fashion as the starch primers (see Chapter Six on how to prepare animal glue).

Soft goods also may be primed with *acrylic* or *latex paint*, but a polymer paint finish does not take paint as smoothly as starch and animal glue primers. Paint used as a primer also makes the drop heavier and creases will be more persistent when folded. It also retards any shrinkage later on. Drops primed with starch or glue, however, keep a resilience and usually can be unwrinkled after storage with a spray of warm water.

Applying Primer

Methods of applying primer coats to soft goods may vary, depending on how the goods have been stretched, but one rule never varies: *when priming a drop, the job must not be left until it is finished.* If the drop is partially primed at break or quitting time, a seam will be evident where the primer was allowed to dry between the first and second attempts. Have enough crew members available to ensure the priming is applied quickly and evenly. A drop that is mounted on a paint deck or framed out on the floor should be floated as soon as possible to keep the surface of the fabric from acquiring the pattern of the floor. Drops stretched on the floor can be primed very efficiently with a broom and sprayer. Spray the primer on with a garden sprayer in a large swath about three feet wide. Then, smooth out the starch with a clean, soft bristle push broom. At the end of each swath, before the next swath is begun, the broom should be pulled across the whole length of the drop so the broom marks are smoothed out. I have found, after having a bad time with garden sprayers one day, that the primer can be just as easily spattered on the drop as sprayed. This method actually goes a little faster. The difference between spattering and spraying is that the spatter marks may continue to show through the finish as successive layers of paint or dye are applied, more so than if the primer was sprayed. An airless sprayer also may be used to prime a drop stretched on the floor. A pitfall of priming with an airless sprayer is that it is very easy to put too much starch in one spot. Constant movement, an even speed, a repetitive pattern side to side, and an overlap on each pass by half will help ensure the even application of starch or primer. When priming a drop on the floor with an airless sprayer, it is necessary for two people to work together because the hose of the sprayer needs to be reeled in so that it does not drag through wet starch.

It is possible to apply primer with a brush when working on the paint frame, but there will be drips and brush marks, which may not result in a clean finish. Primer sprayed on with an airless sprayer results in the cleanest finish on framed drops. When priming a drop on a frame with an airless sprayer, each pass made should overlap half of the previous pass, just as on a deck. Each pass made with the airless should be as long and even as possible. The sprayer should be in constant movement so that starch does not pile up in one spot.

If a drop is sized and primed with paint on a paint deck, the same care must be taken to ensure that it does not stick to the deck when it dries. The paint should be applied in swaths starting at the paint bridge, working outward. Paint can be applied as a primer to a drop on the paint frame with an airless sprayer or large brushes. The paint should be no thicker than necessary to seal the fabric. White latex commonly is used, because it is cost effective and can be tinted to a color close to the primary local color of the drop for even application. Many scenic paint manufacturers sell a brand of primer in their scenic paint line. Often these primers are formulated for hard scenery more than soft goods. A quick phone call to the district office of the manufacturer will clear up any questions you might have about the firm's products and their intended uses.

Once the primer is dry, the drop will be ready to cartoon and paint. If the drop has a paint bridge in the edge, the bridge should be removed and that edge stapled down. Some puckers and wrinkles will be left from where the bridge was placed, which should shrink out when sprayed with hot water.

Problem Solving

If the fabric used for the backdrop is behaving oddly, not shrinking to size when it dries for some unknown reason, the problem may be reconcilable. Astringent alum, which can be purchased at a local pharmacy or grocery store, will increase the shrinkage of natural fiber fabrics such as muslin, canvas, and linen. The alum should be dissolved in hot water at the ratio of about one tablespoon per gallon of water. It should then be loaded in a garden sprayer and sprayed on the trouble spots. Alum should not be used on dyed drops, particularly in humid climates. Because it is an astringent, it will absorb and hold humidity. This can cause the dyes to get fuzzy edges or, if it is humid enough, even imprint a pattern from one section of the drop onto another while it is folded.

While a drop is drying from its primer coat, it should be watched closely for the first hour or two. This is the time when it is most apt to pop its staples on one side or another. If an edge begins to pull, it will be easy enough to reinforce the staples if you catch it early. Pull the edges that have popped back into shape with canvas clamps, pliers, or vise

grips and staple them down again. Canvas clamps are pliers with a set of textured paddles, designed to grip and hold canvas or muslin. Once the drop has been primed and is dry, the risk of it popping any staples is very low.

If you are priming a drop on a paint frame that drops down into a well, keep an eye on the seams as the drop is raised up. If you notice a seam bowing up, the bottom of the drop has pulled loose. Don't panic if disaster strikes and the drop pops the staples along several feet or an entire side. First, reinforce the staples that have not popped on either side of the gap. Add staples along the edge of the gap, about every foot, to keep the drop from stretching further out of shape. Then begin working in from either end of the gap, pulling the edge of the drop back into shape. One or two people should pull the drop with the canvas clamps while another person staples the edge as it is stretched back into shape. Pulling a wet drop and stapling at the same time is much too difficult.

If the drop resists all human efforts to be stretched back into shape, or if you are alone when you discover the mishap and can only hope to localize the damage on your own rather than repair it, do not despair. Later, when the drop is completely dry, it can be blocked back into shape with the help of one or two crew people armed with staplers, canvas clamps, and a large garden sprayer full of cold water. First, remove the staples from the edges that pulled loose. Next, dampen the drop along the bad edge and ten feet or so in from that edge. Do not soak the drop or it will begin to stretch in again; if the fabric is just dampened, it will become more elastic. Methodically pull the drop back into shape from the sides of the gap to the center and staple along the line that is its intended shape. Once stretched back into shape and dried, the drop will be ready to cartoon and paint. If the starch on the drop was particularly heavy, there may be a network of stretch marks on the drop that will show with dye or transparent paint. These marks will not show under opaque paint.

Priming Translucent Drops

A *translucency* is a drop or an area of a drop intended to allow light through the muslin for a special effect, such as a sunrise or a lighted window at night. To prime a translucency, the drop may be laid down and primed on the back with clear starch only, no tints. While priming the back of a translucency with seams, be careful not to glue these seams down with the starch as they will have puckers or welts when the translucency is viewed from the front.

After the primer is dry and the bridge has been removed, the back of the translucency should be cartooned using a reversed line drawing to lay out the translucent areas. The designer will have provided an elevation and possibly a line drawing that will very clearly show where the translucent areas are. This cartoon must be accurate because the masking process is irreversible. The lines of the cartoon should be made with a heavy ink marker so they are visible from the front when the drop is flipped over. When cartooning clouds or color shifts in the sky of a translucency, one must be very careful about imposing the hard-edged lines of an ink marker on the design. These lines will become visible when the drop is lighted from behind.

The opaque areas of the drop should be painted over, after the cartoon is completed. This creates a lightproof mask. Use a color similar to the local color used on the front of the drop. If backpaint showing through to the front is a concern, these areas can be primed first with white paint.

The front of the drop also must be primed after the drop has been flipped onto its back and stapled down again. If not, the painting will be arduous, due to the absorbency of the muslin; the paint job, as a result, will be splotchy. The starch used on the front of the drop can be very thin, as the drop already has been sealed from the back. It will not be necessary to put in a paint bridge to float the drop if it has been sealed on the back. The cartoon then should be restored on the front of the drop and completed, if parts were left undone. This process may be abbreviated to one step. The process of opaquing a drop from the back may be difficult with very complex images. It is possible to do all the work on the front surface. Two coats of heavy front paint will opaque it fairly well, if not as flawlessly as opaque paint on the back and the front.

The translucent areas of the drop first should be painted using dye or very thin, high-quality paint. Poor-quality paint contains fillers that impair the translucency of the muslin. Aniline dye is completely transparent, but if paint is used, thin it as much as possible and avoid using white—white paint will interfere with the translucency.

If the front of the drop is painted in a watercolor style, requiring relatively translucent paint, then it may be cartooned and entirely opaqued from the back despite the opaque areas. The opaque areas on the front of the drop can be covered with a base coat of a solid muslin color so that the backpainting is not visible.

If the opaque area on the back of the drop is different than the design on the front of the drop (for instance, storm clouds that are revealed in a clear sky), then the back must be primed and cartooned first. Use white or pastel chalk for the cartooning if visible dark cartoon lines are a problem when the drop is lighted from behind. The opaque areas must be given a base coat in a white, muslin, or local-color-tinted paint, depending on the design of the front of the drop, and then may need to be recoated in gray to ensure opaqueness. If the areas of opaque color need to be very soft along the edges, then the opaque paint can be applied with a spray gun.

Priming Scrims

The magic of scrim is that any image painted on it appears opaque until it is lighted from behind. Then, it becomes transparent, revealing what is behind the scrim, be it a three-dimensional version of the scene on the scrim itself, another scene entirely, or the ghosts in the walls. The open weave of the scrim allows this to happen.

Scrims may or may not be treated with a primer. The fabric cannot be completely soaked down if it is primed, or it will stick to the surface below and become very stiff, because scrim fabric is very absorbent. Scrim may blot paint as it is applied, making the lines blurry. A measure some scenic artists take to gain a little more control over the fabric is to spray the scrim with thin starch or animal-glue size water. After working with scrim for a time, most painters develop a habit of blotting the brush on a rag after it has been charged so that lines are crisper. The viscosity of the paint will effect control when painting a scrim. Very thin paint or glazes will tend to blot or wick into the scrim more than heavy bodied paints.

Before a scrim is painted, a full-size cartoon of the elevation is made on another surface as a reference. The gauzy and stretchy nature of scrim makes it very difficult to cartoon on. It is simpler to follow a cartoon that is drawn out on the deck or on paper underneath the scrim. If you are drawing directly on the paint deck then the area must first be painted white so that the cartoon will be discernible; paint decks can be very splotchy due to previous paint applications. Kraft paper and bogus paper are often used under scrims because they absorb some of the moisture from the scrim, which helps somewhat with the problem of blurry lines. Kraft paper is a heavy brown paper similar to the paper that grocery bags are made of. Rolls of brown paper can be purchased from local industrial paper goods supply houses. Bogus paper is a heavier brown paper that is more absorbent. Bogus paper may be obtained through theatrical paint and fabric suppliers. To create a surface for a cartoon, lengths of paper should be laid across the entire area of the paint deck that the scrim is to be stretched out on. The sides of the paper should be taped together, edge to edge. Once taped together, the entire drop-size piece of paper can be flipped over so that the lines of the lighter colored masking tape are hidden underneath. In either case, working on paper or directly on the deck, the scrim can be stretched over the cartoon once it has been completed and the line work has been set with ink.

If the scrim is to be painted on the frame, it will be necessary to first hang and stretch a full-size backing drop for the cartoon. After the cartoon has been completed on the backing drop the scrim can be stretched in front of it. The backing drop also serves as a solid surface behind the scrim, which helps the scenic artist to focus on the scrim itself instead of the paint frame and the wall behind it. The backing drop can be made out of nearly any kind of light-colored fabric. It can even be made out of scrap fabric since, once it has served its purpose as a scrim backer, it will not be good for much else. Scrims can be painted with either dye or paint. The point simply is not to fill in the weave of the scrim, or it cannot work its magic when backlighted. Dye and high-quality scenic paints work best on scrim, delivering good-quality color without having to be overly thick.

Priming Floorcloths

Floorcloths usually are constructed of the heaviest material available, canvas duck. Care should be taken to secure floorcloths extremely well when stretching them. Canvas can generate tremendous force as it shrinks. Pneumatic staplers are preferred over handheld staple guns for mounting the floorcloth, because of the strength of the staple itself as well as the reliable force of a pneumatic gun. If the ground cloth is mounted to a frame rather than a paint deck, the frame must be very sturdy. Canvas

stretches so tautly that it easily could warp or break a paint frame.

If the canvas floorcloth is painted on a deck, it can be stretched and primed in a manner similar to priming a drop. The floorcloth will not need to be floated because not enough paint will seep through the heavier fabric to create problems. The cloth should be primed and painted with acrylic, vinyl, or latex-based paints, because of the heavy use it will receive. Protein-based paints and primers, like caseins, do not hold up to foot traffic as well and break down if liquid is spilled on them. For this reason, and because the floorcloth will come in direct contact with the performers, aniline dye should never be used.

After the floorcloth is painted, it should be sealed with a spray coat of clear acrylic or water-based urethane to increase its durability. Do not use a brush to apply the sealer on canvas floorcloths because brushing will trap air bubbles, giving a white or milky appearance when dry and possibly ruining the paint job. Also, never put a fan on clear water-based finishes while they are drying, as cool air blowing across the finish may cause it to cloud.

Preparing China Silk

China silk has a distinct tendency to bleed paint, so details and line work become blotchy. One way to inhibit this is to give the silk a light spray of gum thickener, also called methocel, or Irish moss mixed into a solution of size water. Either one of these must be applied in moderation. If applied too heavily, it will stiffen the silk, compromising the quality of flow and grace. (Methocel and Irish moss are both discussed in Chapter Six.)

Only aniline or batik dyes should be used to paint china silk. Any paint, no matter how thin, will stiffen and flatten the finish of the silk. The dyes may be mixed into a vehicle of methocel or Irish moss to thicken the dyes. This will reduce the problem of blotting and wicking somewhat. It may be best to dye an entire panel in a vat before it is stretched, if the background color of the silk must be altered.

Priming Monk's Cloth

Monk's cloth can be painted just as it is or after a light coat of starch to help reduce bleed. However, the surface of monk's cloth never truly can be sealed.

PREPARING HARD SCENERY

If a scenic unit is not a piece of soft goods then it is *hard scenery.* Typical flattage, platforms, sculptural items, metallic frames, and plastics fall under this umbrella. Hard scenery, like soft goods, requires considerable preparation and a primer coat is absolutely essential for most items. It is very rare that any material is seen on stage in its raw form, without at least a sealant and flame retardant. The materials that constitute hard scenery are as various as can be imagined. However, milled lumber, plywoods, composite boards, plastics, plastic foams, aluminum, and steel probably make up 95 percent of hard scenery today.

Working with Flattage

Flattage, or walls, represents the vast majority of hard scenery. Flats may be hard- or soft-covered. Hard-covered flats have a thin, rigid skin over the frame. This skin is generally one-quarter- or one-eighth-inch thick lauan, an inexpensive three-ply mahogany. Other common skinning products include heavier plywoods, wall paneling, composition board, and even rigid cardboards. It usually is preferable to cover any sheet stock with a layer of muslin to hide the texture and the seams of whatever material is used. The seams of lauan are difficult to hide, often cracking and showing through any paint application no matter how well patched. Soft-covered flats are just empty frames covered with muslin, duvetyn, velour, or other fabric. Muslin is the most common fabric for soft-covered flattage as it is with backdrops.

Flat frames usually are wood, aluminum, or steel. The construction styles vary with the material. *Standard* or *Hollywood* construction are the primary options for wood- and metal-frame flats. Standard flat construction uses milled lumber laying flat, joined together, with plates of plywood on the back over the joints. This makes a frame about one inch thick. Because these flats are so thin they can torque easily under the stress of fabric shrinkage. However, they take up very little space in storage and during transport. Hollywood flat construction places the same milled lumber on edge for a much more rigid, but thicker frame.

Flats should be laid out on the shop floor or secured to the paint frame for painting in the order that they will be joined, from stage right to stage left. Flats for different scenes should be stored together and painted as a group to avoid redundancy of time and effort. The bottom of the flats should be set in a parallel line if they play together on the same level, or adjusted so that the bottom of the flat is the correct distance above the baseline of the rest of the flats, as it would be on stage. This is so measurements that need to be carried across all the flats can be marked without having to stop and recall relationship of the flats to one another.

A foot of space or more should be left between the units for walkways if the units are being laid out on a floor or paint deck. If a unit is wider than four feet, it may be necessary to walk on it to paint and do detail work. "Walk on the wood not on the goods" is an old and practical adage in scenic painting when working on hard scenery. A scenic artist must have an ear for and sense of the stress on flattage when working on it. Special care must be taken when working on Hollywood flats. These flats are framed with one-inch by three-inch stock lumber used on the edges. A foot in the wrong place can put a hole in the flat. If you must work out into the middle of a Hollywood flat, lay an eight-inch plank across the flat to give yourself a surface to walk on. If a unit is particularly bulky then a bridge or scaffolding may need to be constructed, so the scenic artists can access the areas that need to be painted. Naturally, one of the missions of the scenic artist is to return the scenery to the construction department undamaged, especially if he or she wants to encourage the same consideration.

Preparing Hard-Covered Flats

Lauan is the most common sheet stock used to cover hard scenic flats. A lauan surface has to be primed with a solvent-based primer such as an alkyd primer or white-pigmented shellac. Like any other wood product, lauan tends to stain through the paint in varying degrees from one sheet to another. Lauan also has a very distinct texture and hard edges. A yellow rectangle of lauan may begin to stain through painted baroque drawing room wallpaper if improperly primed. A cover of muslin will eliminate the staining problem; this is called *skinning* a flat with muslin. Yet, if the set is a location on the seamy side of life, a dockside tavern for instance, unprimed lauan may add a beneficial aspect to the paint job. If it is intended to be stained for a wood deck or paneled walls, it should not be primed.

One way to hide the lauan finish without a muslin cover is to put a fine silicate sand in the base coat. This kind of sand is sold at brickyards for pennies a pound, in forty-pound or eighty-pound bags, as a mortar additive. The paint with sand in it must not be too thin and should be stirred every few minutes while in use. The proportions should be about two cups of sand to every gallon of paint. It should be brushed out with an omni-directional paint stroke when applied, so as not to develop a grain. The sand will leave behind a fine, consistent finish once dry (very much like fine sandpaper) that helps defeat the grain of the lauan. This treated sand paint also helps hide the grain of other sheet stocks such as plywood.

If a hard-covered flat has a skin of muslin on it, it can be primed with a regular water-based paint, latex, or acrylic house paint. The muslin will provide the barrier between the lauan and the painted finish so there will be no staining through to the top coat. Solvent-based or heavy-duty primers are not necessary.

A main problem with muslin-covered hard flats is the need to use glue to adhere the muslin cover. Dried glue resists paint and shows up as glossy spots once painted over. A little glue overstepping its bounds is hard to avoid while covering a flat. The flat will take paint better if the glue spots are pounced with whiting (dry white pigment) before they dry. Use a pounce bag (see Chapter Eight for more on pouncing) filled with whiting while the glue is still tacky. White pigment commonly is made from calcium carbonate or chalk. This breaks the surface of the glue and makes it much more accepting of paint. If the scenic artists are not covering the flats, it would be in their best interests to mention this technique to the carpenters and provide them with pounce bags of whiting.

Preparing Soft-Covered Flats

Some soft-covered flats are covered by gluing the fabric to the face of the flat frame with casein-based glue (wood glue, white glue, or fabric glue) or scenic dope. The casein-based glues must be thinned down for gluing muslin. When the glue is dry, trim the excess fabric off the edges. When covered in this fashion, glue that may be on the surface of the flat can be fixed with a pounce of whiting. Scenic dope is animal glue mixed with a paste made from whiting and water. Scenic dope accepts paint very well and does not need to be pounced with whiting. Soft-covered flats also may be covered by stretching the fabric around to the back of the flat and stapling it to the frame, but this may cause the seams between flats to be wider than desired.

All soft-covered flats may be primed with any water-based paint. Always consider if the primer should be tinted to a hue related to the local color of the base coat. A tinted prime coat will help in achieving even coverage of the base coat, particularly if the base coat is a deep or saturated color. A tinted prime coat may even serve as the base of the paint treatments to follow. The flats also may be primed with starch. The starch will take differently to the areas where the muslin covers the frame and those where the muslin was glued to the frame. The primary reason to use starch instead of paint to prime a flat is for translucencies. If this is the case, the flats should be treated like a translucent drop, as described earlier in this chapter.

Dutchmen

Hiding the seams between adjoining flats is part of the preparation. This can be done by gluing on a strip of cloth, known as a *dutchman*, made out of the same material as the flat covering, which is usually muslin. The strip of cloth should be as long as the seam that it is intended to hide and about four inches wide. The edges of the dutchman strip should be frayed a quarter of an inch or more along the edges so that they blend into the surface. The back of the dutchman should be brushed with glue, scenic dope, or wallpaper paste, being careful all the while to keep the glue off the front of the dutchman. The dutchman is laid in position on the seam, glue side down. The dutchman should be smoothed over the seam with a damp sponge from the center out to the edges. Sponge up all excess glue that seeps out from under the dutchman. Smooth the frayed edges of the dutchman to blend into the surface of the flat. If glue is used to attach the dutchman rather than wallpaper paste or scenic dope, then the entire dutchman should be pounced over with a bag of whiting while it is still tacky. The dutchman should be allowed to dry thoroughly before the flat is primed, or it may shrink and leave gaps in the prime coat.

Preparing Floor Coverings

Painted stage floors are common, but rarely are they painted directly on the stage itself. A temporary cover can be prepainted and easily installed.

The most common materials used for a *painted deck* are ground cloths, sheet stock, and covered platforming.

Floor Sheet Stock

Masonite and *MDF* are common choices for painted stage decking, because they are thin, smooth, sturdy, and relatively inexpensive. The two materials are virtually the same from a painter's point of view. Masonite is a more commonly known word, and it is also a brand name. If a paint treatment is one color or a color and a finish, then painting a full stage deck of Masonite is a simple issue. It can be painted several sheets at a time in a corner of the shop and the process can stay more or less out of the way of everybody. More complex patterns or treatments require that the Masonite be laid out and treated as a whole either in the shop or in the theatre during load-in if the schedule allows. The Masonite deck may be loaded in early and left for few days to be painted before the rest of the load-in proceeds. If any deck is painted on stage, the entire stage deck needs to be covered with visquene before the painting surface is installed. Otherwise, the paint will seep through the seams of the Masonite and ruin the floor underneath. Later, the visquene can be trimmed away from the edges of the painted deck so that it does not present a hazard during the run of the show.

Normally, a deck is painted on Masonite before the load-in. A fully painted deck then can be installed in a matter of a few hours. A Masonite deck painted at an earlier point in the schedule, either in the shop or on stage, will be pulled up and stored until load-in. Each sheet of Masonite must be numbered and referenced to a deck plan. When the stack of Masonite is brought in during load-in, the stage carpenters have a clear guide for assembly.

Priming Sheet Stock for Floors

Raw Masonite has two finishes that require some preparation before they will accept paint evenly. Masonite is made by heating and compacting wood chips with graphite. The result is a product that is very slick on one side and rough on the other. The rough surface takes paint so poorly that only rarely is it used on a stage deck. Because the smooth surface of the Masonite is slick and slightly oily, water-based primers will not bond well to its surface. Prepare the smooth surface for painting with an alkyd-based primer. Shellac-based primers are very brittle and may chip off the Masonite when it is flexed or under compression from casters on heavy stage wagons. MDF is smooth on both sides and should be prepared like Masonite (see Chapter Four, Safety and Health Regulations).

For the best coverage, use a roller to paint Masonite. Masonite has such a smooth finish it difficult to get good coverage with a brush without leaving streak marks. When applying a base or primer coat with a roller, take care to work the roller in many different directions, so that the paint job does not develop a directional grain.

Priming Wood

When dealing with any wood or wood-based product, the primer has to serve as a barrier between the natural stains in the wood and the paint. Tree resins and natural color in lumber and plywoods will show through any water-based primer. If a primer coat has a different solvent base than the scenic paint (something other than water-based), the stain will not be able to travel between the two layers, but will stop at the primer coat. White-pigmented shellac and alkyd primers are excellent sealers and easily available through commercial paint suppliers. Water-based primers on the market now are reputed to stop the natural stains in wood from penetrating through to the finish color, but these are relatively new and I have observed that stains from knot holes and darker woods still can come through these primers.

PREPARING AND PRIMING OTHER SCENIC MATERIALS

A wide variety of materials are used for scenic construction and, therefore, a wide variety of methods are used to prepare materials for painting. The common thread to this preparation is that most materials need a primer just as fabrics and wood do. Some of these materials will not accept standard scenic paints at all and must be coated in advance with another adhesive or sealant. Many sculpted surfaces must be primed or skinned first before applying paint. Other surfaces need to be smoothed, and still others need to be reinforced so that they can stand up to trucking, loading, or hard use.

Preparing Noncellulosic Materials

Noncellulosic materials, such as plaster, metals, plastic, and foams, are common in set construction, and their use is increasing constantly. This section discusses how to prepare these materials for painting (additional treatments of these materials may be found with the techniques discussed in Chapter Ten).

Plaster

Plaster must be primed before it is painted, because the surface is too absorbent to take paint evenly. Plaster can be primed well with a water-based primer. If the finish of the plaster still needs smoothing, joint compound mixed with clear latex or acrylic binder can be added into the primer to give it more body. When dry, vinyl, latex, or acrylic primers serve as a barrier to the water-leaching tendencies of plaster, smoothing the way for the paint techniques to follow. Casein-based paint does not form this barrier but behaves like a fresco, by penetrating and absorbing the minerals from the plaster. In European countries, casein-based fresco paint is still used to paint the stucco finish on the exteriors of buildings.

Several options are available for reinforcing the brittle finish of plaster. Fiberglass and two-part resin is a time-consuming but long-lasting process, but they present health hazards. More simply, plaster can be primed first with undiluted flexible glue. Do not use regular white glue or a wood glue, because both are very brittle and do not accept paint. After the glue coating is dry, coat the plaster entirely with a vinyl-, latex-, or acrylic-based paint. After the base coat is dry, the plaster can be painted in any fashion with any common binder or medium.

Priming and Sealing Metals

Steel straight from the distributor has an oil coating to inhibit rust or corrosion. The first step in painting it is to clean off the residual oil. Solvents such as mineral spirits and lacquer thinners will clean off most of the oil, although they will leave a little residue of their own and present health hazards. The metal may be cleaned off with a concentrated cleaner/degreaser.

If the metal has been further fabricated into a unit by welding, the welds must be cleaned first before priming or painting. The welds can be cleaned by scrubbing them with a wire brush. To prime coat steel use a solvent-based primer that can cut through the residual oil still on the metal. A shellac- or alkyd-based primer works well. After the primer has completely dried, the unit can be painted with any standard water-based scene paint (see Chapter Four, Safety and Health Regulations).

If the natural sheen of steel is desirable, use a clear shellac, lacquer, or solvent-based urethane to seal the steel and keep it from rusting.

Preparing Plastics and Foam Plastics

Plastic, Plexiglas, and *PVC* by themselves will resist most water-based paints. Shellac or alkyd primers will adhere to most plastic surfaces, but if the surface is very smooth and even slightly flexible, they can easily be scratched or flake off. Water-based contact cement will adhere very well to most plastic surfaces (see Chapter Four, Safety and Health Regulations). If a Plexiglas surface must be paintable but remain clear, water-based urethane will not cloud up when it dries and will adhere beautifully to Plexiglas. The urethane also may be tinted with aniline dyes and thinned with acrylic floor wax.

The many kinds of *foam plastics* used in scenic construction fall into two broad categories: rigid and soft. Rigid foams include styrene foams, such as bead boards and blue foam, and urethane foams, like florist foam and two-part AB foam. Soft foams include ethafoam rod and foam rubber used in upholstery and weather stripping.

Rigid Foam

Styrene and *two-part urethane* foams are used for fabrication of sculptural elements and three-dimensional scenery, because they are lightweight, rigid, and cut and carve easily. These qualities become liabilities when used on stage, where they may receive a fair amount of abuse. Hence, when preparing foams it is necessary to create a surface that is both paintable and durable.

Usually, a scenic artist is apt to deal with two types of polystyrene foam. One is *beadboard*, so called because it is made of compressed polystyrene beads. Large beadboard blocks, up to 128 cubic feet, commonly are used for carving sculptural pieces, such as stone detail, rocks, and stone blocks. Lengths of large profile molding often are cut from beadboard because it is lightweight and inexpensive. These lengths of molding are normally eight feet long, so it may be necessary to spackle the seams or skin the

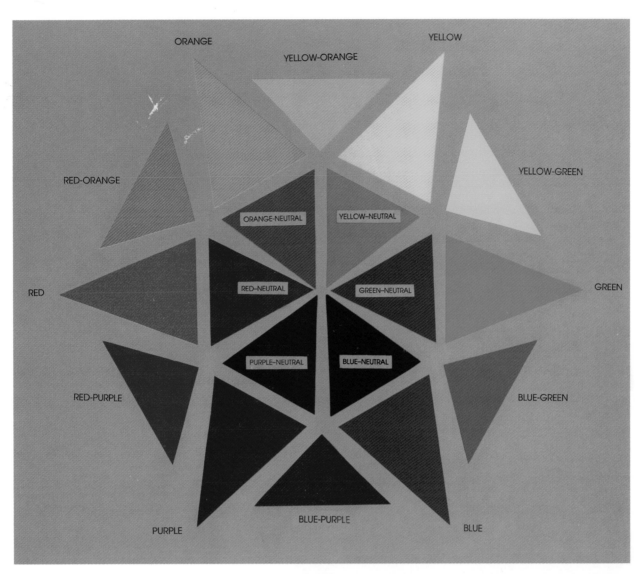

Plate 1
Color wheel. Designed by Toni Y. Auletti.

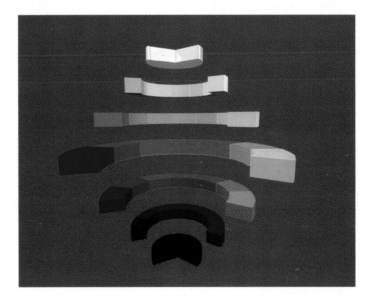

Plate 2
Color model.

Plates 3–7
Technique photos from the Lyric Opera of Chicago (courtesy of The Historical Scenic Collection, School of Theatre Arts, Northern Illinois University, DeKalb, Illinois, Alexander Adducci, curator).

Plate 8
Aging techniques, Linberg Gun Shop, "Grand Rapids 1890s," Buffalo Bill Banner painted by Mary Evers, Public Museum of Grand Rapids, Michigan.

Plate 9
Trompe l'oeil fresco, Museo Dell'Accademia, Florence, Italy.

Plate 10
Mural detail from the Cabot Theatre at the Broadway Theatre Center in Milwaukee, Wisconsin, designed by David Birn, painted at Cobalt Studios by David Zinn and Rachel Keebler.

Plate 11
Castle drop detail, Tobins Lake Studios in Brighton, Michigan, painted and designed by Susan Crabtree.

Plate 12
Giacomo Torelli, design for a "wooded scene" from *Venere Gellosa*, 1643; Act I Scenes 2–6. This design of the early Italian baroque shows the contrast beyween landscape and architecture keeping a symmetrical composition (see also Plate 13). Tobin Collection of the McNay Museum of Art.

Plate 13
Giacomo Torelli, design for "The Elysian Fields" from *Venere Gellosa*, 1643; Act II Scene 10–Act III Scene 4. A diagonal axis in this stage design is an innovation of later Italian baroque stage painting. Tobin Collection of the McNay Museum of Art.

Plate 14
Giuseppe Galli Bibiena, design for "Gallery of Mirrors." Tobin Collection of the McNay Museum of Art.

Plate 15
Auguste Alfred Rubé, design for a city rain scene from an unknown production. Light and shadow play a greater role in the romantic style of this nineteenth century French work. Tobin Collection of the McNay Museum of Art.

Plate 16
Illustration #1, Twin City Scenic Collection, sketch designed by John Z. Woods (courtesy of the Performing Arts Archives, University of Minnesota Libraries, St. Paul, Minnesota).

Plate 17
Illustration #2, Twin City Scenic Collection (courtesy of the Performing Arts Archives, University of Minnesota Libraries, St. Paul, Minnesota).

Plate 18
Illustration #3, Twin City Scenic Collection (courtesy of the Performing Arts Archives, University of Minnesota Libraries, St. Paul, Minnesota).

Plate 19
Illustration #4, Twin City Scenic Collection (courtesy of the Performing Arts Archives, University of Minnesota Libraries, St. Paul, Minnesota).

Plate 20
State Fair, midway backdrop daytime scene, designed by James Joy, painted at Cobalt Studios, 1992.

Plate 21
State Fair, midway backdrop nighttime scene showing translucency effect, designed by James Joy, painted at Cobalt Studios, 1992.

Plate 22
Mechanically painted reproduction of a translucent drop. The "Olio" stage backdrop ca. 1928, Savoy Theatre, Grand Rapids, Michigan. "The Furniture City" exhibit, Public Museum of Grand Rapids, Van Andel Museum Center. (The original backdrop was painted with dry pigments and animal glue on canvas; windows and light were cut out and backed with silk ribbon.)

Plate 23
Garden scene backdrop, Armbruster Scenic Studios, Columbus, Ohio. Courtesy of Dale Seeds, College of Wooster, Wooster, Ohio.

Plate 24
Bavarian village painted with aniline dye, Tobins Lake Studios, Brighton, Michigan, painted and designed by Susan Crabtree.

Plate 25
Turn-of-the-century interior painted with aniline dye, Tobins Lake Studios, Brighton, Michigan, painted by Susan Crabtree.

Plate 26
The King, University of Michigan Scenic Studio, Ann Arbor, Michigan, collage by Bill Abbott.

Plate 27
Pittsburgh skyline painted with aniline dye, designed by Anne Mundell, painted by Susan Crabtree, Kenmark Studios, Las Vegas, Nevada.

entire molding with fabric. The texture of hand-carved beadboard is very pebbly and appropriate for simulating the texture of rough or carved stone. This surface is very weak and needs to be sealed. If a smooth texture is sought, for simulating wood or plaster, the foam can be skinned with a texture compound or fabric. An explanation of texture compounds and fabric skin occurs later in this chapter.

Polystyrene foams are manufactured in solid, even-density sheets known by the trade name *Styrofoam*. Many scenic shops use this blue or pink sheet foam, sold as insulation in the construction industry, for deep profile lines on scenic units. Foams are easily built up and carved for bas relief. Because of the density of these foams, they can be sanded down to a smooth finish. Furthermore, these foams are so dense they are not as fragile as beadboard. They can be coated with a texture compound or sculpture coating.

Urethane foam is a two-part foam that sets up a crisp density that can be carved. It can be purchased in sheets and blocks. The two-part resins also may be purchased, mixed at will, and poured into your own molds. Either the premade blocks and sheets or the two-part resins of this foam are available in a range of densities from very firm to the soft foam that florists use as the foundation for arrangements. The two-part resins you mix yourself may be less evenly dense and show a honeycomb of large air bubbles due to inconsistencies in the mixing process. All of the urethane foams tend to be somewhat brittle and fragile. Once carved and sanded they will have to be skinned with either texture compound or fabric. Always use proper safety precautions and protection when carving Styrofoam, beadboard, or urethane foam, and when mixing two-part urethane foam (see Chapter Four, Safety and Health Regulations).

Vacuformed and Premolded Plastics

Vacuforming is the process of heating sheets of either *polystyrene* or *PVC* until they become malleable. The softened sheets are dropped over a positive mold made out of a dense heat-resistant material. These molds may be made out of particle board, thoroughly cured molding plaster, hydrocal cement, or any strong, heat-resistant material. The mold is prepared for vacuforming by drilling small diameter holes through all the areas of low relief. The mold sits on a sealed vacuum bed connected to a vacuum chamber. The vacuum action quickly pulls the softened plastic onto the mold. Once the plastic has cooled to its new form it can be lifted off the mold and the process can be repeated. In this way hundreds of copies can be made of an intricate architectural detail from a single mold. Commercial vacuform machines can handle objects approaching 4' x 8' large.

Polystyrene and PVC plastic used in vacuforming can be primed with a shellac-based finish. Alkyd-based primers should be avoided, as they may soak into the plastic and soften the impression (see Chapter Four, Safety and Health Regulations). Vacuform pieces have a matte finish and can be prime coated with water-based primers. Acrylic-based stain blockers are sold by house-paint suppliers. These primers have a high binder content and are very tough. They adhere very nicely to polystyrene or PVC vacuform. After vacuform pieces have been primed they can be painted with any water-based paint or medium. The plastic sheets used for vacuform may also be prepainted with acrylic-based paints. The advantage of prepainting the plastic sheets is that a wood grain, for instance, can be painted on a flat surface very easily. Once the plastic sheet has been molded, executing the wood grain technique becomes more problematic. Prepainting works best on forms that will have a low relief. If the prepainted plastic is stretched too far, gaps will appear in the paint treatment.

Premolded elements may be purchased from theatrical and architectural supply houses. Some elements are vacuformed and may be painted in the same manner already discussed. Molded elements from architectural supply houses are frequently cast with PVC, plaster, or urethanes. These element are marketed to be paintable, and in some cases they are cast out of polyresin material and tinted to a wood grain color that can be stained.

Flexible Foam

Ethafoam rod is a flexible foam rod used in building construction as a temporary expansion joint in concrete work. These long, round, flexible foam cords come in a variety of diameters from one-quarter inch to three inches. They are ideal for many three-dimensional applications in set construction.

Ethafoam has a slick flexible finish that resists almost all effort to paint it. P.V.A. and vinyl-based binders do not adhere to ethafoam: they easily can be peeled away when dry, as the ethafoam is handled or scraped. Shellac and alkyd primers will adhere to it, but they will crack when the ethafoam is compressed. The best choice is water-based contact cement, which adheres to the surface and flexes when the foam is handled or compressed. Once it is dry, the ethafoam can be painted with standard scene paint. Some theatrical paint manufacturers have developed a primer specially formulated to adhere to foams of all descriptions. These primers adhere well even to ethafoam and have the added benefit of being tintable. To be made even more durable, ethafoam can be skinned with cheesecloth or cotton scrim after priming.

Foam rubber, being very absorbent, first must be primed with something that will seal it. Often one coat of primer is not enough to provide a paintable surface; two coats of primer generally are necessary. Water-based paints of all descriptions will adhere to foam rubber, but if the foam is bent or dented after it has been painted, the surface may crack or the dent may remain evident. A flexible primer, like water-based contact cement or a theatrical paint manufacturer's durable primer coat, will work best for application on foam rubber. Several scenic manufacturers supply durable primers (see the Reading and Resources Chapter).

Sealing Plastic and Plastic Foams

Rigid foams can be painted with water-based paints. Vinyl, latex, and acrylic binders adhere best to these foams. However, paint alone will not strengthen the surface and smooth the finish. Primers are sold by theatrical paint manufacturers specifically for priming and sealing foams. Joint compound can be added to a water-based primer to give it more body, which will help smooth the finish of the foam. Joint compound works best when added to vinyl-, latex-, or acrylic-based paint. A prime coat with a lot of body may be made by mixing clear latex-, acrylic-, or water-based glue and joint compound. This will make the joint compound less brittle and more resilient. Water-based roof patching is another good viscous coating for foam. If the finish of the foam needs to be smoother than a heavy brush coat will accomplish, the foam can be coated with straight joint compound on top of a primer coat. After the joint compound has dried, it can be sanded to a very smooth finish and then another primer coat applied before painting. Water-based contact cement gives the foam a more resilient surface and serves as a good base for all water-based paints. Once the surface is covered with contact cement, it no longer can be sanded, nor will contact cement fill in and smooth the surface of the foam.

Fabric Skins, Sculpture Coatings, and Other Preparations

Fabric Skins

Fabric skins are applied to reinforce fragile surfaces and conceal porous or very distinctive textures. Almost all sculpted items are skinned after the carving process. This skinning can be with fabric and adhesive or just an adhesive. When covering sculpture, a looser-weave fabric must be used, so it will stretch on the bias and mold to the contours of the piece. Loose-weave fabrics are less apt to pull away from recesses of the form as they dry. Cheesecloth, gauze, and cotton scrim frequently are used for fabric skins. For small pieces, plaster or fiberglass bandages, purchased through medical suppliers, make an excellent skinning material. These must be soaked in water for a minute or two and then applied and smoothed over the form; they require no additional binder. Cheesecloth is one of the most commonly used and inexpensive skinning fabrics. It is sold by the yard or by the fifty-yard box at most fabric stores. Cotton scrim is a woven, gauzelike scrim and should not be confused with the more expensive sharkstooth scrim. This scrim is available from theatrical suppliers by the yard or bolt. Muslin produces a very durable coat, but it is not well suited for intricate detail, because it is relatively thick.

Rigid foams may be covered with other materials to give them a more durable and paintable finish. Materials can be adhered to the foam with thinned flexible glue, vinyl wallpaper paste, or clear polymer binders. A papier-mâché can be made using newspaper, cellotex insulation, or even paper towels. In some cases, a crinkled texture may be desired and paper towels or even toilet paper will do this nicely.

Smooth Sculpture Coatings

Some foam carvings are finished to a smooth surface by sanding. Foam details that are cut, such as hot-wired foam moldings, also have a very smooth surface. If these scenic elements are to be loaded in and used on stage in such a fashion that they will not receive much wear and tear, then simply coating these elements with a heavy primer coat, such as sculpture coating, flexible glue, or reinforced joint compound, may suffice.

Foam-Coating Materials

Commercial foam coatings are available through theatrical paint suppliers, either Foam Coat from Rosco, or Sculpt or Coat from Sculptural Arts Coatings in North Carolina (see the Reading and Resources chapter). These highly viscous coatings are formulated to fill in the pores of foam and dry to a smooth, paintable finish. Foam-coating products are formulated with water-based polymer binders. They can be applied straight or thinned as needed. Most water-based foam coatings can be tinted with paint or colorants. A homemade sculpt coat may be mixed with a drywall compound and a flexible polymer glue, which will give the coating a matte, opaque finish. Always try a small test sample before mixing large quantities of these coatings with other mediums, in case they are incompatible with each other.

Roof Patching

Latex-based roof patching and roof coatings are sold at lumber yards and home remodeling stores. Roof patching is more viscous than roof coating. These products can be tinted with colorants. Do not use asphaltium-based roof sealers as bases for texture. These tar-based products do not dry completely and will stain through any top coat as well as soften under the heat of stage light.

Two-Part Epoxy Resins

Two-part epoxy systems consist of a resin and hardener. Until mixed together, these elements will not dry or set up properly. When mixed together in the correct proportions, these resins do not air dry but rather cure through strong chemical reaction. Epoxy systems are used in adhesive, paints, and hard-shell coating processes.

Present-day two-part epoxy systems are much easier to use than their earlier counterparts. The resin and hardeners can be purchased in kits that range in volume from one pint to five gallons. Two-part resins must be carefully proportioned, and you cannot add universal tinting colors to the resin or it

will not harden properly. Some manufacturers of epoxy resins have tints available for their products. If a resin is too thin for the desired texture, most manufacturers sell fillers for mixing into their systems. Inert materials and fillers also can be mixed or coated with the resin, such as vermiculite, natural fiber fabrics, or chopped polyester fibers. Mix the resin and hardener thoroughly before adding the filler. If you are unsure whether a particular filler is compatible with the two-part system you are using, do a sample beforehand.

Once cured, epoxy finishes are very hard and durable. When reinforced with fiber, they stand up well to the most punishing moving and trucking schedules. These systems are excellent for coating scenic sculpture that otherwise might be damaged easily. Use proper safety precautions and protection when using these products (see Chapter Four, Safety and Health Regulations).

THE TOOLS AND MATERIALS OF TEXTURING

Creating a layer of texture on scenery is the work of the scenic artist. A texture coat transforms the construction materials underneath into a unified surface resembling stone, plaster, wood, or simply a unified mass. A texture coat may fully conceal the materials underneath or enhance and unify the natural texture of the surface at hand.

When a texture is part of an overall paint technique, it needs to be handled before the painting is done. The texturing should be executed separately from painting and allowed to dry before paint is applied. Occasionally, paint is applied directly to wet texture by spraying or spattering. The paint then mixes into the texture to some extent, which works particularly well with stone or rustic textures.

Texture Tools

Textures can be applied with all manner of tools. As in applying paint, tools can be either traditional or handmade. As in painting, each tool used to apply texture has its own signature of patterns it creates.

Wood

One of the simplest and most effective tools used to spread and create texture is one-inch stock board.

The board, cut to short lengths, can be used like a paddle for scooping and spreading a texture medium. The board can be used to stipple small peaks into the surface of the texture once the mix is spread. Boarding may be used over texture after it has been stippled or to spatter with, creating a stucco effect.

Knives

Drywall knives are useful for paddling out and spreading texture medium. These knifes are used to create a smoother fresco texture or a fan pattern stucco. Tiling adhesive knifes are made in various sizes and configurations of teeth, ranging up to one-quarter inch deep. These knives are used to create more elaborate patterns and textures.

Grainers

Graining tools are used to create texture grains in the same manner as with paint (see Chapter Ten). After the texture compound has been applied to the surface, a rough wood texture can be developed by graining it with graining combs or rubber grainers. The stiffer the texture compound is, the more pronounced the grain will be. Other types of rough wood textures may be developed by graining a texture compound with straw brooms, stiff brushes, or wads of newspaper. A technique called *roping* is traditionally done by dragging a loop of hemp rope through texture compound; a brush may be used for roping as well. The result of roping is a texture that looks like a heavy paint build-up such as you would see on surfaces that have been painted many times over.

Sponges

Sponges can be used to apply texture or pattern a textured surface. Like the paint techniques, texturing done with a natural sponge will have an organic feel. This texture works well for stone or rough concrete. Stippling the surface of a texture with square cellulose sponges creates a pattern that looks more humanmade and regular, like brick or block.

Rollers

Fleece rollers can be used to apply texture medium as well as to stipple the surface of texture. Some texture rollers are made not to apply the texture but to stipple the texture medium once it has been brushed or sprayed on the surface.

Sprayers

Some pneumatic spray guns (discussed in Chapter Five) are specifically for spraying textures. No spray gun should be used for the application of texture other than those made specifically for it. Caution must be taken in the choice of material put through the gun, as some substances described next cannot be used with a gun or they will ruin it.

Texture Mediums

Texture frequently is the key to creating a surface with a realistic appearance. If texture is involved in the overall paint treatment, it should be the first consideration of the scenic artist's process. The scenic artist must plan a texture thoroughly from a standpoint of function as well as the visual effect. Textured scenery still must be handled and installed in a theatre. A flown unit, for example, cannot exceed the weight limit of a batten, and often a large unit will rapidly increase in weight as texture is applied. The unit must still be gripped, and the weight of the texture cannot outstrip the strength of the structure. The texture must stay on the unit and pose no health threats to the stagehands or performers through dust or overly abrasive surfaces. Of course, the texture must take paint well and dry thoroughly in the amount of time available for the painting. For all these reasons and more, samples must always be done for texture.

A medium should be mixed with enough body to hold the texture pattern. Texture mediums are mixed from a spackle or drywall compound reinforced with water-based adhesive. Texture mediums should be applied to a clean, primed surface for a good bond between the medium and the surface. Texture mediums can be tinted to a hue that approaches the base-coat local color of the intended finish. Then, if the scenery is scraped in moving and trucking, the texture coat revealed will not be too different from the local color. Once the texture medium is dry, the surface can be painted, glazed, and given a finish.

Viscosity in texture mediums is very important. If the texture medium is stiff the resulting texture will be very pronounced. If the texture compound is thinned the texture will settle out and have a softer appearance.

Note that some compounds discussed here harden through evaporation, like paint, and others cure through chemical processes. It is critical with compounds that cure that no additive, other than those sold by the manufacturer, be added to a curing compound or it will not set up properly.

Line Thickener

Line thickener is a medium used to thicken polymer-based paints. A very small quantity of line thickener will thicken a full gallon of paint. Paint may be thickened to the consistency of paste. One drawback to using line thickener and paint for texture is that thickened paint is a very expensive texture medium. Paint thickened with line thickener loses a lot of its volume when it dries. However, texture done with line thickener is a very durable and can be mixed to the color desired.

Drywall Treatments

Drywall Compound

Drywall compound is available at paint supply stores, lumber yards, and home-supply stores. It is sold two ways: premixed and dry. Normally used in the construction industry, drywall compound is a very useful texturing medium for theatre and display work.

Premixed drywall compound is available in regular weight and lightweight. The lightweight mixture is made with air mixed in, so when mixed into paint it loses its volume. Drywall compound in dry or powdered form can be mixed with water or paint to the desired consistency. Regular-weight drywall compound should be used for texture mediums. All drywall compounds are water-based, porous, and sandable when dry. They are intended to be used on permanently installed surfaces and not formulated for surfaces that are frequently handled or that flex in any way. Drywall texture compounds must be reinforced with flexible adhesives or polymer binders or it will crack or chip off the surface. Flexible polymer glue, latex binder, and P.V.A. all work well in this respect.

If straight, undiluted drywall compound is applied too thickly, it will crack when it dries. For thick applications of drywall compound, additives can be mixed in. Drywall compound should never be mixed in with concrete, plaster, or any other compounds that cure.

Latex Spackle

Latex and vinyl spackle are used to patch drywall. They are premixed with binders to be durable. Because this spackle is polymer-based, it is more expensive than drywall compound. Because it has a very durable texture, latex spackle is useful for treatments on sets and displays that will have to undergo a fair amount of moving and trucking. Polymer-based spackles can be purchased at lumberyards and paint supply stores. They can be tinted to an appropriate base color with colorants or scenic paint.

Quick Textures

Quick textures, or Q.T. mixes, are available through contracting suppliers. These mixes are available in different grades of texture: fine, medium, and coarse. These textures produce a pebbly texture that covers most imperfections and seams. Quick textures are designed to be sprayed through a hopper gun. The spray tip of the gun can be adjusted to accommodate the grain of the Q.T. mix to be sprayed through it. Most commonly, Q.T. mix is sprayed on ceilings. The Q.T. mix comes in forty-pound bags and should be prepared according to the instructions on the bag.

Q.T. mix is not designed to endure much wear and tear. It may not hold up well through the rough handling that the scenery receives from trucking and load-in. A main component in Q.T. mix is polystyrene beads. When the surface covered with this texture is scraped, these granules break up and leave a white mar on the finish. The Q.T. mix can be tinted with colorants and the texture can be reinforced with flexible white glue, which will make it more durable and less likely to show the inevitable scrapes and scratches.

Plaster

Plaster of Paris is gypsum baked to reduce its natural water content. When remixed with water, it regains the lost water content and hardens to a solid mass. Plaster warms as the gypsum rehydrates. Plaster sets quickly, so there is no shrinkage. This makes plaster very useful for molding. After plaster has set, any extra water trapped in the plaster will evaporate slowly. While evaporating, the plaster will remain cool. Once all the extra moisture has evaporated the surface of the plaster will feel warm to the touch. The plaster now is completely cured.

Hydrocal cement is made of thoroughly burnt gypsum mixed into a compound with salts. It has a smooth texture that looks and handles like plaster but is much more durable. It will cure to a very hard mass that can be used for coating surfaces and building up layers on three-dimensional elements. Both hydrocal cement and plaster can be reinforced by mixing them with polyester fibers or by layering them with webbing or screen.

Neither plaster nor cement can be tinted with universal tinting colors or mixed with additional binder, as these interfere with the ability of the compounds to set up or cure. Dry tinting colors can be purchased from construction suppliers for use with plaster or hydrocal cement. Plaster can be carved, but the hydrocal cement is more rigid and can be used as surface treatment only.

Adhesives for Texture Mediums

Some adhesives can be used as textures themselves or added to other compounds for elasticity. Most texture compounds are not formulated to be used on anything other than stable, rigid surfaces. Scenery has a tendency to flex, because it is made of lighter materials and undergoes considerable handling after painting, which makes the addition of flexible adhesives necessary.

Polymer Glues and Theatrical Coatings

Some polymer adhesives are formulated to a thick pastelike consistency, such as Sculpt or Coat. These adhesives are useful as coatings for polystyrene foam, foam rubber, or texture coats that need to be protected. They may be used to reinforce drywall compound or Q.T. mix. The thickened adhesive itself can be used as a texture but is somewhat costly. Theatrical coatings can be tinted easily.

White polymer glue can be used to strengthen the bond and durability of texture compounds. Because the glue is liquid, be careful not to thin a texture compound too much before adding the glue itself, as the liquid glue also will thin the compound. When using glue to strengthen a texture medium, it is important to use only glues that remain flexible after they are dry. Glues that dry to a brittle finish result in a rigid texture, which actually could pop off

hard-covered scenic units or crack on soft-covered units when they are handled.

Contact Cement

A great variety of industrial adhesives are available through contracting suppliers and adhesive manufacturers. One adhesive commonly used in theatre and display is contact cement. The primary use of contact cement is to permanently bond together two surfaces. Both surfaces are coated with the cement and allowed to dry thoroughly before the surfaces are pressed together. Contact cement works well for bonding wood, plastics, foams, and plastic laminate. There are many varieties of contact cement. Some varieties work best for certain applications. If you have any questions about what type of contact cement to use for a given application, call the manufacturer for information about its line of adhesives.

A texture medium reinforced with water-based contact cement is useful for texture that must be particularly durable, such as texture for floorcloths and decks. It also is useful for texture applied to flexible surfaces like ground cloths and soft sculpture.

Contact cements may be either solvent- or water-based. Solvent-based cements are used primarily to bond materials, because solvent-based contact cement cannot be mixed into any sort of texture medium. Water-based contact cements can be mixed with almost any water-based compound, such as drywall compound. Not all water-based cements are compatible with other binders, such as acrylic or vinyl. If you are going to try to tint or mix the contact cement with any paint that has a binder, do a test first to make sure the mixture will not clot. Water-based contact cement can be tinted with colorants (see Chapter Four, Safety and Health Regulations).

Rubber Latex

Rubber latex dries to a flexible rubbery surface. Rubber latex is excellent for mixing with particulate mediums, such as clay or vermiculite. A texture medium made with rubber latex as the sole binder dries to a very soft, durable surface. Rubber latex-based textures are particularly useful where a texture may come in contact with human skin, for instance bare feet on a floorcloth. The rubber latex will hold up to dancing, stage combat, or similar activities. Many particulate additives soak up a fair amount of water from rubber latex, making the medium thick and difficult to spread. Thin it with water to keep the mixture pliable. Bear in mind that, if a rubber latex surface is folded face to face, it must be sealed with a thin coat of paint or flat sealer to prevent the folds from bonding. Note that, although most texture compounds can be sprayed through a hopper gun, absolutely no mixtures containing rubber latex or contact cement can be, as they will bind up the gun and ruin it (see Chapter Four, Safety and Health Regulations).

Tile Adhesive

Tile adhesives are sold through tile-supply stores and lumberyards, with a fair range in the type of tile adhesive available. Adhesives used for installing asphalt floor tiles set up to a malleable, tacky finish that works well for laminating surfaces. Asphalt tile adhesive should not be used to reinforce texture mediums, because it remains in a tacky and malleable state.

Adhesives designed to adhere ceramic tile to drywall dry to a tough, rigid finish. This adhesive works very well for texture that must stand up to a lot of wear and tear, such as the texture on stage decks and platforms. This texture is so rigid it cannot be used where performers will be in bare feet. The adhesive may be used by itself as a texture, added to drywall compound, or mixed with most any dry particulate. Water-based adhesives are easily thinned and tinted with universal tinting colorants to the desired color.

The adhesives used for adhering marble tiles to concrete or durarock sheets are silicate-based and have latex or acrylic binders premixed in them. These compounds are sold in dry form and should be mixed according the manufacturer's directions. Some marble tile adhesives are designed to be mixed with a separate liquid binder for even greater strength and durability. Some marble tile adhesives cure rather than simply dry. Any additives mixed into the compound such as colorants or extra binders may interfere with the curing.

Texturing Additives

Many texture compounds discussed have a pastelike texture. The substance or character of these compounds can be changed by adding dry materials or particulates. Depending on the material added, the texture can resemble brick, stone, mortar, tree bark, or other textures that a scenic artist may need to emulate. Remember that concrete, marble adhesives, plasters, and other materials that need to cure cannot be mixed with additives (Figure 7.6).

Clay

Dry clay can be purchased in bulk form through pottery suppliers. The dry clay can be added to other texture compounds, such as drywall compound or Q.T. mix. Because clay, when dry, has no

Figure 7.6
Textures: joint compound with trowel, cellulose insulation, joint compound and sand, joint compound and vermiculite, joint compound and cocoa mulch.

binders, these compounds must be strengthened with binder or adhesive. Clay may be mixed with water and binder for use as a texture compound on its own. An advantage of using clay is that it is earth and keeps its natural hue. Also, when a texture compound based on clay dries, it will develop cracks and cupped plates like clay earth does in nature (see Chapter Four, Safety and Health Regulations).

Sand

Sand is an additive that gives a variety of finishes depending on the variety of sand used. Sandbox sand easily is available and renders a coarse, pebbly texture. Coastal sand, which is available to some readers, is a finer sand. An even finer grade of sand is white silicate sand, sold at brick dealers and hardware stores. This sand is made to mix into brick mortar. Clean sand can be purchased from sandblasting suppliers. This sand is strained carefully according to its coarseness and is much more expensive than other kinds.

Straight sand can be used to simulate soil. Real soil will dry out in the theatre and may create a distracting and hazardous dust cloud. Sand is a reasonable alternative, because it is not as dusty as soil. Most readily available sand is either a yellowish-brown or off-white. Sand can be painted as needed with water-based paint. To paint small amounts of sand it can be spread out thinly on visquene and sprayed. It should be mixed and spread out to dry several times until it approaches the right hue. Small amounts of sand- also can be put in a gallon bucket and paint drilled into the sand to coat it. In either case, be careful to not overly moisten the sand so that it clumps together.

If a large amount of sand is to be painted, doing it by hand would be too tedious and strenuous. A rented mortar mixer will do the job. Small mortar mixers with a thirty-gallon barrel are easy enough for one person to move around and operate. The difference between a mortar mixer and a concrete mixer is that, even though both have barrels that rotate, the mortar mixer also has arms that rotate in the opposite direction to thoroughly mix the mortar. This tool works very well for coating sand with paint. After the sand has been blended with the paint in the mortar mixer for several minutes it can be poured out and spread over some visquene to dry. Use proper safety precautions and protection when working with silicates (see Chapter Four, Safety and Health Regulations).

Perlite

Perlite is a very lightweight white synthetic grain particle that can be mixed easily into many texture mediums. It is available in a variety of pellet sizes, from a grain about the size of coarse sand to a pellet the size of large-curd cottage cheese. Fine-grain perlite is sold through paint suppliers specifically for use as a texture additive. It is mixed directly into the paint. As light as it is, perlite will float to the top of thin paint mixtures so it must be stirred frequently. Perlite also is available through landscape suppliers, where it is used as a soil additive. It is available in large quantities, four square feet to the bag. Bulk perlite is categorized by the size of the pellets: 1 is a fine grain, 5 is the coarsest. A disadvantage to using perlite in a texture compound is that the white pellets leave a noticeable white mark when the scenery is scraped. For this reason, perlite works best for texture applications with naturally light colors, like stucco, rock, and mortar.

Vermiculite

Vermiculite is another useful texturing product available from landscaping suppliers, where it is used as a soil additive. The pellets of vermiculite are angular and light bronze to gray in color. Vermiculite is available in different size pellets from fine to coarse, like perlite. Vermiculite also is an excellent soil substitute for the theatre. The surface of the pellets are somewhat reflective, like the surface of mica, so for simulated soil the vermiculite may need to be sprayed with paint or a flat acrylic finish.

Vermiculite is an excellent texture compound. Its extremely light weight makes vermiculite ideally suited for extensive use in the theatre. The overall weight of even the largest scenic units will remain manageable when textured with vermiculite. Even when the scenery inevitably is scraped during load-in, the color of vermiculite will be far less pronounced.

Cocoa Mulch

Cocoa mulch is a landscaping product sold through landscape-supply houses and garden nurseries. It is packaged in bags of four square feet, like perlite and vermiculite. Cocoa mulch mixed with drywall compound renders a very distinctive, coarse organic texture that is excellent for simulating the appearance of tree bark and stone. The cocoa mulch bleeds stain unevenly through the drywall compound and any paint applied over it. So this compound must be used only for textures that will be enhanced by the brown dappled stain.

Paper and Fabric Textures

Papier-mâché is made by saturating paper with glue or any binder and then layering it onto a surface. Papier-mâché can be used as a texture itself or it can be used to strengthen a textured surface or sculpture. Most any paper can be used in papier-mâché. A paper used for this process should be rather absorbent, so that it completely soaks up the glue or binder. Newsprint is the standard choice for papier-mâché, being absorbent and abundant. White or brown commercial paper towel, available in quantity from janitorial services, makes an excellent paper texturing product. Brown paper towel is excellent for emulating tree bark and particularly that of palm trees. The color of the brown paper towel functions as a base coat for the paint treatment. White paper towel works equally well as a base for birch tree bark. Stucco texture can be made in a papier-mâché process by using toilet paper. Because toilet paper is so thin and fragile, the binder should be sprayed or brushed first on the surface, the dry toilet paper applied to that, then a final spray of binder applied.

Fabric

Erosion cloth, burlap, cotton scrim, cheesecloth, and nearly any fabric can be dipped in thin glue, vinyl wallpaper paste, or wheat paste, then applied or sculpted to some degree directly on scenery. Once dry, it can be painted as needed. The same process used for paper can be used with fabric to create texture. Highly absorbent fabrics are the easiest to handle. Fabrics like cheesecloth, felt, and gauze should be cut into easily manipulated pieces and treated like the paper just described. Textures like bark, shingles, and even bas-relief architectural details can be done this way.

Sculpture can be reinforced with fabric. Cheesecloth is a very common supply in the scenic shop for this sort of work. The weave of cheesecloth is very loose, so it can be applied smoothly around complex curves and worked around contours. Theatrical cotton scrim has a weave tighter than cheesecloth but still loose enough so that it can be used in much the same applications.

Binders

Wheat paste has been the traditional binder for papier-mâché. Note that you should never use glue in combination with shellac-based mediums. This combination may cause the papier-mâché to peel away from the surface. Shellac-based mediums applied over a wheat paste finish is an age-old recipe for a crackle or peeled paint finish.

For the most part, wheat paste has been replaced by contemporary vinyl paste products. Other binders for papier-mâché and fabric can be made with joint compound reinforced with glue. Thinned water-based glue may be used as well.

Cellulose

A papier-mâché paste made from pulped paper can be used as a texture or skinning product. Some art supply stores sell pulped papier-mâché that has a binder mixed into it; just add water. This product is not packaged in the volumes often needed for theatrical applications. A good substitute is cellulose insulation. It usually is available from lumberyards or a construction materials supplier in bags of three square feet. When working with cellulose, be very careful to contain it well and always wear a respirator with dust cartridges while handling it.

Cellulose can be used as a papier-mâché by mixing it with wheat paste or vinyl binders. Paint also can serve as the binder with cellulose, so that when the texture is applied it is the desired color. The binder in the paint will be sufficient to hold cellulose to most surfaces. Before using a texture compound mixed with cellulose, let it sit for about thirty minutes. Cellulose will soak up a fair amount of water from the binder, and it may need to be further thinned out.

Texture Stencils

Textures can be applied through stencils to create specific, repeating patterns like bricks and cinder blocks. The stencil itself must be cut out of a flexible, durable material. Polysytrene, the same material used in vacuforming, is an excellent choice for the heavy-duty demands of a texture stencil. Polystyrene is sold in 4' × 8' sheets through wholesale plastics suppliers. Polystyrene is made in a wide range of thicknesses, from a few millimeters to one-half inch thick. Select a thickness based on the depth of the impression needed. Polyethylene is available in the same sizes and is equally flexible and washable.

Prepare a texture stencil in the same manner as paint stencils described in Chapter Five. A texture stencil should be cut to register right up to the edge of the last repeat. The reason for this is that most heavy textures take somewhere around twenty-four hours to dry, so it would be inconvenient to have to wait that long to do the adjacent repeats. The stencil should be hosed off and scrubbed well at the end of the day. Any texture allowed to dry on the stencil will be very difficult to clean off.

A texture compound for bricks can be made with drywall compound reinforced with glue. Sand, perlite, or vermiculite can be added to give the compound body and texture. The compound can be sprayed on with a hopper gun or dropped directly onto the stencil then smoothed out so it is more or less even with top of the stencil. The compound can be smoothed with the edge of a board, a trowel, a drywall knife, a silkscreen squeegee, or a tar squeegee.

The texture stenciling process for large surface areas must be planned to maximize time and effort. Normally, stencils are made in a size that can be handled by one person. When faced with hundreds of square feet of surface area, however, the stencil should be cut out of a full 4' × 8' sheet of polystyrene or polyethylene. Two people are needed to work with this large a stencil. The ratio of texture compound to surface area may be as much as five gallons for every one hundred square feet covered, based on a coverage depth of one-quarter inch. This ratio could result in hundreds of gallons of compound being mixed for a reasonably large production. A mortar mixer should be used to mix large volumes of texture compound, which can be stored in plastic garbage cans for convenience.

CONCLUSION

It is important for a scenic artist to understand the preparation of materials as thoroughly as possible. Sound preparation is essential for the painting that will follow. The paint's adhesion, flexibility, durability, and the strength of its surface are crucial for the scenery to survive handling in the shop and on stage. The natural quality of a material, such as the transparency of scrim, can be ruined by poor or uninformed preparation.

A myriad of new products are available to theatre artists for making scenery and props. Many of these products are synthetic or extensively processed natural materials. Some may contain dyes or binders that could react with common theatrical paint products. When using a new product or material, take the time to investigate how best to approach preparing the surface of that material for paint while preserving its desirable qualities. If you and your colleagues are stumped, call the manufacturer of the material in question or a paint manufacturer for advice. Keep in mind actors will be using your product (the scenery), and their safety and comfort is a serious consideration. Exercise caution and use common sense when handling unfamiliar products.

Part Three
The Techniques of Scenic Painting

Forest Drop, Monument Valley Drop. Drops are property of Kenmark Studios, Inc., Las Vegas, Nevada (painted at the Power Center Scene Shop, University of Michigan, Ann Arbor).

chapter 8

Cartooning, Layout, and Lettering

INTRODUCTION

Drawing the cartoon is the next step in scenic painting after priming. A *cartoon* is the line drawing of an image representing the visible edges or intersecting planes of objects, sometimes known as a *contour drawing*. The cartoon seves as a guide for placement of shade, shadow, and color. Cartooning precedes painting, in most cases, and gives the scenic artist a reference for painting on the surface of scenery. Cartooning is done after the scenery is stretched and primed and may be drawn freehand or mechanically drafted. Cartoons may be drawn onto paper and then transferred to the scenery in a process called *pouncing*.

An accurate cartoon is an essential guide to accurate painting. A poor cartoon usually cannot be corrected by subsequent painting because of the physical size of the scenery. The scenic artist paints at arm's length from the scenery, and it is awkward to step back to check the painting continually. The scenic artist should be able to paint with confidence in an accurate cartoon. If good preparation of the scenery is the first step toward high quality, then cartooning is the next, equally important step. Even a relatively simple painting, such as a gradient blend or wash of color, can need a guide. Reference points are placed where color values shift and guidelines are drawn to establish the direction of washes.

To paint well you must learn to draw well. Cartooning is not something to be rushed through so the "real work" of painting can begin. Cartooning is the first point at which the scenic artist begins to interpret the scenic designer's intent onto the scenery. The cartoon forms the foundation for all work to follow. There are many instances in scenic art when the cartooning process takes as much time and effort as painting. For example, a scenic element might depict a complex line drawing of an Italian Renaissance street scene that is painted with thin color washes. In this case the cartooning may constitute the majority of the work. Effort made to do an accurate cartoon results in a better looking product and more professional looking scenery.

Cartooning is best after the scenery has been properly primed because that priming (discussed in Chapter Seven) not only prepares the unit for painting but also prepares it for smooth cartooning. Drops should never be cartooned before they are stretched and primed or lines will warp and distort as the fabric shrinks. Hard scenery could be cartooned before a primer coat, but the primer would obscure a cartoon. Unprimed scenery is difficult to cartoon due to uneven and inconsistent texture, so with hard scenery as well as soft, the cartooning is done immediately after the prime coat.

THE TOOLS OF CARTOONING

The tools for cartooning fall into three categories: measuring, drawing, and transferring. These tools, like the tools of painting, are somewhat specialized for scenic art, mural, and display painting, but they are different from the painting tools. A scenic artist usually keeps cartooning tools in a cabinet or storage locker separate from the painting tools. In some shops where it is convenient to do so, the cartooning tools are kept on a cart that can be rolled to the project being cartooned at the time so they are always together and accessible (Figure 8.1).

Measuring Tools

Scale Rule

Scenic designers work in scale, that is, proportionally reduced, so their work can be done on a drafting table. One job of a scenic artist is to "read" this scale drawing and recreate that image in full scale, or its actual dimensions.

The *scale ruler* is the measuring device used to transfer measurements from the drafted scale of a paint elevation to full scale. A scale ruler may be in either feet and inches or in metric scale, depending on the country where you or the designer work. Theatres in the United States still use feet and inches, although most of the rest of the world, including Canada and Mexico, use the metric scale. A scale ruler generally has two scales on each edge of the ruler that are compatible, such as one-inch and one-half-inch scale or three-quarter-inch and three-eighth-inch scale. A scale rule may have two or three sides with two scales noted on each edge and up to eight or twelve different scales on it. Although many different scales are used in theatrical scenic design, the two most common scales used by scenic designers for paint elevations are one-half inch to one foot and one inch to one foot. Half-inch scale is roughly equal to 1:25 metric scale. Other scales may be used to delineate detail drawing, simpler forms, large formats, or by preference of the scenic designer or technical director.

Paint elevations often need to be adapted to a new shape or size. A drop may get built shorter and wider than designed. A scenic designer might solve size alterations by telling the scenic artist to move the height of a skyline to eight feet instead of eleven feet and ask for some clouds to fill in on either side, where three feet of additional muslin is exposed. Sometimes, the proportions of the scenery do not change but the actual size is different. Imagine a drop

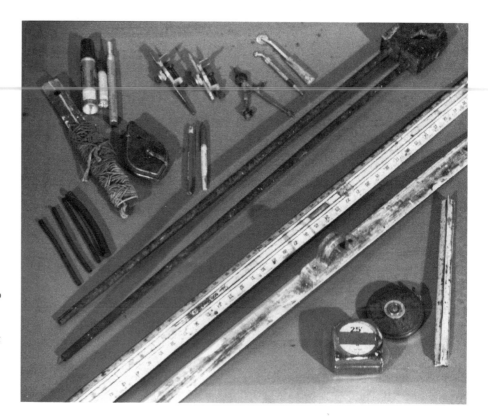

Figure 8.1
Common cartooning tools: top left, vine charcoal, snap lines, ink markers, trammel points, compass, and pounce wheels; center, large compass, ruler with levels, and lining stick; bottom right, tape measures and scale ruler.

becomes 10 percent larger. What the scenic artist needs is a scale to fit the new dimensions. A simple solution is to take a scale ruler to a copy machine, enlarge the scale 10 percent and print it out. That copy of the scale can be used to read the measurements throughout the elevation, and the elevation will stay in proportion. Another solution would be to make an enlarged or reduced copy of the elevation that corresponds to a specific scale.

> Never assume you know the scale of an elevation. If the scale is not noted on the elevation, check it before you begin. Often you can verify the scale by measuring the scenery and the elevation to see which scale fits. It is disastrous to have assumed the scale when ordering materials and supplies then come up short when it is time for work to commence.

Tape Measures

Flexible *tape measures* are commonly used measuring tools for a scenic artist. A paint shop needs twenty-five-, fifty-, and one-hundred-foot tape measures. Smaller tape measures work well for small projects but are exasperatingly useless for most needs. Most paint shops need several twenty-five-foot, two fifty-foot, and one or two one-hundred foot tape measures. The longer tape measures are needed for large backdrop cartooning. Equip yourself with a good-quality tape measure, because it needs to hold up for a while. A good tape measure should have a replaceable tape or blade. Be certain to get twenty-five foot tape measures with one-inch-wide blades as any narrower blade is too flexible for the kind of work a scenic artist does (Figure 8.1).

Rulers and Squares

Rulers come in several varieties and lengths, from the common wooden *yardstick* to six-foot-long *steel rulers*. Rulers can be used in place of a tape measure for measuring long lengths but are less accurate. Over the course of long measurements, in addition to wasting time, small errors add up; these are made each time the ruler is picked up and laid down. A tape measure is more accurate and far more efficient with long lengths, especially when working on the floor.

When cartooning on a paint frame, however, tape measures are not as useful as yardsticks. A four-foot-long plastic ruler with vertical and horizontals levels is very useful when working on a paint frame and easier to handle. You can establish true vertical and true horizontal any place on a drop by using the levels in the ruler. You can avoid having to take two sets of measurements, over from center and up from the bottom, to find a single point. Care should be taken when using the shorter rulers to not distort a long measurement while moving the ruler end to end.

Steel rulers come in a variety of lengths from one to six feet. The shop should have a complement of various-size steel rulers for small cartooning and layout tasks. Steel framing squares also are used for cartooning. Steel-edged rulers have other uses, particularly as a guide for cutting cardboard stock. Flexible steel and plastic rulers, available from sign-painting supply stores, are useful for patterning, because they bend evenly. They are used as a guide for drawing curves, called *splining*, on smaller cartooning and layout projects.

Drawing Tools for Cartooning
Vine Charcoal

Medium-density *vine charcoal* is the standard cartooning medium for scenic painting. The advantage to using vine charcoal is that when it is flogged or blown off the surface of the scenery or paper it comes away fairly cleanly. Vine charcoal is made from fired sticks of soft wood. Real vine charcoal is made from lengths of fired grape vine. Real vine charcoal is not as consistent in density as charcoal made from soft woods. Avoid using compressed charcoal, which is made from finely ground charcoal formed into sticks. Compressed charcoal is sooty and will not come off the surface cleanly. A light oil is added to compressed charcoal to help bind it, which explains why it does not erase.

Vine charcoal is sold by some theatrical suppliers and art supply stores. It is usually available in small, medium, and large, sometimes called *jumbo*, sticks. Most scenic shops stock at least two if not all three sizes of charcoal. The size of charcoal most commonly used in the shop may depend on the scale of the work the shop most often does. The size of charcoal may be a personal choice: one artist may prefer to work with medium and another with jumbo. Because of differing applications, it is sold in soft, medium, and hard densities. For application in scenic art, medium density charcoal works the best. The hard density charcoal etches the surface and will not clean off well, and the soft charcoal wears down too fast and smudges easily.

Chalk

Some materials cannot be cartooned with vine charcoal. Black charcoal lines can get lost on a dark-colored surface, such as velour. Even a faint charcoal line might be distracting if used to cartoon clouds in a translucent sky drop. *White blackboard chalk* is an excellent cartooning medium for these applications. In other situations, the cartoon is best rendered in a contrasting, or less distracting, color. Multicolored chalk is useful for those applications.

Charcoal Holders

In cartooning, just as with brushwork, extensions (described in Chapter Five) are used when working on the floor. Charcoal and chalk can be used with extensions, but they break off easily in a bamboo extension, so the solution is a chalk holder. Charcoal and pencil holders can be bought or ordered at art supply stores. These are made from brass or nickel-plated steel and have two prongs to hold the charcoal with a ring that slides over the prongs to grip the charcoal. Charcoal holders are used by artists to hold charcoal or pencils down to the nub while providing a handle for leverage. In scenic art, they are used in the same way. By inserting the holder into a bamboo or attaching one to the end of a wooden dowel, they make using charcoal very convenient.

Floggers and Air Nozzles

A *flogger* is used to clean charcoal lines off scenery. A flogger is a simple tool made of a short handle, between two and three feet long, with strips of fabric, either muslin or canvas, about eighteen inches long, secured to one end. It resembles a short-handled mop. Floggers are used not just to clean off charcoal but to clean off dust, footprints, and assorted grime that would otherwise mar the finish of the paint. Flogging means to beat or whip, and that is how you use it: you beat the charcoal or dirt off the scenery. It is best to start flogging from one end of the scenery and work in a single direction, so that you are not just spreading the dirt and charcoal dust around. Floggers cover a fairly large area in one swipe, so if you want to clean up only a little of the drawing and not annihilate it, a dry flannel rag works well for carefully wiping away specific lines.

Compressed air is great for blowing charcoal thoroughly off a drop. Some air nozzles are equipped with a cut-off tube used to roughly aim the pressurized air, but with these you may end up blowing away more charcoal than you intended. Automotive paint stores carry pinpoint air nozzles with cone-shaped tips. These nozzles, manufactured to blow dirt out of crevices and small opening in car parts, work beautifully to selectively blow away charcoal lines. When using air nozzles you can control the strength of the air flow more or less by feel, so you can carefully delete a line or blast away everything in your path. Most paint studios will stock both floggers and air nozzles for cleaning off charcoal and dusting off scenery.

Ink Markers

After the cartoon is drawn in charcoal, it needs to be set. The term *set* means to clean up the cartoon so the correct lines can be distinguished from the mistakes. It also means to make the lines permanent or to trace over them in a permanent medium. Charcoal lines that have not been set may mix into the paint or be inadvertently wiped off. If the lines of a cartoon are set in ink and the charcoal is flogged or blown off the surface, then the cartoon will be crisper for the painting that follows. Also, charcoal lines by themselves may disappear under layers of paint. A cartoon set in ink usually will be retrievable under several layers of paint. *Felt-tip ink markers* are perfect for inking and widely available. As ink markers are made with a variety of inks, the best markers for scenic art use a solvent-based ink. The solvent usually is naphtha or alcohol, easily identified by a chemical-solvent smell. Most art markers are solvent based. The advantage in using a solvent-based ink marker is that lines drawn with it will lightly "ghost up," that is, reappear faintly, through layers of paint, even after application of an opaque color. Any line set with a water-based marker will mix into paint applied over it.

All the lines of the cartoon should be traced over with ink markers. Line work around organic shapes that do not have a solid contour, such as clouds and clumps of foliage, needs to be traced with a dashed line. Dashes are used so the ink does not reappear through the paint as a solid line to distract from the brushwork or spray work that defines the leaves. The contour of the leaves then can be rendered more realistically with paint. Other types of foliage, such as palm and fern leaves, should not be cartooned in solid outlines either. These leaves can be drawn in the cartoon with a single line defining the spine of the frond or leaf. The shape of the leaf can be filled out later with brushstrokes when the base colors are painted.

After several applications of water-based paint, even an inked cartoon may become invisible. To retrieve a cartoon, spray the surface lightly with denatured alcohol where you expect the lines of the cartoon to be. Always wear a respirator when doing this. After a few minutes the lines will soak up through the paint in those areas treated with alcohol. Many different solvents will bring the lines to the surface; however, denatured alcohol is preferable because it is one of the least toxic solvents. Nor does denatured alcohol melt or change the surface of water-based paint or leave behind a residue as it evaporates.

A cartoon set in solvent-based ink will reappear, whether you want it to or not, with any solvent-based paint treatment over it. Water-based markers can be used under solvent-based paint if you do not want the cartoon to be seen. However, water-based inks dissolve in the first application of water-based paint and the lines will disappear as you paint. Water-based ink lines are not retrievable, like the solvent-based are ones, after they have been painted over with opaque mediums.

Most shops keep a good supply of black markers specifically for cartooning. Different color markers can be used to set cartoons, too, just like different colored chalk. A black marker ghosting through a transparent or very light paint application could be distracting, depending on how close the audience is to the scenery, so a colored marker might be preferred. Various colors of markers are used for some kinds of detail painting, such as making the seam lines in a plank floor or for graphic line drawing. Art markers are available in a wide range of colors, including earth tones, warm and cools grays, and subtle tints and shades to meet most needs.

Markers also come with a variety in tip size, marker function, and the marker size itself, depending on the brand. Standard chisel-tipped felt markers are fairly common and frequently stocked in scenic paint shops. Felt-tip markers have a case filled with felt that is saturated with ink. The tip is an extension of that filling. When the tip of the marker is worn down to the metal collar, the marker must be discarded whether it still has ink in it or not. Other ink markers are made to be recharged. Rechargeable markers have a case filled with liquid ink. The marker has a cone- or chisel-shaped tip that can be replaced when it has worn down. In the metal collar of the marker is a valve to control the ink flow to the tip. Jumbo-size ink markers have a large chisel tip, about three-quarter inch square. Jumbo markers currently are available only in bright colors and black. These markers come in handy for the occasional odd job where the line work must be exceptionally wide or pronounced, but they generally are not used for cartooning. Permanent laundry markers have a finer, cone-shaped tip, useful for any fine-line cartoons and scenic applications. They may also be used for writing notes on the clear protective covers of scenic elevations. It is useful to keep a few of these in stock in the shop.

Dye

Most cartoons need to ghost through the paint to some degree to be useful. *Aniline dye* was the standard medium used to achieve this ghosting before ink markers became available. Once the cartoon was drawn in vine charcoal, it was set with aniline dye, painted on with a small lining brush. For each job, the aniline dye was mixed to an appropriate color, depending on the local color of the final image. Today, aniline dye still is very useful for some cartooning, particularly in situations where a color other than black is desired to set the lines. Aniline dye can be thinned down to make a much fainter line, something you cannot do with a marker. Drops entirely painted in dye should have the cartoon set in an appropriate color of dye, as the solvent-based ink cartooning would show completely through a dye drop. A cartoon can be set with dye in the same manner as with markers. Do not use crystal black aniline dye to set a cartoon, because it is very soluble in water and will mix into subsequent layers of paint.

Graphite

Most theatrical painting is done knowing that the audience will see it only from a distance and that the scenery is not intended to last forever. Most scenery is not needed beyond the run of a given production. If made to last any longer, it rarely is expected to be used for too many years. Ten years is a fairly long life for a piece of scenery; and even at that, it will need to be touched up and refreshed from time to time. But a scenic artist also might work in areas of the arts where longevity is an important consideration. Many techniques and materials in scenic art cross over to other areas of the visual arts, but setting a cartoon in ink or dye does not. Neither of these is suitable for long-term display, exhibition, or mural work. Dye will quickly discolor subsequent layers of paint. Ink, even if completely obscured by layers of paint, will slowly and inevitably ghost up through the top layer of paint. For these reasons, all cartooning for murals or exhibits that are to be permanently installed should be executed or set with *graphite*. The cartoon may be worked out in charcoal first and the lines can be set with graphite, just as they are set with ink or dye in other circumstances. A graphite block or soft pencil, 4B or even softer, can be used depending on the size of the line desired.

> It is possible to seal dye or ink cartooning from showing through by covering the cartoon with a coat of shellac or oil-based sealer in situations where an unwanted cartoon could ghost through after a long period of time. This method also is useful for covering a cartooning mistake on hard scenery. This should never be done on soft goods of any kind.

Fixative

The issue of the cartoon ghosting through paint is irrelevant when a transparent, or nearly transparent, medium is to be used to paint a piece. It would be a waste of time to set a cartoon in ink when charcoal would be perfectly visible throughout the medium. It is necessary only to fix the charcoal lines so that they do not smudge. In these cases, the charcoal is set with a *fixative*. Smaller pieces may be sprayed simply with workable fixative purchased at an art supply store. Always wear a respirator when doing this (see Chapter Four, Safety and Health Regulations). As the name implies, this product will fix the charcoal to the surface and dry in a finish that does not alter the workable surface of the piece.

Large cartoons drawn on scenery that has been primed with paint may be set by spraying the cartoon with a very thin solution of either the primer, the base color, or clear flat acrylic sealer. Cartoons drawn on drops primed with either starch or animal glue can be set by simply spraying them with hot water. The hot water melts starch or glue primer, which is absorbed by the charcoal lines. When the drop is dry the line will be permanently set in the primer. If the drop is to be painted with aniline dye the first few sprays of local color will accomplish the same thing. If the cartoon has been set into the primer with water or dye, the line may still be inadvertently scrubbed off if over worked with wet brush techniques.

> Before setting the charcoal lines, either with ink or fixative, always check the cartoon carefully to make sure the lines are correct. Inking over the lines to set them also is a way to check each line individually for accuracy. Mistakes are easy to miss when the whole cartoon is sprayed over. When fixing the lines with hot water or a fixative, clean up the charcoal lines so that the correct lines are very clear and any incorrect lines are flogged or blown off as cleanly as possible.

Mechanical Drawing Tools for the Scenic Artist

Snap Lines

When cartooning a large area, the first lines that need to be drawn are the base, or reference, lines. A *snap line* is used to make these long straight lines from point to point. A snap line is a length of string coated with powdered charcoal, chalk, or pounce powder. It is held firmly at the two points at either end of the line to be drawn and pulled taut. When the line is released, it snaps back into place leaving a perfectly straight line.

Snap lines simply may be a piece of cotton string coated along its length with a stick of charcoal or chalk to "chalk" it. The string is stored wrapped around a stick when not in use to keep it from getting tangled. Commercial snap lines spool the line up into a case filled with powder. These are far more convenient to use, because they recharge the chalk line every time they are wound or unwound. Doubled-geared snap lines that reel in twice as fast are very handy. The lines in commercial snap lines can be replaced if they get frayed or knotted, or if the color of chalk needs to be changed.

Snap lines commonly are called *chalk lines,* because carpenters load them with various colors of powdered chalk. Carpenter's chalk is not used in scenic painting because it leaves a permanent mark. Often snap lines are used for laying out the cartoon on a drop; these are guidelines that will need to be cleaned off later. So the snap lines in a paint shop are filled with either pounce powder or powdered charcoal. Talcum powder works well for snapping lines on dark surfaces. Pounce powder can be purchased from sign-painting supply stores or ordered through sign-painting supply catalogues. Available in black or white, they are very economical and clean off surfaces easily. Powdered charcoal was the standard filler for snap lines until the advent of pounce powder. The main drawback to powdered charcoal is its expense. Store pounce powder or powdered charcoal in a plastic squeeze bottle for refilling the snap line case.

It may not be possible for one person to hold each end of the snap line when laying in vertical lines while working on a frame. Tie the head of a safety pin to the end of the snap line so the pin can be inserted at top of the drop, then raise the drop or lower the bridge to snap the line from the bottom. The snap line case doubles as a plumb bob so it will be necessary to measure the verticals only at the top of the drop. Gravity will accurately extend the line to the bottom. One person, using several snap lines, can set several verticals each time the drop or bridge is raised and lowered. Safety pins in the end of a snap line make it possible for one person to snap lines alone while working on a deck.

> One drawback to commercial snap lines is that they generate a lot of unwanted powder as they unreel. The powder can make a mess of a drop stapled to a deck. Snap lines should be unreeled away from the edge of the drop and carried to where they are needed.

A *snap bow* is made for one person to snap lines alone. It is a length of lumber, square aluminum, or conduit with a large corner block at each end. The snap line is stretched between them. The snap bow can be as lengthy as can be handled comfortably. Because they are easy to make, a snap bow can be assembled for a specific project. The line of the snap bow can be chalked by rubbing it with charcoal or chalk (Figure 8.2).

Lining Sticks and Straight Edges

Lining sticks are guides for drawing or painting straight lines. Lining sticks can be short or very long, used in painting up or down. They are made of wood, beveled on the bottom edges. This bevel keeps the edge of the lining stick from touching the surface of the scenery. This way, paint will not draw under the lining stick and blemish the surface. Lining sticks for use on a vertical surface should be made out of lightweight materials; oak trim molding works very well because some profiles already have a bevel and these trims tend not to be warped as often as one-inch stock lumber. Finding straight lumber for lining sticks out of one-inch stock can be a challenge. Buying a better grade of lumber for building lining sticks will help.

The shop should be equipped with lining sticks for use on the deck and the frame. A lining stick for use on the frame or vertical surfaces can be a maximum of six feet long; if it were longer, it would be beyond the painter's reach. Shorter lining sticks are useful to have on hand for tighter work. The handle, placed in the center for balance, is just a block of wood or a drawer handle placed away from the edge

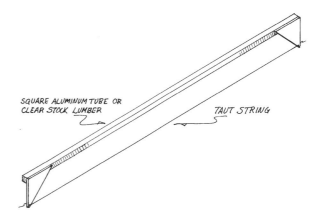

SQUARE ALUMINUM TUBE OR CLEAR STOCK LUMBER

TAUT STRING

Figure 8.2 A snap bow.

so as not to be in the way. Often lining sticks can be made for specific projects as needed (Figure 8.3).

Lining sticks used on the deck or horizontal surfaces must have handles that extend up to the standing painter's grasp. The base of the handle needs to be reinforced with angle braces where it is attached to the line stick. Some scenic artists prefer the handle to be bolted to a joint in the base, so it can fold up for easy transport. These extended lining sticks should be able to stand up on their own because they are a real nuisance if they are forever falling over. Lining sticks for floor use can be quite long, because the painter need not hold the handle while drawing the tool along the edge. Most shops have lining sticks in a variety of lengths, from six feet for tight work up to sixteen feet. Eight- to ten-foot-long lining sticks are very useful, and many shops have a fair amount of these.

Splines

Splines are guides for drawing or painting curved lines. A spline is a piece of flexible thin wood or plastic bent to meet points of a curve. Splines bend smoothly and conform to almost any shape. With a few points plotted, and the help of two people, long irregular curves can be drawn quite easily. The spline also may be used as a guide for inking or painting a circle that has been drafted with a compass.

A shop usually will have splines of various lengths and flexibility. A ten- to twenty-foot-long spline is handy to have around. Good wood splines must be free of knots to bend evenly. Once found or made, these splines should be stored carefully, like any good tool. Shorter, more flexible splines can be made from one-eighth-inch-thick Masonite or Upson board. Metal rulers and curves for very tight work, sold at sign-painting, drafting, and art supply stores, come in very handy as well. Other materials work well for splining. Long sections of plastic molding and rubber hose may all be used to draw curves. On the paint frame lines that curve downward, such as the curve of a window valance, can be drawn by using a chain or a rope secured at either end of the curve with safety pins. A long, small-link chain works very well because it hangs in a smooth curve; rope often tends to have kinks in it.

It may take some practice to learn how to hold a spline so the curve it describes is natural looking. By holding the spline only at the ends and adjusting the pressure, the spline will shift into a curve that will intersect the points that have been drafted for the curve. When several points have been drafted to delineate a curve, some of them will be slightly off. Adjust the spline so that it hits as many of these points as possible. Forcing the spline to hit every point will warp the curved line.

Compass

A scenic artist needs a drafting compass for drawing and geometric analysis of an elevation. For actually

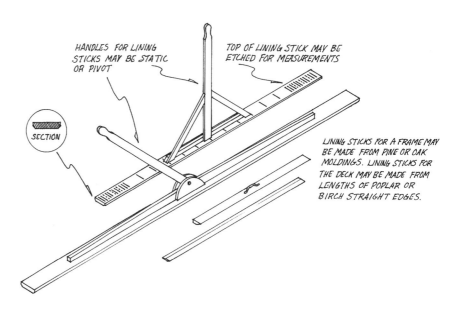

Figure 8.3
Lining sticks for the floor and the frame.

HANDLES FOR LINING STICKS MAY BE STATIC OR PIVOT

TOP OF LINING STICK MAY BE ETCHED FOR MEASUREMENTS

SECTION

LINING STICKS FOR A FRAME MAY BE MADE FROM PINE OR OAK MOLDINGS. LINING STICKS FOR THE DECK MAY BE MADE FROM LENGTHS OF POPLAR OR BIRCH STRAIGHT EDGES.

cartooning circles or arcs on scenery, the painter will need an *oversized compass*. Some sign-painting and art supply stores may carry oversized wooden compasses made for blackboards. These are useful but usually too small for scenic painting. A homemade wooden compass is a good solution. A compass can be made easily with two pieces of 1" × 2" stock lumber and a wing bolt. Leave a round profile at the top of the lumber, so there is enough surface area for tightening the wing bolt. The compass can be as tall as is comfortable to work with; two to three feet tall is a useful height. One leg of the compass should end in a nail, the other leg should be cut off one foot shorter and have a short length of narrow bamboo inserted into a hole drilled in the end. The end of the bamboo will be split and have a rubber band grip for charcoal, a pencil, a brush, or a laundry marker for different applications. Alternatively, the end of a scenic lining brush can be inserted into the hole of the short leg of the compass.

String

To draft any size circle, all you need is a string, a nail, and something to mark with. Pound the nail into the compass point of a circle, and pull a string taut to the length of the radius. Tie a slip knot in the string to mark the radius in case the line slips. You also may tighten the slip knot over your marking tool and extension so you can stand while drafting the circle. The problem with using string is that it tends to stretch as it is pulled, so as the circle is completed, the lines might not meet up. If your circle is twenty feet in diameter and you have a discrepancy of two inches in the length of the radius, this may not be enough to be perceived on stage once the lines where the difference has occurred have been smoothed over. Some cords and string stretch more than others. Nylon stretches less than cotton string or cord.

String is used as a guide for plotting points when working with linear perspective. By putting a nail in the center of a geometric form or on the vanishing point of a perspective cartoon, the string can be used as a guide for extending a line from one point through another.

Walking a line is a technique of cartooning a straight line using a string. Walking a line is not a very efficient way to draw a straight line, but it can be useful in some situations or when working alone. To walk a line, attach one end of a clean line at the endpoint with a nail or hook it with a safety pin, and pull the other end of the line past the far point. Holding the line behind you, line it up on the point and pull it tight. Put your foot on the line to hold it in place. Begin marking the line lightly, being careful not to move it. Work on the same side of the string so the marked line does not jump side to side. Slowly walk forward as if on a tightrope, being careful not to disturb the position of the line and keeping it tight, while marking the line in front of you.

Trammel Points and Bar Compasses

Trammel points are used for drafting large circles accurately. Trammel points are a pair of small clamps mounted to any rigid bar, the trammel bar. If the trammel bar needs to be very long, then two pieces of wood can be clamped or screwed together. The clamps hold pencil-thin rods of steel that end in sharp points; these are the trammel points. The point can be taken out of one of the clamps and replaced with a pencil. The other point can be set and actually hammered into the radius point. As the trammel pivots, the pencil marks the circumference. If the circle is very large, it usually is necessary for one person to hold down the compass point while another person walks the pencil around the circumference. If the trammel points are clamped to a lining stick with an extended handle, then, after a little getting use to it, one person can draft circles on his or her own. *Bar compasses* work in the same way as trammel points only on a smaller scale. Bar compasses are used primarily for drafting.

Triangles and Templates

Any paint shop should have a selection of drafting templates for intricate projects, such as patterning and signage. During cartooning and layout, there will be call for larger triangles. The shop also needs assorted sizes of standard 45° and 30° drafting triangles at least eighteen inches long. Large circle and oval templates with assorted sizes on them and a variety of sizes and styles of lettering templates also are useful in the paint shop. Large 45° and 30° triangles and circle templates, suited to the scale of scenic painting, can be drafted out of Masonite or lauan. Very large triangles can be framed out of lumber or steel.

TRANSFERRING A CARTOON OR REPEATING PATTERN

Many times a scenic artist chooses not to cartoon directly onto the scenery but to cartoon a pounce and transfer the image. There are a whole host of valid reasons for transferring the cartoon to the scenery from a prepared pounce or stencil, but this almost always is done to save time. It would be foolhardy to accurately cartoon dozens of identical copies of an intricate pattern without a stencil to trace. A single large image may be completely cartooned onto paper so it can be transferred to a drop quickly by a team of painters. Obviously, this would save time in cartooning the drop itself, as well as making a permanent copy of the image for later use. Many designs are symmetrical. A perfectly symmetrical design can be made by drawing half the design on a pounce or transfer screen. Then the mirror image can be traced or pounced. Entire drops can be cartooned in this manner. This process is called reverse and repeat. The layout of almost all lettering is best prepared on a drafting table, off the scenery, where the scenic artist can work in more controlled conditions with a T-square and triangles.

No matter how simple it is to draw on muslin, it is far easier to work complex images on paper with pencils or charcoal. Almost any cartoon can be transferred, and several simple ways to do that are described here. The cartoon transfer, usually using a pounce, also guarantees the scenic artist more control over the cartooning. A pounce normally is drawn on paper, away from concerns of priming and stretching the soft goods.

Using a Pounce

The pounce is a centuries-old means of transferring an image and still one of the most common methods. Fresco painters in the past worked by cartooning an entire fresco on paper first. Because a fresco must be painted on a wet plaster base, there is a limited amount of time to work on it. The image would be divided into small sections that could be completed in a day's work. The paper was then hung in front of the section of freshly applied plaster. The pounce was transferred by either jabbing the paper along the cartoon lines with a sharp point, creating a trace line of indentations in the plaster, or by perforating the paper first. Ther perforations were rubbed over with a bag of powdered charcoal. When the pounce was taken down, an impression of the lines remained on the plaster as dotted lines. Then, the day's painting would commence.

Today, in the theatre, a very similar approach is used. A paper pounce is not jabbed with sticks, but it is perforated with a wheel so that all the lines are traced by a series of little holes. A powdered medium is dusted across and through the perforations, leaving behind a fine dotted line pattern of the cartoon on the surface to be painted.

The cartoon for a pounce usually is drawn on butcher or kraft paper. The cartoon is marked with ink and given registration marks for positioning the pounce on the scenery. The perforations are done with a tool called a *pounce wheel*. This is a little wheel ringed with spikes, held in a metal or wooden handle. Several types of pounce wheels are available. The larger wheels, one-half inch diameter and up, work the best for scenic painting. Select a pounce wheel that has good, long spikes, as smaller spikes will overperforate and tear kraft or butcher paper. Small pounce wheels are designed for much finer work. The paper needs to be perforated on a surface that gives a little bit, such as a piece of velour or homasote. This allows the spikes of the pounce wheel to sink through the paper. After the paper has been perforated, the back of it should be lightly sanded with fine sandpaper to open the perforations on the back of the pounce.

Once positioned on the scenery, the pounce may need to be taped, tacked, or pinned at the corners so that it does not shift while being dusted. The powdered medium used to dust a pounce can be anything that is fine enough to drop though the perforations. Pounce powder, recommended earlier to use in snap lines, works very well. Powdered charcoal works very well also, but it is expensive. To pounce on dark backgrounds, white pounce powder is available or use talcum powder. Blue carpenter's chalk in chalk lines is usable for pouncing, but it leaves a permanent mark. Pounce powder is put in what is called a *pounce bag*. This is a bag made from several layers of cheesecloth or gauze, holding pounce powder, charcoal, or chalk. The powder evenly sifts through the layers of gauze as the bag is lightly pounced and rubbed across the perforations.

Pouncing works somewhat better when done flat rather than up, because gravity works for you. In either case, before the pounce is removed, a corner of it should be lifted, keeping the rest in place, to make certain that the cartoon can be seen easily. If not, replace the corner and go over the cartoon again with the pounce bag.

If the pounce is being used for a reverse and repeat, then it should be moved away from the scenery and thoroughly flogged off before flipping it over to pounce the reverse image. When doing a fair amount of work with large pounces, wear a dust mask, because pounce powder and charcoal are very fine and can take a while to settle out of the air. When finished with the pounce of a particular cartoon, roll it up, label it, and store it away until the show is out of the shop. Pounces are easy to store, and once in a while, that cartoon may be needed again because of an added piece of scenery or paint treatment, loss of the cartoon lines, or damage to the scenic unit.

Pounces also can be made out of visquene plastic sheet. These pounces are more difficult to make and work with, but they are useful for some applications because they are transparent and waterproof. Positioning a pounce can be a problem sometimes, particularly if the image must work together with other elements. In this case, it would be a great benefit to see through the pounce to position it or to trace an image already there. Another occasion when plastic pounces are useful is when working up on a paint frame. Because the fabric of a drop gives in places where no framework is behind it, getting the pounce powder or charcoal to penetrate the perforations can be difficult. The image from a plastic pounce using pounce powder is not as crisp as that from a paper pounce. A visquene pounce can be lightly sponged over with a thin solution of dye, however. Thin black aniline dye works well, and it is one of the most forgiving colors of dye. Black aniline dye is water soluble so it will not stop up the holes in the pounce. It can also be washed off more easily than other colors of dye if a mistake is made. The dye should be only as dark as is necessary to see. Do not use paint for this, because if the pounce needs to be reused in the future the paint will have dried up and blocked the perforations. Use a cellulose sponge to apply the dye and wring out most of the dye, then press the sponge along the perforations. It may take a while to get the knack of this technique.

To make a plastic pounce, draw the image on paper first, set it with ink, and label it with the necessary registration marks, as usual. Then smooth out and tape the visquene over the drawing and trace the cartoon with an ink marker. Just as with a paper pounce, the visquene will need to be perforated on a surface that gives a little. Because the visquene tends to stretch rather than puncture, a firmer backing surface such as homasote works best. The back of the visquene pounce also must be sanded carefully to smooth the perforations.

The Transfer Screen

Another method of repeating a pattern is with a *transfer screen*. This is a screen made from linen scrim stretched tightly over a frame that has no interior braces. Once the repeating image is drawn on the scenery, the screen is laid over it and the cartoon is traced onto the screen with vine charcoal. Then the screen is laid down in its new position and the cartoon is traced once again with vine charcoal applied with a heavy hand. When the screen is taken away, a charcoal impression will be left on the scenery. The transfer screen works well enough for repeating an image maybe half a dozen times, by which time the original image has become obscured and the screen very messy. This is not a highly accurate tool. If the design needing to be transferred is very intricate, use a pounce. The screen will need to be blown off with an air nozzle for its next use. The expression "quick and dirty" is a propos for the transfer screen, but it is useful for some situations.

Templates, Stencils, and Stamps

A template works well for a simple repetitious pattern or outlines such as finials or balusters. Templates can be cut out of any stiff board such as bristol board or Upson board, or they can be cut from sheet stock. The same stencils and stamps used in painting may serve as a cartooning tool, and might be helpful in quickly applying an outline of a pattern in a contrasting color to the base.

Early in the building of a production, the technical director should confer with the charge painter about pieces of scenery that have profiles, so the scenic artist can make the final decision on the shape of any contours. Often, the scenic artist is responsible for drawing all contours. Ultimately, the scenic artist will match the paint treatment to the constructed contour. What appears as a simple curve in the construction drawing may be a critical shape within the painted image as well. The scenic artist should inspect the paint elevations as well as the construction drawings to correct any discrepancies. Often, the paint elevation contains information crucial for the contour. The scenic artist also may need to generate templates for the carpenters.

PREPARING THE SCENERY FOR CARTOONING

Preparation for cartooning starts with a thorough reading of the information supplied by the scenic designer. A scenic artist can expect a complete set of draftings for the production to supplement the paint elevations. Once you have assembled the information needed to execute a cartoon, lay out the scenery so it is in a logical order to itself and establish that it is properly aligned. With these steps completed, the actual work of cartooning can begin.

Preparing the Design Information

The scenic designer supplies the scenic artist with a full set of ground plans and drafted front elevations of the entire design to complement the set of paint elevations. The ground plans will tell the scenic artist how all the units relate to one another on stage. It is certainly worth knowing, for instance, that intricate marble paneling is downstage in full view, as opposed to half-hidden behind a window. From this information, the scenic artist can set priorities in the painting schedule.

A scenic designer usually provides three types of information, or some combination of these three, that are specific to the painting and cartooning information: the paint elevation, a cartoon, and a model (refer to Chapter Two for a full description of the scenic designer's information and how to interpret it). These are in addition to the drafted front elevations, which may hint at paint information or even function as the cartoon. The drafted front elevations essentially are construction drawings and may not contain all the information required for cartooning. The front elevation of a typical drop can be as simple as an empty rectangle or contain a line drawing of the painted image in scale. Many scenic designers like to do a separate cartoon for the line work of the drop.

Make certain that you have an elevation of all the scenery to be painted. Look carefully at the ground plan and count the units and cross-reference them to the elevations.

Paint Elevations

The color elevations should match, in dimension, the front elevations. In some instances, the designer will cut the front elevations right from a set of bluelines and laminate them to an illustration board for painting color elevations. The paint elevations are the most important guide to painting and cartooning the scenery. Often copies of the color elevation, and cartoons, if provided, are made so that several people can paint simultaneously. Color copies frequently differ in color from the original. For this reason, color always should be mixed only from the original paint elevation.

A soon as the color elevations come to the shop and the copies have been made, they should all be given a protective cover of clear vinyl or acetate. This protective cover should be sealed on all edges to prevent spilled paint from seeping under the edge of the protective covering and damaging the paint elevation. The elevation, in spite of being a working guide, is an original work of art and should be returned to the designer in good condition. If notes need to be made on the elevation, they should be written on the protective covering or on tape or note paper taped to the cover.

Additional drawing may need to be done on the protective cover of the elevation for cartooning. The center line or a grid may need to be to be applied for reference during cartooning. China markers, laundry markers, acetate markers, and ballpoint pens all work well for making notations on vinyl or acetate. If a lot of reference-line work needs to laid out on the paint elevation then a separate black and white copy should be made for cartooning. Take care to make sure that all copies of the elevation used by the painters involved in that project have identical notations and layout on them. If you are superimposing a grid, center line, or layout of any kind over an elevation on a black and white copy, use a pen or marker of a color that will stand out to avoid confusion.

The Scenic Model

A color model may be provided by the scenic designer instead of paint elevations. The scenic artist may need to disassemble the model because each piece of the model is used as a guide for the scenic painting on specific units of scenery. Ideally, the designer has engineered his or her model with this practicality in mind. These model pieces still need to be treated as works of art and carefully wrapped with a protective layer of cellophane or kept in a vinyl pocket. Models frequently are rather delicate, and in spite of the care given them, constant handling may damage the pieces. After the production, the charge painter should see to it that the model is repaired as necessary and returned to the designer.

> One other aspect of the scenic staff relying on a model as the color elevation is that, as mentioned before, the model is very useful to the director and performers. When the set is being painted, the scenic art staff must have primary possession of the model to do its work. The stage management staff should clear it with the charge painter before removing the model from the paint shop for any period of time.

Preparing Hard Scenery for Cartooning

Hard scenery should be laid out so that similar processes are done at the same time. All the flats and pieces that relate to one another in any given scene should be laid down together, all the backing flats for one off-stage room together and so on. This helps speed up cartooning and painting as well as maintaining stylistic continuity. A paint technique done by one person on a flat on a Monday may look very different from the flat it plays next to if that flat was painted by someone working on the other side of the shop on the following Friday.

When the flats or units of hard scenery are laid out, the charge painter or lead painter should check through the front elevations and the floor plan carefully to make sure he or she has a clear understanding of how the units are assembled. The scenery should have all hardware, reveals, and trim either installed or easily accessible, so it does not need further painting later and so the separate elements of a single unit are painted together. Most carpenters are not painters; most painters are not carpenters; both may have needs and limitations that will need to be discussed. The more complex the set, the more crucial is this communication. Issues may need to be addressed when the scenery goes from the construction shop to the paint shop. Scenery may need to be made more accessible, stiffeners removed, a paint scaffold assembled, and so forth. If a hard scenic unit is large, a very important question will be, "Where is it safe to walk and stand?"

In terms of cartooning hard scenery, the shape of the scenery itself serves as a frame of reference for the cartooning. The top, bottom, and sides can be used as references in cartooning. Often horizontal lines of painted molding extend across a group of walls or an entire box set. The alignment of those lines is crucial. Care must be taken to assure that the lines correlate from one flat to the next. One way to assure continuity in cartooning is always to measure up from the bottom of the flat. That way any discrepancy in the height of the flat will not affect the cartooning. If the measurements of the horizontals are complex, draw the lines on one flat, double check measurements for accuracy, then lay a piece of lumber along that edge and transfer all the measurements to it. Use this piece of wood as a measurement template for all the other flats sharing those lines (Figure 8.4). If there is not room to lay out all the flattage that has these measurements in common, save the measurement template for use later. Be aware of any flats that are placed on the platform but have horizontal measurements in common with flats that sit directly on the stage deck. If complex verticals progress across a series of flats, such as wallpaper stripes, butt the flats together to make measurements for these verticals, then pull them apart to make room to walk between them.

Frequently the painting area available is not large enough to accommodate all the related units. The technical director and the charge painter together will decide what is to be laid out in what order. A box set may have to be painted in two groups, stage right and stage left, depending on the constraints of the shop space. After the first group of units is done, a unit adjacent to the next related group of flats should be retained for reference while the next group is being cartooned and painted.

Imposing a ruled design on irregular three-dimensional scenery can be a challenge. Any surface that is curved in one direction can be approached by making a pounce that covers the surface area of this curve or a section of the surface area of a repeated design. The pounce can be cartooned, inked, and perforated while flat, then laid on the contour of the surface and transferred to the scenery.

If the scenery is contoured in two directions, cartooning on it can be approached in a couple of ways. First, if it is possible by using flexible rules and tape measures, the cartoon can be gridded out and cartooned directly on the scenery. Second, it

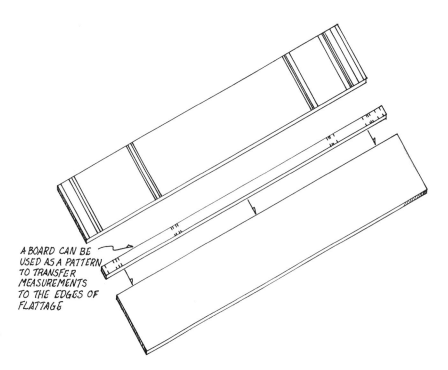

A BOARD CAN BE USED AS A PATTERN TO TRANSFER MEASUREMENTS TO THE EDGES OF FLATTAGE

Figure 8.4
Transferring a continuing horizontal wall pattern.

may be feasible to project the image to be cartooned on the scenery and transfer the image, if the scenery can be moved into a position where it is convenient to work with a projection. Using a projector to cartoon scenery is discussed later in this chapter.

Preparing Soft Goods for Cartooning

Cartooning soft goods requires first that specific and accurate reference lines are drawn onto them. No point can be accurately placed without horizontal and vertical baselines to guide the cartooning. Any point can be located by taking measurements perpendicular from each of these baselines. The two most common baselines that are used as a frame of reference for cartooning are the vertical center line and the bottom edge of the drop. All lines cartooned on the drop in one way or another will have been plotted from these two baselines.

When a piece of soft goods is stretched and primed (see Chapter Seven), it is important that the top of the drop is stapled in a straight line. If the bottom of the drop is a finished edge, it should be stapled to a straight line parallel to the top. If the sides are finished edges, they should be stapled to straight lines perpendicular to the top and bottom. Not all soft good pieces are conveniently rectangular. The sides and the bottom of a piece of soft goods may not be straight, parallel, or perpendicular because the piece has unfinished sides. Drops often are finished after they have been painted. A drop may have uneven contour or may not span the centerline of the stage, yet vertical and horizontal baselines still need to be established. These horizontal and vertical baselines must be parallel to the stage floor and the centerline. All you need to locate the baseline of a piece of soft goods is one straight line. The baselines usually are measured or found with a geometric equation (described later in this chapter) from the top edge of the drop.

When cartooning a drop the horizontal baseline is usually the bottom of the drop, which, when it plays on stage, rests on the stage floor. If the bottom of the drop is stapled in a straight line parallel to the top, you have already found the horizontal baseline. If the bottom of the drop is uneven or unfinished, you will need to find the baseline by measuring down from the top of the drop (Figure 8.5). Scale the

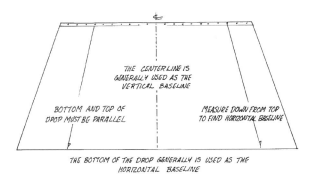

THE CENTERLINE IS
GENERALLY USED AS THE
VERTICAL BASELINE

BOTTOM AND TOP OF
DROP MUST BE PARALLEL

MEASURE DOWN FROM TOP
TO FIND HORIZONTAL BASELINE

THE BOTTOM OF THE DROP GENERALLY IS USED AS THE
HORIZONTAL BASELINE

Figure 8.5 Finding a horizontal baseline on a drop.

If you are working in a shop that has a square paint deck and the drop is laid out square to the deck, the baselines can be located by measuring in from the edge of the deck. Make absolutely certain that the deck is square. Do not assume it is if you are working in an unfamiliar shop.

The Pythagorean theorem (described later in this chapter) also is very useful in establishing that either baseline is perpendicular to the other.

height of the drop off the elevation. If the bottom of the piece is an uneven contour, for example a foliage border, scale out the longest vertical length on the elevation. Then measure this distance down on either side of the drop or soft goods. Snap a line between these two points and that will be the baseline. It may be necessary to ink this line so that it is not inadvertently rubbed off.

The vertical baseline may be the center line of the drop, the center line of the image, or the offstage edge of the soft goods. To find a line perpendicular to the horizontal baseline, first locate the intersection of the vertical and horizontal baselines, often the center of the drop. If the piece is very small, a framing square or triangle can be used to find a perpendicular line. If working on a paint frame, just use the snap line as a plumb bob for a perpendicular line. If working on the floor, use trammel points and a piece of stock lumber as a trammel bar (you may also use a measuring tape if someone will assist you by holding the end of it for you) to do the following (Figure 8.6):

1. Measure the width of the drop at either the top or the bottom to find the center. This will be point A.
2. Strike an arc from point A equal distance on either side of the point. Points B and C will be at the ends of the arcs.
3. Strike a slightly larger arc from each of the new points B and C. These arcs must cross the imagined perpendicular point below point A.
4. Snap a line between the intersection of the arcs and point A extending as far as needed. This is the vertical baseline.

Measuring the Drop

Now that you have horizontal and vertical baselines, you can find the dimensions on the sides of the drop, if needed. Often a drop will be a few inches shorter, wider, narrower, or taller than listed on the elevation. This variance is common because of the properties of unsized muslin. Also, many shops order or build all soft goods a few inches larger to cover errors. The finished dimensions of the drop need to be marked on the back of the webbing when the drop is pulled up if they differ from the elevation. The change in the size of the drop should not change how the elevation is scaled out unless the scenic designer specifies a change. It may be that there are simply a few extra inches of sky at the top of the drop, or a few less. It may mean that the scenic artist will need to improvise some tree limbs or architectural detail if the drop is too wide. If there are major discrepancies between the size of the drop and the elevation then the scenic designer should be consulted.

If the sides are unfinished, the side edges of the image are found by measuring half the width of the finished dimensions of the drop from either side of the center line, at the top, and at the bottom of the drop. If the bottom edge is unfinished, measure these points down from the top of the drop to create the horizontal baseline. Make sure to leave enough extra fabric for a turnback or pipe pocket, if needed. To make certain that the drop is square, measure the inside dimensions diagonally from corner to corner. If these measurements are the same, then the drop is square (Figure 8.7). Once the outside dimensions are done, the drop is ready to cartoon.

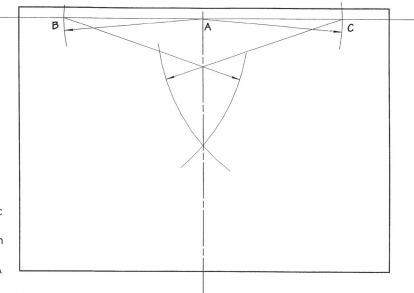

Figure 8.6
Three steps to creating a vertical baseline perpendicular to the horizontal: (1) strike an arc from A to find points B and C; (2) strike arcs that intersect from B and C; (3) connect the intersection of these arcs to point A to find the perpendicular.

Make sure to mark the center line and the sides of the drop well at the top and bottom. You will need to locate these lines again when the drop is taken up. The center line will need to be marked on the back of the webbing. If you put your marks on the deck and cover them over with tape, they can be retrieved after the many coats of paint. A nail bent over at the top and bottom of the center and sides works, too. On the frame, nails or safety pins can be used to relocate your marks.

DRAWING THE CARTOON

Artists and writers often say that the blank canvas, or page, is the greatest challenge. Where do I start? For the scenic artist that same challenge comes in a very large form. A cartoon is just a very big drawing. The scenic artist has many avenues of approach to the cartoon. An architectural layout is much like large-scale drafting and will render a crisp, highly accurate copy of almost any image, but this approach to car-

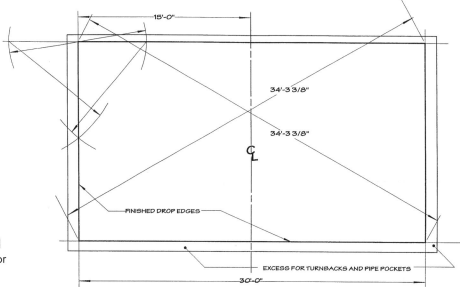

Figure 8.7
Finding the side edges and using diagonals to check for squareness.

tooning clearly is best suited for rectalinear forms. A grid transfer may be better for organic forms. Mechanical devices like a projector or a pounce are useful for certain types of cartoon layout. The knowledge of the rules of perspective and geometry will aid you in any type of layout.

> Do not forget to keep a thorough record of all reference lines on the elevation. In cartooning, this means recording all superimposed reference lines or marks. When using a grid, the grid must become part of the elevation the scenic artist uses.

Architectural Layout

An *architectural layout* is a very direct approach to cartooning an image. This works best with images having a lot of straight geometric line work that can be plotted off horizontal and vertical baselines. Essentially, it is the same process as drafting the image on paper, only in a larger scale. Instead of a T-square and triangle, your tools are a measuring tape and snap line. Horizontal and vertical lines can be scaled off and referenced to the baselines on the elevation and transferred full scale to the scenery.

The horizontal baseline should correspond to the bottom of the elevation. If working on a paneled wall, for example, plot all major horizontals, such as chair rails and cornices, from the baseline. The same is true for plotting vertical lines, such as doorframes and the sides of buildings, working from the vertical baseline. Once these primary vertical and horizontal lines have been marked on the drop with a snap line, the drop is effectively sectioned into smaller areas in which details can be refined. Odd-shaped elements, such as wall sconces, arabesques, or picture frames, can be placed and drawn in relationship to these major lines. An angled baseline can be drawn to serve as a major reference point if the drawing is at an angle (Figure 8.8).

Using a Grid for Cartooning

Cartooning with a *grid* involves creating a frame of reference over an image as an alternative to the architectural layout. This method of cartooning is very useful for organic shapes and sketchy or abstract images that are more easily approached when broken down into small units.

A grid is a network of squares evenly laid over the elevation that corresponds to a full-scale grid on the drop. There is no standard grid size; it is based on personal preference and the complexity of the image. When first working with a grid, one is inclined to use a grid small enough to ensure absolute accuracy, like one foot square. Rarely is a one-foot grid necessary; a four-foot grid usually is adequate. If you have to keep track of your place and fill in all the grid squares of a one-foot grid, it will take you much longer to transfer a design than with a four-foot grid.

A four-foot grid is an excellent size. Most forms easily can be proportioned and transferred in this grid. If a section of the image is more complex, the grid can be subdivided, so tighter detail can be transferred easily. If you generally use grids of either four feet or two feet, then you will develop a pattern of eye-hand coordination that naturally fits into that size. You can

Figure 8.8 Example of an architectural layout.

adjust easily enough into a three-foot or five-foot grid, but there may be fits and starts where you just cannot seem to get the proportions right.

Grid lines should be labeled because losing track of your place when working on a full-stage drop is easy. Avoid labeling the grid line with some fancy Able-One, Baker-Two labeling system. It is better to label the grid lines with their actual dimensions; measurements will help you keep track of where you are in distances. The center line is labeled CL just as it is on the elevation, which makes it reference dimension zero. The vertical grid lines are labeled out from the center line, according to distance: four, eight, twelve feet, and so on. The horizontal baseline also is zero. Adjust accordingly for whatever grid size is used (Figure 8.9).

As soon as the center line and the outside dimensions of the drop are found, it is time to lay out the grid. A snap line is the fastest way to lay out the grid over a large area. Make sure to use pounce powder or powdered charcoal so the lines can be erased after the cartoon is set. Once they have been flogged or blown off, and the scenery has been painted, grid lines no longer are noticeable on stage. If sections of the scenery should stay clean, such as a translucent sky, then grid only the portions of the scenery where it is necessary. If a grid is necessary in some portions of a drop, such as a light-value translucent sky with complex cloud forms, and yet there is real concern that a grid may blemish these areas, then a string grid can be set up for cartooning. Pound in a nail at all the marks for grid lines around the outside dimensions of the drop. Wind string back and forth around the nails for a grid. All the nails should be tagged with bright ribbon or construction tape so they are more visible and less likely to cause injury from tripping or being stepped on.

Perspective

Scenic designers rely on perspective to create depth in two-dimensional and three-dimensional scenic compositions. The scenic artist needs to understand the rules of perspective to fully translate the designer's work.

Atmospheric Perspective

Atmospheric perspective is based on the observation that objects seen at a distance are affected by the atmospheric haze and the eye's reduced ability to perceive detail. Faraway objects usually appear lighter, less colorful, and less detailed. Scenic designers manipulate atmospheric perspective in backdrops, and sometimes ask a scenic artist to make some part of a drop look "farther away." This normally is done in the painting process, but it can be important in the cartooning. The amount of detail of

Figure 8.9
Grid layout.

the cartoon should be adjusted so that faraway forms are less detailed (Figure 8.10).

Linear Perspective

The concept of atmospheric perspective and the observance that the size of objects and forms diminishes at a distance was not lost on the Medieval artist. What was missing, until Renaissance Italy, was a convincing method of methodically plotting in a drawing the effect of objects and shapes receding, both in distance and size. This method is called *linear perspective*, and has been refined and used to great effect by artists throughout the world, and it has changed the expectations of form and content in the visual arts. Linear perspective has been an integral part of scenic design and scenic painting since the Renaissance.

In cartooning scenery, linear perspective, along with the grid method and architectural layout, provides a very useful way to reproduce a line drawing. In many ways, linear perspective is the most accurate method of plotting lines, because it replicates the manner in which a perspective drawing was created.

The Principles of Linear Perspective

Linear perspective creates an illusion of depth in cases where the image represented spans no more than 60° of the field of the viewer's vision. This field corresponds approximately to the field of clear sight of the human eye. Beyond this span, one has to rotate one's head to view a larger expanse, which changes the point of view. Believable perspective depends on a stationary point of view.

Linear perspective is predicated on the perception that straight lines of vertical and horizontal planes converge to a single point on the horizon. If you continued the lines of the side of a square plane from the forward edge to the distant edge and beyond, these lines would appear to meet at the vanishing point. This vanishing point is the place in the distance where objects have receded to a size so infinitesimal that the human eye is no longer able to distinguish forms (Figure 8.11).

> Linear perspective does not take into account the curvature of the earth. A nuisance of the vistas we see in reality is that planes in the distance subtly curve away from us, like the observation that Columbus reportedly made of ships on the ocean. Only very rarely are we aware of this slight curve, as forms in the foreground, the atmosphere, or the terrain occlude this subtle occurrence from us.

Figure 8.10
Atmospheric perspective.

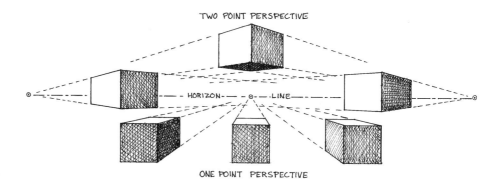

Figure 8.11
Linear perspective.

The Method of Perspective

Gaining a working knowledge of the application of linear perspective is a skill that every scenic artist must master. You can interpret and reproduce a linear perspective drawing only if you understand it. Once you have a working knowledge of linear perspective you will find that it all fits together and has a logic governing it.

The *picture plane* represents a stationary point of view, which generally relates to a human viewer based on an average height of 5'6" and a 60° range of human sight. From this stationary point of view, there is a fixed horizon, which is a straight line across the picture plane at about the height of the viewer's line of sight. In theatre the picture plane is the stage. All objects appear to recede uniformly in size until they disappear into the distance at this horizon line. As objects recede into the distance, the distance between these objects appears to recede as well. In a theatre, the height of a person's line of sight may depend on the viewpoint of the average audience member, as well as the rake of the auditorium seats and the height and rake of the stage. The illusion of perspective may not work as well for a person seated in the balcony as it does for the person seated in the center of the orchestra (Figure 8.12).

The edges of planes parallel to the picture plane do not converge to a point, but remain parallel to the picture plane. All lines perpendicular to the picture plane converge on the same point on the horizon line at the center line of the picture plane. If these lines are the edges of square planes that are perpendicular to the picture plane, then the lines on the front and back edges of the square planes will remain parallel to each other and the picture plane. The lines on the side of the square planes will, if extended, converge

on the center line/horizon line intersection. Two of the edges of all square planes that are perpendicular to the picture plane converge on the same point on the horizon line. This is called *one-point perspective* (Figure 8.13).

All square horizontal or vertical planes not parallel or perpendicular to the picture plane have two edges whose lines converge on the horizon line, while the other two edges remain parallel to each other. This may result in *multiple vanishing points* (Figure 8.14).

All parallel lines that are not vertical, horizontal, perpendicular, or parallel to the picture plane converge at some distant point, called an *oblique perspective point*, sometimes called the *uphill* or *downhill perspective point*. If the top and bottom edges of a square oblique plane are horizontal, they converge on a point on the horizon line. These oblique vanishing points can be used directly for oblique planes such as roofs or as guides for inclined planes such as steps and staircases (Figure 8.15).

All *spheres in perspective* appear as perfect circles that diminish in size as they recede in space

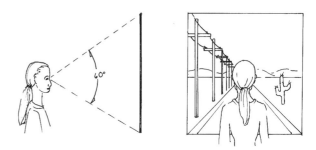

Figure 8.12 The picture plane.

Figure 8.13 One-point perspective.

Figure 8.14 Multiple vanishing points.

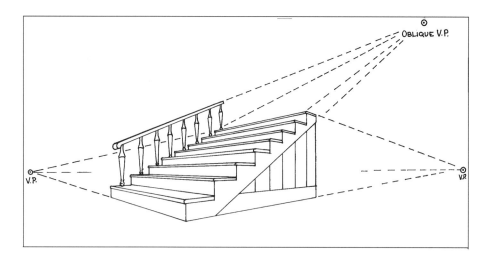

Figure 8.15
Oblique perspective.

(Figure 8.16). All circles not parallel to the picture plane appear as perfect ellipses, unless seen on edge, in which case they are a straight line. All sections of a sphere not parallel to the picture plane also appear as perfect ellipses. All perpendicular sections of a perfectly round cylinder appear as perfect ellipses. The spatial relationship of ellipses foreshortens, but the perfect shape of the ellipse remains. An ellipse can be plotted into a square plane that is drawn in perspective. By doing this you can determine how much the ellipse should be foreshortened. Drawing the bottom of a round column sitting on a square base is a circumstance where you might need to do this. If you are drawing a tall urn with several segments, you may need to plot an ellipse into a square plane for each segment—at the top, the bottom, and in-between. These plotted ellipses should be drawn on a central axis.

An object or form drawn as compressed in length because it tilts away from the viewer is called a *foreshortened* form. To plot foreshortening, first draw the form straight on with no attempt to fit it into perspective. Next, impose a grid over the form or draw in lines of reference. Then, plot the grid into the linear perspective drawing, boxing it out for the depth of the form, and redraw the form in this shape (Figure 8.17).

Drop-Point Perspective

As a guide to working out more complex forms, an elevation or ground-plan view of that form, in full

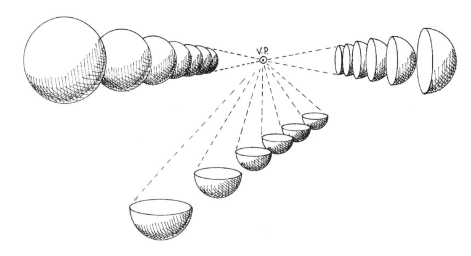

Figure 8.16
Circles in perspective.

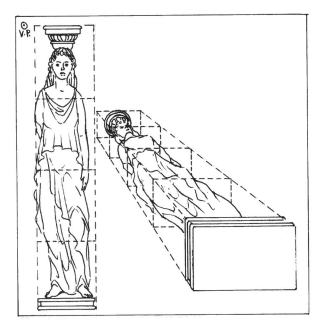

Figure 8.17 Foreshortening.

scale, can be set on the side or the bottom of the picture plane, then the lines of the form carried straight up or over to the edge of the picture plane. This *drop-point perspective* also can be used to plot the height and proportions of a form through varying depths in the picture plane. From the bottom or the side, the proportions of the form can be projected back to the vanishing point, and when parallel to their position of depth, they can be carried across to their position in the picture plane (Figure 8.18).

Finding Depth

A method of finding depths for any series of equidistant forms made up of squared planes is to section the plane that has been drawn in perspective corner to corner with diagonals. The center of the square plane as it appears in perspective will be where the diagonals cross. Draw a vertical or horizontal at that point. Draw diagonals again in these subdivided planes to find the centers of both those planes (Figure 8.19). Another method of achieving the same end, which gives you control over the width of the receding depths, is projecting a center line through the plane, drawn in perspective, back to the vanishing point. Place the first two verticals at the distance that looks proportionally correct, then draw a diago-

nal from the top corner of the first vertical through the center of the next vertical and on down to the bottom of the plane. At that point on the bottom of the plane, draw in the next vertical. From the top of that vertical repeat the process. The verticals will then become evenly spaced posts, columns, or evenly divided squared planes receding into the distance.

The distance between forms that are receding in perspective may be drawn by dropping points down to the baseline (Figure 8.20). First find the points where the outside edges of the columns intersect the baseline at the bottom of the columns. Draw a line from the vanishing point that intersects these points and continues to the baseline at the bottom of the picture plane. Between these two points measure the equal widths of the columns and the equal widths between the columns. From these points, which represent the widths of the columns, project lines back to the vanishing point. These lines will intersect the baseline at the bottom of the columns and establish the widths of the columns as these widths recede into perspective.

Perspective for the Stage

Linear perspective works very well in a flat picture. But, if you enlarge this picture, put it in a box, and have people walk back and forth in front of it, the illusion could fall flat when people wander into areas of the picture plane where the receding forms make them look like giants. Part of the challenge of manipulating perspective on stage belongs to the director, who may have to avoid blocking performers in areas where they appear out of proportion to the scenery. But the designer, along with the scenic artist, must create an illusion on stage by subtly manipulating design and painting so that the vista and the performers merge gracefully.

One of the realities of the stage is that any stage image is in a three-dimensional volume, not a flat picture plane. The lines of an image as it comes into the foreground may be cut off by the floor. All lines and planes can be related to the perspective point, save the stage floor and platforms, which may need to remain level for safety. Generally in stage design, the most obvious perspective technique is reserved for the background, and these images of depth are merged carefully with the elements in the foreground. All elements in the acting area of a stage need to be carefully designed in regard to human proportion.

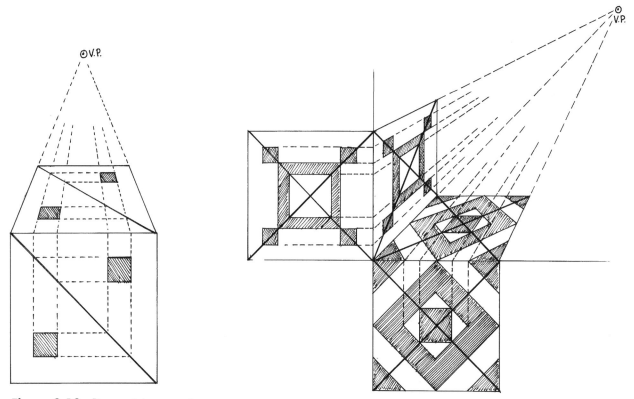

Figure 8.18 Drop-point perspective.

When creating an interior using perspective, one method of keeping the stage in human scale is to keep all elements close to the ground, such as base-

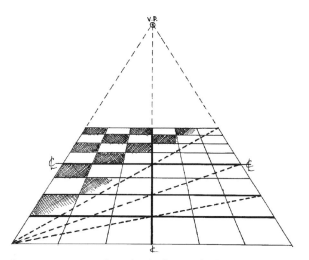

Figure 8.19 Finding depth, first method.

boards, wainscoting, and pillar bases, at a constant height and begin the linear perspective at about four feet above the deck (Figure 8.21). That way whatever piece of scenery the performer approaches will appear natural. The design of the stage scenery cannot be disassociated from the performers, unless the point of the design is to place the performers in an artificial environment.

The Raked Stage and Traditional Wing and Drop Perspective

The traditional use of perspective on stage is an arrangement of wings, drops, and borders on a raked stage creating a perspective box. This approach to the stage picture is now antique and occasionally is revived, but for a span of two centuries, it was the most constant of approaches to stage design (refer to Chapter Twelve for a discussion of perspective stage design). In this genre, the methods of perspective are used to their utmost potential, no longer relegated to the backdrop and singular elements. Every compo-

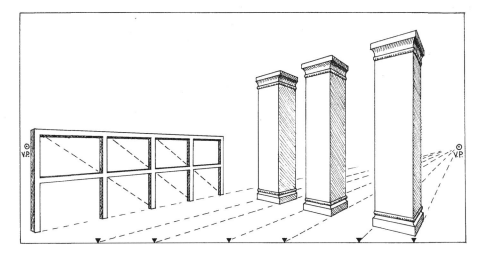

Figure 8.20
Finding depth, second method, and by dropping paint down to the baseline.

nent on stage relates to the horizon line and the vanishing point. In this case, the raked stage deck in addition to all the vertical elements becomes a consideration in the application of linear perspective. The basic format of the design remains standard from production to production although additional elements may be added. The stage picture is set with a

vanishing point that, in some theatre houses, related directly to the center balcony box, where the most prestigious members of the audience would sit. The rake of the stage and the position of the wings lined up with this vanishing point. When these set pieces were cartooned and painted by being plotted off of this vanishing point and horizon line, the illusion was

Figure 8.21 Perspective for the stage.

very convincing. Staging performers on these designs was necessarily shallow, for as soon as someone moved too far upstage, the effect unraveled.

Contemporary scenic artists may encounter projects designed in this way, where every piece of scenery on stage must relate back to a very specific vanishing point and horizon line. In a project like this, although the scale of the image should relate to human scale, there is less concern about manipulating the image so that it works with the human performers because the designer has the additional agenda of creating a seamless illusion of depth.

Methods of Doing Linear Perspective in the Shop

The tools and approach to doing linear perspective full scale on theatre sets are the same as the tools for cartooning. Straight edges are needed for plotting out the vanishing points and the horizon line. Once again, the same lines of reference will need to be marked out on the scenery. Mark the vanishing points with nails so that strings can be attached to them or they can be used as swivel points with the edge of a line stick. Mark the nail with ribbon or construction tape so it is easy to find and avoid stepping on. When plotting lines back to their vanishing points, it is practical to use straight edges, but there are limits. When the lines are beyond the sixteen-foot length of the longest lining stick, or when two or three people are trying to plot lines on a drop, a lining stick will get in the way. A length of clean string or cord attached to the nails at the vanishing points can be used to plot lines from point to point. A design may have several vanishing points. The strings should have a loop on the end so they can be moved from point to point easily or removed so that you do not end up with a web of strings on the scenery. If you are working on hard scenery and the vanishing point is off the scenery, the nail may need to be driven into a section of 2" × 4" wood that is weighted down so that it will not slide around. This way, the string or cord will not snag as easily on the edge of the scenery. Be careful not to let scenery shift once a vanishing point is established. Do not overdo using the string or cord as a guide to walk the lines. String is flexible, no matter how tightly it is pulled, and lines using the string as a guide are apt to be warped. Use the string to plot the points of the line that extend to the vanishing point; then, use a lining stick or snap line to actually draw these lines.

Perspective itself works as a method of enlarging an image to full scale by plotting the point where lines originate and extending them to their terminus. You need to know only at what measurement the line stops; relating it to the vanishing point will plot it in the right place. As in an architectural layout, start with the major lines and define the primary planes, then locate and define the elements and keep working into ever-tighter detail. If, at first, the primary parallel lines are laid in—these are frequently verticals—it will be easy to locate the points on these lines from which perspective lines need to be plotted and to know just where they must end. A full-stage drop completely in perspective can be rather intimidating at first glance, but if it is broken down into specific elements, it is less overwhelming. Frequently, elements drawn in perspective are combined with compositions that primarily are in an architectural or grid layout.

Remember that, in perspective, many of the lines are interdependent. A line that is out of place may throw off many other lines throughout that section of the drawing. Be aware that, if lines are not meeting as they should, it might be time to take an objective look at the image and search for an oversight.

It is not always simple to plot large perspective drawings in a scenic shop. One of the first things an art teacher will tell a student about drawing in perspective is that you should have plenty of room around the page for plotting out the horizon line and vanishing points. In the scenic shop it is not uncommon for a drop to be wedged between a post and the wall. There may be no room to plot vanishing points unless they were placed in the parking lot next door. Many designers, when they choose to use perspective in their designs, bear in mind the limitations of the shop space. If the shop has an expansive 150'-long paint deck, the designer will take advantage of it; but if the shop has barely enough room to accommodate the drop itself, he or she may keep the vanishing points within the confines of the drop.

When arranging scenery or stretching a drop that has an image on it in perspective, the charge painter should plot out the vanishing points beforehand on paper. Depending on the placement of the horizon line and vanishing points, the scenery might need to be arranged so enough space is left in one direction or another to plot vanishing points. Obviously, this factor should be considered before and not after the scenery is in position. In spite of thoughtful shop arrangement, a scenic artist may need to plot perspective where there is not enough room to do so. In some cases, a vanishing point cannot be plotted out because there was no way to avoid a post or wall. In other cases, the design was not plotted out with linear perspective, but an agreement with the designer has decided that the application of perspective will clean up the lines of the design. The dilemma is how to do the perspective when there is not enough room. Often, there will be room enough for some vanishing points but not all. First, try to get around the problem. If plotting a point is only a matter of moving it in on the horizon a foot or two, get the scenic designer's approval. That would be the easiest solution. You cannot move the point above or below the horizon line because that would warp the design.

Another way to get around the problem is a pounce. Cartoon the drop or part of the drop in a space where there is enough room to plot the points. After the cartoon is done on paper it can be transferred to the scenery. A full-stage drop-size pounce may be the best solution for this logistical problem, or you may need the pounce to create only part of the image. If only one side of an image is dependent on a vanishing point you cannot reach, the major lines and forms on that side can be cartooned on a pounce. After it has been transferred to the drop, the other side can be cartooned to merge into it. Also, in many cases, one-point perspective is used for a symmetrical image, which can be done as a reverse and repeat. The pounce should be used as a time saver because exactly half of the image can be cartooned, then the pounce can be flipped over to do the other half.

If all else fails, you may have to rely on your educated knowledge of how these forms will behave in spatial depth. First, work on the copy or line drawing of the elevation to make sure the line work is very clear and easy to measure. The line drawing also should be examined to eliminate any mistakes that, once blown up to full scale, will look odd. When drawing perspective on a drop, the points are scaled off lines of reference and then plotted back to the vanishing point. As lines are drawn in this manner, they must be double-checked against the elevation to make sure they end about where they were

expected to. Frequently, there will be some differences—differences that are subtle on the elevation but amount to several inches in full scale. Proportions of some elements, such as doors, windows, and other architectural details, can appear to be perfectly natural when on the scale of the elevation but look at odds with other elements when transferred to full scale. These are the kinds of incongruities that the scenic artist will encounter and work out in linear perspective. So, when you are denied working out the perspective image in full scale, make sure to go over the elevation or line drawing carefully. Draw in lines of reference that you can transfer to the drop. These lines of reference may be the top, lower, and middle lines of the plane that you cannot plot off the vanishing point. There may be a vertical scale on the side of the drop, from which your lines, should they continue past this scale, would meet up more or less at the vanishing point. You can sight along the length of your line stick using this scale as a guide. A grid may be very useful, as long as the elevation that you are working from is correct.

The final tool you will have to rely on if working without access to a vanishing point is your own innate sense of what looks natural. This sense will develop over the years you spend drawing and observing.

Using Projectors for Cartooning

Projectors are useful for the direct transfer and enlarging of almost any image in cartooning. In fact, cartooning complicated images can proceed very quickly by using a projector. However, projecting an image does not mean that you can dispense with the straight edge and compass. The projected image is just a guide to show you where the lines should be. If the form is a drafted pattern or lettering, then the projected cartoon usually needs to be carefully worked over with a straight edge. In some cases, the cartoon will be broad and sketchy enough that you can trace the lines straightaway with a marker as you are projecting the image. In rare cases, a scenic artist can use the projection itself as a cartoon and paint directly onto canvas with only the projection as a guide.

Three projectors commonly are used in cartooning: opaque, slide, and transparency. Only the opaque projector is capable of projecting directly from a traditional elevation or drawing. These are versatile and convenient, as any source, even books, can be projected from an opaque projector. The slide and transparency projectors require that the elevation or image be copied to film or an acetate transparency first. The opaque projector is the bulkiest and least bright of the three types. It also generates heat, which could endanger the elevation. Slide projectors have many advantages. They are quite bright; a broad selection of lenses is available; they have superior optics; and they are very compact. Slide projectors require that any projected material be photographed in advance and made into a slide. Theatrical slide projectors, which often use large 4" × 5" transparencies, are even brighter and better than the typical 35-mm carousel projector. These large-format slides are expensive to produce. Transparency projectors, or overheads, offer a happy medium. They are uncomplicated machines that can produce fairly large images. They require that the image be copied onto a transparent acetate sheet as close to elevation size as possible. That sort of copying is easily done with a copier onto xerographic acetate. The 35-mm slides are too small for the overhead projectors. Overhead projectors work particularly well for projecting simple line drawings, where shade and color are not present.

Projectors make cartooning easier, when finally set up. The preparation is considerable, however. First, almost all projectors function best in very low-light situations. Other workers may balk at having the lights out. An alternative space may be necessary. Projectors need to be isolated from vibration. Even foot traffic on some shop floors can cause a projected image to gyrate wildly. Projectors need to be focused dead-center on the drop or flat. This sometimes means that the projector must be twelve feet or more off the ground, depending on the scenery. If the projector aims up from floor level, the projected image will keystone; that is, it will distort abnormally as it projects away from center. What appears to be in proportion at ground level will be oversized and distended at the upper edges. Projectors must not be moved once set. It is very difficult to perfectly realign a projected image. Finally, the beam of light itself must be unobstructed. Even when the projector is on and aligned and the lights are out, a scenic artist standing in front of the drop to draw will discover that his or her own body blocks the light. One needs to develop a side-arm drawing technique and a good short-term memory.

Projected images will distort toward the edge of the image, unless the optics of the projector and lens are of top quality. For very large images, a scenic artist may choose to work in segments of the drawing and slightly overlap one portion to the next as the work progresses. It is helpful to grid the projected elevation and the surface onto which it is projected as well. The grid helps maintain alignment and scale as the artist works.

Remember when using the projector that you are still the artist and the interpreter. Do not draw every single little line, only the ones that mean something and are applicable to the form. It is very important not to use the projector as a crutch, as more often than not, the scenery will have to be cartooned by the other methods discussed here. When studying scenic artistry, become adept at all methods of cartooning if you want to be a viable professional. The opaque projector is a time-saver, but your value as a professional will depend on your alacrity in all methods and techniques.

USING GEOMETRY FOR CARTOONING

The ability to draw shapes accurately using geometry is a powerful tool for a scenic artist. Large arcs, ovals, polygons, and architectural shapes frequently must be reproduced on a very large scale, and only with geometry can these things be drawn absolutely accurately. Geometric analysis of a shape may render seemingly complicated forms into a series of simple arcs and polygons, easily replicated. Very large geometric shapes can be drawn easily with the simplest tools, a string and a straight edge, provided the proper points are located. The following are some useful formulas for creating shapes using geometry.

The Pythagorean Theorem

The Pythagorean theorem may be used to square a large area. The Pythagorean theorem states that the sum of the squares of the lengths of the two sides of a right triangle are equal to the square of the length of the hypotenuse. If you can measure the length of the horizontal baseline of a drop (either top or bottom) and the length of the vertical baseline (the centerline), this formula can be applied to check if they are perpendicular to one another. On your drop, plot a triangle with a vertical side (equal to the vertical baseline) AB, a horizontal side (equal to half the horizontal baseline) BC, and an hypotenuse AC. If AB and BC are perpendicular, the length of AC squared will equal the sum of the squares of AB and BC:

$$(AB)^2 + (BC)^2 = (AC)^2$$

An even simpler means of expressing the Pythagorean theorem is the three, four, five method. That is, A3, B4, C5 also will plot a right triangle. To use this method to find the center line on a drop, find the center point at the top of the drop. Measure down 18 feet ($3 \times 6'$) from the center point and draw an arc that crosses the area where you think the center line will be. Measure 24 feet ($4 \times 6'$) over from this center point. From the point on the drop that is 24 feet over from the center, measure 30 feet ($5 \times 6'$) over to the center of the drop and strike a second arc that intersects the first. Snap a line from the center point at the top of the drop through the intersection of the two arcs. This is your center line. Someone may assist you with this or you can use nails driven into your points at the top of the drop to strike the arcs. For smaller drops multiply the numbers three, four, and five by a smaller factor. If you used a factor of 4 feet your measurements would be 12 feet, 16 feet, and 20 feet.

Geometric Construction

Finding a Perpendicular from a Given Point, First Method

From point C as center on a line, strike an arc of any convenient radius R_1, finding points A and B. With any convenient radius R_2, longer than R_1, strike arcs from A and B equidistant from C, describing D. Connect C to the intersection of those arcs, D. CD is perpendicular to the base AB.

The Perpendicular Bisector

Given line AB, strike two arcs from A and B slightly longer than the distance to what appears to be center. The arcs intersect at C and D. Line CD is perpendicular to AB and perfectly bisects it (Figure 8.22).

Finding the Center of a Circle

Draw any line inside a circle to the edge, finding points A and B. Erect two perpendicular lines from A

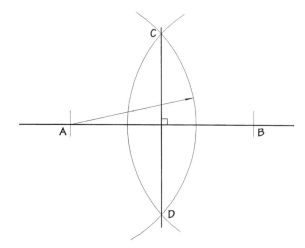

Figure 8.22 The perpendicular bisector.

and B. The intersection of these perpendicular lines with the circle finds points C and D. Connect AD and BC with diagonals to locate P, the center of that circle.

Describing a Circle Through Any Three Points

Given points A, B, and C, draw lines AB and BC. Draw the perpendicular bisector for both lines at the same distance from point B. Their intersection at P is the center of the required circle.

Constructing a Hexagon: The Compass Method

Given line AB, find its center, P. Draw a circle with AP as the radius. From A and B, strike arcs through P, finding C, D, E, and F. Connect the six points around the edge of the circle to describe the hexagon (Figure 8.23).

Constructing a Pentagon and Pentastar in a Circle

Draw diameter AC and radius OB (Figure 8.24a) perpendicular to the center of AC. Bisect OC to find X. From X, strike arc BY. From B, strike arc YZ. Line BZ is one leg of the pentagon. Walk off the other four legs with a compass, string, or trammel points. Connect all five corners of the pentagon with diagonals, as shown, to construct a pentastar (Figure 8.24b).

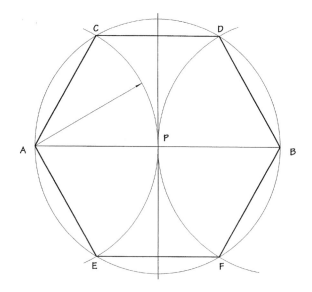

Figure 8.23 Drawing a hexagon, using a compass method.

Drawing an Ellipse

An ellipse, or oval, is a shape generated by a point moving around two fixed points, always maintaining a distance equal to the added distances to both points. A simple construction method illustrates this easily. This is the pin and string method.

Describe line AB (see Figure 8.25) and the perpendicular bisector CD; note their intersection at E. Strike an arc from C the length of AE to find R_1 and R_2. Place pins in points R_1, C, and R_2. Tie a nonelastic string tightly around these three points. Remove the pin at C and carefully draw the ellipse by moving the marker around R_1 and R_2 while maintaining even tension.

To plot an ellipse, draw the horizontal and vertical axes and mark their intersection as X (see Figure 8.26). Strike an arc from X to find the radius points A and B. The length of XA is one quarter of the major axis of the ellipse. Draw a circle lightly from A and B using the same radius, XA. Describe an equilateral triangle from AB to find C and D. Note the intersection of the triangles and the circles. Strike an arc from C and D to those points and redraw the arcs from A and B to finish the ellipse.

Drawing Accurate Architectural Shapes

Most architectural forms are based on geometric construction. The following is a guide to the creation of some of the most common architectural shapes.

The Roman Arch

Draw the horizontal baseline, or spring line, through center point C (Figure 8.27). Mark AB equidistant from C. Strike a semicircle from C connecting A and B.

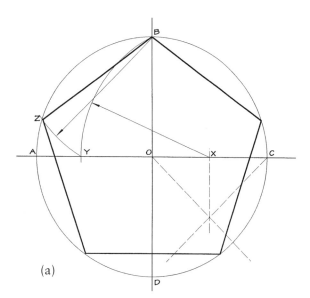

(a)

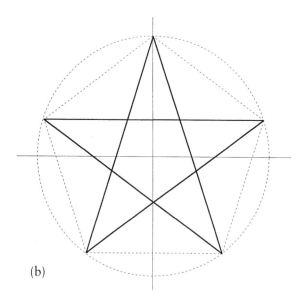

(b)

Figure 8.24 Drawing (a) a pentagon and (b) a pentastar.

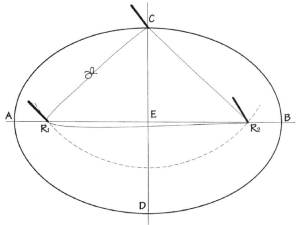

Figure 8.25 Drawing an ellipse with a string.

The Gothic or Ogive Arch

Draw the baseline, or spring line, through center point C (Figure 8.27). Draw a perpendicular vertical through C to the assumed height of the arch. Mark AB equidistant from C. Strike arc AB up to the center line and repeat for BA.

The Tudor Arch

Draw horizontal and vertical baselines and label the intersection X (Figure 8.27). Draw a half circle below the horizontal baseline from X, the width corresponding to the desired arch width and mark the endpoints A and B. Bisect AX and XB to find points C and D. Draw an arc from X to find C and D, the diameter is AX. Describe a equilateral triangle from CD down and extend the legs until they intersect with the half circle, finding points E and F. Also extend the legs upward to intersect with circles lightly drawn from C and D, this finds points G and H. Strike arcs CG and FG; repeat for the other side.

The Moorish or Horseshoe Arch

Describe the horizontal and vertical baselines, label the center point R_1 (Figure 8.28). Lightly draw a semicircle from the center point as a guide for finding A and B; and lightly draw vertical side lines through them. Draw 45° guidelines from R_1 to find R_2. Strike arcs from R_1 and R_2 meeting at C and D. Draw guidelines 30° from vertical down from R_2 until they touch a horizontal line that connects C and D; label those points E and F. Draw an equilateral triangle from EF,

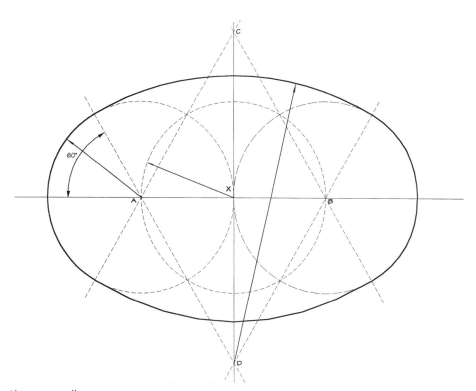

Figure 8.26 Plotting an ellipse.

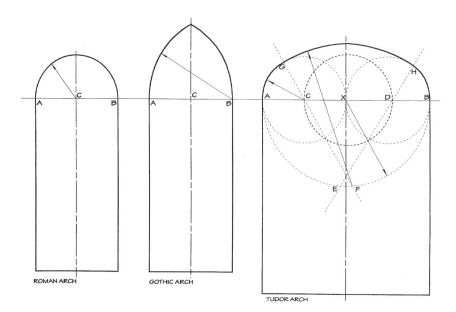

Figure 8.27
Drawing arches.

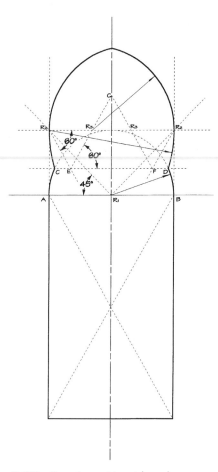

Figure 8.28 Drawing a Moorish arch.

and draw a horizontal guideline connecting R_2. At the intersection of the triangle and line R_2 are points R_3, strike an arc from them to complete the arch.

The Russian Reverse-Ogee Arch

Draw horizontal and vertical baselines, label the intersection R_1 (see Figure 8.29). Draw 45° guidelines from R_1 up, and strike arcs from R_1 to A and B (the width of the desired arch) to meet the guidelines. Label those points C and D, and construct an equilateral triangle up from there. From the center of CD, draw guidelines 30° from vertical upward a good distance. Label the intersection of the triangle and the guidelines as R_2, and draw arcs from there as shown, stopping at the guidelines. Transfer length CD further out on the 30° guidelines to find G, and strike the final arcs from G; repeat on the other side.

SIGNS AND LETTERING

Lettering and proper sign painting is an art in itself. Many extremely skilled painters are lettering specialists. The craft relies on tools similar to those of the scenic artist, but the investment in good lettering brushes can be considerable. A theatrical scenic artist will be called to do signage often and must be prepared for it by knowing some basic rules of the craft.

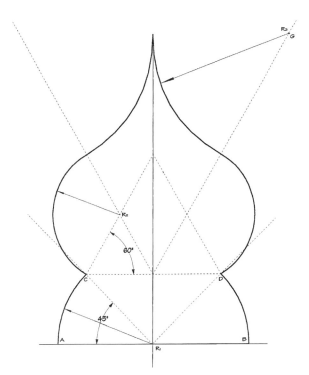

Figure 8.29 Drawing a Russian or reverse-ogee arch.

We see signs every day in shops, on the road, in advertising—everywhere. We know no set of symbols better than the alphabet. Therefore, it is obvious to lay people when these symbols are laid out incorrectly, although they may not know why. When learning to draw and cartoon, signage should be given a lot of attention. Once the rules of signage are clear, they will make logical sense. When apprenticing sign painting, most students are encouraged to learn one font or lettering style first. The object is to learn one style completely before moving on. We encourage the scenic painting student to do the same. Once you are thoroughly acquainted with one lettering style and can do it without referring to a guide, other styles and variations will come easily.

Lettering styles for scenery are chosen by the scenic designer. Many designers include copies of the fonts they have chosen for the signage in the research pack they present to the scenic artist. Unless the signage is very large, it is much too difficult to render lettering accurately in half-inch scale. If signage on the elevation comes through to the shop with no research and its style is not evident, the

charge painter should ask the designer to choose a font. Most shops keep several books on hand of lettering and font styles from which the designer can make a selection then and there. If the designer has some of the same font style books, this decision can be made over the phone.

The Rules and Methods of Sign Painting

In the scenic arts, there are two types of painters: those who can do sign painting and those who cannot. As most scenic artists can spend a lifetime of education and study on the skills of painting alone, a great many scenic artists would not venture to say that they are sign painters as well. Also, in this day and age, a good hands-on sign painter is getting hard to find. Most sign work is generated by computers now. The best way to learn signage is to do it. Embrace the opportunity to work on several sign painting projects until you feel comfortable with your skills.

Layout Tools

For the most part, the tools used for the layout and cartooning of signage are the same as the tools discussed earlier in this chapter: scale rulers, measuring sticks, straight edges, and triangles. At sign-painting supply stores, you may be able to pick up clear plastic straight edges that have a grid printed on them. These sign painters' rulers are very useful in three ways. First, they come in a variety of widths so that they can be used for drawing the widths of the down strokes and cross bars of larger letters. Second, their width and the grid can be used for figuring out spacing between letters and words. Third, these rulers are very flexible and can be used for splining the tight curves of letters being cartooned. Frequently signage work will involve drafting the cartoon of the sign first on paper. A drawing bench should be set up in the shop for complex cartooning projects like signage. A simple drawing bench can be just a 4' × 8' piece of AB plywood. The drawing bench should be tilted up steeply at a 60° angle or better to relieve back strain (see Figure 8.30). The bottom of the bench should be about two and a half feet off the floor. This way you can work more comfortably and look at your work objectively from a distance. If space is a problem in the shop, then the drawing bench can be designed to fold up against the wall. If

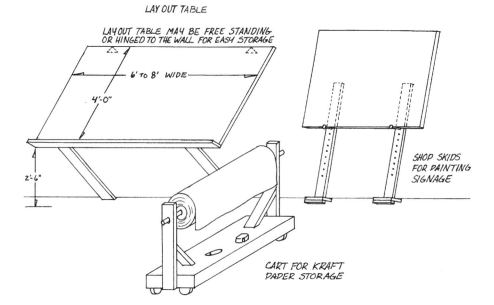

Figure 8.30
A drawing bench,
shop skids.

built carefully and thoughtfully, it can be used like a drafting board. Horizontals and verticals can be set using T-squares and triangles.

If a great many signs need to be done for a given production, shop skids can be used to prop up the signs against the wall at a good working height. The shop skid is simply a five- to eight-foot piece of 2" × 4" stock with bolt holes drilled in it at regular intervals. The 2" × 4" needs a foot to stabilize the skid against a wall and keep it from falling sideways. A pair of shop skids with bolts inserted at the same height can hold a sign at a comfortable working height.

Sign Painting Brushes

When buying lettering brushes, remember what trade you are in. Chances are that any lettering that you will be doing will not be seen from closer than twenty feet. Also keep in mind your own skills. The best brush in the world will not make you a terrific sign painter. It will help, but it has no brain; you do.

When you are buying brushes ask for brushes that are made for use in water-based mediums (refer to Chapter Five for a full discussion of lettering brushes). If you have cause to use a lettering brush in an oil-based medium at some point, do not bother

trying to revive it for use in water-based mediums again. The bristles will start to get frizzy and lose their snap. Store brushes that are used with oil-based mediums in lard oil or olive oil. Lard oil does not dry out, so it is very good for storing and conditioning oil-medium brushes. Lard oil can be purchased through sign supply catalogues and stores.

The Rules of Lettering

There are hundreds of styles of letters, called *fonts*. Most of these fonts have their own drawing conventions. The primary division between the common styles of fonts is the distinction between block letters and script or sans serif and serif. Beyond these there is a huge range of specialty and trick lettering. Some fonts have been designed for uppercase (capitals) and lowercase letters, some have been designed for only one or the other. The following are some simple guidelines.

Gothic Fonts

The one-stroke gothic alphabet is one of the most commonly used, straightforward lettering styles. It is a block or sans serif style. The uppercase and lowercase letters are made up of lines of equal width. Once

Figure 8.31 Fundamental painting strokes for lettering.

this font is mastered it can serve as jumping-off point for all other block-style letters.

Certain practice strokes will aid you in developing prowess as a sign painter. These are the strokes that are repeated in different combinations to create the alphabet (Figure 8.31). Do not indulge in personal variations. The purpose of learning a font is to master a style that is inseparable from professional signage work.

Here are some general rules of lettering that, if followed, will add a professional polish. These rules are applicable to most fonts but may vary in some styles of lettering.

1. All letters based on circles or ovals should use the same shape of circle or oval. So, if you laid a template of the letter O over a C, the contours would be nearly identical except where the C is broken.
2. All round uppercase letters O, C, Q, G, and S and lowercase letters o, a, e, c, d, b, p, q, and g should be drawn slightly above and below the top and bottom guidelines. If these letters are taken right to the guide lines, optically they or parts of them will look smaller than the other letters. This is an optical correction and should not be exaggerated to the point where it is perceptible without applying a straight edge to bottom or top lines.
3. The bottoms of the B, the R, and the S should be slightly larger or wider than the top so that the letters look grounded. Once again this increase should not be exaggerated to the point where it is noticeable; it is an optical correction.
4. The crossbar on the uppercase A should be lower than the center guideline or middle bar

lines of the other letters. If the crossbar of the A is too high, the letter will appear to be top-heavy. The crossbar should not be dropped down too far, as the letter will appear to droop.
5. All letters, and in particular the square letters H, N, M, Z, and X, should be boxed in when laid out so that the letters do not lean.
6. The letters W and M will need about one and a half times the width of other letters. Round letters such as O, C, Q, and G will need about one and a quarter times the width, or they will appear to be crowded and narrower than the other letters.
7. If spacing is a problem the E, F, and T can be somewhat diminished from a full width without appearing too narrow.
8. Embellishments of font serif, the little flags sometimes added at the top and bottom of letters, should be done consistently or not at all. Doing these embellishments half and half will make the lettering look amateurish.
9. Any variation done in a given font on a given piece of signage should be consistent throughout the signage. So, for instance, if there is a G of a certain style, then that G should be used throughout the font.

Roman Fonts

Building on the gothic fonts one can move to roman fonts. In these fonts, the letters are composed of thick and thin strokes. The basis here is that, if the letters were being generated with a lettering pen, the downstrokes would create thicker lines. What started perhaps as function of the tool or brush some millennium ago has become a convention (Figure 8.32).

Either gothic or roman fonts can be built on further by adding serifs, playing with the widths of the letters, putting in drop shadows, or italicizing them by placing all the letters on a slant toward the right. This slant must be kept consistent throughout the italicized letters in the layout.

Script

Script lettering is as much about the way the letters connect to one another as it is about the shape of a letter itself. A fair amount of variation is allowed from one script to another. When working with a script, maintain any conventions of letter shape or connection throughout the font on that piece of signage, so

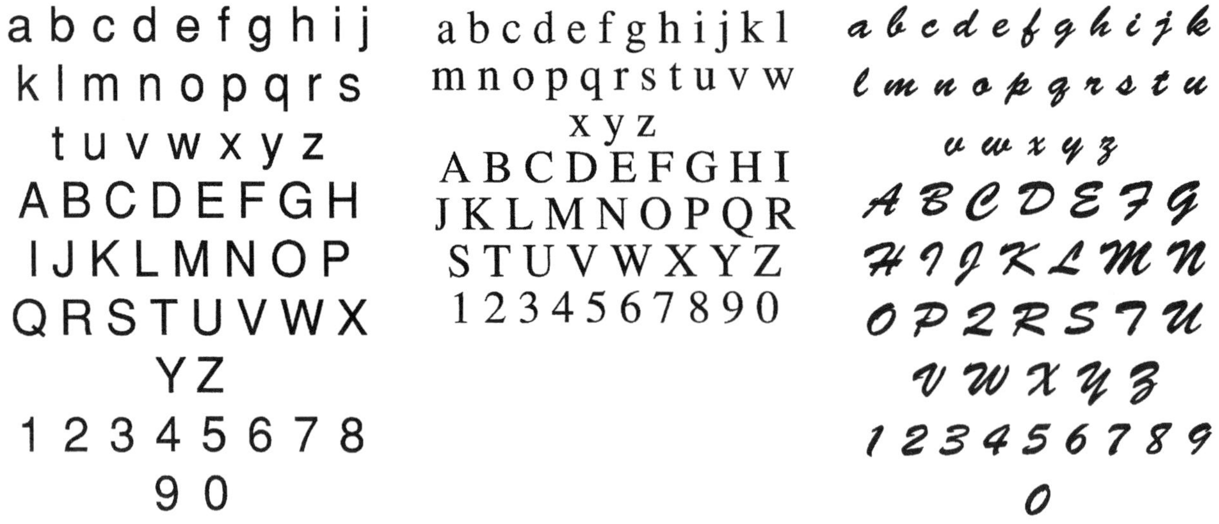

abcdefghij
klmnopqrs
tuvwxyz
ABCDEFGH
IJKLMNOP
QRSTUVWX
YZ
1 2 3 4 5 6 7 8
9 0

abcdefghijkl
mnopqrstuvw
xyz
ABCDEFGHI
JKLMNOPQR
STUVWXYZ
1234567890

abcdefghijk
lmnopqrstu
vwxyz
ABCDEFG
HIJKLMN
OPQRSTU
VWXYZ
123456789
0

Figure 8.32 Gothic, Roman serif, and script lettering.

that the script has an overall uniform appearance. The emphasis in a script is that it have a grace throughout the sign; the letters should appear to flow together smoothly.

Signage Layout

In signage the lines you do not see are as important as the lines you do see. The negative spaces around the letters and between the words are as essential as the letters themselves.

General Layout

As in any kind of complex layout and cartoon, take the time with signage to work it out on brown paper first and then make a pounce of it. This process also is a convenience, because once the signage is pounced in position it then may have to be moved or shifted. It is easy enough to blow off the charcoal and repounce a sign moved up two inches; it is a different matter entirely if the sign was drawn in place. Also, the a whole sequence of letters may need to be erased and reworked. If this is done on the scenery, that area will get smudged and dirty from being overworked. Another reason to pounce signage is that the layout can be done on a work-

bench or in a clear space rather than hunched over a piece of scenery.

Layout on Transparent Surfaces

Frequently a designer will call for signage on a window. In theatre, Plexiglas is usually used instead of real glass for safety reasons. The advantage here is that you can ask the construction department to leave the protective paper cover on the Plexiglas and do your cartoon directly on that paper. Later, the letters can be cut out with an X-Acto knife. The paper cover will serve as a spray mask, also called a *frisket*. Frisket paper is available for this sort of work anywhere airbrush supplies are sold.

Often lettering is placed on the back of a sheet of Plexiglas. Do not try to lay out signage backward. You will be unaware of several mistakes until you view the piece from the front. Do a pounce, then simply flip it over to use it.

Spacing

Letterspacing is done in two ways. In mechanical spacing, the boxes around each letter are exactly the same distance apart from each other. This spacing works well for an H that is next to an E, but when an A is next to a Y, the letters will look like they are too far apart. It looks mechanical. The appearance can be corrected with optical spacing. In optical spacing, the A and the Y would be moved closer together so that comparably they look like they are the same distance apart as the H and the E.

Before inking the lines or applying paint to the layout take a moment to actually read what has been written. First, see if optically the sign flows together. Second, check your spelling or, better yet, have someone else check it for you. In sign painting, it is easy to become so involved with the layout and style of the letters that you may be oblivious to having spelled Taylor instead of Tailor. Yes this is a true example, and it was discovered on opening night.

Margins

Margins are very important to the flow of a sign. To make a sign clearer and easier to read, it may be more useful to sacrifice a little on the height and the width of the letters so that there is adequate space around the letters and words. Crowded, unplanned layouts are more difficult to make sense of regardless of the size of the letters.

CONCLUSION

The cartooning of scenery is as important as painting itself and as enjoyable. It allows the scenic artist to become completely immersed in the design. This is the time to explore and understand the work of the scenic designer before committing to the more permanent painting ahead. Cartooning is a satisfying job as the scenery begins to take on the form it is intended to have.

Cartooning calls on the skill of drawing, a skill that good scenic artists need. In this step, the scenic artist transforms the often tiny squiggles and gestures in the paint elevation through his or her understanding of art and a sense of the scenic designer's style. Only after the cartooning is done can the work of applying color begin.

chapter 9

Two-Dimensional Scenic Painting Techniques

INTRODUCTION

Here you are at last. The scenery is primed and cartooned, the colors are mixed, and you are ready to paint. The first piece of advice is simple: just put the color where the color goes. The second piece of advice also is simple: make every brushstroke count. Proper application of paint is not about smearing color around until it ends up in the right place by chance, nor is it drowning the scenery in glaze coats all day long. It is the careful, thoughtful application of color in the proper sequence with the right tools. This chapter illustrates the proper methods for many traditional painting techniques. Learning and practicing sound methodology will help you realize the two simple rules just stated.

The basic two-dimensional paint techniques discussed and illustrated in this chapter are the fundamental building blocks for how to paint almost anything on scenery. Two-dimensional painting techniques are one third of a triad that forms an image, with color and line being the other two. These techniques also form a vocabulary of scenic art and are a means of communication between artists. All scenic artists should be proficient in these techniques and understand the full meaning of them. A scenic artist in New York can talk to a scenic designer on the phone from Los Angeles, describe the color and opacity of cast shadows for a drop, and execute the work at hand without needing the designer actually to be there, because they speak the same language. The individual techniques described here are fairly simple on an individual basis. A good

scenic artist knows how to use them repeatedly, consistently, and with appropriate adaptation to whatever medium is used. These techniques are part of the trade of a scenic artist, the artist's skills. Two-dimensional painting techniques range from simply covering a surface with a color to creating the illusion of three dimensions on a flat surface. Specific textures and patterns also are created with two-dimensional painting techniques.

BASE PAINTING TECHNIQUES

Every paint job starts with the *base coat*, which is the foundation of color and texture. Choosing which style of base coat to apply depends largely on what materials are being painted as well as the result desired. In a few cases, no base coat will be needed, as the primer serves as the base in certain techniques used on backdrops, such as working with aniline dye or painting a translucent area. However, almost always there is a base coat, and it has two important functions. First, it is the foundation of color for the techniques to follow, which might be a single color or several blended colors. Second, the base coat also creates a pattern of grain or texture. Every brushstroke has direction and creates a texture signature. Creating wood in paint is the most obvious example of this texture, as it is natural to pull the brush with the direction of the wood grain. Many other grain patterns can be made in base coating as well as random patterns of texture. Smooth, grainless bases can be painted as well, using the proper technique.

A base coat of paint can be mixed out of any water-based painting medium, such as dry pigment, casein, latex, or acrylic. Always be certain the paint has sufficient binder, if working with dry pigment. When mixing lighter colors, the base may be mixed from a less-expensive paint, such as household latex or acrylic, because so much of it is needed. Large painting suppliers offer very inexpensive off-white contractor's paint, which can be ideal as a base coat for hard scenery.

Brush Techniques

Base Painting Large Areas without Leaving a Grain

The brush used to paint the base coat should be the largest brush you can handle and should hold a large charge of paint, particularly when base painting a large piece. Covering a large area each time you charge the brush means a more efficient base painting technique. A typical brush for large jobs is a six-inch- to eight-inch-wide flat-ferrule brush with two or three paint wells. A brush such as this covers about ten to twelve square feet with each charge. The direction of the brushstroke makes a difference, as most paints develop a grain when applied in one direction. A simple figure-eight stroke or a sort of omnidirectional paint stroke leaves virtually no grain when dry (Figure 9.1). Changing the brush direction, as with the figure-eight stroke, provides better penetration of the paint, particularly on rough surfaces. The viscosity of the paint is important as well. It should be thin enough to spread easily but thick enough to cover. Paint the viscosity of heavy cream works well for a base coat.

Creating a Grain Pattern in the Base Coat

Some materials emulated in scenic painting have a distinct grain, such as wood or marble. Creating a grain in the base coat is an advantage in convincingly simulating these materials. Loosely follow the direction of the grain intended for that surface, even when working with only one color, so the grain of the base coat does not interfere with subsequent paint techniques, such as dry brush or glaze treatments (Figure 9.2).

Cutting a Hard Line in a Base Coat

Landscapes or architectural details may have several different colors of base coat for different areas of the

Figure 9.1 Omnidirectional stroke and brush.

scenery. A light single-color base coat may have areas of different colors painted over it later. Base painting the scenery area by area with different colors is called *cutting in* a base. In either case, cutting in calls for careful painting up to the cartoon line, where the color shift takes place.

The natural inclination when cutting in is to do the edges first, then fill in the rest with a large brush. The problem with this approach is that the initial cut-in lines dry quickly. The overlapping larger brushstrokes used to fill in leave a different texture, which may show through subsequent techniques. Avoid this problem by cutting in the line for a few feet and filling in with a bigger brush while the paint still is wet. Another solution is to cut in all around the cartoon first, but break up the cut-in strokes as you go, so that a sharp dry edge does not form.

When cutting in an edge always use the largest brush possible that still gives control. Larger brushes

Figure 9.2 Creating grain with the base coat.

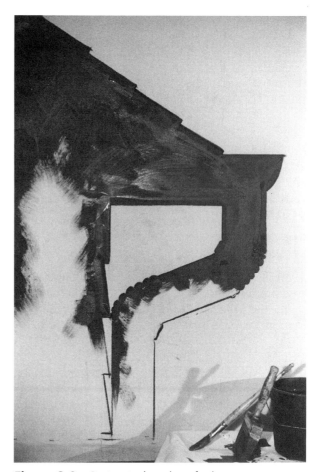

Figure 9.3 Cutting in the edge of a base coat.

hold more paint, have to be charged less often, and get the job done faster. Edges can sometimes be cut in with a four-inch flat ferrule or even a priming brush (Figure 9.3).

Wet Blending

Wet blending is the technique of blending together two or more colors while they are wet (Figure 9.4). The blend can be done with any consistency of paint, from glazes to opaque. A wet blend often serves as the base coat. If a very large area needs to be wet blended, then the leading edge of the blend can be kept moist by spraying it lightly with a garden sprayer. Generally, the blend is done by laying in all the colors save one in the right proportion and pattern. The last color is used to blend together the other colors. This last color is the dominant color of the blend.

Smoothing or Feathering a Wet Blend

A wet blend can be patchy or quite smooth (Figure 9.5). If the blend is to be very smooth, then a large dry brush should be used to do the final smoothing in order to give the surface a feathery finish. Wet blends also may be done on surfaces that have been moistened with water first, so that the colors melt into one another more readily.

Wet Blending for a Grain Pattern

If the wet blend is part of a treatment that emulates a grained material, such as wood or marble (Figure 9.6), then the blend should be done in the same direction of the grain. When painting grained materials, this wet blend forms the basis of the final paint job. When doing a wet blend for specific effect, always try to capture the characteristic of that material in that first blend.

Figure 9.4
A typical wet blend.

Graded Wet Blending or Ombré

Graded wet blending, or an ombré blend, is a smooth even transition from one hue or value to another. In a wet blend this is done by laying the separate colors or values in stripes across the width of the blend and systematically brushing one color into the other (Figure 9.7). Then, blend one color field into the next with a clean dry brush working from the lightest color field to the darkest. Usually, this final blend begins in the lightest value color and works toward the dark. If the area being blended is a little too large, the paint can be kept moist by lightly spraying it with water. Do not use too much water when keeping an area moist. Too much water will cause control problems. Very large areas that need to be covered with an ombré blend should done with sprayers rather than brushed.

Scumbling

The terms *scumbling* and *wet blending* often are confused. There is no sharp division between these terms; on some projects you may be hard pressed to say whether it is a wet blend or a scumble. But, there can be a great difference in the resulting texture.

The object of scumbling is to let the colors mingle together without necessarily making an effort to blend them. Sometimes, the paint strokes in a scumble can have the quality of being drawn or sketched, so that one layer of paint shows through the gaps of another layer. A scumble is done on a dry surface rather than a moist surface that will melt the edges of the paint strokes. A scumble may be done over a large area for color shift and modeling or it can be done in a tight and specific application for detail work (Figure 9.8). Areas of one color may even dry before another color is scumbled into them.

A scumble can be done with a brush of any size or style. Scumbles can be done with any consistency of paint. So, whether the treatment is to be done with a glaze, a thin wash of color, or opaque paint will depend on the needs of the project and the elevation.

Figure 9.5
A smooth wet blend.

Washes and Glazes

A wash or glaze is a thin coat of transparent paint. Washes and glazes are used for dozens of reasons, to tone down a harsh color with a shade, to make an image soften or recede, or to faintly color an area like the panes of glass in a window. Generally, a wash refers to a large area of transparent color, while a glaze is more localized. Washes and glazes are made by working with very thin paint, or by using normal strength paint and dipping the brush into water to thin it. Washes and glazes can be applied to wet or dry surfaces; the wet into wet wash yields a smoother result, like watercolor. Many techniques rely on wash work, such as wood graining, perspective effects, and stone and marble. Washes of color also can be built up in layers to give flat color fields greater depth.

Any water-based paint can be used as a wash. The wash can be applied with a large brush, sprayed on and brushed in, or even rolled on.

Base Coat Painting with Rollers

A roller is a very efficient tool for covering a large flat area with paint. Beyond this, the roller may be used for a variety of paint techniques, such as lining work and painting texture, as it has characteristics that are very different from brushwork. Rollers have their own signature and can be used in such instances where a more organic quality is desired. (Rollers themselves are fully described in Chapter Five.)

Roller Techniques

The most common purpose for a roller is to quickly cover a lot of square footage with paint or finish. Like brushes, rollers can leave a grain if worked in the same direction. So, as in base-coat painting with a brush, the roller should be worked in different directions and the strokes should be overlapped to spread the paint evenly.

When working with finishes, the opposite sometimes is true. Overworking a finish can trap air bubbles in the finish, which will dry cloudy. This can be particularly noticeable if the finish is on a dark paint treatment. In the case of finishes, particularly fast-drying ones, it is sometimes best to apply the finish with even, minimal strokes. Two layers applied in this manner should result in a polished finish.

Figure 9.6 Wet blend for wood.

TEXTURE PAINTING TECHNIQUES

Additional texturing steps are often called for after the base coat. The texturing can use a variety of tools including sponges, brushes, rollers, rags, feathers, and other tools you may create for specific projects.

Texturing with a Roller

Rollers also are used to paint two-dimensional texture. After charging the roller, wring out the excess paint on a flat tray or flat scrap of wood; screens and roller trays may leave an imprint in the fleece of the roller cover. A mostly dry roller will leave a grainy pattern of paint that will be more pronounced if you do not comb out the fleece with a brush before using it. The roller is worked from several directions so a direction in the grain does not develop. A dry roller can be used with a stencil or by itself (Figure 9.9).

A fleece roller can be segmented with strips of any waterproof tape wrapped tightly around the nap. If evenly segmented with tape, the roller will leave a stripe pattern that works well for an ink block or crosshatched effect. A roller segmented so the tape crisscrosses it leaves a broken pattern not unlike tree bark or other organic textures.

Some techniques relate to specific types and styles of roller covers. For example, foam covers come in a variety of naps, from one-quarter inch to three-quarter inch. Foam roller covers hold less paint than fleece covers, but foam rollers can be carved into an imprint or a specific design. One very useful variety of foam roller is manufactured for painting over rough surfaces. This roller is covered with a three-quarter layer inch of foam with slits in it for working into the nooks and crannies of a textured surface.

Other types of rollers not made specifically for paint can be very useful in creating textures (Figure 9.10). So-called texture roller covers have a looped nap and render a texture coat with very uniform grain. These make an even texture in the thick wall surfacing compounds used in homes. The texture compound is applied first with a brush or a fleece roller, then reworked with the texture roller before it sets up. If the texture roller is used with plaster, it must be washed out immediately after use. Glue roller covers are surfaced with looped carpet. These rollers work well with highly viscous materials. Scenic supply houses sell mottled leather roller covers that leave their own particular imprint when used with paint or texture.

Which paint should be used with a roller? Any standard water-based scenic or house paint can be used with rollers. All standard solvent-based paints may be used as well, just remember to get extra roller covers when purchasing these paints. It is not worth the expense to clean these.

Dry Brushing

Dry brushing is done by separating the bristles of a charged brush and dragging them across a wet or dry surface to leave a very streaky, linear paint stroke. Dry brushing implies that the brush itself has very little charge, but this is not the case. A brush for dry brushing should be fairly well charged with paint, so that

Figure 9.7 The steps of an ombré blend: (left) the colors laid in next to each other and (right) finished ombré blend with stripes to show contrast.

Figure 9.8
Broad scumble.

Figure 9.9a
Dry roller technique:
detailed.

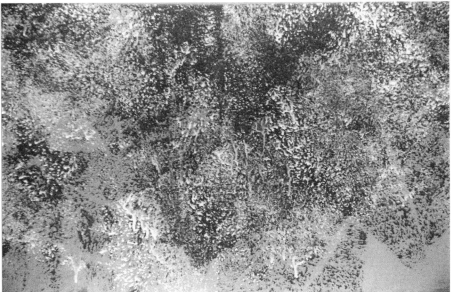

Figure 9.9b
Dry roller technique:
broad.

you can pull out as long a stroke of paint as possible (Figure 9.11).

The Tools and Paint for Dry Brushing

Usually, flat-ferrule brushes are used for dry brushing. Because the bristles need to be separated, this technique is very hard on liners and nicer brushes. If you are using a good-quality flat-ferrule brush to dry brush, the bristles will tend to clump together, just as they have been designed to. Gently separate the bristles by combing the brush across the lip of the paint bucket. The bristles of some older, much-used brushes usually separate out on their own, and these could be the best choice for dry brushing. Any brush can be cut up to give the bristles a specific pattern.

Which paint should be used when dry brushing? The paint used in dry brushing should be thin enough to flow smoothly. If you use a paint that is too thick, you will not be able to get a very long paint stroke out of your charged brush. The paint can be either opaque or a glaze, depending on the technique at hand.

Figure 9.10a
Variations of roller types.

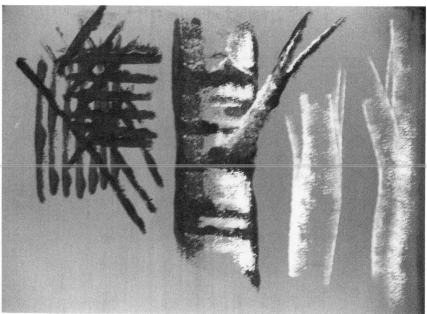

Figure 9.10b
Variations of rollers used
on edge.

Dry Brushing Techniques

Dry brushing can be used to represent a variety of materials, like wood grains, tapestry fabric and other coarse materials, grasses, or conifer trees. A very important aspect to good dry brushing is paying attention to where it starts and stops. If you lay the width of the brush down and start a stroke in the middle of what is intended to be a heavy wooden plank, this obvious paint stroke will remind the view-

ers that they are looking at a poor paint job and not a wooden plank. Generally, begin a dry brushstroke at the end of the plank or a natural division in the material. Finesse also comes into play (Figure 9.12). You might do nothing but dry brushstrokes using the full width of the brush from the beginning to the end of a stroke. In some instances that is what is called for. Often, some variation in the technique will enhance the treatment. Learn to begin the dry brushstroke with the corner of the brush, then ease the rest of the

Figure 9.10c
Variations of taped rollers.

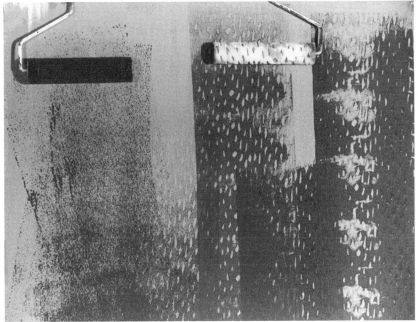

Figure 9.10d
Variations of cut foam rollers.

brush down while pulling through on the stoke. You also can end a stoke in this manner, by rolling one corner of the brush up and trailing off the stroke.

Graining

Wood and stone, particularly marble, have very distinctive grain patterns (Figure 9.13). The patterns evolve in the actual material through normal growth or formation. When wood or marble is cut for use, it reveals a variety of grain patterns. We all know wood develops a ring pattern during normal growth. Dozens of different grains are revealed in wood when the tree is cut for use. Trees are cut lengthwise, widthwise, or shaved while being rotated. Each type of cut produces a distinctive grain, and the grain also

Figure 9.11 A standard dry brush technique.

will vary depending on the type of wood and the part of the tree from which the wood is milled. Painted wood grain could be a long, stringy grain or semicircular arcs, or small bull's eye pattern, to name just a few.

Stone and marble can produce an equally wide variation in grain pattern. Marble is a mixture of stone pieces and liquid bands of minerals, formed by centuries of compression. The original fluid state of marble lends itself to endless variations of pattern. Marble, like wood, might be cut in different ways. Sheets are the most common architectural format, whereas a large carved block is the basis for a sculptural piece. With either of these materials, or any naturally formed material, the scenic artist needs to understand the logic behind the pattern. These grains may appear completely random, but they are not. Marble and wood evolve along rather clear lines, which the scenic artist should understand.

A tricky aspect to painting the grain of naturally formed materials is that the grain follows no set pattern yet is repetitive in form. It is completely human to apply a grain with a repetitive motion, producing a pronounced repetitive pattern. When the same pattern repeats itself over and over in an image, it reminds the viewer that they are just looking at paint. Crosscut wood has rings that give the grain a V-, U-, or oval-shaped pattern. A scenic artist may be tempted to return to these patterns frequently when graining wood. When these patterns are overdone, they may appear ludicrous and the graining will become a parody of wood. In graining marble, the tendency is to keep forking off the grain until it looks like tree branches or to interconnect the grain until it has a cellular pattern. Make comparisons frequently between your work and the research. Avoid mechanical repetition when graining and always think of how the material actually was formed. Understanding its structure will give the scenic artist an insight into how it may be recreated with paint. Remember that less is more; sometimes, a suggestion of grain will be more convincing than a densely grained surface. It is like an actor finding a motivation for any action. Method painting—imagine that!

Graining Techniques and Tools

A variety of tools are used for creating grain. Brushes are a reliable choice for many graining projects, because they can create a natural pattern when handled correctly. A brush is handled differently for graining than for other techniques. Whereas normally you would have a firm hold on the tool, in graining you hold the brush loosely and roll it around in your hand to alternate between painting with the edge and the width of the brush. This works particularly well when graining marble. The type of brush used for graining will vary, sometimes a liner will do or a small flat-ferrule brush would be preferable. As with other techniques, always use the largest brush you can, for theatricality and efficiency. When graining is first painted with a brush, it can look a little hard-edged. To soften the wood or marble, you can drag another brush through the painted grain, following its direction, while the paint is wet.

Other painting tools are used to create the effect of naturally occurring grains. Using a tool other than a brush may help you avoid repetitive patterns in the graining. Feathers have been used to grain marble for

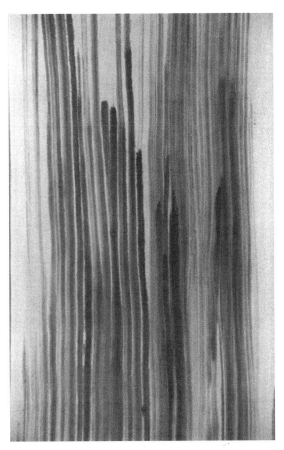

Figure 9.12a Standard dry brush technique: dry brushing in an area moistened with water

centuries (Figure 9.14). A large bird feather is used by dragging it through a fresh wet blend or by dipping it in grain-colored paint and dragging across the surface. As you turn the feather over while dragging it, the grain will abruptly change direction, as it would in the marble. This technique works well enough for small-scale faux finishes. The problem with using this technique on a scale correct for theatre is that a bird feather does not hold a lot of paint. Having to recharge the feather every few seconds really can slow down a process, especially with an entire deck to paint. One solution is to use a feather duster of turkey, pheasant, or ostrich feathers. Several feathers will hold a great deal more paint then one scrawny feather. A muslin flogger or a rag may also be used in this manner. The grain lines from these will be somewhat softer than the graining done by a brush.

A variety of faux finish tools are used for graining wood. Some of these tools work well for the larger scale of theatrical painting. Many of these tools are available at paint and decorator supply stores and through some theatrical supply houses. The *grainer* is a tool that makes wood grain with paint. A grainer may be a rubber pad adhered to a curved block, sometimes called a *rocker*, a hollow rubber tube, or a rubber pad that has been molded into a grain pattern in relief. Such tools are available in some variations of grains. These tools selectively squeegee a pattern off the surface, leaving a pattern

Figure 9.12b
Standard dry brush technique: crosshatch and basket weave.

Figure 9.13a
Example of wood graining
with a brush

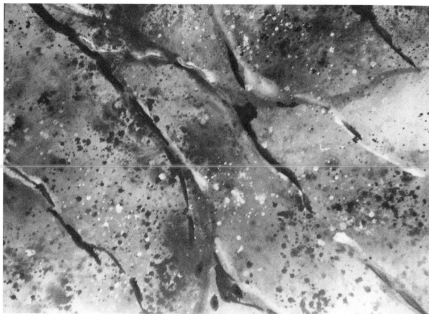

Figure 9.13b
Example of marble graining
with a brush.

reminiscent of a crosscut wood grain. The grainer is dragged through the paint or tinted transparent glaze medium while it is wet. The tool works best if the base paint is a satin finish or has a satin finish applied over it so that the glaze medium squeegees off easily. While working with this tool, occasionally rotate it in relation to the direction of your stroke for more variety. The finesse in using this tool comes in not overdoing it. Because it leaves such a distinctive pattern, a little goes a very long way.

Combs, made out rubber or stainless steel, are used in conjunction with a grainer or by themselves to squeegee or scrape wet paint off a surface in a linear grain pattern. Combs retailed as faux finish tools have been cut into uniform widths so there is no sense of natural variation. Rotate the comb in relation to the direction of your stroke to add variation. Also the teeth of these combs tend to be spaced too tight to read well for broad theatrical style. One solution may be to cut gaps in the teeth. However, it goes against the grain, so to speak, to cut up a set of costly stainless steel combs. You can easily fashion your own combs out of rubber or plastic sheets to fit the type and scale of wood grain needed. Wadded newspaper also works well as a comb of sorts. Because every wad of paper will leave a different grain, there will be no repetitive patterns.

A *checker grainer* is an odd tool made up of several stainless steel rings that swivel on a small roller carriage. These rings have indentations cut into the edges so that, when charged with paint and rolled across the surface, they will leave a series of choppy lines, much the same as you would find in an oak grain. A similar pattern can be created by lightly spattering the surface with paint and dragging a dry brush through the paint to create a series of small choppy lines. This technique is called *spatter and drag*.

Which paint should be used when graining? The paint used for brush-applied grain in a marble or wood can be standard scene paint. The paint can be thinned down to whatever consistency is most workable. A glaze medium is necessary for working with faux wood graining tools. The glaze medium may be a clear finish such as water-based urethane, P.V.A., or clear latex. Add tints to the glaze medium to create the desired hue and saturation.

Lining

Lining simply is painting lines. They can be straight or curved, done freehand or guided with a lining stick. Lining technique is useful for creating emphatic shadows, architectural moldings, linear patterns, or any image that looks "drawn." Using a lining brush and a lining stick, either vertically or on the floor, is a key skill for a scenic artist.

Lining sticks are used to aid the scenic artist in making perfectly straight brushstrokes. They come in a wide variety of lengths (as described in Chapter Eight) and are made for use on a paint frame or on the deck with extensions. A lining stick can be almost anything, from a 2" × 4" to a stir stick, but the better ones have three important characteristics: they are lightweight, easy to hold and move, and are beveled underneath to prevent paint from running under their edge onto the scenery.

The spline and a compass are useful lining guides for curves and arcs. A spline of any reasonable

Figure 9.14 Marble graining with a feather duster.

length takes at least two people to set down and hold for the painter. Splines (as described in Chapter Eight) often are homemade tools and will not behave as well as conventional lining sticks in preventing paint from running underneath them. Use splines very carefully as a lining stick. A shop compass can be fitted with a brush on one leg (Figure 9.15). Smaller circles can be painted evenly in this manner. A lining brush may work better than a flat-ferrule brush to paint curves with a compass. When painting any kind of tightly curved line, a flat-ferrule brush may not be able to track the curve while maintaining the width of the line.

About Lining Brushes

Brushes used for lining can be of nearly any sort to suit the demands of the particular task. A four-inch-wide transparent cast shadow and intricate crosshatching both are lining tasks, but each of these jobs calls for a very different brush. A lining brush must have bristles that are tight and do not splay out. Errant bristles will cause linework to look sketchy. Always use a brush that gives the desired line width and holds as much paint as possible. Oddly enough, fitch brushes sold by theatrical supply companies as liners are not always the best choice for doing line work because they do not hold a large charge of paint like other styles of brushes. Flat-ferrule brushes, particularly sash brushes, often

Figure 9.15a
Lining with a spline.

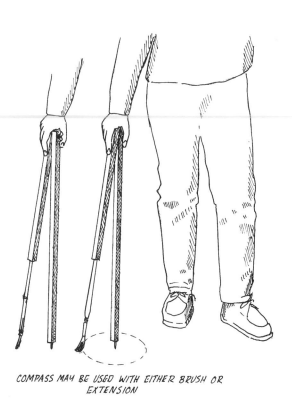

COMPASS MAY BE USED WITH EITHER BRUSH OR
EXTENSION

Figure 9.15b   Lining with a compass.

Figure 9.15c   Painter working with a lining stick. Drop
designed by John Schak, designer of Carmina Burana,
presented at the University of Michigan.

are an excellent choice for lining. These brushes hold a good charge of paint, so they can go for a long distance between chargings. A one-inch sash or flat-ferrule brush used on edge can deliver a good one-quarter- or one-half-inch line.

Lining is easy to practice, and any scenic artist not used to lining should do so. It is relatively easy to pull a brush along the edge of a lining stick. Always use the thinner side of the brush if possible to get as much as possible out of each charge. For example, a four-inch sash brush held sideways should generate a one-inch-wide line that is several feet long, but a one-inch-wide brush will give up the ghost pretty quickly. Remember to keep the brush as vertical as possible, keeping the bristles from running under the lining stick. Keep your eyes slightly ahead of the brush. This avoids mistakes and makes the brush go to where you are looking. Keep an even pressure on the brush so the line stays the same width. Do not tilt the brush over, toward, or away from the lining stick while drawing out your line. Doing this will cause the line to waver. If you are merging one painted line into the end of another, begin moving the brush along the edge of the lining stick before the tip of the bristles comes in contact with the surface. In this way the separate paint strokes will taper and merge into one another.

Which paint should be used when lining? Any scene paint can be used for lining. Keep in mind that the paint should be as thin as possible but still keep the quality of color desired. If paint is too thick, the line will not pull out well. The stroke will get sketchy and quickly start to skip. If you must do line work with an oil-based paint, thin the paint with the appropriate solvent. Use proper safety precautions (see Chapter Four, Safety and Health Regulations).

Sponging

Sponging simply means applying paint or texture with a sponge. Sponges can be used to create a very convincing organic texture. They may also be used for blending fields of color and chiaroscuro shading. Various types and styles of sponges should be stocked in the shop and the scenic artist's kit.

Sponge Technique

A natural ocean sponge often is used to create the illusion of texture on two-dimensional surfaces because of its natural texture. Sponging can be used to create the appearance of a variety of materials such as rock, tree bark, distant tree foliage, coral reefs, and so on. A surface may be moistened with water first to soften sponge work. The sponge, not as heavily charged, also may be used for applying color through a stencil. Natural sponges frequently are used to soften edges and blend in painting. The natural sponge works well putting paint on a real texture. A sponge dabbed over a surface after texture compound has been applied gives it a more natural or organic appearance (Figure 9.16). It is important to rotate the sponge between dabs so that a pattern does not develop.

Sponges are an important cleaning tool. A scenic artist should keep a bucket of water and a natural sponge nearby for cleaning up drips while working. When a bucket of paint gets spilled on a drop, a soft natural sponge is the first tool to reach for. Be sure not to rub a spill. Dab up the spilled paint and clean out the sponge thoroughly each time it is wrung. If necessary, spray the edges of the spill with water to keep them from drying before they can be cleaned up.

Figure 9.16 Various ocean sponges and ocean sponge textures.

Synthetic sponges are manufactured out of cellotex or foam rubber. They can be torn up so they have a more natural texture. Both the cellotex and the foam rubber sponges give a specific texture when torn up that may be applicable for particular surfaces. They also can be cut up or used in the block shape to print or texture repetitive shapes like bricks and tiles. They may be carved into a pattern to be printed on scenery. Because of the limited size of foam rubber and cellotex sponges, it may be necessary to use sheets of foam rubber and make paint stamps for larger pattern work.

> Which paint should be used with sponges? Any kind of water-based paint can be used with sponges. This paint can be of any consistency, from very thick and opaque to a glaze. Sponging also may be done with any water-based clear medium. Joint compound can be sponged to make a three-dimensional texture. Do not use a sponge with plaster or solvent-based paint unless you are prepared to throw it away afterwards. Never use a sea sponge with bleach.

Rag Rolling

Rag rolling is exactly that, a paint-soaked rag loosely twisted and rolled around on a surface. This creates a broken texture that is even but not repetitive (Figure 9.17). Nearly any kind of fabric can be used for rag rolling. To soften a texture, the edges of the rag can be frayed. Burlap and muslin are terrific for rag rolling and almost always found somewhere in a scene shop. Another rag rolling technique involves wrapping and tying rags around a roller cover. Use this in a multidirectional fashion or in a single direction to create a grain on the scenery.

> Which paint should be used when rag rolling? Any kind of paint can be used for rag rolling, from thin glazes to fully opaque paints, depending on the desired effect. Rags commonly are used to spread and work in stains and finishes on wood and in some faux finish aging techniques.
>
> CAUTION: A note about using rags with solvent-based paints. Rags soaked in solvents and oils, particularly cotton rags, can and will combust spontaneously. Many fires have been started by solvent-based rags left in a pile. Once, when working with a cotton rag and linseed oil, the rag began to heat up in my hand while I was working on a scaffolding. I tossed the rag to someone on the deck, who got it to the sink just as it caught fire. Solvent-soaked rags should be disposed of in buckets of water or spread flat and allowed to dry out outside. They should be labeled as toxic waste and disposed of through an OSHA-approved agency. Always use proper safety precautions (see Chapter Four, Health and Safety Regulations).

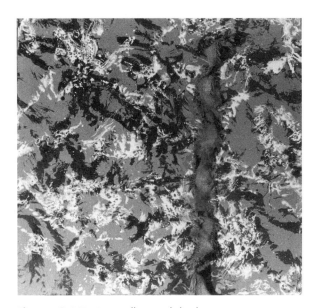

Figure 9.17 Rag rolling with burlap.

Flogging and Schlepitchka

Flogging as a paint technique is similar to flogging done in cartooning except that paint is applied rather than charcoal cleaned off. Flogging is an excellent approach as a base coat for foliage and grass. *Schlepitchka* is a texturing trick done by twirling a feather duster or flogger around gently and dabbing it on the surface of the scenery. This is difficult to do on a paint frame. If working vertically with a rag flogger the handle length should be short, so that the tool is easy to manage (Figure 9.18).

Tools and Paint of Schlepitchka

Flogging and schlepitchka can be done with a flogger made of any material you can imagine, such as burlap, netting, fishing line, muslin, or sash cord. Feather dusters commonly are used as tools for flogging and schlepitchka. The types of feathers used are chicken, ostrich, pheasant, and turkey. Feather dust-

Figure 9.18
Examples of schlepitchka with various feather dusters.

ers can be found in most discount and grocery stores, but the longer and more elegant feather dusters of ostrich, pheasant, and turkey can be found primarily at janitorial supply stores. The type of texture created in flogging depends on the type of feathers or material the flogger is made from.

> Which paint should be used with floggers? The paint used for these techniques can be any consistency necessary, from thoroughly opaque to thin glazes. Floggers drip a lot when working with glazes. It will be necessary to wring a fair amount of paint from the tool after charging it. If a flogger or feather duster is sopping wet, the feathers or rags cling together in a bundle rather than separate.

Spattering

Spattering involves flinging paint on the scenery so the paint lands in blobs. It may sound reckless but is quite controllable as well as a lot of fun. A scenic artist with a good spattering brush can make spatter from extremely coarse to extremely fine textures or can toss the paint quite a distance. Spattering is used both up and down and in almost every imaginable circumstance. Spattering is one of the most commonly used techniques in scenic painting. Manyscenic paint treatments involve spattering in at least one, if not several, stages of painted development (Figure 9.19).

Spattering Techniques and Tools

Basically, there are three techniques of spattering. One is to gently shake or rock a charged brush over an area and let the drops of paint fall in an evenly dispersed pattern. The second is to pitch or fling the paint from a charged brush so that it falls in a line or an arc. The third is to slap the ferrule of a charged brush against your hand or a piece of wood so the bristles snap and paint flies onto a surface. Each of these methods will result in a different texture. The first two techniques are primarily for work on a horizontal surface. Coarse spatter will run if attempted on vertical scenery (Figure 9.20).

Water or dirty water spatter may be done over wet paint to soften or add texture to a blend or graining. A finished piece of scenery frequently is given a dirty water spatter as the final paint application to break up the crispness of the paint job. Objects in reality usually do not have perfectly sharp edges or surfaces that reflect light seamlessly. The dappled grain of a dirty water spatter adds to the realism of the piece.

The technique of spatter and drag, discussed as a graining technique, involves spattering the surface and dragging a dry brush through the spatter to elongate its pattern before the spatter has dried. (Figure 9.21). This can be done more heavily with coarse spatter for other texture applications.

Larger brushes, four inches wide and up, should be used for spattering. It is difficult to get a

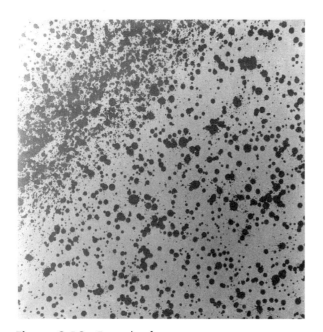

Figure 9.19 Example of coarse spatter.

while spraying to diffuse the paint over a wider area. It may take some getting used to, but this method will cover a large area with a fine spatter quickly.

Which paint should be used when spattering? Paint used for spattering should be thin enough to drop off the brush with ease when working down. If the paint is too thick, it will be particularly difficult to get an evenly dispersed spatter. When working up, the opposite is true. If the paint is too thin, then it is likely to run once it hits the surface. If a glaze or transparent spatter effect is necessary on vertical scenery, try adding a flat acrylic, methocel gum thickener, or wheat paste to the paint to give it body without adding to its opacity.

well-dispersed spatter pattern with smaller brushes. Brushes with longer bristles have more snap, making it easier to throw and disperse the paint. A garden sprayer can be used for fine and even spatter. The sprayer can be pumped to a very low pressure to spray fairly large droplets. Point the nozzle up

Boarding

Boarding is a technique used in conjunction with other techniques, such as spattering or scumbling, but boarding can be used on its own to create a texture

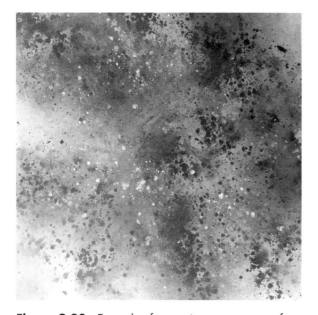

Figure 9.20 Example of spattering onto a wet surface.

Figure 9.21 An example of spatter and drag.

(Figure 9.22). Boarding uses the edge of a board to smear wet paint across a surface, creating a texture or adding dimension to what is already there. Paint also can be applied to a board and smeared straight off it. Any flat-sided board will work for this technique. If a great deal of boarding is to be done, then a tool can be improvised by fastening a handle or extension to a board for convenience. Spattering and boarding are excellent ways to create a linoleum pattern or the appearance of peeling and distressed paint.

> Which paint should be used when boarding? Paint of any consistency can be boarded. The thinner the paint, the farther it spreads. More viscous paint is preferred with boarding. It has more impact than glazes, which tend to spread too thin.

Stippling

Stippling is applying paint by dabbing or lightly dry brushing a surface with only the tips of a brush's bristles held perpendicular to the surface. Theatrical and decorating supply houses sell stippling brushes made expressly for this purpose. The bristles in these brushes are very short and set in a wide ferrule. They are trimmed to the same length so all of them can hit the surface at the same time. Until the advent of sprayers and rollers, stippling was the primary technique used to stencil (Figure 9.23). Stippling can be used to create very fine texture, too. The stippling brushes sold for use in decorating tend to be small, so they are not as useful for broad theatrical applications. Some theatrical supply houses carry large stippling brushes useful for theatrical techniques.

Pointillist painting techniques rely heavily on stippling (Figure 9.24). Smaller brushes, such as a small theatrical liner, can be used to apply color dot by dot for detail work. There are many ways for providing a broad coverage of paint in pointillist dots. Foam bottle brushes, foam orthopedic mattresses, and bundles of ethafoam rod all can be used for stippling the general areas of color.

> Which paint should be used when stippling? Paint or glaze medium used for stippling techniques should be rather thick. If the paint is too thin, it will be difficult to keep the texture consistent and even. If the paint needs too be transparent, then the color can be mixed into a flat acrylic medium so that the paint will have body. Stippling must be done with a rather dry brush. If the brush is fully charged, there will be no stipple patterns, only blobs.

Figure 9.22
Examples of boarding.

Figure 9.23
Stippling through a stencil.

A bunched-up rag or newspaper also can be used to stipple. The technique is very similar to sponging, but the different material gives various textures. With this application, it is important to rotate the wad of cloth or paper between each dab so that a pattern does not develop.

Garden Sprayers

The kind of sprayer made for gardening is an indispensable scenic art tool. These sprayers are used for smoothing and blending color over large areas. Seen from a distance, the pattern of the spray blends together smoothly into a solid wash or even gradation. Sprayers are much easier to use on scenery painted on the floor; however, with practice, they can be used on vertical scenery or drops on a paint frame.

Sprayers are available in many different, useful varieties. A paint shop should stock the two-and-a-half and three-and-a-half gallon sprayers as well as the smaller one-half-gallon size sprayers. The larger sprayers are equipped with a short hose and spray wand with a nozzle on the tip of the hose wand. The nozzle offers considerable control of the spray shape, and the hose allows the user to aim the spray in any direction. The small sprayers are very convenient for smaller jobs, because they hold less paint and are lighter and easy to clean. They spray a tighter pattern suited to detail work and toning small areas. Larger sprayers are essential for large-scale work, such as toning an entire drop.

Garden Spraying Techniques and Tools

Smoothing the texture of brushstrokes in a base coat or wet blend can be done by spraying over the brushwork with the same base colors (Figure 9.25). If two or more related colors are sprayed on the base coat, such as cooler and warmer variants of the base colors, the resulting colors are more brilliant under stage light. This is standard practice when painting flat color fields, so that the color fields are smoothed and respond well to stage light. Altering the value or hue of the base coat also can be done easily by spraying.

To spray evenly over a large surface, use a large-volume sprayer with a wand. The pressure and the spray nozzle should be set so that the spray does not come out too fine. A heavier spray will go where it is aimed, whereas a too-fine spray will be turned into wispy patterns affected by air drafts. For an even spray, the person spraying should traverse the drop or scenery in a very methodical pattern, walking

Figure 9.24 Stippling pointillism.

slowly in straight lines while taking care always to keep the spray nozzle high and the same distance from the scenery. The wand should be rotated in a small circle while keeping the nozzle perpendicular to the surface or object being painted. This rotation helps avoid uneven spray buildup and keeps the pattern of the spray much smoother. Overlap every pass of spray pattern over one half of the preceding pass.

Work methodically and take time when blending different hues or values by multiple applications of spray. Always let all spray applications dry before applying the next one. Widen the revolutions of the wand and walk more quickly to lighten the density of the spray while progressing through the blend. When doing a blend with a sprayer, it helps to have the paint hues or values shift in several stages for a smoother blend. For example, a shift from blue-violet to emerald may take four or five steps in color shifts.

Small garden sprayers are used for tight or detailed spraying jobs, such as contouring clouds or spraying into foliage. Their small capacity can run out quite quickly, so do not attempt to spray a large surface with a small sprayer. The small sprayers produce a tighter pattern and create less pressure as well, so your range is limited. They may also be used in places where space is limited or in painting small areas, as when working inside fully assembled scenic units.

Figure 9.25 Smoothing and blending with an overspray.

A common problem with garden sprayers occurs each time the spray is started. The initial spray forces out the entire contents of the spray nozzle, resulting in a splattering of paint drops. Always start the spray aimed away from the scenery, if possible. If you are working in the middle of a drop and have nowhere to aim but on the drop itself, carry a sponge to catch the drips or start the spray in a bucket.

A mask or template can be used in conjunction with a sprayer to paint along a contour or pattern. Evenly placed strips of a masking can form the basis for a wallpaper pattern. If there is an object, such as a mountain in the distance, where the spray must not go into the adjacent sky, the area around the mountain can be masked out with paper or plastic. Masking along a straight edge can be done with strips of lauan or Upson board, which can be shifted and reused repeatedly. When using visquene, or any plastic, mask on a deck, the edges should be taped down to keep the lightweight mask from moving or floating while spraying. Safety pins can be used to hold a mask in position on a paint frame. Be careful that the edges of masking do not get too wet. Visquene masking takes longer to dry than the surface of the scenery. Excessive paint built up on the masking will bleed onto the scenery.

Normally, solvent-based paints should not be used with garden sprayers, because they will shorten the life of the tool considerably and require a large amount of solvent to clean the sprayer. If the need arises, take care not to use one of the shop's favorite sprayers. French enamel varnishes (F.E.V.s) made with denatured alcohol, shellac, and dye are the most common solvent-based mediums used in garden sprayers. These can be cleaned out fairly well with denatured alcohol.

Which paint should be used in a garden sprayer? The paint used with garden sprayers should be water-based scenic or house paint. The paint must be strained through a nylon strainer. Dye also can be used with a garden sprayer. After spraying with dye, it may be necessary to clean the sprayer with a 25 percent solution of bleach before using it again with paint. Do not use bleach to clean out a sprayer before using it with another color of dye. The residual bleach will ruin subsequent dye colors.

Pneumatic Sprayers

There are three basic reasons for painting scenery with a *pneumatic sprayer*. First, some three-dimensional forms are too complex or lacy to be painted with a brush and are covered more easily with a sprayer. Second, an airbrush style demands the smooth coverage and even blend of a sprayer. Third, smooth application of a medium such as dye is accomplished more easily with a pneumatic sprayer. Pneumatic sprayers are capable of applying much thicker paint than garden sprayers. In general, these two types of sprayers are used for very different applications.

Pneumatic Spraying Techniques and Tools

A pneumatic sprayer is passed slowly back and forth across a surface to evenly coat it with paint. Each stroke should overlap by about one quarter of the preceding pass to ensure good coverage. When spraying a three-dimensional form, the recesses should be sprayed first, then the raised areas of the form to avoid excessive paint buildup.

An airbrush technique can be done on a large scale using pneumatic sprayers (Figure 9.26). Separate areas of color can be filled in and blended using masks. The masking discussed for working with garden sprayers, visquene or lauan, also work well in pneumatic spray techniques. Kraft or butcher paper masks will tend to curl when the paper gets wet, so

Figure 9.26a
Example of masked spray with a template.

Figure 9.26b Example of pneumatic spray gun technique.

use them on a limited basis only. Do not rush the painting when working with a mask, particularly if the area being sprayed is highly saturated or a blend of several applications of color. If too much paint is sprayed on the mask at a time, paint will seep under the edges of the mask. To avoid this, take the time to spray two coats of saturated colors. Areas of large color fields are difficult to lay on evenly, particularly with dyes; spraying on the color in two applications of lighter dye results in a smoother fill. Do not apply the second coat until the first coat is completely dry, or the result will be a patchy surface. If you are working with any mask, be careful not to spray at an angle that forces the paint or dye under it. Conventional artists' airbrushes can be used in scenic painting when the demand is for extremely fine or detailed work. Photo-realism is one such style where the exacting control of an airbrush is particularly useful.

Pneumatic sprayers used as tools are discussed in Chapter Five. Quart- and pint-size sprayers are the primary types used for these applications. They offer great control and are easily held in the hand. Airless sprayers should be confined to covering large areas with paint. They should not be used for work where finesse is called for, because of the high pressure and volume delivered. All pneumatic sprayers should have regulated air lines for even more control. Whenever working in a masked spray technique, the spray pressure should be set at the

lowest setting possible so the masking is not blown around.

Which paint should be used with pneumatic sprayers? Paint used in a sprayer must be thin enough to flow through the sprayer evenly. Paint that is too thick will not atomize evenly. If the paint is too thick, it will come out in droplets rather than a spray or the volume of the spray may change rhythmically, which generates a pattern on the scenery. All paint and mediums used in a sprayer should be strained through a nylon strainer. Staining is very important when working with scenic paints, as the paint is mixed up in buckets that have been used several times before. Some remnant of old paint in the bucket can stop up a sprayer if the new paint is not strained thoroughly.

Paint Stamps

A *paint stamp* is a tool similar to a giant rubber stamp and ink pad that makes repeating patterns (Figure 9.27). These stamps are custom-made and assembled in the scenic shop by the scenic artists from foam rubber glued to a piece of rigid sheet stock. Paint stamps easily can be used on both vertical and horizontal flat surfaces. A paint stamp may have an irregular, broken texture, such as foliage, or a specific pattern, like wallpaper. Stamps are charged by setting them into a shallow tray of paint. Because paint stamps can be large, it frequently is necessary to create a tray to fit each stamp. A paint tray can be made of visquene draped in a one-inch stock lumber form.

Stamp Registration

Registration in printmaking means aligning one print plate to another so the different colors of the image merge accurately. Registration of a paint stamp guides the scenic artist in repeated and accurate placement of a pattern, although in terms of theatrical scale the registration need not be as perfect as in printmaking. Yet, it does need to be thoughtfully worked out and tested before applying the stamp to the scenery. The pattern for a paint stamp is drawn and pounced first on a piece of kraft paper. If the pattern is a repeating wallpaper design then use the pounce to check the alignment and registration of the pattern top, bottom, and sides. Because you look at the back of the stamp base as you work with the stamp, the registration will have to relate to the outside edges of the stamp base. A ref-

Figure 9.27
Patterned paint stamps. (See Chapter Five for more information about paint stamp construction.)

erence line normally is snapped on the scenery and the registration marks are made on the snapped lines relating to the top and bottom registration marks on the back of the paint stamp (Figure 9.28). A detail of the actual pattern near the edge of the stamp can be used as a registration mark. It may be possible to cut part of the stamp base away around this detail. Multiple paint stamps for color separations should be shaped and registered in exactly the same way.

Which paint should be used with paint stamps? The paint for paint stamps should be fairly thick. Paint that is too thin will seep to one side of the stamp and leave an uneven print. If the paint is to be transparent, then the color can be mixed in flat transparent medium for body. The paint also must be water-based, as any solvent-based paint will melt the foam rubber of the stamp. It may take a few applications of paint for the paint stamp to get evenly charged. Because the paint used with a paint stamp is so thick, the stamping is not a good technique to use with materials that need to stay soft, such as silk or scrim. A stencil might do a better job.

Stencils and Templates

A *stencil* is an intricate painting mask made of flat material with the negative area of a design or pattern cut out. Paint is applied through the stencil. Like the paint stamp, a multicolored design can be done with a stencil by drafting out the color separation on separate stencils and registering them all in the same manner. Registration, color separations, and pattern reconciliation need to be cartooned and checked first just as with paint stamps. (Figure 9.29). (See Chapter Five for an explanation of stencil construction.)

What Tools to Use with Stencils

One of the most common paint tools used with a stencil is a pneumatic sprayer. In this case, the paint used should be thin enough to go through the sprayer. A stencil to be used with a sprayer should be adequately masked on the sides, so the scenery is protected from overspray. When spraying a stencil, it may be necessary to experiment with the color and consistency of paint so that the least amount of paint can be sprayed on the surface and on the stencil and still do the job.

The stippling brush is primarily used as a tool for stenciling. But stippling is a time-intensive technique. If there are three colors to repeat a pattern over two hundred times, stippling is much too slow. For the most part, this tool is best left to home decorating.

Rollers work very well with stencils. When working with rollers, it is easy to work with two or more colors. Another advantage of rollers is that the texture that they leave works very well with some common stencil applications. A dry roller technique is convincing in creating the appearance of a velvet wall paper. Large brick stencils, often cut from a 4' × 8' piece of tin, work very well with rollers. The rollers cover the area quickly, and by blending two or more colors across the stencil, a good start is made on the color variation in bricks.

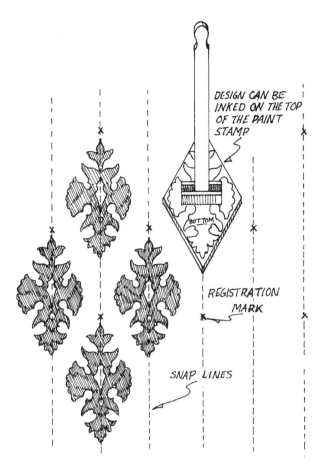

DESIGN CAN BE INKED ON THE TOP OF THE PAINT STAMP

BOTTOM

REGISTRATION MARK

SNAP LINES

Figure 9.28 Paint stamp registration.

Which paint should be used with stencils? Any water-based paint can be used with a stencil. Solvent-based paints also can be used, but paint buildup on the stencil may be a problem. The viscosity of the paint depends on the paint technique to be used. Do not rush work with a stencil. It is a slow process, and if there is much to do, it will take time. Concentrate on doing a clean and thorough job rather than rushing through it and having a lot to clean up afterward.

MASTER PATTERN

COLOR SEPARATION

GOLD

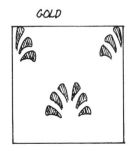

GREEN

WHITE

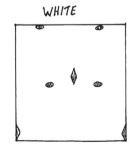

Figure 9.29
Stencil and stamp color separation.

To clean the stencil between repeated uses, set it on a moist towel or rag and carefully dab it off with a damp sponge. Do not let paint build up on the bobbinet. Make multiple copies of the stencil if the pattern repeats a lot. While one stencil is used for two or three repeated instances, the other stencils can be getting cleaned and dried.

Stencil Registration

Stencils in a repetitive pattern need registration marks (Figure 9.30), such as grooves or diamonds cut into the stencil to guide it to corresponding marks on the scenery. If different stencils are used for color separation, the registration marks must be in the same place for all stencils. Registration marks on the scenic units are made along guidelines laid on the scenery prior to stenciling. The guidelines should not be inked in any permanent way. If the pattern has a stripe or a border, it may be painted prior to stenciling and used as a guideline for registration. Carefully position the registration marks on a stencil so that the stencil can be placed easily and accurately.

When preparing to apply the stencil to the scenery, think through the actual work. Make sure your paint tools and air hose are placed so you may avoid tiptoeing over or dragging the hose through freshly stenciled areas. Place the registration marks on the side of the stencil that you can see while painting. Also consider whether you need to do every other repeat and then return to do the missing patterns, so the stencil need never rest on a wet area.

When deciding on the steps involved in painting the scenery, it is important to consider at what point the stenciling is to be done. Normally, stenciling should be painted as early as possible, so other painting, such as cutting in moldings and cast shadows, will be placed over the pattern. Similarly, with hard scenery, all three-dimensional elements should be applied after the stenciling has been done so the stencil can lay flat.

Templates and Spray Masking

Templates are similar to stencils in that they create a mask for painting, but templates are painted around rather than through, like a stencil, and issues of registration are not as critical. A leaf template or various patterns of templates can be used to spray leaf patterns. Templates were illustrated, along with spraying techniques, earlier in this chapter. *Spray masking* comes into play when an area of scenery needs to be isolated from another for contrasting techniques. Spray masking allows the scenic artist to work on a misty, distant sky next to a more crisply painted building by placing a mask over the building. Several contours in a complex city scene might need toning along straight edges. If two scenic artists work as a team, one person can place the masking and move it as necessary while the other sprays. This way several colors can be worked through the scenery at the same time.

Some shapes are small enough to be masked with one or two widths of tape, such as windows in a city scene. Masking tape can be a very effective template, although time consuming if the forms are round. Tape templates can be cut out right on the scenery, which will speed up work on curving shapes. Lay the tape over the contour to be cut out, overlapping the cartoon only as much as necessary. You should be able to see the cartoon through the tape. Cut through the tape with a fresh razor blade along the contour. Be careful to apply only enough pressure to cut through the tape and not the muslin underneath. The muslin will give just slightly, so the right pressure will cut through the more rigid tape and not the muslin. Practice on something small and inexpensive first. If you are working on a thirty-foot piece of seamless goods this can be terrifying. Once you develop the touch, this method of cutting contour masking will be a very useful technique.

Spraying Masking with Fabric

Erosion cloth, burlap, lace, and extruded plastic fencing may be used as a spray mask of sorts. A piece of cloth can be laid over scenery that has been base coated and another color sprayed over it. The pattern left behind, depending on the fabric used, will be distinguishable from some distance away. In this way, one piece of cloth can be used to paint a texture on an entire set.

TROMPE L'OEIL PAINTING TECHNIQUE

Introduction

Trompe l'oeil, a French term that means "deceive the eye," is a means of painting any surface employing

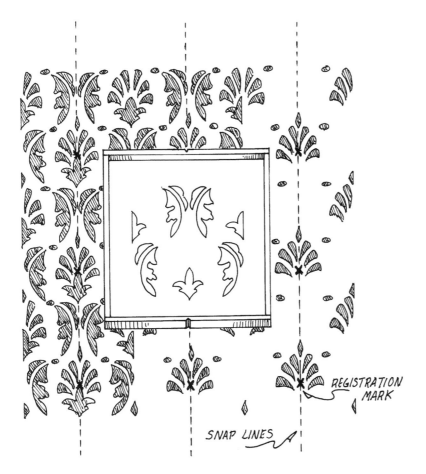

Figure 9.30
Stencil registration and repetition.

the pictorial devices of perspective and foreshortening combined with the painting techniques of chiaroscuro and cast shadows. The result is to trick observers into believing they see three-dimensional objects on a two-dimensional plane. Successful trompe l'oeil technique results in stunning results of illusion perfectly suited for the theatre.

The techniques of trompe l'oeil were developed and widely practiced during the Italian baroque period as a way of satisfying the increasing demand for sumptuous and fantastical interior decoration, reaching a state of perfection in the grand palaces and theatres of Europe. Increasing use of trompe l'oeil coincided with the development of theatrical design and painting. The two grew together, and trompe l'oeil became synonymous with scenic illusion itself. The wing and drop staging of European theatre served as a perfect vehicle for the scenic art-

ist expert in the technique of trompe l'oeil. Illusions of elaborate and exotic locales portrayed in stunning trompe l'oeil techniques became the standard for over three hundred years. The history chapters of this book concentrate fully on this development, but here the technique is explained for the painter.

The three hundred years of use instilled sound understanding of trompe l'oeil practices in scenic artists working in England, France, and Italy. These practices remain in use today as standard procedure for many scenic designers and scenic artists. Trompe l'oeil technique is the correct combination of many individual techniques, some of which already have been discussed in this book. Foreshortening forms and drawing in linear perspective are discussed in Chapter Eight. Both skills are intrinsic aspects of trompe l'oeil.

The Theory of Practice of Trompe l'Oeil

There are three overall aspects to making a successful trompe l'oeil painting. The first step is a complete and accurate cartoon. The second step is painting convincing representations of real surfaces and materials like wood, stone, or printed fabric. The third step is modeling the form with carefully applied light and shadow, sometimes known as *chiaroscuro*. *Chiaroscuro,* meaning "light-dark" in Italian, is the technique of modeling form by painting gradations of value relating to a specific light source. This "light-dark" describes the shape of the object. The relationship of form and light was further analyzed by Camille Pissarro, the French Postimpressionist. Pissarro observed that four fundamental geometric forms are the basis of all shapes, both humanmade and organic: the sphere, cube, hollow cylinder, and pyramid. Pissarro asserted that an artist could adeptly model any form based on combinations of these four elemental forms.

Modeling the shape of each object is where the painting of trompe l'oeil begins. Each individual form contained in a composition must be treated separately. Later in the process of trompe l'oeil, these forms will be treated as an overall, unified picture with lighting and shadowing. Certainly, trompe l'oeil scenic painting is done systematically. Random execution of these steps will lead to nothing but confusion. Cartooning, texturing, modeling and lighting are the way to build the image. One reason for this is that if more than one artist works on a project all the artists should share a common visual vocabulary, so the work of any one artist is indiscernible from another. Another reason is that, with so much area to cover, only a systematic approach will get you through the process.

A description of a basic system of painting trompe l'oeil follows, to serve as a guide to the execution of the technique. This basic structure has room for finesse and variation. Some possible variations are discussed, others you will discover on your own as you employ and perfect your technique.

Light and Shade

Identifying the light source within an image is absolutely essential to doing trompe l'oeil. The scenic artist must be fully aware, from the first step, where the

Figure 9.31 Placement of shade on Pissarro shapes.

light source is and where the objects are in relationship to it. In reality, nothing is visible without light (Figure 9.31).

Begin with the correct placement of *shade*. Remember, shade is the part of a form not facing light. The shadow projected from the object is dealt with later. The color of shade is a step down in value from the base, or local, color of a form. In conventional theatrical trompe l'oeil, the shade is an opaque paint. This helps establish shade as a part of the form itself, not its cast shadow. The color mixed for the shade usually is a modification of the primary base color. Before applying the color, lay a swatch of it next to the base color and look at it through squinted eyes. It should "read" as a shaded version of the base.

This first step, the shade, determines the placement of all the steps that are to follow. The shade is brushed in those areas of the form that do not receive direct light. Each of the forms in the picture plane should be treated separately from the others when determining where the shades are. The object of this step is to model the form. Remember, do not be concerned whether the form has a shadow cast across its surface.

The placement of shade on a square form is a good example. Any given plane is either in shade or not. If you are having difficulty deciding whether a plane would be shaded or not, try drawing a sketch of that form in a ground plan view that includes the placement of the light source. By projecting lines from the light source, you will see which planes receive direct light and how much of them. All that remains is to determine whether the form is above, below, or level with the light source.

The placement of shades on rounded forms can be trickier to figure out. A diagram of a ground plan view also can help with forms such as cylinders. One trap of describing rounded forms occurs when the shade and local color areas are an even half and half: the form may begin to look square rather than round. The classic approach to modeling a cylinder is to divide it more or less into thirds. One third of the cylinder would be in shade. This is by no means a hard and fast rule, but it is a good place to start when creating the illusion of a rounded form. In the case of a sphere or a cylinder, this theatrical cheat can be used to help round out the forms even more. On the lighted side of both forms, you may notice a sliver of shade along the edge facing the light. This contrivance is a subtle trick that furthers the illusion of a rounded form.

Bear in mind when dealing with rounded forms such as spheres that, as the edge of shade approaches the center of the form, the contour will become less pronounced because it is viewed on edge. Imagine cutting an orange in half. Then, holding it in front of you, rotate it so that the flat section becomes an ellipse. This ellipse will become ever shallower until you have an edge view of the orange half. The same effect happens to the contoured edge of shade as it progresses around a curved form. When a rounded form also is contoured, as in a capital base or vase,

the shade and following lowlight must follow the contour of the form. (Figure 9.32).

When the shades are finished, step back for a moment, and look at the picture through squinted eyes. Squinting your eyes diffuses the image, which helps you see the shift of values more completely and objectively without focusing on specific details. At this point the shape of the forms should be clearly, not dramatically, defined. Plan the shading of all forms carefully and execute it consistently.

Lowlight

The *lowlight* is a step down in value and neutrality from the shade and should be of a color related to the shade. There should be a natural progression in value and neutrality from the base to the shade and then to the lowlight. Once again, make a swatch of the lowlight and, through squinted eyes, look at the swatch on top of the shade to see the relationship of the two colors objectively (Figure 9.33). Like the shade, the lowlight conventionally is an opaque color.

The lowlight is placed in shaded areas on the planes or curves of the form that receive no direct or ambient light. In the case of the cylinder or the sphere, you may notice another contrivance much the same as the trick of putting the sliver of shade on the lighted side of the forms. By leaving a sliver of the light showing on the shade side of the forms, the illusion of a curved surface is more complete. This is called a *creeping light*. The trick of doing shades in thirds on curved forms may be applied to the proportion of shade to lowlight areas. Lowlights should be applied only in shaded areas.

The lowlight, like the shade, is used only to model the forms. It should not be placed in areas of the form that could receive direct light from the light source because it is in the shadow of another form. Once the lowlight is done, you should be able to look at the forms through squinted eyes and see a crisp illusion of dimension. If some forms in the picture are not "reading" as intended at this point, you

Figure 9.32
Sections of curved forms.

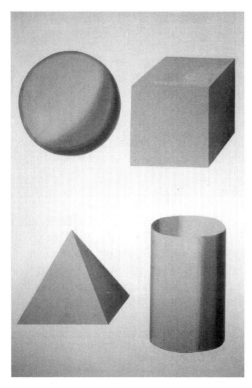

Figure 9.33 Placement of lowlight on Pissarro shapes.

may wish to rethink the shades and lowlights before continuing.

Cut Lines

Cut lines are dark accentuation lines that delineate the change of planes or edges. They should be placed primarily along the joint between receding planes. Beyond this, cut lines should be used minimally to describe the contour of the forms. The cut lines are not a cartoon. If the cut lines are applied like a cartoon along every profile, they will flatten rather than enhance the illusion. Never fully outline an object. Keep in mind that less is more effective. A complete cut line should not be placed along the profile of a form that does not join another plane. For instance, a freestanding column may have a dash of a cut line that strikes up from the bottom and down from the top, particularly on the shade side, but no solid cut line. However, a pilaster would have a solid cut line along the entire length of the shade side of the form where it joins the wall. The cut line on the lighted side of the pilaster may be

dashed or broken. A sphere sitting on the ground would have only a dash of a cut line on the shadow side of the form. On the other hand, a half sphere in a bas-relief would have a cut line that would go nearly all the way around the form, breaking on the highlighted side (Figure 9.34).

The cut line should be the darkest value in the image, but if too dark, it may look cartoonish. Frequently, the cut lines for the scenic units in the same scene are the same color throughout the entire composition. While the shading and lowlights need to be predicated on the local color of a form, the process of unifying the composition begins with the cut line, which is another reason it may be the same color in the context of a scene or a backdrop. The paint for cut lines should be opaque.

Cast Shadow

Cast shadow truly establishes the depth of field in a picture. The cast shadows unify all the various planes and surfaces in the picture plane by placing them in the same light at the same moment of time.

Figure 9.34 Placement of cut lines on Pissarro shapes.

A single light source casts very specific shadows. They have a clear direction and indicate the relation of the object to the light. The light has character itself. It may be bright or dim, cool or warm, and so on. The light reveals the texture and shape of objects in the painting. Scenic artists are excellent observers of light; most have a fascination with the different effects of natural light. Look closely at how shadows fall on a wall and how colors are affected by shadow. Try to understand interior lighting, as it is almost always from multiple sources. Through close observation of light you will be able to discern when light is depicted correctly in a painting. In trompe l'oeil, the light and shadow play two key roles. First, they are used to define the form of individual objects in relation to the light source as described here. Second, light illuminates the whole scene and projects cast shadows, bounces off surfaces, and further describes the dimension of the objects we see (Figure 9.35).

A cast shadow is placed on the sides of forms as well as in the areas of forms blocked from receiving direct light. Cast shadows may be placed only in the shadowed areas across a surface that would normally receive light if it were not blocked, or the shadows may be placed in the shade areas as well. A normal convention is to do the former in interior scenes and the latter in exterior scenes, where light is harsher and shade areas may be deeper in value. In some cases, natural light is soft and indirect, perhaps, filtered through clouds. However, it will still be necessary to spray or brush soft shadows into the shade areas of forms. If the light source is soft, the cast shadow color should be lighter in value. If the appearance of a strong light source is desired, then a darker cast shadow should be used. Some compositions have multiple light sources. A lighter or slightly different version of cast shadow color can be applied for the secondary and tertiary light sources.

Because cast shadow describes only the quality of light and must work with all the surfaces represented, the paint used for the shadow must be transparent. A field of snow on a sunny day is an excellent example of how a cast shadow describes the quality of light. This hue is a very distinct cast shadow color: the color of the sky. All that one sees is the sky reflecting off the snow where the direct sunlight is blocked. Cast shadow paint should be thinned to the desired value. Do not add white to a cast shadow color. Some deep colors in more economical brands of scenic paint have white filler in them that settles out once the paint is thinned. These colors should be avoided when mixing cast shadows. It may be necessary to mix the cast shadow out of a higher-quality line of paint to obtain the desired transparency.

Highlights

When you begin painting *highlights*, the illusion of dimensional form should be evident in the painting (Figure 9.36). Highlights should not be necessary for

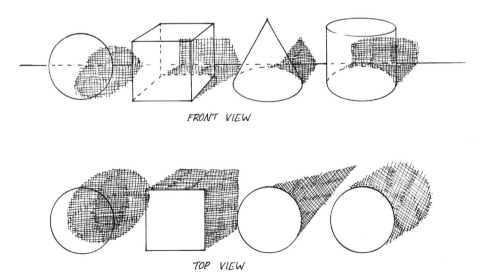

FRONT VIEW

TOP VIEW

Figure 9.35a
Projecting cast shadows.

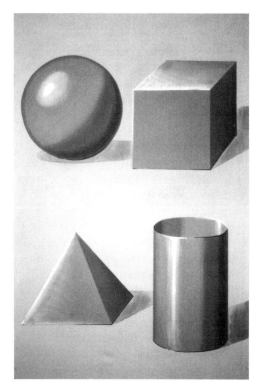

Figure 9.35b Placement of cast shadows on Pissarro shapes.

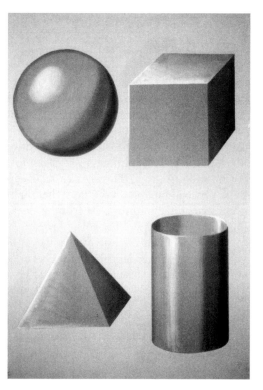

Figure 9.36 Placement of primary highlight on Pissarro shapes.

this illusion but rather enhance it. Conventionally, a highlight may be simply a lighter version of the local color of a form. However, the color of the highlight also may serve as a description of the light striking the form. Cool or warm, soft or bright, light resonates with the color and placement of a highlight. If the value difference between the highlight and the local color is subtle, it will give the appearance of a soft light source, such as candlelight. A broad difference between the highlight and the local color will give the appearance of a strong light source, such as sunlight.

Highlights may be placed on either a plane or the forward edge where two planes join together. Often, two different values of highlights are used, so that the first value is painted on the plane of the object as the primary highlight, and an even higher value highlight is used on the edges as a secondary, brighter highlight (Figure 9.37). The placement of highlights on spheres and cylinders is very important. If the highlight is not placed in the proper relationship to the shade and lowlight, these shapes may

look warped. If the highlight is too close to the edge, the sphere or cylinder will look flat; if the highlights are too close to the middle, the shapes will look pointed or squared off. As with the shade and lowlight, a good general rule is to place the highlight about one third the distance from the lighted edge of the shape. When dealing with round forms, such as capital bases or vases, the highlight must follow the contour of the form in the same manner as shade and lowlights. Also, different colors of highlights may be positioned slightly differently from one another to indicate multiple light sources.

Highlights, like cut lines, are applied very sparingly. Too much highlighting will flatten an image and render the dimensioning meaningless. Look at highlights glancing off surfaces in the real world. They actually are very minimal. Even after you exaggerate these highlights for the stage, they are still modest in proportion to the surface area of the form. The highlights do not need to be applied along the entire length of an edge or form. Often, highlights will only glance and skip along an edge or a plane.

Figure 9.37 Placement of secondary highlight on Pissarro shapes.

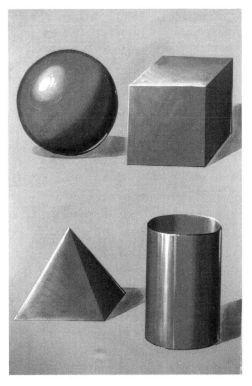

Figure 9.38 Placement of reflective light on Pissarro shapes.

The paint used for a highlight is opaque, to stand out against the local color. Some acrylic-based paints may not stand out against the background. If an acrylic-based paint or dye is being used on the scenery, it may be necessary to switch to a latex or casein for the highlight work.

Reflective Highlights or Bounce Light

Reflective highlights, also called *bounce light*, describe colors reflected on a form from other lighted surfaces. A highly reflective surface will reflect back not only a light source but also the color of other surfaces and forms around it. Imagine how a fresh field of snow in sunlight reflects light. Watch people walking on a very light cement sidewalk on a sunny day around noon. The strong top light of the sun bounces off the pavement and acts like a footlight illuminating the face from below. A brightly colored shirt can reflect light and its own color back onto you. All these are examples of bounce light. Reflective highlights need not be painted only in the highlight areas but may be placed

anywhere on the form, including the shade and low-light areas (Figure 9.38).

Like highlights, reflective highlights should not be applied over the whole length of an edge or plane. One convention is to apply reflective highlights in approximately oval-shaped areas. These ovals tend to be on an angle, creating the impression of a slash of color. Across the length of a wall, there may be two or three of these oval areas of each reflective highlight. Across a large surface or a flat plane, the reflective highlight color can be sprayed over a section to create an oval or a slash of color. This may be done before any of the other steps of trompe l'oeil are done.

Reflective highlights may be several different colors. If a surface is highly reflective, such as glass or metal, as many as five or six colors may overlap one another. Some reflective highlights may reflect off one side or another of the form specifically, while others reflect from underneath this color, perhaps related to the color of the stage deck. To offset these areas of high concentration, there may be areas with no reflective highlights at all. The more reflective highlights used, the more reflective the surface will appear.

Reflective highlights may be related or complementary to the local color. In most cases, the reflective highlights are related to the local color of other forms in the composition. However, some surfaces work very well with certain colors of reflective light; for example, gold or gilt surfaces work well with turquoise and orange reflective highlights. Commonly, refelctive highlight is more chromatic than the local color of the form. In some cases, a more neutral color may be used for reflective color as a means of integrating the form into the composition by means of reflective light.

Reflective highlights, like primary highlights, should be opaque so that they "pop." They should be mixed from the more opaque mediums, latex or casein. In some cases, the reflective light may be a glaze coat that is used to give areas of the form a wash of color, once again as a means of integrating the form into the composition.

Color Theory and Trompe l'Oeil

The standard rule for shades and highlights is cool shades with warm highlights and warm shades with cool highlights. If you play the complements of the colors off of one another, the results will be more interesting as well as apparent. In general, shades, lowlights, and cast shadows should not be more chromatic than the local color (see Colorplates 3–7). Then these areas recede or pull back. Cast shadow is most effective if it is a deeper value and the complement of the color of light illuminating the scene (Figure 9.39).

The converse of this approach is to make the highlights more chromatic, so these areas push forward. The highlights may be related to a greater extent to the light striking the surface of a form than to its local color. Thus, if a warm light is striking a cool color form, the primary highlights would be related to the cool local color and the secondary highlights would be related more to the warm color of light.

Application Techniques

There are several ways to apply trompe l'oeil. A chosen style may depend on the size of the theatre and the style of the painting. An operatic approach to this technique is the method of applying paint very broadly with little effort made to blend the steps into one another. If a broad operatic style is desired, the trompe l'oeil is applied directly with a brush, making no attempt to soften the edges of the individual colors. If a realistic style is desired, the edges of the shades, lowlights, and highlights may be softened by

Figure 9.39a
Trompe l'oeil bricks.

Figure 9.39b Trompe l'oeil stones.

Figure 9.39c Trompe l'oeil stucco alcove.

dry brushing, with water, or by spraying in the color with a pneumatic sprayer. Rounded forms require the most finesse, if a more realistic trompe l'oeil is desired. For a photographic appearance the steps of trompe l'oeil may be applied with pneumatic spray guns and airbrushes.

When working on trompe l'oeil, each step should be completed across all the units laid out before going on to the next step. For instance, if several pieces of scenery laid out simultaneously have various gold or gilded details, then the shade will be applied to all the elements of gold detail at the same time rather than each element being treated individu-

ally. This is done to save time and to integrate the technique on all elements of the composition.

The final step is to view the composition as a whole. Once the units of scenery are in their configuration on stage, it may be necessary for some corner of the scenery to recede. Backing units may be sprayed down so that they are not a higher value or more chromatic than the primary scenic units. Backdrops or the sides of scenic units in cast shadows may need to be sprayed down so they, too, retreat into the shadows. The edges of drops may need to be sprayed down with a deeper color of the cast shadow to focus attention on the composition.

chapter 10

Creating Aging, Decorative, and Faux Finishes Using Multiple Mediums

INTRODUCTION

This chapter addresses some of the newer techniques of scenic painting, many of which have developed in this century with the advent of new painting and finishing substances. Called *multimedium techniques*, these include faux finishes like marble and wood grain, aging and staining techniques, and some texturing effects. Included in this chapter as well are some of the traditional approaches to the same problems of faux finishes and aging. Beyond the issues of faux finish and aging techniques, this chapter discusses a wide range of newer paint products and their uses. Included are texturing compounds, sealants, and adhesives. Paint application problems with materials such as metal, plastic foams, rigid plastics, and fabrics are addressed. The chapter discusses many of the special products a scenic artist will encounter on an occasional basis.

We use the term *multimedium* because many contemporary faux techniques rely on mixing paint mediums to purposely contrast finishes or textures for more realistic results. In many other instances, the ability of one product to repel another will be used to create wonderfully accurate aging effects. Not all scenic painting follows the traditional paint on canvas routine. Modern scenic artists must have a broad knowledge of many unusual combinations of mediums to get the look desired and must be willing to experiment a little and perhaps discover a new

approach. It is obvious that not all paint or texture techniques have been discovered nor are all the solutions to covering and painting scenic materials already known. Hundreds of products have been adapted for scenic uses that were never intended for the stage at all. Many techniques are discussed in this chapter that involve the use of organic chemical solvents, toxic dusts, and toxic mediums. Proper safety precautions and protection must be used in every circumstance where toxic materials are involved (see Chapter Four, Safety and Health Regulations for more information).

THE LAYERING PROCESS: GLAZES AND RESISTS

Many painting techniques, theatrical or otherwise, use paint in thin built-up layers because only through layering relatively transparent paints can some deep, rich, and vibrant colors be achieved. Scenic paints may be thinned down and used in layers, called *glazes*. Several glazes of flat-finish paint provide a deeper color, due to the layers of paint. When pigment or colorant is suspended in a medium such as a polymer or shellac and applied in successive layers, the result is a strikingly rich color and glowing surface. Glazes form the basis for many faux techniques. The actual mediums used to suspend the pigment may vary widely, but the primary technique is consistent throughout all the glazing processes.

Glazes with Pigment or Dye and Finish Mediums

The combination of a pigment or dye and a transparent medium creates a useful painting tool for faux finishes. In the years before the appearance of modern polymer mediums, solvent-based mediums were the mainstay for such layering or glazing techniques. French enamel varnish (F.E.V.) is one such traditional approach. An F.E.V. is a solution of shellac, thinned with solvent alcohol, and tinted with alcohol-soluble aniline dye. Amber, or orange, shellac with no added pigment is a useful glaze in itself, particularly with wood finishes, and it may be thinned with solvent alchohol to use as an F.E.V. An F.E.V. works well for layers of color or as a finish coat in glaze applications on faux woods and marbles. It will slightly cloud reflective and transparent surfaces, so it is a good technique for aging mirror or glass. An advantage of working with shellac is that it may be redissolved with later applications of solvent alcohol to further alter the glaze or even remove it. The F.E.V. can be given a cloudy or gouache appearance by adding white pigmented shellac to it.

The tint in an F.E.V. typically comes from alcohol-soluble aniline dye. The aniline dye provides brilliant color without clouding the shellac, but not all aniline dyes are soluble in the alcohol solvent. Japan colors and some universal tinting colors are soluble in alcohol and shellac to some extent; they may be purchased or ordered through commercial and theatrical paint suppliers. These colorants will result in a cloudy glaze color when mixed with shellac. Always try a sample of colorant with the shellac and alcohol for compatibility before mixing a full bucket.

A substitute for F.E.V. can be made by combining colorant with clear acrylic, latex binder, or P.V.A. However, these water-based glazes do not penetrate porous surfaces, such as wood or muslin, as deeply as solvent-based mediums, so the finish may not be as rich. These water-based mediums may be tinted with water-based paint, aniline dyes, and colorants, which make them easier to use. They can be used straight or thinned considerably with water or acrylic-based floor wax.

A shellac-based F.E.V. glaze dries to a semigloss finish that increases in sheen as more layers are painted. Glazes made with satin or semigloss urethanes and flat acrylics also will develop a sheen after several layers, but it will not be as pronounced.

Additional glaze mediums are sold specifically for faux-finish work, particularly at paint suppliers that specialize in interior decoration. These mediums have a high viscosity, so that they "set up" well on vertical surfaces, without sagging or running. Glazing mediums that are oil-based take upward of four to twelve hours to set or become dry to the touch. Such slow drying may make it difficult to use these mediums for application in the theatre. Glazing mediums dry to an eggshell finish and may be covered with alkyd finish if a glossier sheen is desired. Water-based glazing mediums are available through most paint and theatrical suppliers. Water-based glazing mediums perform in much the same way as oil-based mediums do, but they dry faster and are safer to use. These mediums contain drying retardants so they remain workable for thirty minutes to an hour and take four hours to dry completely.

Finishes

All clear mediums used as a finish over an F.E.V. or glaze may be tinted to add an extra dimension to the treatment. Finishes are available in a variety of sheens ranging from high gloss, gloss, satin, and flat. White shellac and solvent-based urethanes dry with a faint yellowish tint that, in addition to sheen, adds depth to a painted surface. Amber or orange shellac can be used as the final finish for a deep warm tint. As discussed before, shellac may be tinted only with alcohol-soluble dyes and tints. Colorants added to water- or oil-based finishes serve to "pull together" a paint treatment, faux wood, or faux marble, like the application of stain on fine wood. These finishes may be brushed, rolled, or sprayed on.

Resists

A resist is a paint process using two or more mediums that repel or slide off of one another. A glaze or finish applied to a flat medium, such as scenic paint, normally will cover it smoothly. However, one technique entails wiping the glaze medium or finish off the base surface to create a texture or grain pattern. This is one form of a resist. It is difficult to separate the finish medium from a flat-finish base coat. If the finish of the base coat is a satin or a gloss sheen, then any glaze medium can be wiped or combed off easily. If the base coat was done with a flat-finish scenic paint, it can be covered with a clear coat finish of gloss medium before doing the resist technique.

CREATING FAUX FINISHES

The word *faux* is French for "false, forged, or imitated." A faux-paint technique is the realistic imitation of a specific material, such as marble or wood, onto a less expensive surface. Faux finishes are very popular interior decoration techniques for obvious places like doors and walls; and they are found, with a postmodern touch of ironic wit, on improbable objects like computers and telephones.

Faux treatments are created through a process. Once the process is established, it must be carefully followed to maintain consistency. The process may be a simple one-step application of mixed mediums or carefully applied successive paint layers. Any artist creating a faux treatment first should closely examine the material to be mimicked to understand how that material was created. The artist should then determine, by doing samples, how best to create the faux finish. The techniques used to create faux finishes are standard painting techniques of wet blend, glazes, dry brushing, graining, and others that have been discussed in Chapter Nine. The mediums used for faux finishes may vary greatly, depending on desired qualities of transparency and permanence. Standard scenic paint may be used as a base coat or to tint some of these mediums, but rarely is a faux finish executed satisfactorily when it is made up entirely of flat opaque mediums. The discussion in this book clearly is focused on theatrical work, not interior decoration. (Consult the Reading and Resources chapter for sources of faux and decorative finish texts.)

Wood

Most experienced scenic artists focus their painting technique on creating the apperance of a specific type of wood, such as oak or walnut, rather than a generic wood grain. In determining how to emulate wood grain, a scenic artist first must understand the pattern of wood as it is cut from a tree. It is well known that, as trees grow, rings are formed as the trunk widens over the years. When a tree is harvested and cut into board or veneer, these rings become the grain of the wood. If a board is cut along the length of a fairly straight tree trunk, the board will be composed primarily of a straight, parallel grain. Oblong and elliptical grains are created from crosscuts of the tree rings. Knots in the grain come from where branches sprouted from the trunk. Veneers are made by shearing a thin sheet from around a section of the trunk in a continuous spiral, yielding a soft marblelike grain. Some trees, such as pines and poplars, tend to grow with very straight trunks. Consequently, the boards they yield have a great deal of straight grain. Other trees, such as oak and walnut, which often have curved trunks, yield boards with more crosscut grains. Because mahoganies yield a supple fine-grained wood, they often are used in veneers. With proper technique and graining tools, all of these variations can be produced in faux wood. In addition to the proper tools, layers of transparent color in glossy or satin mediums create a depth of color akin to stained or oiled wood.

Graining

A faux wood grain is done by initially painting a base coat that is the hue of the lightest grain of the wood either in a single color or a wet blend. The finish of the base coat will effect how much of the top glaze can be squeegeed or combed off with a graining tool. If the finish of the base coat is slick and smooth, a subsequent coat of glaze will come away very cleanly. This means that surfaces given a faux wood treatment must be very carefully prepared and sanded (Figure 10.1).

The dark grain of the wood is created by tinting a transparent medium that dries to the desired hue. Although not as common, for some light colored woods it may be effective to tint the graining color to a lighter hue than the base coat. In either case, the grain is created when a top coat is painted over the base coat in a streaky grain pattern or painted on and squeegeed off with a rocker or comb before it dries. Any clear medium can be used for the glaze medium, but shellacs and solvent-based finishes do not work as well for wood grain because of their tendency to spread out once applied. Commercial faux mediums sold specifically for graining and overglaze

Figure 10.1
Various faux wood graining techniques and tools: rocker grainers, tube grainers, combs, and rubber pad grainers.

techniques work very well, because they are highly viscous. For large volume theatrical applications, clear acrylics, latex, P.V.A., and water-based urethanes work well and are more affordable.

Rockers, graining pads, and tube-style grainers are used to create crosscut grains. Grainers of this sort come in a variety of patterns for different types of grain or variations within a grain. Tube grainers sometimes are sold with a wire handle and wooden dowel for holding and manipulating the grainer. Many scenic artists prefer simply to hold this grainer from either end so that it can be bent and curved for more diversity in the grain patterns. In addition to rocking or rolling the grainers as they are pulled through the medium, they also may be twisted from one edge to the other to vary grain widths. Combs for graining are available in rubber and steel with different widths of teeth. These are used to comb off a straight grain and usually are used in combination with the pattern grainers. Homemade combs can be made from many different materials, such as rubber tread, carpet scraps, a torn edge of cardboard, or wadded newspaper. The advantage in using homemade combs is that irregular patterns can be cut into these to produce more realistic random patterns than their commercial counterparts.

Commercial grainers, combs, and patterns used exclusively to paint a wood grain technique leave a distinctly even and regular grain pattern. When used

in combination with commercial tools, homemade tools add a dimension to the technique that lends a hint of realism. When preparing a wood graining project, consider what tools can be made from materials found around the shop to augment commercial grainers and combs. A scenic artist should become adept at using commercial and homemade graining tools, blending the paint swaths together and twisting the tools while etching the medium to manipulate the grain realistically.

Checker rollers are interesting devices used to create the short choppy straight grain that speckles the surface of some woods. This type of grain is very common in oak and some mahoganies. The medium used with the checker roller must be fairly viscous or it will drip off the roller. When the roller is passed across a surface, it may splatter a little as well as leave the short choppy grain it was designed to do. If the spatters are not desirable, they can be brushed out in the direction of the grain with a dry brush. An even coarser short grain may be achieved by simply spattering over a base coat with the grain color and dragging through the wet paint with a dry brush.

Brushed graining may be done in lieu of the grainers or to augment them. Grain may be painted on with a small brush and dragged through with a larger brush to soften it. Dry brushing may be done to create a simple straight grain through and in addition to a crosscut grain. A crosscut grain also may be created by dry brushing. By tilting the brush from one edge to the other while it is being pulled through the stroke, it will feather out from one edge to the other. Once the scenic artist becomes accustomed to this technique, a broad feathery crosscut grain can be created quickly.

After graining has been completed it may be necessary and desirable to soften or deepen it with layers of glazes, so that areas of the grain appear to sink into the surface of the wood. These glazes may go over partial areas or the entire surface. Generally, it is best if the glazes are deeper in value. In some instances, particularly in the case of light-grained woods, a lighter glaze made with white pigment is effective. Finally, a gloss or satin finish over the completed faux wood will add depth to its appearance.

Marble

When creating faux marble, the scenic artist should understand how marble forms its appearance. Just as with wood grain, a scenic artist must know the structure of the material in question, not just the image. Marble is formed by compression, heating, and upheaval, singly or in combination. One of the most common marble types is drift marble. Drift marble is formed by layers of silt settling together and hardening under compression over thousands of years. The solid mass is colored by the various shades of silt, which we see as veins. The veins intertwining through the stone may be either feathery or well defined. Serpentine marble forms with stone pieces broken up into various sized nuggets. This rubble then is filled in with molten rock or silt. When this hardened mass is sliced open, it results in a dramatic two-tone marble. Luminous crystalline marbles are formed by the intense heating of minerals, resulting in layers of dazzling crystals and ribs of color, as found in malachite marbles.

Faux marble, like faux wood, may be the application of several separate layers or a one-step process. A challenge in creating a faux marble is to replicate the chaotic nature of the marble grain and finish without creating a repetitious pattern. The techniques and tools used in the process may help to ensure that results look natural rather than contrived. In addition to brushwork tools, techniques frequently used in faux marble that add to its depth and character include wet blending, feathering, sponging, spattering, and glazing.

The grain pattern in painted marble is often its most conspicuous component. If a faux marble is poorly done, the grain usually is what gives it away. A poorly executed marble grain tends to look somewhat like tree limbs or repetitious diamond patterns. When painting the grain in a faux marble, keep in mind that a marble veneer or object was cut from a larger marble block and so the grain may pass down into the depth of the stone or up into a cutaway layer. The grain in drift marbles generally is directional, like wood. Some varieties of marble also have a cross grain, nearly perpendicular to the primary grain. Marble used on floors or walls sometimes is cut in successive sheets and laid as cut off the block: face to face and back to back. The faces are finished and laid adjacent to one another on the site so that the sheets mirror one another along the seam.

The surface to be painted with faux marble technique should be carefully prepared: all seams must be filled and sanded, any grain covered, and material edges filled and sanded. This is particularly important if the faux marble is seen close up. It is somewhat difficult to separate the various stages and steps to painting faux marble. The order in which these steps are done may be grouped together and executed in a wet-on-wet sequential technique or done in individual, careful steps allowing each application to dry before the next one is applied. Glazes may be blended together over the top of the finish for color variation, or the base coat may be blended for this same purpose, or both may be necessary.

The first step in a marble finish is the base coat. The base coat may be one color or a blend of several colors. This wet blend may be done in various ways, as best suits the planned marble. The blend may be very soft and well blended, or loosely blended on a damp or fully wet surface so the colors mix of their own accord. The colors simply may be laid in next to one another so that very little mixing occurs. It may or may not be necessary for the base coat to dry before successive steps are done. Depending on the faux marble pattern, you may want to spatter, grain, or sponge directly into the wet base coat so that the paint seeps and mixes together. Working paint this way, wet into wet, may be fast, but it is not very controlled. The use of brushed graining, spattering, and sponge work may be better controlled by allowing each application to dry completely before beginning the next step. An application may be softened by first dampening a surface with water or spraying the still-wet paint with water. Any application may be further softened by working into the still-wet paint with a damp sponge.

The grain of drift marble usually is brushed on. It is natural when painting a grain over a large area to unconsciously develop a pattern. Scenic artists must be continually aware of this as they work. Nearly every text written on faux finishes will discuss the use of a feather for creating marble grain, a method that is not as useful for theatrical applications. Over a large scale, feather graining would be too time-consuming. Occasionally, a feather duster may be used instead of a single feather to effect a marble grain over a large area. Graining over a large flat area also may be done with the edge of a three-inch roller, but this method does not work over moldings and three-dimensional surfaces. A serpentine marble has a strongly defined grain, which can be done with careful brushwork. It also may be done by laying down a base of the primary marble finish and then masking out everything but the grain. The masking can be made from torn-up sheets and bits of newspaper. The grain color can be sprayed or spattered over the top of the masking. Once it is dry and the masking has been removed, the grain can be enhanced with some brushwork. Once again, over a large area, this masking approach to a serpentine marble, discussed in many books on faux techniques, may be too time-consuming for theatrical applications. A large paint stamp cut into the pattern of the base marble in a serpentine or grain can be used to quickly cover large areas with a serpentine pattern. In addition to the stamp, the grain may be refined with some brushwork. This technique will not stand up to close observation but may be fine for viewing from a distance.

After the base has been done and graining completed, it may be necessary to break up the surface with some transparent glaze work, which will enhance the natural appearance of the faux marble. One of the prized qualities of marble is its soft, translucent crystalline base. Because of this translucency, it seems as if one can see into the stone. Glaze work adds the necessary variation and depth to the surface by breaking up brushstrokes and opaque color. Glazes may be applied over the entire surface or over partial areas for more variation. Glazes may simply be thinned paint, or they can be suspended in a water-based medium, such P.V.A. or water-based urethanes. Commercial faux-finish glazes work very well for layering color. But, as mentioned previously,

consideration must be given to the amount of drying time involved in using these mediums. The glazes can be brushed, spattered, sponged, or sprayed on, as best suits and approaches the marble finish being mimicked. Particularly in lighter colored marbles, a great deal of depth frequently may be added by applying partially opaque or cloudy glaze work over a higher contrast base and graining. Glazes made from pearlescent paint or interference color will be very transparent but catch or play with the light over the surface of the stone. Interference colors and pearlescent paint are available from Golden Artists Color, Inc. (see the Reading and Resources chapter). As well as being used as overglazes, these may be used directly over the base coat, and in some cases they may work well as one of the graining colors. Pearlescent and interference glaze colors work best on lighter colors of marble and can be very effective.

The finish coat over faux marble adds great depth to its faux-marble surface and gives it the appearance of being polished. A finish for work seen at very close range should be sprayed on in several layers until it is glossy. If the finish is brushed or rolled on, the brush or roller grain will be discernible to the viewer. If the faux marble is meant to be seen only from a distance, as in a theatre, then-brushed or rolled on finish will suffice. If desired, the finish can be tinted to add depth by subtly changing the hue of the faux marble.

Even though there may be a great deal of variation in creating a faux marble, all the steps must be carefully noted and followed throughout. Before beginning a complex faux-marble process, work through the process by doing samples until a satisfactory approach is found. Complete the sample all the way through to the finish to see how that final step affects the color of the marble.

Metal

Real metallic surfaces and finishes are generally too expensive or heavy to be used in theatrical applications. The scenic artist is called on to replicate a wide range of metals, from common to rare, on a regular basis. Architectural and decorative details such as gold filigree are replicated by gilding or painting with bronzing powder mixed into a medium. Large surfaces of industrial or commercial materials, such as stainless steel or aluminum, also can be replicated in paint but through a longer process.

Gilding

The term *gilding* means overlaying a surface with a metallic leaf. This is done to give the surface a grand or rarefied appearance. The metal used in gilding is either gold or silver leaf. The leaves usually are three to four inches square and sold booked between layers of tissue paper, which holds them until the gilder is ready to use them. Metallic leaves have been hammered and rolled until they are tissue thin. This is all that is necessary to coat the surface with the precious metal. Because the leaves are so thin and delicate, they must be handled with special care and tools.

True metallic leaves cannot be handled with the fingers because the oils on the skin are enough to snag and tear the leaf. Out of necessity, a system of tools has been developed for handling and applying the leaf (described in Chapter Five). Gilding also must be done in a very stable environment. Drafts and dust will made the work difficult or impossible. The surface to be gilded first is given a coat of a gilding medium. This is a binder that sets up a tacky surface that adheres the metallic leaf. When in place, the leaves are pressed down into the medium with a gilder's mop. This soft, full-bristle brush is used to press the leaf onto the medium and work the leaf into the details. Burnishing tools then are used to fully adhere the metallic leaf to the medium and further work the leaf into all the nooks and crannies of the object. Burnishing is important, as it also adds a significant shine to the leaf.

It usually is unnecessary to use real gold and silver leaf for the theatre. First of all, the expense is prohibitive. Second, working with genuine gold leaf requires time and a undisturbed environment, two conditions in short supply in the theatre. So rarely is true gold leaf used in theatrical work that acquiring these specialized tools may be necessary only for the most discriminating of property painters. However, the knowledge of these tools and the tools of any craft that the scenic artist may need to represent always is helpful.

Composite gold leaf, sometimes called *Dutch gold*, is much less expensive and much easier to handle, because the leaves are not nearly as thin. Dutch gold, commonly used in theatrical work, actually can be handled and placed with clean dry hands. Even though the leaf is easier to handle, this work still should be done on a clean surface with little or no air draft. For theatrical use, Dutch gold also may be placed on freshly applied shellac while tacky. Metallic leaf adhesive size is a glue formulated to use in the gilding process. The size is applied to the surfaces that are to be gilded. Once dry it remains tacky so the leaf will adhere to the surface.

Bronzing Powders

Bronzing powders are particulates of dry metallic tempera. They can be mixed with a broad range of mediums and applied with a brush or sprayer. These powders mix directly into shellac, oil-based urethanes, and lacquers. They may need to be pulped with solvent alcohol before being mixed into water-based mediums, such as P.V.A., water-based urethane, clear acrylic, or clear latex. All bronzing powders are very lightweight, particularly the silvers, which are made with aluminum. The dust from mixing these paints will permeate the air. It is best to mix the bronzing powders in a spray booth or hood, where the dust can be vented off. No one not wearing respiratory protection should be in the vicinity while bronzing powders are being mixed.

Premixed metallic paints are available at theatrical suppliers, sign-painting suppliers, and retail paint stores. However, the last two sources carry only a very small selection, primarily gold and silver, with little choice in intensity, color, or richness. Bronzing powders are available in a wide range of colors from theatrical supply houses. The selection in these lines covers a broad range of metallic finishes. For instance, there are many different qualities of gold: pale gold, bright gold, rich gold, and Roman gold, to name a few. The silvers come in varying shades of aluminum, silver, and stainless steel. With so many selections of golds and silvers, a scenic artist or faux-finish painter can be very discriminating when selecting a metallic finish. Bronzing powders also are available in a wide spectrum of colors, such as purple, green, and red and various shades of bronze, brass, copper, and deep brown statuary hues. If a color of bronzing powder must be altered, the powders can be mixed with one another to create a desired hue. These paints also may be tinted with aniline dyes, colorants, and universal tinting colors. Keep in mind that universal tinting colors and colorants will dull the gleam of the metallic paint, depending on how much tint is added to the paint.

Bronzing brushes may be used to apply bronzing powder mixed in medium. These specialty brushes are used by faux-finish artists and furniture decorators. It is not absolutely necessary to use specialized bronzing brushes with bronzing powders. In theatrical applications, nearly any soft bristle brush will suffice.

Graphite

When bronzing powders are applied to a surface they can be quite lovely but not a thoroughly convincing metallic finish. One explanation for this is that the particles of bronzing powders have a random alignment once applied. The finish of a surface coated with bronzing powder is glittery and the highlights are soft due to this randomness. Real metallic structures, sheets, and leaf are made through combinations of heating and extrusion, rolling, or polishing. The result of these processes is that the molecular structure of metallic surfaces is organized so the surface of metal takes on a deeper glimmering sheen that we equate with well-polished metal.

Gilded gold and silver surfaces can be burnished and polished until they shine, but bronzing powders cannot be polished. They may be coated with a gloss finish that will help give them the appearance of polished gold, silver, or brass. Faux finishes of stainless steel or aluminum made with bronzing powders alone never will have that gleam. Graphite powder can be used with bronzing powders to make a more realistic metallic surface. The molecules of graphite can be aligned after it is applied through polishing and friction so the surface takes on the distinctive appearance of polished steel. There are two ways to use graphite in a paint treatment. One technique is to polish a surface with graphite once it has been painted with aluminum bronzing powder. This surface must be well primed and sanded prior to painting. The graphite is mixed into a transparent glaze of lacquer or a water-based urethane. Two or three layers of this glaze is applied to the surface and each allowed to dry thoroughly. After these have dried they can be hand-sanded with very fine sandpaper or buffed until the surface forms a sheen. A buffing pad used on an electric drill or a machine buffer will polish the graphite coat to a glossy sheen.

Another method of working with graphite is to mix it directly into a silver paint, which, once it is dry, can be buffed to a high sheen. This method is effective for large surface areas that need to have the appearance of sheet metal or stainless steel.

The medium for the graphite must not be too elastic. Water-based urethane, solvent-based lacquer, or oil-based paints work best. Acrylic, P.V.A., and latex-based paints do not work well because they cannot be sanded or polished as easily. When preparing a metallic treatment of considerable quantity, it is more economical to start mixing the paint from commercial brands of silver paint rather than fabricating it completely from dry bronzing powders. Add about one pound of powdered graphite per gallon of metallic paint. Silver bronzing powder may then be added to the paint if the graphite darkens it too much or just to adjust the color. This paint should be applied to a surface that has been well prepared by being carefully spackled, sanded, primed, and sanded again so no trace of a wood grain or seam is visible. Apply this graphite-treated paint with a sprayer rather than a brush or roller to avoid visible brushstrokes. Two to three solid layers should be sprayed. After the graphite paint is thoroughly dry, it can be lightly sanded with a fine sandpaper or buffed to a high sheen.

Imitating Commercial Decorative Materials

Frequently, a scenic artist is asked to mimic modern synthetic materials through a paint process. It may sound strange to say faux linoleum or faux Formica, but this often is called for in realistic dramas. Many distinctive patterns of these commercial finishes are no longer available, so it is up to the scenic artist to replicate them. All of these faux treatments can be created with water-based paint and finished with water-based or solvent-based urethane of any sheen. These finishes can be tinted with umber, ocher, or even white colorant to age or create the appearance of a yellow or cloudy wax buildup on the surface.

Linoleum Flooring

The earliest linoleum floor patterns often replicated carpeting. These can be mimicked easily enough by laying down a two- to three-color sponged base and stenciling on top of it. The pattern will remain feathery by dabbing with a coarse sponge through a

stencil. More contemporary extruded plastic linoleum with abstract patterns can be painted with a
base of the dominant color and spattered with the
other colors that run through the linoleum. The
spatter is boarded while still wet to draw it out. If a
long strip of linoleum is being done, then a board
with an upright handle attached to it comfortably
may be drawn through the entire length of linoleum. If a very wide area is being painted, do it in
three-foot-wide sections.

Linoleum tiles usually are laid in alternating
directions. Assuming the floor is painted onto 4' × 8'
sheet stock, cartoon the tile grid after the base coat.
Cut a board the width of the tile so that each tile can
be boarded without disturbing the tile next to it. For
more exacting work, it may be necessary to individu-
ally mask every other tile. Masking may be done for
extremely fine detail or if the deck is in forced perspective. Once the complete process is done and dry
for the tiles going in one direction, the completed
tiles are masked out and the alternating tiles are
painted. For further realism, the seams between the
tiles can be scored with a sharp awl guided along a
metal straight edge.

Of course, real linoleum tiling commonly is
used. This is installed by the carpentry staff. After it
has been installed, it may be up to the scenic artist to
age the floor, covering it with a glaze of grime in the
corners and creating a sense of traffic patterns.

Plastic Laminates and Ceramic Tile

Plastic laminate surfaces, like countertops, are treated
much like linoleum surfaces. The pattern may be an
intricate intermingling of finely drawn shapes, like
the famous boomerang design of the 1950s. These
patterns can be recreated with stencils or paint
stamps. More abstract speckled patterns may be done
simply with sponging or spattering. As with linoleum,
plastic laminates can be bought and installed as
needed. A pattern can be added and the laminate
aged as needed.

Ceramic tile may be painted on, using stencils or
paint stamps, and enhanced with two-dimensional
texture techniques and trompe l'oeil for highlights
and lowlights. Ceramic tile often is painted on
pressed board tile paneling, which helps render the
tile pattern. These panels are not altogether very convincing, so it may be necessary for a scenic artist to
do some glaze work with shellacs or water-based
urethane for variation. Individual tiles can be cut

from quarter-inch Masonite for greater realism.
These tiles are primed with a shellac or oil-based
primer. Spraying the primer and base coat may be the
most efficient method of handling all the edges of the
individual tiles. The base coat, any pattern, and texture techniques can be done with water-based paint.
After the tiles have been painted, they can be given
the desired sheen with water-based urethanes. Then
the tiles are installed with ceramic or linoleum tile
adhesive. If the tiles need to look truly realistic, they
can be grouted with tile grout or a mixture of drywall compound and fine silicate sand.

PAINTING ON MISCELLANEOUS MATERIALS

There is no apparent end to the variety of materials
used to create stage scenery. New materials are
adopted constantly by ingenious designers and technicians. The scenic artist must learn the qualities of
these materials, so they may be painted and their true
identity disguised. Some materials may be used in
new combinations, requiring new approaches to
preparation.

Simulated Glass and Plexiglas

Actual glass rarely is used on stage because it is hazardous. Bobbinet and window screen sometimes are
used to suggest glass panes, but in most contemporary productions, Plexiglas is used as a glass substitute. Frequently, a scenic artist is called on to paint
signage on Plexiglas or give it the appearance of
antique rolled glass or stained glass. Fortunately,
Plexiglas bonds well with water-, solvent-, and oil-
based urethanes; lacquers; polymer-based glues; and
shellac.

To create the effect of rolled or antique glass,
solvent-based gloss urethane can be rolled over one
or both sides of the Plexiglas. When dry, the gloss
urethane will not cloud the Plexiglas. Satin urethane does cloud Plexiglas somewhat, which may
be desirable.

The effect of thick bottle glass can be simulated
by coating Plexiglas with polymer glue in any pattern desired. The glue can be poured on in circles,
so that when it dries it thickens toward the edges or
the center, like bottle glass. It also may be rolled
over the Plexiglas to create a very uneven surface.

The polymer glue can be tinted with aniline dyes or colorants.

Tinted shellac, amber shellac, or French enamel varnishes tinted with dye can be used to simulate stained glass, although an F.E.V. will cloud Plexiglas. Shellacs can be tinted with dyes or universal tinting colors.

Lacquers adhere well to Plexiglas. Lacquers can be mixed to custom colors at the paint store or tinted in the shop with universal tinting colors. Clear lacquers can be tinted with universal tinting colors and Japan colors for transparent colors.

Water-based gloss urethanes dry to a smooth, transparent finish that does not cloud Plexiglas at all. Water-based urethanes can be tinted with colorants or aniline dyes. These urethanes bond well to the glass and are excellent for simulating stained glass and painting signage. Water-based urethanes may be thinned with acrylic floor wax for glaze techniques.

If a cartoon must be laid out on uncovered Plexiglas, the cartoon should be executed on a piece of kraft or butcher paper that is then taped to the back of the transparent Plexiglas. Then, the Plexiglas may be painted from the front in the same manner as a scrim, while it lays over the cartoon (see Chapter Eight for more discussion of cartooning signage).

It is difficult to get even coverage of a medium on Plexiglas when working with a brush. Windows often are lit from behind, making any irregularities in coverage apparent. Spraying the paint medium across a cut frisket masking is the best way to acheive a smooth coverage. Spray the medium on in two or three even coats. The protective paper covering on Plexiglas may be cartooned, cut, and peeled in the appropriate areas for spray techniques. If the paper masking has already been removed from the Plexiglas and you must cut your own out of masking tape and paper, it is important to spray the medium on in several very light layers to avoid paint seeping underneath the masking.

If you are working with Plexiglas that, given a tight budget, must be saved for use in future productions, tints can be mixed into vegetable oil soap or dish detergent. This mixture of tint and detergent can be sprayed or brushed on in the same manner as paint then washed off after it has served its purpose. Spraying glass with straight soap is excellent for clouding mirrors or glass. Commercial glass frosting also may be purchased at paint suppliers. An interesting winterlike glass frosting can be made by letting Epsom salts dissolve in puddles of beer on the glass. The frosting will form as this dries. Plexiglas may also be frosted by sanding the surface of it with a fine grit sand paper.

Using Caulk on Plexiglas for Texture

Some texture may need to be applied like a drawing as a raised pattern, or delineation between colors in a design, such as in stained glass. Over small areas or for delicate patterns, hot glue can be used. Paintable latex caulking can be used for larger areas of raised texture. Latex caulk is available in a great variety of colors from lumberyards, hardware stores, and home improvement centers. This caulking can be purchased by the tube or by the case for large jobs. When simulating stained glass, caulking can be purchased in colors that will give the effect of leading, such as gray, brown, graphite, and black. This caulking adheres well to Plexiglas.

The pattern for the leading first should be cartooned on a piece of kraft paper. The glass, stripped of its paper cover, should be laid on top of the paper. The caulk has to be applied using a caulking gun. As you work with the gun, you will become adept at squeezing it with just the right amount of pressure to get a steady, even flow of caulking onto the glass. It is very difficult to lay down a straight line of caulk while squeezing the gun, so any straight line should be laid on using a jig as a guide. The jig can be as simple as two spring clamps and a board. If straight lines break up the glass in two directions, only one direction should be done at a time, because the caulk may take several hours or a full day to dry. For instance, all the horizontal lines of leading should be done on each pane of glass one day, and all the vertical lines should be done the next. If freehand work is to be done with the caulking gun, take the time to practice on an extra piece of Plexiglas before starting on the set pieces. After the caulk has dried, the stained glass tints, urethanes, or polymers can be applied.

Metal

The metals used in scenic construction generally are steel or aluminum. Steel stock usually is coated with oil at the mill where it is manufactured, so that it will not rust while in stock at the steelyard. Before steel can be painted, it should be washed down with mineral spirits or a degreaser to clean off the residue.

After a steel frame has been welded together, all the joints must be cleaned with a steel brush. To paint the steel use a solvent-based paint or primer; either alkyd- or shellac-based paints work well. Steel sanded down to a bright finish must be protected so that it will not rust or corrode back to a dull finish. Clear lacquer, white shellac, or solvent-based urethane can be sprayed or brushed on to protect a bright steel finish.

Aluminum need not be cleaned off before it is painted. However, like steel, it must be primed with solvent-based paint or primers. Once welded together, the joints of the aluminum frame must be cleaned with a steel brush. If a bright aluminum finish is desired, it can be polished with a sanding pad on a grinder or orbital sander. Once polished, aluminum will keep its finish for many months. If the finish must hold indefinitely it can be sealed with clear solvent-based finishes.

Foam Rubber

Foam rubber is a very useful sculpting material. It wraps around almost any form and can be carved or adhered to soft goods with contact cement. Foam rubber can be painted to a certain extent by spraying it with scenic paint just as it is. However, wherever it is seamed with glue or there is a change in material, the paint emphasizes the change in the surface. To avoid this problem, foam elements should be coated to create an even texture throughout. The foam can be skinned with fabric, either cheesecloth or cotton scrim. It also may be covered with a heavy, flexible primer. Some theatrical suppliers sell a foam coat product that can be used on foam rubber as well as polystyrene foam. Commercial polymer-based sculpture coats will work as well. Latex-based roof patching is a less-expensive alternative to these products. A homemade foam coat can be made of drywall compound mixed in even proportions with either contact cement or a polymer-based glue. The most important quality these foam coatings have in common is that they must be flexible.

Carpeting

It is not uncommon to paint or stencil a pattern onto carpet. This works best with short pile carpet. Regular scenic paint can be sprayed or stippled through a stencil on synthetic carpet fibers. Extra binder should be added to the paint used on ground cloths and carpets because of the foot traffic. French enamel varnishes also may be used on synthetic fiber carpets and rugs.

Aniline dye is the best for wool carpets. Because the aniline dye does not set up, care must be taken to keep any carpet painted with dye completely dry.

When an entire carpet must be toned down, a challenge is to coat the fibers thoroughly so the original color of the carpet is not revealed when the nap is brushed. An F.E.V. works well for toning carpets. The color should be sprayed on in even passes and then worked in with a push broom. The color should be thinned and applied in two or three coats. Several light layers of color help ensure even coverage.

Upholstery

Occasionally, a scenic artist has to tone upholstery fabric. Modern upholstery fabrics often are treated with stain guards. Because the stain guards will repel paint as well, it is necessary to work out the intensity and medium of the toner on a sample of the upholstery fabric first. If working with a water-based paint, add extra binder to it for better adhesion. If the water-based paint does not adhere to the fabric, an F.E.V. should be used. Never tone down upholstery with aniline dye, as it may transfer to the costumes or the performers' hands. If the fabric can be stretched and treated before it is tacked on the furniture, it can be sprayed down easily. If an upholstered piece must be toned down, the fabric should be sprayed with several layers of thin color.

Dried Plants

When dried plants, grasses, and foliage are used on stage, one of the main concerns is to ensure they have been treated with fire retardant. Suppliers of fire retardant should be consulted to determine what product will be best suited to these materials. Dried materials should be dipped in a flame retardant for complete coverage. Dried foliage too large to dip should be sprayed with flame retardant from two or three sides. After flame retardant has been applied, dried foliage can be painted with water-based paints, stained with aniline dyes, or toned with an F.E.V. The simplest ways to paint dried foliage are with a pneumatic or garden sprayer, or simply dip the foliage in the paint and let it drip dry.

AGING TECHNIQUES AND MEDIUMS

Aging refers to any technique or combination of techniques used to render the appearance of age and weathering. The most important goal is to realistically simulate the effects that the years and weather have had on real materials. For instance, barn wood will bleach out in the weather while the nails that hold the barn together may rust and stain the wood. Wallpaper in an old buildings may be stained by water marks. The underside of limestone cornices and lintels on the exterior of an old building may be stained and streaked with soot.

Peeling and Cracked Paint

The most obvious way to make a painted surface look aged is to give the paint a cracked appearance. There are a few ways to make fresh paint actually crack or to give it a cracked appearance.

Sodium Silicate

Sodium silicate can be purchased at some theatrical supply houses by the gallon. Mann Brothers is one supplier (refer to the Reading and Resources chapter). It also is available through chemical suppliers in bulk quantities of fifty-five-gallon drums, far more than what would be called for in most theatrical endeavors. When sodium silicate is mixed with polymer binders, particularly acrylics, the two mediums will react chemically, causing a dramatic resistance that cracks the paint (Figure 10.2). The surface to which the silicate mixture is applied first should be painted with the hue that is to show through the cracked finish coat. This undercoat should be covered with shellac. The shellac undercoat will accomplish two things. It will give the sodium silicate mixture a smooth surface to slide off and the alcohol in the shellac will accelerate the evaporation of the mixture.

The sodium silicate should be mixed in equal proportion with the desired hue of paint. The two mediums should be mixed together just before they are to be used; because they are not compatible, the mixture has a very short shelf life. While the shellac on the undercoat is still tacky, the sodium silicate mixture should be brushed or sprayed on with a pneumatic sprayer. While the sodium silicate mixture is setting up, spraying it with solvent alcohol from a garden sprayer also will accelerate the drying time

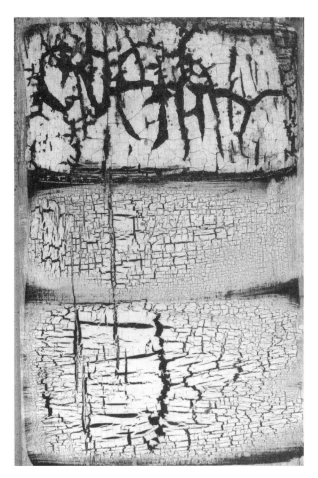

Figure 10.2 Paint cracking samples: sodium silicate (top), animal glue undercoat (bottom two).

and cause the cracks to be more dramatic. A second application of shellac and sodium silicate mixture, after the first one has set up, will result in more profound cracking and aging.

The cracks caused by sodium silicate may look somewhat unnatural because the mixture tends to separate on diagonals while weathered paint tends to crack on verticals, horizontals, or in the direction in which the paint most commonly was applied on that surface. The sodium silicate mixture can be encouraged to crack in a more uniform way by combing it with a wire brush or paint scraper while it is setting up and being sprayed down with the solvent alcohol.

When straight sodium silicate is used as an undercoat, the paint used as a top coat will sag if applied while the surface is vertical. After the top coat has dried, the sagging can be accentuated by spraying it with water or a dirty water glaze.

Glue Base

Polymer-based paints are not stable on an undercoating of animal glue. The paint or polymer varnish will separate and crack on this base. The cracks caused by this technique are very regular and natural looking, but the glue base that is revealed by the cracks will be shiny. This sheen may be eye-catching and unnatural looking. If the surface is vertical while the paint or varnish is drying, it will sag too. The sagging may be desirable in some circumstances, but one of the drawbacks of this technique is that the sagging is very difficult to control.

Boarding

The technique of boarding can be used to give the appearance of chipped paint. Several layers of closely related colors spattered on the desired background color and boarded out can have a very effective appearance. This technique is particularly useful if a large area is to be treated. A boarded base coat may be combined with other aging techniques for cracked or peeling paint.

Distressing

In scenic painting, the term *distressing* means giving a material the appearance of age, wear, and grime. Any technique that contributes to this effect can be termed *distressing*. The peeling and cracking techniques just described are but one form of distressing. The key to convincing distressing is to observe how various materials age and understand the nature of the wear on these materials as they are subjected to use, age, and weather; for instance, how rust from nails or support brackets streaks down the side of wood planks or a brick wall (see Colorplate 8).

Fabrics

As fabric ages, its color fades in areas exposed to light. This fading can be simulated with a spray of a light opaque glaze. Dust and grime in the atmosphere yellow fabric over time. A dirty-water spray of umber or ocher can accomplish this. When spraying fabric with a glaze, it is best to use a very watery glaze applied in two or three passes and allowed to dry between each application so that there are no hot spots. If the fabric to be aged is upholstered on a piece of furniture that is to look tattered, the arms and seat can be worn down with an orbital sander or a rasp.

Other Organic Distressing

Types

Dirt and Soot

Dirt on an exterior usually is the soot and dust that has accumulated in corners and under overhangs that has not been washed off by rain or weather. In productions that are set in eras and areas where coal was used for heating and in industry, the collection of soot will be especially heavy and dark. Soot collects on the sides of building exteriors, particularly if the buildings are located in large cities or towns where coal is used or has been used in the past for heat. Soot streaks may be very dark after many years of being exposed to polluted city air. When distressing interiors most of the dirt collects and spreads through contact with people and inept attempts to clean. Dirt will collect in the corners. Smoke will yellow ceilings, and soot will streak the walls and ceiling above wood- and coal-burning stoves and fireplaces. Grime will accumulate around the corners of walls, along chair rails, and around doorknobs.

Rust

Whenever there are steel nails in wood or iron fixtures on the side of a building, exterior rust will streak down the side of the boards or stone below them. If the rust stain has deepened over the course of many years, it will be a dark blackish brown.

Wood

Wood siding on the side of structures, such as houses, outbuildings, and city structures, ages quickly due to the effects of the weather and the sun. Aged wood tends to simultaneously deepen in color and bleach out. The result is that the exposed wood turns varying shades of gray. The wood under overhangs, protected from the elements, will age more slowly and become darker from mold, moisture, and pollution. The color of the wood in these areas tends to deepen in color and bleach out less.

Wood can be aged by using glazes made from Payne's gray, raw umber, and light gray hues. When the colors are washed on unprimed wood, they will penetrate the wood somewhat and alter its surface color.

Techniques and Mediums

Asphaltum

Asphaltum is a tar-based resin. When thinned with turpentine, the resin will yield a deep sepia-colored glaze that makes a very convincing patina of age and grime. Use proper safety precautions when working with turpentine; it is one of the most toxic solvents commonly used (see Chapter Four, Safety and Health Regulations).

Paint

Scenic paint can be used for aging and distressing techniques. The paint can be thinned and used as a glaze for most applications. If the finish needs to be durable and enduring, the paint can be mixed into a dull-finish acrylic- or water-based urethane.

Wood Pickling

To alter and deepen the actual color of the wood, it must be oxidized. This process can be emulated through pickling. Pickling is not instantaneous. The color of the wood will not fully deepen for nearly eight hours. If the wood is being treated out-of-doors, sunlight will accelerate the process. A few different washes can be used to pickle wood. One solution can be made from steel wool and vinegar. First, immerse the steel wool in water and set it aside to rust. Repeat this once or twice, until it is thoroughly rusted. Then, drop the steel wool in a bucket of vinegar and let it sit overnight. The next day, strain the remaining fragments of steel wool out of the solution. This is your pickling solution. When sprayed or brushed on most woods, it will cause them to oxidize. Denser woods, such as oak, will not absorb or deepen as much as coarser grained woods, such as pine and cedar. Always test the pickling solution on a sample to ascertain its strength and how it will affect the wood being treated. If too strong, it can be cut with water.

Pickling solution also can be made from iron sulfite. The iron sulfite can be mixed into water and sprayed or brushed on the wood. This pickling solution is unpredictable, oxidizing coarser grained woods more darkly. This works very well with cedar. Iron sulfite, also called *copperas*, a soil additive, can be purchased at garden-supply stores.

Wood and Metal Patinas

Patina solutions for metals are sold in paint stores. These corrosive solutions oxidize metal and wood. The solutions are formulated differently so the resulting patina is of a desired color. These different patina solutions will result in slightly different colors on woods as well. Because these solutions are somewhat costly, they may not be the first choice for large-scale projects.

A patina is the pleasing result of corrosion that occurs when metal surfaces are exposed to air and weather. Artists and architects rely on this when they specify bronzes or copper in their work. The sepia, deep greens, and cerulean blues are the result of exposure of these metals to the elements.

Oxidizing Patinas

Products can be purchased through paint supply stores that specialize in faux-finish products that accelerate the oxidizing of many metals. Patina products are available in different solutions that will result in various colors of patinas, such as blue, green, black, and burgundy. These products work on composites of gold and silver leaf and bronzing powders. The patina will form on the metal as the solution dries. If a deeper patina is desired, the solution may be applied again. The patina finish will be fragile and easily wiped off, so if the scenic units or props are to be handled frequently, the units should be sealed by spraying them with water-based urethanes.

Paint

Paints or tinted glazes reinforced with water-based urethanes may be used to simulate patinas. These glazes can be sprayed, brushed, sponged, or ragged on for the desired appearance and sheen.

WALLPAPER

Stencils or stamps may be used to simulate wallpaper. However, if the designer desires very complex patterns or the naturalistic appearance that can come only from actual wallpaper, it will be more time- and cost-effective to select a wallpaper pattern (Figure 10.3).

Conventional Wallpaper

There is not much difference between hanging wallpaper in an actual room and on a set. Wallpaper comes in differing widths; twenty-one inches up to thirty inches is standard. When ordering wallpaper you must include enough extra in the order to cover the linear footage lost when matching the patterns on each seam. When ordering the wallpaper, the information in the catalogue will state how much extra length must be added on per panel.

It is simpler to hang the paper on an assembled set in the shop or on stage. If the units are laid out on the shop floor or paint deck, then the lap joints of the flattage must be carefully measured and cartooned so that the seams of the paper will match when the set is assembled. When actually hanging the wallpaper, a long work table should be set up in the middle of the set or shop. The tools necessary for the job will be sponges, a bucket of water, a metal ruler, a ruler with levels on it, a nine-inch roller and roller tray, a straw wallpaper brush, and a hundred count box of razor blades. Because the wallpaper will be wet with wallpaper paste when it is cut to a width, a fresh blade should be used for each cut. Used blades will have dried paste that can snag the paper. Tape each blade before disposing of it or col-

lect them in a paint can that can be sealed and thrown away.

For centuries, wheat paste was used for pasting up wallpaper. In the later part of the twentieth century, vinyl wall paste has become the new standard for installing wallpaper. Because the paper will expand from the moisture in the paste it must sit for a time after the back has been rolled with paste. Once the length of wallpaper has been measured, cut, and the back rolled with paste the paper should be carefully folded, both ends into the middle, and then folded once again in the center. This is called a *book*. The book of wallpaper should sit for five minutes while the paper expands. Some wallpapers actually must be soaked in water before they are pasted. The manufacture usually will include instructions on how to handle the variety of wallpaper you purchased.

All surfaces to be papered should be primed beforehand. When hanging wallpaper in a room, you first choose the focal point of the room and center the first book of wallpaper on that surface. Successive books should be pasted up on alternating sides so that the paste has a chance to set up before the next book is pasted up alongside of it. The same is true of wallpapering a set. Using the ruler with levels in it, mark out vertical registration lines for aligning the edge of the wallpaper. To hang a book of paper, keep it folded until you are at the top of the ladder or scaffolding. Unfold only the top of the book and

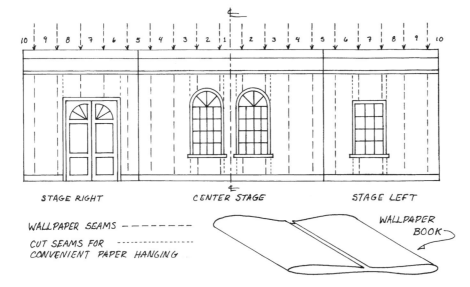

STAGE RIGHT   CENTER STAGE   STAGE LEFT

WALLPAPER SEAMS — — — — — —

CUT SEAMS FOR ·············
CONVENIENT PAPER HANGING

WALLPAPER
BOOK

Figure 10.3 Wallpaper.

position the paper. Once it is in place, brush the paper down from the top and out from the center, being careful to keep the edge lined up on your registration marks. After the top half of the paper is positioned correctly, unfold the bottom of the book and brush the rest of the paper into place. Trim the paper flush to the molding and sponge the excess paste off the molding and the paper before it dries. When working on a set, it may be possible to install the moldings after the wallpaper has been hung.

In a home, the paper must be carefully measured and trimmed around doors and windows. On a set, an additional vertical seam can be added at the corners of door and window casements to speed up the process. The additional vertical seam will not be noticed by the audience. Measure and cut the vertical seam in book of paper using a straight edge. After the first section of the book has been pasted into place along the edge of the casement, the second section can be matched along the new seam and trimmed at the top and the bottom of the casements.

Raised Pattern Paper

Wallpapers with raised patterns and vinyl-based ornamental details frequently are used on sets. When glazed to bring out the detail or viewed with downlighting or sidelighting, these intricate patterns richly enhance the architectural setting. These patterns are available only in their natural white or off-white color. After the patterns have been installed, they can be painted and glazed as desired.

Raised paper patterns installed in commercial and residential interiors must be adhered with a clay-based wallpaper adhesive, usually available through the same manufacturer as the paper. The clay-based adhesive fills and reinforces the pattern of the paper, so that it is not easily dented or crushed during day-to-day wear. When installed in the less permanent situation of a stage setting, regular wallpaper paste may be used to hang the paper. Heavier paper borders and vinyl-backed decorative details also may be installed with wallpaper paste or water-based contact cement, in the case of heavier molded vinyl borders and details.

Laminate Papers

Laminate wall papers such as mylar are made to be used on very smooth commercial wall surfaces. These laminates come in a wide range of finishes and colors and are available from theatrical suppliers. Some of these plastic finishes are adhesive backed, others are paper backed. The adhesive-backed coverings must be applied to a very clean, well-sanded surface. The covering is quite thin and its reflective surface will highlight every imperfection in the surface below it. Air bubbles trapped in thin plastic laminates can be smothed down by carefully pricking the surface with a pin to release the air. The paper-backed plastic coverings are thicker and so are somewhat more forgiving of the surface. However, the seams and dents in the surface still should be patched and sanded before the covering is applied. The paper-backed coverings can be applied with vinyl wallpaper paste. However, the plastic coverings cannot be booked tight and folded along the edge, like wallpaper, because the crease caused by folding will remain. The supplier of the plastic covering also will have a recommendation on the brand or type of adhesive that should be used.

Part Four
The History of Scenic Art

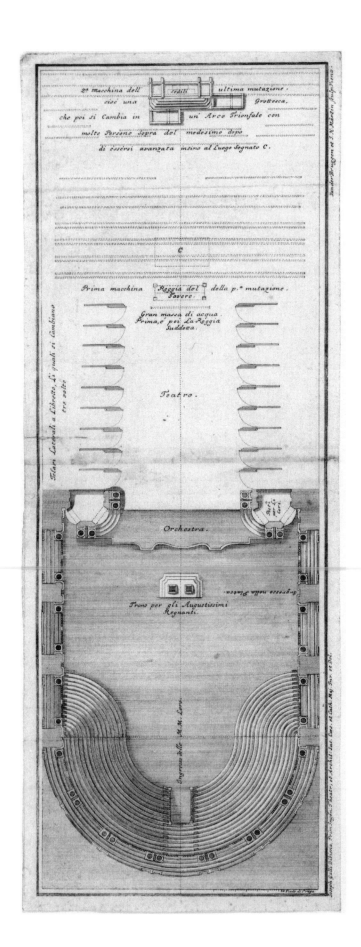

Section of the Teatro Farnese by Pietro Paolo
Coccetti, drawn in 1726; The Tobin
Collection of The McNay Museum,
San Antonio, Texas.

chapter 11

The Ancient Theatre to the Medieval Theatre: 500 B.C.–1400 A.D.

INTRODUCTION

Stage painting most likely was a part of early western drama in the Greek theatre of Aeschylus and Sophocles. From Roman accounts of Greek theatre, we know that the stage had painted decoration to augment the scene. The descriptions suggest a sophisticated illusionistic style. Unfortunately, we have no authoritative record of what painting was like in Greek and Roman theatre. This we do know: once scenic painting entered the stage for theatrical purposes, it remained a significant decorative and dramatic element throughout nearly all theatrical history. As stage decoration progressed through the centuries from this beginning, it consistently explored the exotic, fantastic, and wondrous stage image through painting. Theatre building styles and stage technology evolved greatly in the 2400-year interval from classical Greece to the present, but the fundamental visual relationship between the audience, actors, and painted backgrounds remains.

GREECE: 500–250 B.C.

"The ancients required realistic pictures of real things" (Vitruvius, Book V, 1960). These are the words of the Roman architect Marcus Vitruvius Pollio, written during the first century B.C. Vitruvius's work is the oldest surviving written record with any

reference to architectural practice related to the theatre. This book influenced generations of architects in the Roman Empire and its rediscovery at the birth of the Italian Renaissance has served to inform the world of the practice and aesthetics of Roman and Greek architecture.

Vitruvius reveals much of what we know about the classical Greek theatre, as well as Roman theatre, through his book, *De Architetura*. He describes the site of a theatre, acoustical considerations, foundations, harmonics, use and construction of theatres, and the differences between the Greek and Roman styles. Vitruvius also describes painted scenery and stage equipment. These descriptions were made over 400 years after the time of Aeschylus, Euripides, and Socrates. We cannot be certain of the exact time that the elements he describes were introduced, but we can assume that the Greek theatre used moveable and changeable scenic devices, at least in the later Hellenistic theatres, and painted decoration.

The Greek Theatre Building

Large permanent theatres were built in the fifth century B.C., the classical period of ancient Greece. These theatre spaces were formal structures, placed in very prominent and meaningful sites within a city. Some theatres accommodated thousands of spectators with a good view of the stage and clear hearing of the actor. The earliest of these formal

Greek theatres were placed in carefully chosen locations for two reasons: as a sloping site to aid the seating and acoustics and to situate the view of the audience toward an expansive vista. Nature, in effect, provided the first backdrops.

An elevated stage platform developed in the Athenian theatres later in the classical period. It was placed at the back of the orchestra, the large circular area at the foot of the seating. This stage structure, or *skene*, allowed actors a place for entrances as well as a prominent position for performance. The *skene* was low at first, connected with steps to the orchestra. The height of the *skene* increased and it became an isolated platform for performance, no longer connected to the orchestra. The *skene* also, eventually, had a back wall that was decorated with architectural embellishments common to Greek classical architecture. Temporary decorations were added to it for individual productions. These decorations were

certainly painted, but no examples remain of early scenic art. We must rely on a few written descriptions and the long historical lineage of the form itself. Classical Greek theatre was copied by the Roman Empire and then revived in the Italian Renaissance. Any knowledge we have of the Greek theatre comes from the Roman interpretation and their records of it.

Greek Stage Decoration

Greek theatres are thoroughly documented to have had three essential parts: audience, orchestra, and *skene* (Figure 11.1).

The Skene

The *skene* possibly was built to allow for entrances and to create dressing and offstage areas for the

Figure 11.1 The *skene* and orchestra of a classical Greek theatre.

actors. By virtue of its placement, the *skene* became an architectural background to the stage area and lessened the impact of the landscape as the background. Actors performed in front of the *skene*. The façade of the *skene* was large enough to have doors that served as decoration, as well as for use in the action of the play. The door to a palace, for example, easily could be provided using the *skene*. Vitruvius (1960, Book V) describes this very arrangement: "In the center are double-doors, decorated like those of a royal palace. At the right and the left are the doors of the guest chambers."

Painted Decoration

The *skene* apparently was decorated with temporary and changeable painted pieces. Two types of painted scenic elements, *periaktoi* and *pinakes,* are documented by Vitruvius and Pollux (a Roman architect who described theatres in a book written some two hundred years after Vitruvius). These *periaktoi* were triangular columns, like elongated vertical prisms, that could rotate to present different faces, thus allowing the possibility of on-stage scene changes. Exactly where the *periaktoi* were placed on the *skene* is unknown. Some have theorized that the *periaktoi* were placed within the open doors, others state that they sat on either side of them. Each face of the *periaktoi* could be painted to represent a different scene. In fact, Vitruvius has described three kinds of scenes—the tragic, the comic, and the satyric—which would neatly correspond to the three faces of the *periaktoi*. The other element, the *pinakes,* were simple flat panels, possibly painted either with just color or formal designs (Nicoll, 1966) and used to change the face of the *skene* for particular performances. These *pinakes* probably were placed on the front of the *skene*, between columns, and used like flats are today.

From these written descriptions, it is certain the Greeks used a method of painted decoration. Vitruvius states that Aeschylus invented painted scenery. Aristotle gives the credit, however, to Sophocles. Vitruvius (Book VII) ascribed a document of scenic painting, written by the painter Agatharchos of Samos, that, "Led Democritus and Anaxagoras to write on the same subject [painting], showing how, given a center in a definite place, the lines should naturally correspond with due regard to the point of sight and the divergence of the visual rays, so that by this deception a faithful representations of the buildings might be given in painted scenery, and so that, though all is drawn on a vertical flat façade, some parts may seem to be withdrawing into the background, and others to be standing out in front."

Agatharchos was a painter who apparently worked for the theatre. His work dates from the second half of the fifth century B.C. At that time, there was an understanding that perspective methods of drawing produced effects of depth and contributed to more realistic painting. Furthermore, this indicates a recognition of the role of perspective illusion for the stage. This sort of technique was to have profound importance on the craft of theatrical painting and decoration much later in the Renaissance. It is unknown when these practices actually began, however. The Greek term for scenic painting, *skenographia,* has remained as the modern term for a theatrical designer, scenographer.

ROME: 2550 B.C.–550 A.D.

The Roman Empire spread to enormous proportions throughout Europe, eastern Asia, and northern Africa. The city-states of Greece were one of Rome's most significant early conquests, as it spread outward from the Italian peninsula. The Romans borrowed from Greece an aesthetic sensibility that served as an artistic cornerstone of the prolific empire to come. The theatre was no exception. The written record of Vitruvius underscores the absolute respect Rome had for the arts of Greece. Rome studiously imitated Greek forms of theatre and theatrical building for itself. In this manner, the essential Greek format of audience, orchestra, and *skene* remained and served as the basis for further development and elaboration.

The Roman Theatre and the Scaenae Frons

Rome built theatres in most of its large cities, recognizing that theatre was an important part of cultural life. Their theatres were located close to the center of the city, and they were in constant use. The building resembled the Greek model on many levels; however, Rome brought the building closer to a self-contained architectural unit. The seating was restricted to a half-circle and the orchestra was diminished in size and dramatic importance. The *skene* was replaced by a more elaborate architectural background, called the *scaenae frons*. The *scaenae frons* played a significant role in the decoration and function of the theatre and became the dominant decorative unit. Nearly a building in itself, it was a two- or three-story wall, richly decorated with a program of columns, niches, and statuary. It retained the three doors of the Greek *skene* and sometimes had two more, added for more entrances, particularly as the size of the theatre grew. The stage remained squarely in front of the *scaenae frons*. It became deeper and wider, giving the actor greater freedom of movement (Figure 11.2).

The impact of the *scaenae frons* was tremendous to the building as a whole. The height of it obliterated most views to the natural surroundings of the location. This allowed theatres to be placed at will in the city, no longer dependent on perfect topography. The audience seating was built to a height matching the top of the *scaenae frons*. This meant that the entire building was wrapped in a continuous wall. Effectively, the theatre became an architectural whole, lacking only a roof to completely isolate it from the outdoors. The eventual use of an awning *(velarium)* to cover the audience from the sun virtually created an interior theatre space. The height of the *scaenae frons* allowed two sorts of curtains to be employed in the stage area. One was the *aulaeum*, which functioned as a front curtain. This could be dropped to the orchestra level or raised up to reveal or conceal the stage at will. Another was the *siparium*, which served as a backdrop, concealing the *scaenae frons* and providing a decorative surface. Both curtains easily could have served as painted decoration.

Roman Stage Decoration

There is no question that Roman architects used many types of painted decoration extensively. The remains of Pompeii prove the extent to which painted frescoes were found in the buildings and

Figure 11.2 The Roman *scanae frons*.

homes of the Roman Empire. Mosaics also flourished as a major decorative force to a degree never witnessed before this time. Although no scenery exists from this period, it is safe to assume that stages were completed with the presence of painted scenic elements. Frescoes from Pompeii illustrate full stage settings and use of the *aulaeum* and *siparium*. Certainly, all the machinery known to the Greeks also was used by the Romans. The *periaktoi* and *pinakes* that Vitruvius recorded would have provided Roman stage painters with ample vehicles for their artistic input. Existing paintings of Roman stages indicate that the *scaenae frons* could be further embellished with statuary, paintings, and objects to help delineate a scene.

Vitruvius describes the three kinds of scenes in Book V, Chapter VI, which falls immediately before the chapter on Greek theatres. Perhaps Vitruvius recognized that these scenes are of Roman invention. The description is as follows: "There are three kinds of scenes, one called tragic, second, the comic, third, the satyric. Their decorations are different and unlike each other in scheme. Tragic scenes are delineated with columns, pediments and statues and other objects suited to the kings; comic scenes exhibit private dwellings, with balconies and views representing rows of windows, after the manner of ordinary dwelling; satyric scenes are decorated with trees, caverns, mountains, and other rustic objects delineated in landscape style."

Roman painting explored the world of perspective as a means to represent the real world. Vitruvius's quotation from earlier in this section reflects the demand for real things depicted realistically. Vitruvius noted a degradation of painting away from realism to fantasy. Certainly, in the centuries after Vitruvius to the decline of Rome, there were hundreds upon hundreds of painted embellishments for theatrical productions. Unfortunately, none survive, and we may only speculate as to their content.

THE MIDDLE AGES: 550–1400 A.D.

The Years of Struggle

The Roman Empire crumbled slowly under repeated attacks of the northern tribes, called barbarians. The Roman Emperor Constantine split the Roman Empire in two halves around 333. He established a Western empire centered at Rome and an Eastern

capitol in Byzantium, renamed Constantinople. At this point in time, the city of Rome began to diminish as a cultural power.

Theatre did persist in Rome beyond Constantine. However, after 568 there is no record of further theatrical performances in the city of Rome. The many theatres of the empire fell into disuse, at least for their original purpose.

Important arts, crafts, and skills relevant to theatre were abandoned and forgotten. The books of Vitruvius were ignored and the careful sense of the classical orders of architecture were submerged into distant memory. Architectural development now relied on observation and a naive imitation of the past. This allowed for a completely new aesthetic to develop, one that would reflect the sensibilities of each location. French, German, Italian, and English styles were to come as the world approached the first millennium after Christ.

The transition took centuries. Scores of generations passed from the time of great cultural activity in Rome to the calming of European tribal wars and the growth of Medieval cities around 1100. There were few bright spots in this epoch. Charlemagne made tremendous strides toward recognizing knowledge and learning around 800. His effort to amass the scholars of the known world at the capitol of the Holy Roman Empire in Aix-la-Chapelle (Aachen, at the intersection of modern Belgium, Germany, and the Netherlands) was successful, for a brief period. Within two generations of Charlemagne's death, however, Europe returned to bitter warfare, as small groups struggled for domination.

Warfare, disease, and poverty limited artistic growth in Europe. Theatre was sporadic at best and generally limited to religious spectacle. The development of the theatre building stopped. No theatres were built in Europe for scores of generations. The art of stage decoration and painting, as the ancient cultures knew it, ended. The ability to paint Vitruvius's realism, by means of perspective, was lost. Painting, of course, did not cease and a new sense of "realism" was to evolve in the Middle Ages.

THE REMNANTS OF CLASSICAL TRADITIONS

The Catholic Church was by far the most prominent force in medieval Europe. Politically and culturally as well as by religious influence, Catholicism brought structure to Europe after the fall of the Roman Empire. The harsh existence of this epoch left little time or place for theatrical activity. The Church was one of the few enduring features of the time. It was an intrinsic part of life in the Middle Ages. The act of the mass was in itself a drama and the Church became the source of newer forms of drama, which chiefly revolved around the liturgy. The theatre of Greece and Rome had no place in Catholic theology. Much of what was entertainment to the classical world now was outlawed as pagan.

One might see the Catholic mass itself as a final living remnant of Roman culture. The celebration of the mass developed in Rome, particularly after the division of the empire in 333. It was then that Constantine, himself a convert, legitimized Christianity for the whole Roman Empire. The Church installed its head official, the Pope, in Rome, underlining the enduring importance of the Eternal City. The Church took over many existing buildings of the Roman Empire for use as churches. The common basilica, normally a meeting hall for the Romans, became a church for many early Christians. These basilicas were large, rectangular open spaces, well suited to large gatherings. These Romans, after converting to Christianity, celebrated mass in the basilicas. The people were still Romans, and it is natural to see how a sense of pomp and formality, which is clear in contemporary Catholic mass, would have come naturally to a Roman citizen. Certainly, only in the second half of the twentieth century was the mass finally conducted in a language other than Latin. The mass certainly is a form of drama in itself, and the church would eventually serve as the principal host of dramatic performances.

Liturgical Drama

The Catholic Church had no interest in preserving the performing arts that the Romans knew. Instead, the Church became the source for a new phase in theatre. Christianity used drama to explain more clearly the teachings of Christ. Churches staged liturgical dramas in conjunction with the two great Christian festivals: Christmas and Easter, the birth and death of Christ. This dramatic storytelling took place in the church itself as a part of the mass. These dramas became popular as good entertainment on their own and attracted enough spectators that the entertainment moved out-of-doors to satisfy the demand. Ironically, the Church itself finally created what it had suppressed for so long—theatre.

The Outdoor Stage

The move to the out-of-doors was tremendously significant for the production and the theatre. Indoor dramas had a natural stage in the church itself and needed little visual help. Outdoor performances meant construction of a stage or stages to depict the locations of the drama. After a gap of nearly nine hundred years, theatrical stages were to be built again. Twelfth century texts describe the presence of many locales, called *loci*, which are stages or sets constructed for the outdoor liturgical drama. The crucifix, the sepulcher, a prison, Hell, Heaven, and several other locales are described in the twelfth century French text for *Resurrection*. Each locale appears to be contained in a small stage or mansion. A description of the Anglo-Norman production of *Adam* indicates that paradise was depicted with actors nearly hidden behind curtains and silks, that fragrant flowers and leaves were scattered, and fruit-filled trees completed the scene. These dramas were performed in sequential order, requiring the audience to move from stage to stage. In fact, they were very much like the fourteen stations of the cross common to Catholic churches then and now. In these, the worshipper moves from station to station to observe the fourteen dramatic steps of Christ's imprisonment and crucifixion.

Mystery Plays, Cycles, and Pageants

By the late thirteenth century, these religious dramas appeared in many locations in Europe. Their popularity was immense, and the dramas grew to staggering proportions of detail and spectacle. The growth of liturgical dramas demanded intense activity and effort for their production. Guilds and fraternities were established to produce the dramas. Entire towns devoted weeks of effort to prepare for them. These productions became so elaborate that it took up to four days for the performance of one play. These dramas became known as *mystery plays* or *cycles*. The term *mystery play* is very appropriate to the drama as every attempt was made to realistically stage the mysteries of the liturgy in frightening detail. These mystery plays put remarkable emphasis on theatrical production, which created a need for a unique group of skilled artisans. The chiefly anonymous participants in these productions revived, or created, skills of the theatrical arts that were to become crucial to the revival of theatre in the Renaissance.

The plays, or cycles, primarily had two formats. One form is a stationary presentation, where all the scenic elements are dispersed around an open area, such as a town square. The second form is the pageant. In this form, the scenic elements are moved to the spectators on wheels. This latter form was more common in England, whereas the former style was common in Europe. In both cases, the stages were elaborate, self-contained units, generally called *mansions*. The audience was to focus on the mansion while it was in use and ignore everything surrounding.

Mystery Play Production

Mystery plays served to inspire wonderment and awe in the viewers. Their very existence was to serve religious purposes. We should recognize, too, that these plays were the sole entertainment available for most people. Texts and production notes have survived from some mystery plays in France. We can see from these how the plays grew in scale and spectacle in the fifteenth and sixteenth centuries. The mystery play at Villingen shows that the town square became filled with twenty-two individual stages or mansions, including Hell, the garden of Gethsemane, Mount Olivet, the pillar of scourging, the palace of Herod, the court of Pilate, the last supper, Christ's cross, the thieves' crosses, graves, the holy sepulcher, and Heaven. The mystery of the passion at Valenciennes in 1547 used sixty-three actors. At Bourges, the mystery of the acts of the apostles included 494 characters and required fourteen days of performance. The twenty-two mansions constructed at Rouen were prepared over a period of eighteen years.

These mystery plays and cycles were immense community undertakings. Evidently their popularity was great, as many thousands of people attended these presentations, justifying the tremendous expenses and investments in time. From this work, too, came the revival of the craft of theatre. These mystery plays were loaded with intricate devices to create effects of fire, smoke, explosions, torture, and executions. Clearly, individuals with great skills and talent worked in the creation of these complex presentations. The pageants were popular throughout

much of northern and central Europe as well. France, Germany, the Netherlands, England, and Belgium all saw many of these productions. Through these great liturgical dramas, the actual practice of theatre and great invention in theatrical production spread in Europe. Later, as new kinds of drama emerged in the Renaissance, there would be the knowledge and skills to support the continued growth of theatre and production.

The Scenic Elements of Mystery Plays

The drawings of Lucerne and Valenciennes and records from the pageant at Mons and other productions show us how increasingly complex the scenic elements became. Heaven and Hell were paramount in importance. At Mons, Heaven required complex pulley and winch systems to allow the apostles to rise up. Heaven itself was concealed with painted clouds, and the sky behind Heaven was filled with stars. Hell was often the huge, fearsome mouth of a fantastic creature. From this awful mouth came flames, smoke, sparks, thunder, dragons, serpents, and the devil. The manuscript at Mons describes Hell as a gigantic "mask of a toad face." It took a stone mason and two assistants three days to form it. Then, it was covered in canvas and painted.

The stage at Mons was immense and the play called for sixty-seven different mansions, or settings. The records show that five painters were on salary for the production for a considerable length of time. They used all pigments available, varnish, gold leaf, and silver powder. They were called on to paint the sky of Heaven and the mask of Hell as well as a cloth with the sun and moon, imitation draperies, and architecture. Painting was an extremely integral part of these productions.

Tournaments and Processionals

Stagecraft eventually was kept active by the needs of state, particularly in France and England. The tournament contests often incorporated painted castles for the games. Knights entered on disguised chariots, painted to look like ships at sea or amidst a grove of trees and wild beasts. The visit of a king or queen, a coronation, or a royal wedding demanded elaborate decorations. More painted castles, triumphal arches, gateways, and other embellishments would be erected for these notable events.

The scenic artists and scenic designers of this time mostly were anonymous artists. Their work for theatre was done largely as an outside interest. We have no records of any individual who devoted a career to the visual part of theatre. What their techniques or practices were, we have no information. Certainly the crossover between fine arts, fresco painting, and theatrical decoration was important. Few took theatre as an important and ongoing profession, but simply as an adjunct to other crafts. The "designing" of the era was the effort to create living allegories and make paintings come to life. It would take a broad cultural revolution to restore scenic decoration to the theatre.

chapter 12

The Renaissance Theatre and the Baroque Theatre: 1400–1800

THE FIFTEENTH AND SIXTEENTH CENTURIES: THE RENAISSANCE

Theatrical arts underwent a significant transformation in Europe during the Renaissance, resulting in a variety of entirely new kinds of entertainment. These plays demanded new forms of stage decoration based on a classical ideal. Medieval liturgical dramas gradually were superseded by classical dramas and forms of popular entertainment as secular theatre became viable. In this time, the English theatre went from court pageants and obscure interludes to the works of Shakespeare. The first permanent theatre in Europe since the Roman Empire was built in Italy. Italian artists and architects explored the use of perspective through drawing, painting, and actual building as means to decorate theatrical stages in a new way. Stage decoration itself became a prolific art form of the Renaissance as well as a significant aspect of most theatrical performance.

As construction of theatres revived in the Renaissance, the need also arose for artists to decorate the stages. The scenic designer, a specialist in perspective and painting, in essence, is a product of this time. These happenings are further underscored by the publication of the first book addressing theatrical architecture and design since Vitruvius. The role of specialized painting was important to the theatre and scenery, but the use of perspective clearly was the key element as theatrical performance and spectacle moved from outdoor pageant wagons to indoor stages.

Italy

The Renaissance of the classical civilizations of Greece and Rome began in Italy. This is when the theatrical arts of designing and painting that we recognize today also began. Italian artists created the styles of theatrical decoration that were to become common across most of Europe, as secular drama began to compete with the liturgical dramas of the Middle Ages. The Italian style and technique would become the standard that nearly all other countries would emulate as secular theatrical performance spread in Europe.

The Roman Revival and the Rediscovery of Perspective

Many aspects of the Roman Empire were reexamined in Italy during the fifteenth century, including the arts and philosophy. Italy was the natural place for such study as it had been the center of the Roman Empire and still bore many remnants of the civilization that had died out almost a thousand years before. Influential, wealthy families, such as the Medici of Florence, supported interest in art and history, humanist thought, and creative individuals.

Architecture, literature, and theatre were some of the fields for which interest was renewed. The growth of study and intellectual exploration, the beginning of scientific, methodical analysis of nature, art, and civilization was to have a great impact on the arts, and it affected the theatre for several reasons. First, classical literature was sought for theatrical performances which meant a shift away from the many hundreds of years of only religious or liturgical drama, as other subjects were opened to performance. Second, a tolerance of theatre and performance by the Church allowed, at least in Italy, the theatre as entertainment to grow. As this secular theatre grew in popularity in Italy, it began to spread to the rest of Europe and eventually displaced liturgical drama altogether. Third, the revival of Roman architecture inspired interest in theatre buildings, stages, and ultimately stage decoration. Fourth, the rediscovery of perspective drawing created a device to create two- and three-dimensional indoor stage pictures with much greater impact, requiring a specialist to create them. The primary skill of the scenic designer of the Italian Renaissance was to understand perspective drawing and apply that knowledge to the stage.

Two significant events of the fifteenth century, both of which took place in Italy, are the foundations of Renaissance stage designing. First, the Florentine artist and architect Filippo Brunelleschi discovered the principles and practice of linear perspective in 1425 (Edgerton, 1975). Brunelleschi's discoveries gave artists a system with which the visual world could be scientifically measured and drawn. This new technique had a profound impact on all art, much like photography would four hundred and fifty years later. Second, the Roman architect Vitruvius's *The Ten Books on Architecture* were translated and printed for the first time in 1486. The recent invention of the moveable-type printing press allowed rapid proliferation of this influential work. In the *Ten Books* are evocative references to scenery and perspective painting of the Roman era. Coupled with the new understanding of seeing through perspective, these books provided an inspirational guide for early Renaissance stage decoration.

Early Perspective Scenery

Roman theatrical literature and performance had been explored since the fourteenth century. The printing press allowed greater exchange of information, including performance. The 1486 edition of Vitruvius carries an illustration of recent performances of classical works. An edition of the plays by Terrence, published in Lyons in 1493, features stage pictures, complete with actors and settings. In it, the medieval mansion was still in use but with a small stage in front and a framing device around the edge of the setting.

Performances of *La Calandria* in Urbino and Rome, during 1513–1514, featured a new element. Most likely the first full-stage perspective setting, the design was by Baldassare Peruzzi, the artist also responsible for executing the design. Peruzzi was an architect and painter as well as a set designer and had been greatly influenced by the work of Vitruvius. The design for *La Calandria* was a significant departure from the medieval style of individual mansions. This was a seamless full-stage composition. Houses were grouped together on a center street leading to a distant archway. The four downstage houses apparently were three-dimensional structures; the background was a simple painted backdrop. This may be the first true perspective backdrop in the theatre. The entire composition relies on much greater stage width than medieval style ever permitted. The depth is not astounding in itself but greatly enhanced by the perspective drawing of the background. The scenery demonstrates the ability to unify a stage composition of three- and two-dimensional objects with a background and illustrates the potential of perspective to suggest visual depth.

Sebastiano Serlio and the First Book on Scenic Design

Sebastiano Serlio's *Architettura*, published in 1545, was the first book to discuss stage design at length since Vitruvius. *Architettura* actually is a seven-volume commentary on architecture, published over several years. Book Two focuses principally on theatre architecture and stage decoration.

Sebastiano Serlio was an architect and architectural decorator as well. At the age of fifty, Serlio began study with Baldassare Peruzzi, which is when he probably became influenced by Vitruvius's theories of theatrical designing. Serlio moved to France in 1541 to work for Francis I and died in Paris in 1551.

Serlio's book is a landmark of Renaissance design. The book describes the use of perspective scenery based on the Roman model of the tragic, comic, and satyric settings. Serlio illustrated this scenery in an ideal theatre based on Roman form (Figure 12.1). Serlio's theatre was an indoor theatre with semicircular seating. It had no proscenium arch, however, a small, semicircular orchestra separated the stage from the seats. The stage was wide and shallow and raised up. At the rear of the stage was a steeply raked platform holding the perspective scenic units. At the rear of that was a painted backdrop. The vivid perspective was enhanced by the use of a grid drawn on the floor, which diminished to an upstage vanishing point. The composition depended on perspective construction and painting for an illusion of depth.

The scenery itself, of course, was much closer to the work of Peruzzi than anything Serlio may have known of actual Roman scenery, even though the book attempts to revive classical architecture and theatres. The Roman *scaenae frons* was completely absent, replaced by the wide, full Renaissance vistas similar to what Peruzzi had created for *La Calandria*. Serlio's book, by virtue of its wide publication, created a standard theatre and scenery format that was imitated for decades. The book was published and available in English by 1611 (Rosenfeld, 1973).

The Teatro Olympico

That the Olympic Academy of Vicenza aimed to build a theatre at all was significant in itself. No permanent indoor theatre had been constructed in Europe for over eleven hundred years, since the fall of the Roman Empire. The academy sought to create a replica of a Roman theatre for staging classical plays. It selected the architect Andrea Palladio, who planned and began a theatre building in 1580. Palladio died after three months of construction, and the building was completed by Vincenzo Scamozzi. The theatre was built mostly of wood and is still standing. The Teatro Olympico has an indoor stage that mimics the Roman *scaenae frons* and audience layout. The seating is slightly elliptical, backed by a colonnade with statuary, and the entire assembly is under a curved ceiling painted with clouds. It is as if a Roman theatre was reduced and placed into a museum diorama. The *scaenae frons* is backed by extensive permanent scenery. Each of the five doors of the *scaenae frons* has arched openings to a three-dimensional street behind them. The streets appear to converge on the stage itself, like streets running to a town square. Beyond all the streets and buildings is a painted

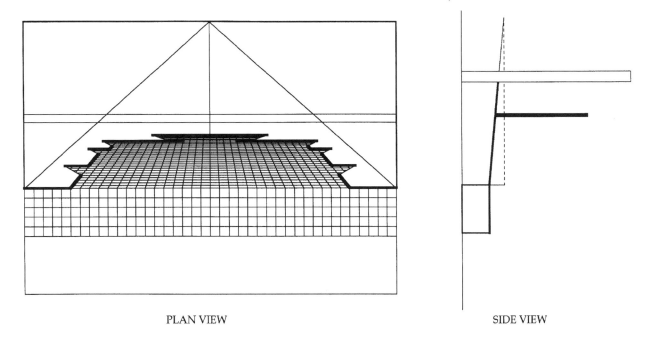

PLAN VIEW   SIDE VIEW

THE PERSPECTIVE STAGE OF SEBASTIANO SERLIO

Figure 12.1 Plan of the ideal theatre of Serlio.

domed sky. The perspective is highly exaggerated, which prohibits using the streets as an acting area. The scenery was the work of Scamozzi.

The Teatro Olympico certainly was a landmark work. It was the first true theatre built after over a thousand years. That it still stands certainly qualifies it as among the oldest existing scenery in the world. Yet, of all the stage decoration of the Italian Renaissance, the Teatro Olympico was among the most conservative. Two more remarkable innovations in this period brought stage decoration to a greater role.

The Introduction of the Proscenium Frame and Moving Scenery

The stage designs of Peruzzi, Scamozzi, and Serlio essentially were views of a city square. We see this image copied during the Renaissance in the work of others. The design by Bartolommeo Neroni (Il Riccio) for *L'Ortensio*, in Siena in 1561, shows us essentially the Serlian tragic scene. The addition of a large frame of formal architecture to this is most notable. Even earlier, a sketch by Antonio San Gallo the Younger, executed between 1515 and 1530, notes a traditional city square, also surrounded by the frame. These have a suggestion of the formal framing device that became the proscenium frame. San Gallo's sketch also indicates *triangulare machina* on the edges of the paper, and plan views of *periaktoi* are evident. San Gallo may have been sketching an idea of moving the scenery in the fashion that Vitruvius referred to but left incompletely described in the *Ten Books*.

The later work of Bernardo Buontalenti incorporated moving scenery. Buontalenti was commissioned by the Medici family to stage an entertainment in the Uffizi at Florence in 1585. The entertainment was *intermezzi*, which are lighthearted pieces first developed as diversions from the ponderous classical dramas. The *intermezzi* took place between acts of the drama and had nothing to do with it. The *intermezzi* became so popular that entire evenings were devoted solely to their production, such as this one that Buontalenti was to have created. It appears that Buontalenti integrated changing stage pictures in this production. Written accounts of the spectacle indicate that, instead of the usual single setting, the audience saw "A continual series of ever-changing and ever startling scenic displays before their wondering eyes. This display featured many scenes. It began with a perspective view of Florence. Then a heavenlike cloud

machine with angelic characters followed by a hellish 'horrible cavern full of the most terrible flames and dark vapours.' Then a winter scene transformed into spring. A seascape and another heavenly scene concluding with a vast plain of trees, grottos and caverns" (Nicoll, 1966).

Buontalenti's sketches survive, but we do not know how these scenic changes were achieved. We do know that *periaktoi* were used in the sixteenth century Italian stage. That in itself is significant, because to use the *periaktoi*, the three-dimensional scenery of Serlio and Scamozzi would have to have been completely translated to the two-dimensional flat surface of the *periaktoi*. This transition must have happened in stages throughout the century. Two-dimensional work had been present in backdrops since even Peruzzi's designs in 1514. Toward the end of the century, moving two-dimensional pieces were common. These were either on the three-sided *periaktoi*, two-sided rotating panels, or one-sided sliding shutters.

France

The visual revolution in theatre came to France far less quickly than to Italy, through the work of Italian designers like Serlio and others. Catherine de Medici, who wed into the royal family of France, brought Italian artists to Paris and elsewhere in France. The influence of Italian Renaissance theatre was less powerful in France at first, because of the immense popularity of the liturgical dramas and passion plays that were so remarkably well produced. These liturgical dramas were more popular and prominent in France than they had been in Italy. The scenic units, or mansions, were the primary scenic element of theatrical performance in France, and it was natural that they should be adopted for indoor use as permanent theatres were constructed. It would take time for linear perspective to have an influence in France and transform the medieval scenic style. Thus, the sixteenth century was truly a transitional period for the theatre in France, caught somewhere between medieval pageantry and staging and the new Italian perspective style.

On November 17, 1548, the Parliament of Paris banned the popular and highly sophisticated mystery pageants, due to religious unrest. Similar statutes were written in other French cities soon thereafter. Although not strictly applied, the ban led to a degeneration of this medieval tradition and allowed secular drama to fill in the vacuum created by the absence of the mystery plays. The same year Catherine de Medici traveled to France for the first time and brought with her the first example of Italian perspective scenery. This took place in Lyons as *La Calandria* with decorations by Nannocio. That performance did not immediately alter French theatrical production, however, and it was a long time before the Italian style became wholly accepted in France. A new theatre was built in Paris, also in 1548, at the site of L'Hôtel de Bourgogne, which was to become the theatrical center of France in this period.

The medieval tradition was deeply engrained in the French theatre, despite the ban in Paris, and that scenic decorative style remained a great influence, modifying the Italian influence. Vitruvius became available in French in 1547, at about the same time Sebastiano Serlio was working for Francis I in Fontainbleau. Serlio, however, lost the patronage of the crown at the death of Francis I in 1547 and did not receive significant commissions or exposure to the French. Italian staging techniques were brought to Paris by Catherine de Medici, when she appointed Baldassarino de Belgiojoso director of all court festivities in 1577. This appointment provided the royalty with some exposure to a new kind of theatrical art, but the general population was entertained more or less by street performances, whose scenic embellishments were few. The royalty continued theatrical entertainment within the confines of their palaces off and on during the reign of Henry IV and Louis XIII. It was for the young Louis XIV that Italian opera made its debut in France in 1645.

L'Hôtel de Bourgogne

L'Hôtel de Bourgogne was the center of public Parisian and French theatre at that time. From the year of the ban of religious plays in 1548, the Confrères de la Passion, who had exclusive right to stage the great mystery plays in Paris, were allowed to continue performing there, although the emphasis was on classical plays and ballads. An Italian troupe was installed in the 1599 season, and by 1600, another French troupe took their place and the name, *Comédiens Royaux*. Eventually they were to become the Comédie Française and the performers of the plays of Molière. This was a traveling troupe that recognized the need for scenic decoration, with a Monsieur Belleroche who played comic roles and worked on painting the decorations of the plays (Decugis and Reymond,

1953). This troupe inherited the theatre and its permanent stock of scenery and stayed for a run of nearly thirty-five years.

The *Mémoire de Laurent Mahelot* is a remarkable testament of the period and one of the best documents of the theatre of the time. Laurent Mahelot, who kept this journal, was director, designer, painter, stagehand, prop master and, happily, diarist of L'Hôtel de Bourgogne. His book records the scenic development of the period through his own work as a designer-painter as well as the work of Georges Bouffequin and his son, Denis. Mahelot describes the repertoire of the company in the 1630s, and apparently the influence of the medieval mansion was still present. Settings reflected the simultaneous method of presentation common in mystery plays, where several locales are present on the stage at once and the action moves from one locale to the next. Perspective was employed within the settings to achieve the compression of space necessary if the scenic units, essentially the medieval mansions, were to be placed on an indoor stage. The imagery of the scenic units still essentially was of medieval origin and sensibility. Mahelot describes a style that was a miniaturization of the medieval space through perspective, resulting in a unique mixture of the two approaches. Later, native French designers would realize their own version of intricate perspective scenery.

England

Theatrical performance in England during the Renaissance was primarily a continuation of medieval traditions. The rich spectacle of tournaments, street pageants, and miracle plays remained vital in this period until nearly 1600. Other spectacular productions, celebrating royal weddings, coronations, royal entries, and other significant moments of the monarch's reign, also were common.

English theatre did not absorb any of the Italian Renaissance style until the work of the architect Inigo Jones, in the early seventeenth century. The sixteenth century was dominated by Shakespeare, the professional actor, and the Elizabethan stage. This stage was decorated relatively simply, relying more on poetry and actor than visual spectacle.

The Medieval Tradition

The presence of the medieval pageants continued in England as well as a greater tolerance of secular performance. Certainly, the crown enjoyed both. There are accounts of preparations for royal weddings, such as the wedding of Arthur and Catherine of Aragon in 1501 in Westminster Hall. It "exhibited a castle drawn on by artificial beasts which held ladies and singers, a pageant ship bearing Hope and Desire, a mount of love from which the knights assaulted the castle, a tabernacle and an arbour" (Rosenfeld, 1973). King Henry VIII was known to participate in royal banquets that included music, masquerades, dancing, and spectacle. Later these were known simply as *masques*.

The Professional Theatre and the Professional Actor

The rise of Protestantism in England reduced interest in the miracle plays. In fact, they formally were suppressed in the 1570s. By 1576, the professional actor officially was accepted into society, and the growth of professional theatre began. By the end of the century, many professional stages could be found in London. The Theatre, the Globe, and the Fortune arose in a form very different from the Italian Renaissance stage. These were open-air theatres with a simple permanent architectural stage and minimal backgrounds. The theatres are very well documented in a wide variety of books, and no doubt are familiar to the reader.

The permanent backgrounds of these theatres incorporated Italian Renaissance architectural details, but were nothing like Italian Renaissance theatres. The stages were small architectural units, having no inclusion of perspective. They provided entrances, exits, and clear exposure to the surrounding seating. The theatre was dominated by a large, nearly square, raised platform. There were entrances at the back and a balcony for overhead scenes. It generally is assumed that very little space was left for additional decoration of any sort, except for an occasional cloth hanging in the doorway. This stage was visible almost all the way around, and the center of the building was exposed to the sky overhead.

Conclusion

The Renaissance was widely varied in terms of theatrical decorative style and techniques. In Italy artists explored the use of perspective for the stage and

applied knowledge of classical tradition to create a unified and somewhat realistic stage picture. The knowledge of Vitruvius was spread throughout Europe, and Sebastiano Serlio wrote an important commentary on scenic design, truly the first of its kind. The resulting Italian Renaissance scenic style had stage compositions chiefly of symmetrical architectural vistas. The scenery was arranged on a steeply raked, relatively shallow stage floor. The scenic units themselves first were three-dimensional buildings, as seen in the Teatro Olympico, and later were translated to two-dimensional shutters (what we call *flats*) through perspective drawing. This allowed the stage picture to be unified into a single, large picture containing many related features. The actual style of painting probably was a minimal application of color in washes over the intricately drawn perspective.

In France and England, however, the medieval tradition remained strong. It was combined with perspective to some degree as French indoor theatres were built. England remained fascinated with outdoor and indoor medieval entertainment in many forms.

The important bond in all these widely varied activities is that the craft of theatre became practiced even more than ever. Clearly, painters, designers, managers, and effects specialists adapted their knowledge to the theatre, contributing to a growing body of skills, knowledge, and talent. This source of expertise was necessary for the remarkable growth that would follow in the coming two centuries. Popular theatre was tolerated by the Church for the first time, and ultimately the popularity and impact of liturgical dramas of the medieval period would be usurped by new texts.

THE SEVENTEENTH AND EIGHTEENTH CENTURIES: THE BAROQUE

Introduction

The Italian Renaissance had seen the development of perspective vistas for the stage through the revival of Roman architectural practice. Peruzzi, Scamozzi, and Serlio found the means to reproduce realistic locales on stage with two- and three-dimensional scenic pieces. The record of Buontalenti's designs at the end of the sixteenth century suggests that scenery had become a significant part of the spectacle of theatre. The stage decoration ideas of the Renaissance were expanded in the Italian Baroque period. Stage designing, stage painting, and stage machinery all matured in a dazzling burst of creative growth in Baroque Italy. The rapid development then spread outward to other European countries, particularly England and France, reaching as far south as Portugal and Spain and as far north and east as Russia and Scandinavia. It did so largely because Italian architects and designers exported their work. Italy so dominated stage decoration in Europe that in France the baroque illusionistic style of scenery is still called *scène à l'italienne*.

The transformation in stage design in the Baroque was one of increasingly complex perspective imagery combined with new technical solutions for on-stage movement of the scenery. The painted world on the stage became awesome and mysterious, as artists explored the potential of perspective painting. Italian Baroque architectural and sculptural style, such as in the work of Bernini and Borromini, was exotic, emotional, and exuberant, thus ideal for the stage and new types of performance like opera and ballet. The stage offered an important new forum for architects and painters of the time, because the compositions made for the stage were free from the practical restrictions of architecture. A stage designer could explore fully the bizarre form of Baroque unencumbered by the reality of stone and structure. The architecture of stage design was realized in paint on flat panels, so it could become almost any imaginable form. The rationality and symmetrical compositions of Renaissance architecture were swept away by Baroque excess and splendor. The canvas that is a stage, with its great height, depth, and artificial light, was the perfect place for the dynamic vision of the Baroque. The theatre became such a vigorous outlet for architects and painters that individual specialists devoted their careers to theatrical designing and painting.

Italy

The Roots of Change

New ideas and practice in theatre placed new demands on stage decoration in the Baroque. First, a new type of performing art developed at the beginning of the seventeenth century. It began as an attempt to understand the mysterious reference to music in the classical Greek theatre, mixing poetic text with music. The result was opera, a performance that centered the drama around singing. The true importance for stage decoration is that operas demanded new types of settings for their drama and created even more public interest in theatre. The formal Renaissance stage compositions of Serlio were inadequate for the more complex dramas that incorporated ballets and masques as part of the overall structure. The second influence is that classical dramas themselves became less popular than the more entertaining *intermezzi* or operas. The *intermezzi* and the operas both demanded much more elaborate and fantastic dramatic settings than previously known, and these settings needed to change during the course of performance. We saw that changeable scenery was introduced in Florence in the late sixteenth century through the work of Buontalenti. Third, there was a recognition that the ability to move scenery and present new scenes would be appreciated and accepted by the audience. This development of mechanized scenic movement led to the fourth influence, the expansion of the theatre building itself. As scenery grew in size and complexity, theatres enlarged the stage area to accommodate it and enlarged the audience area based on the growing popularity of theatre. The final influence in the art of stage decoration and painting is the overwhelming domination in this field by the artists of Italy. All aspects of stage decoration were rooted in Italian effort. Painting, machinery, the operas themselves, the theatres, and the written analysis of the art of stage design came first from the Italian peninsula.

The Science of Perspective

A form of "realism" on stage has been pursued in almost every century of theatrical activity, although each era defines realism on its own terms. Even Vitruvius referred to stage painting as "realism." We also know Vitruvius saw perspective as the key to realism, although modern eyes see the Roman style as rather clumsy and decidedly nonrealistic. In Italy, the rediscovery of perspective in the Renaissance allowed seemingly real images to appear in a lifelike scale on stage. In the Baroque, increasingly complex perspective drawing remained the key to creating illusion on the stage. The understanding of perspective improved greatly in the late sixteenth century through several important scientific studies, some of which were specifically for theatre use. This greatly aided the development of multiple settings during the seventeenth century.

The Importance of Two-Dimensional Scenery

The earliest stage scenery of the Renaissance, like that at the Teatro Olympico, was three-dimensional. Paradoxically, the Baroque rejected three-dimensional units for the seemingly less realistic two-dimensional scenery. This paradox is explained quite easily. With a greater understanding of the science of perspective, the two-dimensional image was every bit as visually effective as a three-dimensional one. The advantages of two-dimensional stage units are obvious. Two-dimensional scenery is far easier to move around on stage than three-dimensional objects and is simpler to construct. It is as true now as it was in the seventeenth century. The only factor that is not easier with two-dimensional scenery is that it requires greater skill to paint. Obviously this trend toward two-dimensional scenery was made acceptable to the increasingly sophisticated audience only because of the availability of highly skilled painters.

Scientific Writing

The growing interest in perspective and two-dimensional scenery is reflected in the scientific writing on the subject. In 1545, the French scholar Philander prophetically interpreted Vitruvian scenic pieces as *scaena ductillis*, or flat panels. Guido Ubaldus specifically studied stage scenery and perspective in *Perspectivae Libri Sex,* published in 1600 (Nicoll, 1966). Giovanni Battista Aleotti was known to employ flat painted scenic panels in 1606 at Ferrara. The famous English designer Inigo Jones relied heavily on flat scenery in his stagings later in the century. A French theorist, Jean Dubrueil, illustrated a simple and straightforward application of flat scenery in *Perspective Practique*, published in 1649. Further works followed, such as *Paradossi per practicare la prospettiva senza saperla* by Giulio Troili in 1672, *De perspectiva pictorum et architectorum* by Andrea Pozzo in 1693 and 1700, and *L'architettura civile preparata sulla geometria e ridotta alla prospettiva* by Ferdinando Galli-Bibiena in 1711. The practical application of perspective for

stage scenery was studied extensively and practiced widely.

The Impact of Perspective Scenery on Theatre Buildings

Permanent theatres reflected the change in staging techniques through their own architectural development during the seventeenth century. The Renaissance stage was wide and shallow, reflecting the Roman theatre model. The Baroque theatre and stage achieved a radically different shape, as the stage became framed by a permanent proscenium arch, visually separating the stage from the audience and isolating the stage picture. The proscenium was considerably taller than what was known before, as theatres grew upward to allow banks of seating boxes to accommodate a growing public. The stage also grew to an immense size, sometimes so much that the total stage space was almost as large as the audience area. The stage became deeper to allow scenery greater depth and, with it, a more convincing illusion. The stage also grew larger, to accommodate multiple scenes.

Comparing two ground plans of Inigo Jones's work shows clearly the importance of flat scenery and its development in this era. The plan of *Florimène* in 1635 features four pairs of stationary angled shutters in perspective alignment (Figure 12.2). The background optimizes flat panels with a system of four pairs of shutters that can close to fill the background, thus providing four separate backings. The design for *Salmacida Spolia* in 1640 illustrates changing Baroque stage technique and Jones's transition. The pairs of angled shutters are replaced by four pairs of bays, each bay with four flat shutters. These shutters can slide out in groups, so the entire stage can change four times, not just the background (Figure 12.3).

The Teatro Della Pergola in Florence

The Teatro Della Pergola was built in Florence in 1656 by Ferdinando Tacca. The plan of this theatre is startlingly different from the Renaissance format devised by Serlio. It shows us several significant changes in the understanding of perspective through the design of the stage area. The depth of the stage is increased nearly three times over that of Jones's plans from the previous decade. This depth was required to enhance the sense of depth of the scene.

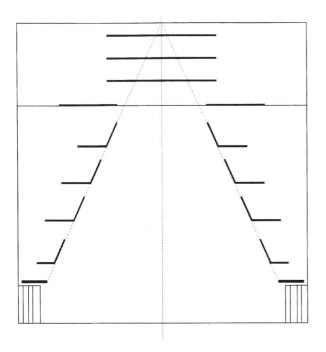

Figure 12.2 Schematic plan of *Florimène* by Inigo Jones.

Without real depth, the perspective depth had to be forced into a shallower space, making the stage itself totally unusable to the actors. A step into the perspective image would destroy the illusion. The Pergola stage allowed for greater flexibility in entrances and action with its enormous size. This deep stage was to become the standard for the Baroque.

The new approach to placement of the scenery bays on stage at the Pergola demonstrated a further sophisticated approach to perspective. The bays were angled slightly toward the viewer at the front. The angling diminished toward the rear of the stage. That aspect of the Pergola stage was not widely adapted by other theatres, however.

Italian Stage Decorators

Italian Baroque stage scenery was created by highly skilled, specialized artists who relied on a thorough understanding of the application of perspective to the theatre. Many of these artists were skilled in architecture, design, and painting. Therefore, they might design a theatre entirely or a set of scenery for a theatre, as well as participating in the actual painting of the scenery. The act of laying out, or plotting, the perspective was recognized as separate from the painting, and often the artist supervised that. The descriptions we have from the Bibiena family and others reflect the deep pride these artists had in their command of perspective as well as a recognition of its importance. The sheer popularity of theatre demanded a growing number of theatre specialists. The scenic painter was one such specialist, and many of them came from Italy, as did the designers and architects. Theatre specialists became somewhat popular in their own right, like many artists of the Renaissance and Baroque. Perhaps due to the relatively rapid production process in theatre, some specialists were sought out and central to the popularity of a theatre. The sheer spectacle of theatre reached previously unknown heights in the Baroque, and

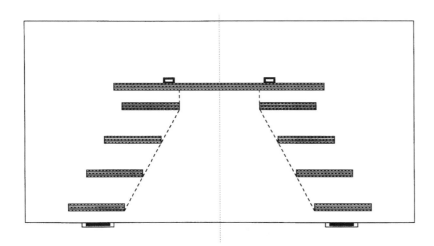

Figure 12.3
Plan for *Salmacida Spolia* by Inigo Jones.

more often that not, this spectacle left a lasting imprint on the public.

Giovanni Battista Aleotti

Giovanni Battista Aleotti (1546–1636) was an important figure in the transitional period from the Renaissance theatres to the Baroque stage. Aleotti was the architect of the famous Teatro Farnese built in 1628 in Parma. This theatre introduced many of the physical aspects of Baroque theatre in a permanent structure. The building is a large, narrow rectangle divided roughly into two halves, one for the stage area and the balance for the audience. The audience seating is a deep U-shaped arrangement of benches. The shape of the seating was novel at the time and became a format that Baroque theatres followed during the seventeenth and eighteenth centuries. The interior of this theatre clearly was influenced by Renaissance decoration surrounding the seating. A sober two-tiered colonnade of Roman arches is topped with statuary, suggesting the wall of the Roman Coliseum. However, the stage itself is a distinct departure. A bold permanent proscenium arch divides the audience and the stage. It is decorated with giant two-story Corinthian columns. Statuary also is present but placed into niches and perched precariously on small ledges. Within the proscenium frame is a startlingly deep stage. Here, Aleotti continued the use of two-dimensional illusionistic scenery he began a decade earlier. The deeper stage and narrow opening of the proscenium were more effective for the perspective imagery.

Giacomo Torelli

Giacomo Torelli (1608–1678), nicknamed *il gran stregone* (the great sorcerer), was one of the most famous and influential theatrical artists of all time. Torelli's use of perspective stage design took the art form of theatrical designing into a totally new realm of dramatic power. Torelli, a student of Aleotti, exploited the increased space offered by theatres based on the Teatro Farnese model. His work, based chiefly in Venice, reflected the architecture and painting of Venice for stronger realistic identity. Torelli designed the scenery for the first publicly performed operas, introducing to the world a method of visualizing the heroic struggles depicted in the new art form. Torelli also created new technical means for moving scenery that allowed highly efficient scenic

changes and encouraged scenic changes in full view of the audience. He had a significant influence in France as well, spending seventeen years there at the height of his career and effectively transforming the French stage from the quasi-medieval style to the Baroque.

Torelli explored the use of perspective in the deep stages typical of the Italian Baroque. The compositions he created for the stage relied on a rhythmic movement of the eye within the individual stage pictures. Torelli's stage pictures were significantly more complex than his predecessors' as the number of individual units increased and compositions strongly contrasted from one scene to another. Rhythm was established in the alternation of compositions, contrasting the symmetrical repetition common in the Renaissance. Architectural façades alternated their compositional axes, and garden or natural settings used the area above the stage as part of the overall picture. This way the composition could alternate between vertical and horizontal orientation (Colorplate 4). Rhythm was established in the image from scene to scene as well as in the tempo of the scenic changes. Opera demanded an increase in settings from classical drama, and the rhythm of the changes was linked to the dynamics of the music itself.

Torelli's innovations included a radical new concept in the use of stage machinery for the movement of the stage picture as well as his mastery of perspective and composition. Torelli perfected a system of moving wings or shutters in unison on the stage, known as the *chariot and pole system*. The side shutters typically had been placed in grooves on the stage floor and slid on or off stage as needed for each scene. An individual was required at each shutter, possibly twelve or more people, and considerable coordination of all hands was needed to change just one scene. Torelli's system put the shutters on carriages that went through a slot cut through the floor to a room below the stage. These carriages were on rollers to move easily, and each carriage was tied to a central winch. When the winch rotated, the on-stage carriages pulled off and the off-stage carriages came on stage, all perfectly coordinated. This giant stage machine could be operated easily by one individual, because the carriages were counterweighted. In this manner, the performance could move forward without interruption by the scenic elements, and scenic changes would be so rapid that they appeared to be magic. The shutters or wings on the carriage then could be replaced and prepared for the next scene change. Torelli's invention allowed a proliferation of settings within a performance without relying on the curtain to mask each change.

Torelli's work as a designer brought significant change to the stage imagery as well as its function. As he progressed in his career, Torelli made a distinct shift away from the emphasis on side shutters in front of a backdrop. The overhead space filled with fantastic imagery of clouds, grottos, heavens, and gods. The imagery of scenic design moved further toward the fantasy through the work of Torelli, suggesting not just real places but exploring the exotic and grandiose in a convincingly realistic style.

The Duke of Parma sent Torelli to Paris in 1645 to satisfy the request for a stage designer made by Queen Anne of France. He arrived in June, and by December, had his first performance in L'Hôtel du Petit Bourbon, which he had renovated to accommodate his carriage system. The performance was the opera *La Finza Pazza*, described later in this chapter. Through this sojourn to Paris and the lengthy period he remained, Torelli changed scenic production and design in France as effectively as he had in Italy. By the close of the seventeenth century, the major countries of Europe had all adapted Italian scenic style, invented by Torelli, as the standard mode of operatic stage design.

Giacomo Torelli returned to Italy in 1661, after his proposed design for Molière's *Les Fâcheux* was rejected by Louis XIV. He continued to work in Italy until his death.

The Bibiena Family

Giovanni Maria Galli (1619–1665) added to his name the town of his birth, Bibiena. He was the first of the Bibienas to create stage scenery and would be followed by a long line of descendants, who dominated theatre design as well as stage design throughout Italy and Europe from the mid-seventeenth century until the closing decades of the eighteenth century. The family's influence was so great that the name Bibiena has become synonymous with Italian Baroque stage design and painting itself. The Bibiena family designed in every major Italian city for many generations and became widely sought after in the major cities of Europe. Their influence is such that the Bibiena family probably is responsible for the tremendous continuity of Baroque style in stage design throughout the world.

The extensive output of the Bibienas has left a well-documented history of Baroque Italian stage design. The family itself was large: Giovanni had two sons who were designers, Ferdinando Galli (1657–1743) and Francesco (1659–1739). His grandsons, Antonio Galli (1700–1774), Giuseppe Galli (1696–1757), Alessandro (1687–1769), and Giovanni Maria Galli (1739–1769) and his great-grandson Carlo (1725–1787) carried on the tradition. The family's career spanned more than one hundred and thirty years in a time period when theatre, opera, and dance became enormously popular entertainment forms. The transformation the theatre had undergone in the seventy-five years before Giovanni Maria Galli Bibiena was extensive, for the Teatro Olympico was not yet quite forty years old at his birth. Opera had only begun to be performed in his youth, and the spectacle of scenery was very much in its own infancy. The Bibienas took the innovations of Aleotti and Torelli worldwide, as the demand for lavish theatre production grew in nearly every major city in Europe and beyond.

The Bibienas were accomplished architects, and they brought the Italian scenic style to Europe through their theatres and the scenery they designed for them. Their style perhaps was the most pervasive force in scenic design in the seventeenth and eighteenth centuries. The large output of the Bibiena family further underscored the sheer importance and appeal of stage scenery throughout Europe. In short, scenery itself was a growing aspect of theatre performance. The Bibienas continued the richly decorative and exotic style of previous designers like Torelli and brought their own influence to the stage picture.

One of the most significant advances the Bibienas created for the stage was a significant sophistication of the use of perspective. One unavoidable aspect of stage designs based on perspective, from the Renaissance to this time, was the center vanishing point. Stage pictures were developed around the center and often completely symmetrical. For example, Torelli's stage pictures soared upward, exploiting the space above the stage in new ways but always remained rather rigid as a line of ordered elements pointed to a central vanishing point beyond. Stage compositions of the Renaissance and Baroque often had a tunnellike effect due to the almost necessary placement of panels in pairs on either side of the stage. The Bibienas broke this symmetry with powerful diagonal views of interiors and exteriors that swept across the stage. The scenic image became composed of layers of architectural units through which the audience looked to the distant and mysterious background (Colorplate 4). The actors were given actual arches and passageways to walk through and around. Through this technique, stage decoration took a step toward a lifelike representation of the world.

The Role of the Scenic Artist and Scenic Painting Tradition in the Italian Baroque

The Italian Baroque produced a scenic style for European theatre that was to remain for nearly two hundred years. The inventions of Aleotti, Torelli, and the Bibienas became the standard operating practices for stage designers. As theatres were built across Europe and scenery was designed to fill them, a need arose for a particular style of painting specific to the stage. In many instances, the theatre architect or stage designer executed the painting. There is no record from any scenic painters of the time, but some scenic designers wrote of the craft of painting. Reading *L'Architettura Civile Preperata Su La Geometria E Ridotta Alle Prospettive* by Ferdinando Galli Bibiena reveals much about the practice of painting scenery.

L'Architettura Civile was published in Parma in 1711, when Ferdinando Galli Bibiena was fifty-four (Ogden translation, 1978). It is a general description of the techniques of a stage designer and his popularity in the "principal Italian cities" (ibid.). In it, he criticizes mediocre design practices and shoddy techniques. The book is exhaustive in its descriptions of the use of perspective for the stage: methods of how to construct scenes at angles, how to draw scenes on oblique wings, and so on. It clarifies the role of the stage painter as compared to an easel painter, particularly in the application of perspective. Bibiena insists that the mastery of perspective is the most essential ingredient to high-quality work by the stage decorator. Stage designs are not so much painted as beautifully drawn in perspective. The references to painting as we know it are very slight, only offhand references to how painting can correct a visual flaw or weak transition of planes.

It also is clear that Ferdinando Galli Bibiena saw himself, without modesty, as a consummate master of the science of perspective. He was meticulous in the application of this scientific method of visualization. He is critical of contemporaries whose perspective work is flawed or unimaginative. Bibiena, in *L'Architettura Civile,* credits himself with devising the method of creating scenes viewed at an angle, a method that was key to breaking the symmetrical rigidity of earlier Baroque designs, as discussed earlier.

The Scenic Artist in the Baroque

Bibiena writes at length about how a stage design is drawn in perspective. Perspective drawing for the stage may have been the most fundamental skill for a stage designer of the Baroque. The drawing process clearly is separated from the painting process and given greater emphasis in the written descriptions from the designers. How did the painting process differ from traditional studio painting? Was there a recognition that painting scenery had different considerations and techniques? Aleotti, Torelli, Bibiena—actually none of the scenic designers discusses scenic painting at any appreciable length, not at least scenic painting that we might recognize. All of these men were painters themselves, but they were designers and architects as well; and their own view of stage decoration indicates a lesser emphasis on painting it than drawing it. For these artists of the Baroque, scenic painting is not distinguished in the way we know. To these Baroque stage decorators, it appears that manipulating perspective in three-dimensional stage space was the most important skill for stage decoration. Ferdinando Galli Bibiena clearly sees himself somewhere between an architect and a perspective painter (ibid.).

The ability to accurately create immense perspective architectural fantasies was a difficult labor that seems to have required the participation of, or at least supervision by, these designers. Work handed off to assistants and apprentices was more than likely the preparation of the scenery and its final coloration. These designers likely went to work like scenic artists and designers do today, in large studios working on huge canvases. The task of laying out perspective for a stage picture requires large amounts of space and well-prepared scale drawings. The scenic designer was expected to oversee the development of the perspective drawing onto the actual scenery, so in this sense they were working much like today's charge painter overseeing a big drop. The emphasis was not yet on beautifully rendered color pictures. It was still the realm of the well-drafted architectural imagery, cleverly knit together in a seamless vista on stage by the master artist, the stage designer. The role of color frankly was secondary to the drawing, or it seems so through the writing of these early designers. Bibiena states in his later *Direzioni della prospettiva teorica* (published in Bologna, 1732) that, when one paints and colors, it is according to the rules of art (ibid.). However, Bibiena does not elaborate further what those rules are.

Baldassare Orsini and Scenic Painting

The writing of Baldassare Orsini (1732–1810), a stage designer and painter, shows a more detailed and expanded recognition of the role of color and, presumably, painting. Orsini's career flourished at a time shortly after the tremendous influence of the Bibiena family and as stage design was developing even newer styles elsewhere in Europe. In Orsini's time, one can begin to see a transition from the architectonic stage pictures typical of the Bibiena family toward a more painterly environment, emphasizing atmospheric effects.

Orsini wrote several books. *Della goemetria e prospettiva practica* (Rome, 1771–1773) included a chapter on scene design. Later, *Le scene del nuovo Teatro del Vezaro di Perugia* (Perugia, 1785) detailed his work as scenic consultant for the new theatre of Perugia, which officially opened in 1781. These books record the methods and thoughts of a modestly successful Italian designer in an age when Italian designers were well in demand. Orsini illuminated the working world of a designer and painter in the last decades of the eighteenth century. The inventions of Torelli and the Bibienas had been fully assimilated by stage designers at this time. Orsini appears to understand the complex rules of perspective construction used to create scenes with great depth, scenes viewed at an angle, scenes of circular buildings, and other complex stage pictures.

Orsini addressed scenic painting in a manner that none of the Italian stage decorators had done before. That he addresses it at all is significant and indicates the rising role of color as a means to enhance the architectural stage picture. Orsini returns to Vitruvius's text as a guide to the role of painting. Orsini and Vitruvius state the same goal of "truthfulness" in the depiction of images on stage. Orsini echoes Vitruvius's recognition that different scenes must be portrayed differently, "Hav-

ing to simulate a temple, a chamber or a dungeon is certainly not the same thing, and an open or charming dwelling place is likewise to be distinguished from a solitary, closed, horrid place" (from *Geometria*, III, Ogden translation, 1978). For Orsini, the pursuit of the character of the scene came through painting and color as much as through architecture. He writes that, "Therefore, the contrasts, the areas of shadow, the diagonal passages of the light, and the coloring are not indifferent matters for a perspectivist. I would propose that the whole scene be defined in three grades of chiaroscuro: that the things which extend from view and occupy the third grade (background) be soft and gentle in their pigments, containing violet; that the pigments which contain greenish and reddish hues be reserved for the middle grade (middle ground) ; and that those things which are placed in front be of yellow pigment" (ibid.).

Baldassare Orsini also clearly recognized the important role of artificial light in the theatre. He insisted that the work be seen with the effects of lighting so that, "The diminishing effect should originate from the chiaroscuro and from the strength of the brush strokes that are determined by the perspectivist" (ibid.). Lighting was not a consideration of the theatre of the ancients, whom he often invoked as the source of inspiration for the theatre of his day. But Orsini admitted that it takes greater skill to paint a scene destined to be seen under artificial light. From Orsini we see, perhaps, the first recognition that theatrical painting is like no other, because of its physical size and depth, the need to visually emphasize space through shading and color, the need to suggest a mood, and the presence of artificial lighting.

Torelli and the Bibienas were master perspectivists, and their stage work grew out of the skillful manipulation of architecture in perspective. Orsini clearly was skilled in these arts, but his writing continually reveals an awareness of equally skilled, and unique, painting abilities. He identified the Bibienas as the reformers of scene design and explained that the work previous to the Bibienas relied very little on color and shading. Orsini stressed the importance of painting, echoing Vitruvius, but detailed the process as no other writer had before this. Certainly, perspective drawing was as important to Orsini as to the Bibienas, but Orsini tended to reject the formal treatises on perspective and advised his students to put them away, for they "in truth only frighten studious people" (ibid.). He advocated a simpler understanding and teaching method for perspective and devoted a third of his second book to painting techniques. Orsini's book easily may be the first to instruct scenic painting principles and techniques.

The writing of Baldassare Orsini draws a link between stage decoration and a specific painting technique, scene painting. The stage decorators of the Italian Baroque more often referred to the importance of perspective drawing. Painting received less attention than perspective in the texts before Orsini. It can be seen that stage decorators needed to fully understand perspective drawing and the role that painting plays to support perspective in the artificial lighting of the theatre. The stage decorator of the Baroque could be architect, perspectivist, theatre machinist, and scenic painter together. From the time of Orsini, it appears that painting began to receive increasing emphasis. We know as well that perspective would diminish in importance, particularly in the modern era. In reading Orsini, it seems that his comments on scenic painting are more relevant to the modern scenic artist or scenic designer, whereas the references to perspective have less immediacy to his modern counterparts. Perhaps, at this point, the role of the scenic artist as we know it began.

France

In the Baroque age, France became one of the most influential artistic centers of the world, shifting the focus from Italy, helped to a great degree by the resources of the state treasury that the last three Bourbon kings—Louis XIV, Louis XV, and Louis XVI—were willing to put toward the development of the arts. Not that this expenditure was done for any reason other than to express the absolute greatness of the French state, which was the monarch himself, of course. But, whatever might be the cause, the effect was a prolific and brilliant period, a hundred and fifty years of remarkable achievement in the fine and decorative arts, of which theatre was certainly a part. France was on the ascendancy in wealth, power, and as an artistic magnet for the world. Although Italy clearly was the originator of Baroque stage design, France would adopt and expand on this style, eventually developing some of the finest theatrical literature of the period around the new decorative techniques.

The Royal Influences

In 1548, Henri II de Valois was celebrated with a triumphal entry into Paris featuring a masquerade on the theme of Orpheus. Unfortunately, Henri was mortally wounded during the festivities, but he might have been somewhat comforted in knowing that the Italian *intermezzi* had made their first appearance in France in his honor. These festivities began a long tradition of extravagant theatrical entertainment for the monarchy in France, in which many highly talented stage decorators emerged. Through exclusive patronage of the monarchy, scenic arts would flourish until Louis XVI and the French monarchy's gruesome end in 1793.

In 1610, the Florentine stage decorator Francini began a ten-year stay in Paris, working for Marie de Medici. By this time, the art of ballet had taken a stronghold in the Parisian life of the monarchy and Francini was brought in to design comic and tragic ballets. For the ballet *Alcine*, performed at the Louvre, Francini created a vast forest painted on cloth that was magically transformed with the appearance of an enchanted castle in the form of an amphitheater, ornamented with several columns, doorways, niches, and antique statues. Clearly, Francini was aware of the innovations of Buontalenti and Aleotti. He impressed the crowd with pivoting scenery in a 1617 production, and by 1619, he had put rolling wings to use. All of this was done without the support of a real theatre space. The French fascination with ballet was such that, in 1651, the young King Louis XIV danced in three productions, which clearly established his own love of the theatre. This was highly auspicious for the theatre in France, as Louis was to remain king for another sixty-four years.

Cardinal Richelieu was an avid supporter of theatrical literature and an author himself. His play *Mirame* premiered in 1641, a year before his death. It featured scenery by Georges Buffequin, the same individual chronicled by Laurent de Mahelot, and seems to have been done in the manner of the late Italian Renaissance; that is, parallel sliding wings with a painted backdrop. The scenery was "classical, influenced by the Italian, but modified by French taste with French innovations; a curtain that opened in the middle and clever lighting device that evoked daylight, moonlight and shadows" (Decugis and Reymond, 1953). With the production of *Mirame*, France was clearly very capable of developing skillful theatrical productions on a level similar to that of Italy.

Italian Stage Decorators in France

On December 14, 1645, opera was first performed in France. *La Finta Pazza* was imported to France by Cardinal Mazarin, then regent. It was performed before the child Louis XIV and the entire royal court at the Salle Royale in the Petit Bourbon Palace in Paris. The scenery was by the great Torelli. Mazarin requested Torelli's appearance and his scenery; Torelli did not disappoint. The prologue of the opera was a significant scenic display from a grove of poplar trees to wagons crossing the Pont Neuf, the statue of Henry IV on the Pont Neuf, Sainte-Chapelle and then Notre-Dame, all before entering the port of Samros, where the action of the story begins. Torelli left the audience awestruck. *La Gazette* reported that "all present were no less than in raves over . . . the scenic decoration and the stage machines, none of which was known in France at that time" (ibid.).

Torelli brought the most advanced Italian Baroque scenery to France, along with opera itself in *La Finta Pazza*. His work inaugurated in the monarchy a passion for great theatrical display and also for a French opera. Torelli spent sixteen years in France and produced several other operas, all with generally great success. After his departure, Mazarin continued using Italian stage decorators with Gaspard Vigarani and his son Charles. Mazarin allowed them the use of the pavilion of the Tuileries garden, which they converted into a theatre known as the Hall of Machines. Mazarin died in 1661 and Louis XIV began his own long reign as king. Louis moved to Versailles and brought his love of opera, dance, and theatre to a palace that had no theatre. Undaunted, in 1664, Louis celebrated at Versailles with seven consecutive nights of performances, including dance, works by Molière, fireworks, and opera, all designed by the Vigaranis. This festival, however, would signify the diminishing of Italian influence in stage decoration. Louis was more nationalistic than Mazarin, and he sought to have a true French theatre with French designers. There would be no more Italian influence in France after the beginning of the reign of Louis XIV. From the time of *La Calandria* in Lyons over a hundred and twenty years earlier, the Italians had played a great part in the French theatre. Most important, they had brought the knowledge of

Baroque stage decoration techniques to France. Now they no longer were wanted. Louis looked to his own country for stage decorators.

Jean Berain I and II

Jean Berain I (1640–1711) became the first significant French stage designer, filling the void left when the Italians lost favor with the monarchy. Berain was an assistant to the architect of Versailles, Charles LeBrun, and a remarkable interior designer himself. He designed the painted interior of the Galerie d'Apollon in the Louvre, where the French crown jewels are currently displayed, as well as the decoration for Louis's private apartments at Versailles. Berain's theatrical career was equally remarkable. He designed over fifty operas in his long tenure as director of the Royal Academy of Music and Dance, which had been created by Louis XIV in 1668. The academy is a government-sponsored institute in which the performing arts—dance, opera, theatre design, and decoration—were studied.

Jean Berain fully assimilated the staging techniques of Torelli and the Vigarani. He understood the processes of perspective drawing and worked in a format similar to that of Torelli, creating the designs of grottos, palaces, and gardens found on the Italian stage. Yet, his work reflects a greater degree of formality and symmetry typical of the French classical Baroque architectural style and reflecting Berain's long career as an interior decorator. Berain's designs employed the statuary, arabesques, drapery, and large cartouches common to the furniture and wall decoration of the time. Berain was a prolific designer and inventive technician. He created many pieces of intricate stage machinery for flying illusions and other effects.

Jean Berain II (1674–1726) was brought into the academy by his father at the age of sixteen. He took over the academy at the death of his father in 1711 and remained its head until his own death in 1726. Both Berains encouraged the participation in stage design for opera and ballet of such well-known French artists as Watteau and Boucher.

Jean-Nicholas Servandoni

The flamboyant Jean-Nicholas Servandoni (1695–1766) was perhaps the greatest of all the French designers in the Baroque age. Servandoni was born in Florence, where he was trained as an artist under

Giovanni Pannini. He studied theatrical design in Rome and traveled to Portugal and England. He received considerable notoriety in London for his work as a scenic designer for operas. Following these experiences, he went to Paris and offered his services to the academy. He would not have an opportunity for two years, until asked to design Act I of the opera *Pyrame et Thisbé*, which was performed in 1726. Servandoni demonstrated his tremendous talent from that start in *Pyrame et Thisbé*, which was very well received; and several months later, in the design for *Prosperine*, his genius began to emerge. Servandoni was a consummate master of theatrical effects as well as a brilliant painter. His *Prosperine* was described as terrifying and overwhelming in its unending string of beautiful images.

In his forty years in Parisian theatre, he employed the most sophisticated Italian techniques of perspective. Diagonal compositions, asymmetrical images, circular and oval buildings—all were commonly seen in his work. But Servandoni understood light and illusion better than perhaps any stage decorator up to this point. He studied lighting and the techniques for creating shadows, moonlight, and strong and faint light. He used local light sources, candelabras, and torches extensively. He imitated sunrise, sunset, and moonlit effects with remarkable accuracy.

Servandoni was famed for his ability to re-create in paint sophisticated materials with almost scientific perfection. His ability to paint marble, stone, and precious metals effectively and in accordance with a specific style of light was one of his gifts. He clearly understood the nuances of perspective and intricacies of stage machinery; moreover, Servandoni's painting technique brought a new aspect to scenic decoration. Servandoni was able to take techniques used by easel painters and expand them to the scale of the stage.

Servandoni represents the apex in French design before the Revolution. He brought to French theatre a fresh style of scenery combined with radically new effects and techniques. Servandoni's world was the world of the painter combined with the perspective techniques common to the Italian Baroque theatre. His style was a harbinger of the trends that stage painting would follow in the nineteenth century, when perspective image, dramatic painting, machinery, and lighting would fuse into even more compelling and "realistic" stage pictures. Servandoni employed painting techniques in a way that Italian Baroque decorators did not. Both were concerned with effective illusion, but Servandoni's style relied on painting over

perspective. Servandoni may have been the first decorator known for his theatrical painting. He was known as a master of illusionistic painting and an innovator in lighting and machinery. His styles and techniques were to become more imitated in the nineteenth century. Perhaps Servandoni's career indicates the diminishment of Italian style. With Servandoni, as with Torelli and the Bibienas, spectators attended the theatre to see his work.

England

Inigo Jones

The work of Inigo Jones (1573–1652) thoroughly overshadows all other theatrical contributors during the early Baroque period of stage design in England. Jones was an architect, painter, stage and costume designer, and the first English designer to bring the Italian technique of perspective scenery to the English theatre. Jones saw the development of perspective scenery in Italy from the earliest steps of the technological movement. He visited the Teatro Olympico shortly after its construction and no doubt was fully aware of the *intermezzi* designed for the Medici family by Buontalenti in the late 1580s.

In 1605, Jones first produced a masque for the court of the English monarch that fully employed the perspective scenery he had seen in his two visits to Italy. During the first decade of the 1600s, Jones moved closer to the adaptation of a proscenium by framing the masques with giant statues, each holding a curtain flanking the stage. Jones was enthralled with stage machinery as well using stage traps, elevators, cloud machines, and turntables in his stage designs.

Jones's stage decorations came closer and closer the Italian Renaissance model of Serlio, using fixed side wings with a changing background of shutters. The plan of *Florimène* (Figure 12.2) clearly indicates this fundamental approach to changeable perspective scenery. In his last masque, *Salmacida Spolia*, staged in 1638, Jones adopted fully moving side wings placed flat to the audience (Figure 12.3). This innovation provided a complete change of four sets of wings and borders and three changeable backdrops (Rosenfeld, 1973).

In a career of thirty-three years of creating masques for the entertainment of the English throne, Inigo Jones brought Italian perspective scenery to England. He also managed to move from the Renaissance technique of perspective scenery to the more complex and moveable forms of the Italian Baroque stage. Jones was truly a visionary artist on the same scale as an Aleotti or Torelli. But, it is significant that the techniques that Jones brought to Great Britain essentially were Italian methods of perspective, which further acknowledges the worldwide impact of the Italian concept of stage scenery.

Scenic development was limited throughout the better part of the seventeenth century in England for two significant reasons. The Elizabethan stage of Shakespeare's time remained as the more durable format for staging in the popular theatre. No new theatres were built in England to accommodate Italiante scenery until much later in the century. The Elizabethan theatres relied on far less scenery and in no way could they support the perspective styles that Jones had brought to the court. The court spectacles were eliminated, of course, during the Puritan domination of England and the exile of the monarchy. Only after the restoration of the monarchy would there be a return to elaborate staging of any description in England.

The English Restoration

The return of the English monarchy through Charles II also brought a renewed interest in theatre. Charles II had spent part of his exile in Paris, where he witnessed the works Torelli staged for Louis XIV and other productions. Charles encouraged the development of the theatre; and he and his successor, James II, were vigorous patrons of public theatre. Their patronage encouraged a theatre for the general public as opposed to the royal theatre and elaborate masques staged previous to the restoration. The Italian techniques practiced by Inigo Jones were continued in these public theatres.

In the latter half of the seventeenth century, a handful of new or newly renovated theatres opened in London, all of which were built to accommodate the Italian perspective style of stage scenery. The Lincoln's-Inn-Fields theatre was adapted for regular performances with full scenic accompaniment by 1661. In 1663, the Theatre Royal opened in London, the first theatre built in England that architecturally supported the Italian form of staging. Later, the Dorset Garden Theatre and Drury Lane Theatre were built, both of which were made so that the stage had full machinery available for perspective scenery as well as for the elevators, cloud machines, and so on Inigo Jones had used earlier in the century. By the end of the seventeenth century, Italian scenic style was common in London and in competition with the Elizabethan theatres for paying customers. The Italian techniques of the Baroque, such as deep perspective vistas and circular perspectives, were known to English audiences. Little documentation survives from that time, and no designer rose up to the stature of Inigo Jones nor did scenery advance much beyond Jones's style. Clearly, the Italian influence took hold and became standard for the stage.

The English Painting Tradition

During the Restoration, several individuals became recognized for their abilities as scenic artists. These were not architects or perspectivists in the tradition of Italy, but chiefly decorative painters whose talents were applied to the theatre. Robert Streeter, Issac Fuller, Thomas Stephenson, and Robert Aggas (ibid.) are recorded as being decorative and scenic painters during the last half of the seventeenth century. Streeter, in fact, was serjant painter to King James II. Their background as decorators and not as perspectivists shows some unique characteristics of the English theatre. One is that the English were far less rigid in the application of perspective than the Italians, who took perspective drawing as a science. In Italy, perspective was the very core of the designers' and painters' art for the theatre. In England, the role of the painter as a decorator developed in this era. Second, English architecture and interior design would continue to demonstrate a greater love of things painted than in most other countries, as that field developed during the seventeenth and into the eighteenth centuries. Ultimately, this trend became very significant for the development of the scenic artist. The lush romantic landscapes of the nineteenth century that are the hallmark of the accomplished scenic artist would arise from this painterly tradition.

The Georgian Period

The eighteenth century, the Georgian era, was a decisive period for stage decoration and painting in England. At that time, scenic art took a turn away from the Italian style to develop its own sensibilities. The English style that developed during this period matured later in the nineteenth century into a form that we are much more familiar with today. The later form is the foundation for American scenic painters of the nineteenth century and a very far cry from the Italian style, where stage decoration had started. The Georgian period is an important transitional phase as well as one where familiar plays and performance styles also emerged. In this time, the decorative sense that we saw in the previous century would become the dominant force in England, despite the overwhelming presence of the Bibiena family on the European continent.

Italian Influence in England

Both Italian and French painters were working in England for very long periods of time early in the eighteenth century, but the predominant group was the Italian. The Italians brought two important ingredients: the Italian Baroque style of design and opera, which was becoming synonymous with that style of design. Opera grew in popularity worldwide and with opera normally came the Italian scenic artists to design and paint the scenery. The Italians were recognized as specialists and masters in the field of design and painting.

Operas, by nature, are very lavish productions. Combined with the absolute necessity to provide brand new scenery for the operas (no stock scenery could possibly suffice), this led to a rather large infusion of energy in building and painting scenery for the theatre in England. Sybil Rosenfeld's (1981) wonderful account of Georgian scenic painters takes note of the theatres that boasted foreign scenic artists. The King's Theatre, London, listed Marco Ricci, G. A. Pelligrini, Roberto Clerici, Jacopo Amigoni, Antonio Jolli, the famous Giovanni Servandoni, and many other Italian artists in service through the century. The rather large number of Italian artists gives us a good indication of the extent to which Italian Baroque scenery had been established as a worldwide standard of beauty. These people clearly were bringing the techniques of perspectivist scenery with their brushes, and the apprenticeship possibilities for native English artists began.

The English Painters

Scenery also was brought in from overseas, with the scenic artists on hand to touch up the wings and drops after they came off the ship. Occasionally, scenery would fall off the dock and require extensive drying and repainting to eliminate the resulting salt stains. Often, the scenery had been used for several performances and was a little worse for wear.

That practice had potential for providing less than first-rate work. It soon was obvious to theatre goers that English versions of the foreign style of scenery were every bit as good as, if not better than, the originals. At least English scenery would not have saltwater stains. Italian and French scenic artists gradually were replaced by their English counterparts during the course of the century. The first English scenic artists to be permanent employees of a theatre were John Harvey and George Lambert (ibid.) around 1725. From this point on, the number of native scenic artists working in theatres in Great Britain grew quickly. By the middle of the century, there are records of families of scenic artists, the profession being handed down from father to son. Scenic artists in Great Britain often were architectural decorative painters or doubled as theatre decorators where they worked. But the numbers of them grew steadily. Covent Garden listed two scenic painters and four assistants in 1767–1768 and by 1794–1795 the number had increased to twenty-seven scenic artists (ibid.). Drury Lane had as many as ten scenic painters working toward the end of the century.

Opera received the bulk of the effort of new scenery and new scenic invention during the Georgian era. Plays often got by with stock scenery recycled from an earlier production or season. This may help explain why so few actual designs, let alone scenery, survive from this period in England. Settings for plays often were combinations of generalized places: tombs, gardens, palaces, walls and gates, prisons, rural settings, and so on. Brand new pieces might be found on stage in the same scene with older ones. Scenery was built to be in service for a considerable period of time, some pieces lasting up to fifty years of service. Scenic artists spent a good part of their time repainting or refurbishing older units.

Scenic artists began to receive recognition for their work in the Georgian era. Program credit normally was given to the artist responsible for painting a particular scene, and the difference between designing scenery and painting it is not totally clear. Philip De Loutherbourg is credited for establishing the practice of recognizing the scenic artist toward the end of the century. De Loutherbourg is the first stage decorator to delineate between designer and painter. Program credit was given to the designer and the executant separately. De Loutherbourg generally was a designer, but that appears to be the exception to the rest of working scenic artists. Certainly, scenic artists were credited as designers when needed, but it was not the overall practice that a person either designed or painted. A sought-after scenic painter might design one work that would be executed by another but, later that same season, find himself painting the designs of another. Scenic designer and scenic artist were not viewed as different trades, merely subdivisions within the umbrella of stage decorator and decorative painting.

Emergence of English Style: Philip De Loutherbourg

Philip De Loutherbourg (1740–1812), a native of Alsace, was the most accomplished and recognized English stage decorator of the Georgian period. De Loutherbourg was brought to England and the Drury Lane Theatre by David Garrick and spent much of his career there. De Loutherbourg may have been the most influential theatre artist of the Georgian period, both in style and technique. In his work, one most easily can see a trend to totally new styles, departing radically from the Italian influence. De Loutherbourg also experimented with lighting and new materials to produce more vivid atmospheric stage images and eventually developed a miniature theatre for viewing his most sophisticated stage techniques.

When De Loutherbourg came to the theatre, the Italian style was still common in England. But, he was to represent most clearly the shift in English style away from the Italian imagery to the far more romantic and turbulent landscape more familiar to the English eye. De Loutherbourg was a romantic and a realist. The trend on the English stage during the Georgian period had been toward a greater sense of historical accuracy for costuming, particularly in the performance of Shakespeare. De Loutherbourg would take strides in the same direction for stage scenery. There also was a growing trend in easel painting for "English" landscapes: the sort of dark, misty, mysterious countryside familiar to the English, which bore little relationship to the clear, sunlit Latin skies of the Italian school of painting.

De Loutherbourg most fully realized a trend in the use of scenery on the stage that differed greatly from the Italian Baroque style. Simply put, the English stage was decorated with freely placed flats in asymmetrical compositions, relying less on the symmetrical wings that Italian stage machinery required. These flats provided a means to break the arrangement used in perspective Italian Baroque dec-

oration yet still produce realistic illusions. It was the first significant challenge to the Italian technique of stage design and ultimately would come to replace it in England and later in the United States. De Loutherbourg had not created the technique; one could point to Servandoni's work in Paris as early as 1728 as perhaps the first practitioner of this new style. But De Loutherbourg's work and the English stage would take this new format and exploit it to its full potential. The physical difference allowed the painter much more flexibility in creating the moody English landscape that was to become the far more common image of the late Georgian period and continue well into the Victorian era.

De Loutherbourg was a multitalented artist as well as a gifted scenic painter. Like Servandoni, De Loutherbourg experimented extensively with stage machinery and lighting techniques. He differentiated between scenic artist and scenic designer in practice and in public perception. He was a star performer at Drury Lane, and he made sure that he received notice for his work, which assured the scenic artists following him that they would receive similar credit. In short, Philip De Loutherbourg put English scenic painters in the public eye. His mastery of the craft of scenic painting created new types of wondrous illusion, reliant on a mix of painting and careful lighting. He was to pave the way for generations of English and American scenic artists to become popular artists in their own field.

De Loutherbourg experimented with pure theatrical painting effects off stage in his own model theatre, the Eidophusikon, exhibited in the 1780s. In its small six-foot-wide and eight-foot-deep stage, he experimented with transparencies, translucency, shifting colors, and moving backgrounds. All of his techniques in the Eidophusikon became standards of the stage of the nineteenth century.

Landscapes and Topographical Scenery

Two stylistic trends began during the Georgian era that would fuel the creation of new scenic pieces for specific events and plays. The interest in topographical scenery, the literal and realistic depiction of familiar places, became a unique English trend during this century. The wonder of seeing a recognizable English site on stage became popular for many theatre goers in the Georgian period, which certainly has continued well into our own time. The beginning of historical accuracy also was seen in this time and became a major force in the nineteenth century.

Two major London theatres, Drury Lane and Covent Garden, were rebuilt in the closing decade of the eighteenth century. Both expanded. Drury Lane became the largest theatre in Europe. It held four thousand spectators and its proscenium was 43' × 38', nearly square. The backstage was a cavernous 83' × 92' with 102 feet of fly space. These theatres needed new scenery made for their immense stages. The result was a resounding acceptance of the English methods and styles that had emerged during the Georgian period. William Capon's designs for Drury Lane featured historical accuracy in their reproduction of Gothic, Tudor, and Medieval locations. Historically accurate scenes arranged freely on the stage were the standard in England at the close of the Georgian period. The scenery was still thoroughly two-dimensional and the work of gifted specialists, called *scenic artists*.

These two new movements perhaps were the greatest legacy of the Georgian stage. Topographical scenery and historicism were essentially English pursuits, having little to do with the Italian Baroque movement, which was at its peak. The English theatre was the mold that formed the American stage and perhaps is why the great scenic inventions of the Italians have always seemed somewhat irrelevant to our stages. America's theatre also began during this Georgian period, chiefly on English exports. Therefore, our history begins halfway through a story already well underway. In America, we jump ahead to the newer trends of the English approach to theatre as we enter the golden century of scenic artists—the nineteenth century.

chapter 13

The Romantic Theatre and the Modern Theatre: 1800–The Present

INTRODUCTION

All the trades that make up the theatrical arts—architecture, acting, costuming, designing, directing, painting, writing, and producing—enjoyed unparalleled popularity during the nineteenth century. In many ways, it was a golden age of theatre, which became a worldwide phenomenon, achieving a broader social acceptance than ever. Famous actors like Kean and Booth worked the stage and raised the social status of the actor. The work of scenic artists and scenic designers reached an apex of public recognition, due, in part, to advances in painting techniques and increased demand for stunning visual entertainment. Technical advances, particularly the more widespread use of controlled lighting, further contributed to increasingly convincing scenic effects. Scenic artists themselves were as famous as many actors, and it became common for a play to be popular because of the scenery. Certain types of elaborate scenic spectacles developed using no actors at all, making the designer and painters famous. Scenic artists worked in greater numbers than ever before, or possibly since, due to growing demand for scenic decoration in the theatre and related entertainments. By the end of the nineteenth century, the scenic arts became a burgeoning industry, dispersing the scenic artist's product throughout the world by railway and sea. By the beginning of the twentieth century, the practitioners of scenic art garnered enough political power to successfully unionize in some countries.

Theatrical styles changed significantly during the nineteenth century and scenic artistry changed with them. The popularity of Italian wing and drop scenery, the bread and butter of European theatre, waned as scenic artists explored asymmetrical stage compositions and the more emotionally striking romantic landscapes. Over the course of the century, new ideas of historical accuracy and realism in the theatre emerged, creating interest in new formats of visual theatrical expression and rendering the Italianate style even less relevant, although Italian style scenery maintained a presence in some theatrical and operatic performances. The craft of scenic painting grew more complex and demanding in the late nineteenth and early twentieth centuries, as lighting and other special effects became common in theatres. Through it all, scenic painting itself remained intensely vital. The forms and format of stage scenery changed, but the love of the painted, two-dimensional image was as strong as ever.

Scenic artistry then changed drastically during the twentieth century. The roles of scenic designer and scenic artist were separated from one another formally by unionization in America and England, reflecting a division in duties recognized around the world. The scenic designer's role emerged as the artistic creator of stage scenery, thus diminishing the scenic artist's role to simply the executor of the vision, not the visionary.

The physical form of scenery changed radically as well. If Italianate style was gradually replaced in the previous century, we witness a more rapid rejection of it, as well as all previous styles, at the beginning of the twentieth century. The scenic revolution at the turn of the century rejected illusionistic, two-dimensional painted scenery, replacing it with a newer, more plastic three-dimensional scenic structure. In a matter of a couple of decades, from 1880 to 1900, traditional painted scenery became characterized as a burden to "real" dramatic action, dishonest, shoddy, and very old-fashioned. Moreover, new generations of modern scenic designers sought texture and shape as their media, not the painted image. Traditional scenic artistry was abruptly condemned by the new generation as a meaningless gimmick. Clearly the theorists of that time were totally accurate in observing the dichotomy between flat, painted scenery pretending to be a room or a garden and the actor's effort at a verisimilitude. The prolific nineteenth century of scenic art generally was rejected and decried by professional designers and theorists in the twentieth century. Unfortunately, as a result, many skills common to scenic artists of the past few centuries were nearly lost from lack of use. The intricate science of perspective scenery, once the chief skill of the Italian Baroque masters, was lost to all but a few curious individuals. Certainly, stage design has been elevated in the twentieth century by probing the emotional, intellectual, and spiritual core of theatrical literature, and many brilliant stage designers have opened new paths through their visionary work. But the craft and art of scenic painting that were commonplace one hundred years ago now are sustained by a much smaller number of scenic artists than previously.

The twentieth century brought significant changes to how a scenic artist actually paints. Electric lighting, at first generally unwelcomed by scenic artists, unmasked poor painting techniques and placed even greater demands on painters. New materials, tools, and techniques have greatly altered exactly what a scenic artist may do on a day-to-day basis, bringing greater ease and convenience to the studio. However, the modern scenic artist generally must have command of a wider range of skills than their counterparts from the previous century. The modern scenic artist may spend as much time sculpting or smearing thick texture pastes as actually putting color on canvas. Traditional painting still exists and is widely used worldwide, but we invariably recognize traditional scenic painting as a specialization. Also, the proliferation in use of digital and mechanical

image reproduction further changed the way scenic artists work. Machines that paint entire backdrops automatically and rapidly are available to the designer and producer. These eliminate the scenic artist entirely. They are expensive and indeed mechanical, but they are in their own infancy and will become far more common, placing a further pressure on traditional painting.

THE NINETEENTH CENTURY

Technical Innovations of the Nineteenth Century

To speak of new technology in the field of painting may seem highly incongruous at first. The actual technology of painting has changed very little in two thousand years: we still apply color to canvas with brushes. No new steam-powered binder infuser was invented in the Victorian age to speed the work of the painter. However, the technology in the theatre changed enough that the painter's art adapted to new potential.

Lighting and Painting Techniques

Philip De Loutherbourg and Jean-Nicholas Servandoni, the leading innovative scenic artists of the eighteenth century, brought an extensive awareness of the potential of controlled lighting to the theatre. De Loutherbourg reworked the lighting system at the Drury Lane Theatre, taking advantage of the newly developed Argand gas lamp specifically to allow for greater illusionistic effects on stage through carefully controlled light. Both De Loutherbourg and Servandoni created dynamic daylight effects with cast shadows, moonlight, clouds passing in front of the moon, sunsets, and variety in time of day or night represented on stage by controlling light. Both designers used colored light, in the form of colored transparent silks, to achieve these effects. De Loutherbourg is credited with the first use of gauze for translucent effects on stage, much as we use scrim today. De Loutherbourg created a moving backdrop in his Eidophusikon to show clouds passing in the sky by slowly unrolling a very long backdrop on a series of rollers. De Loutherbourg also created an effective moonrise by fitting an Argand lamp to a bow covered with the painted orb. With the work of these two men and their successors, the controlled use of light became an important tool of the scenic artist and scenic designer.

In the nineteenth century, the techniques of the scenic artist changed considerably from the time of the Baroque. Many techniques familiar to us now became common in this time. The Baroque painting style was essentially a well-colored line drawing. Color was used carefully to support perspective, as bolder colors were placed in front, tints and shades toward the rear. Late in the eighteenth century, through artists like Servandoni, more illusionistic painting skills developed. Paint imitating marble, metals, and wood became an aspect of the scenic arts. De Loutherbourg and other English scenic artists in the eighteenth and nineteenth centuries also explored color layering with paint for improved depth and sense of realism. Paint was applied to the canvas in thin, translucent layers with this technique. The result is a more lively and lifelike surface, much like the effect of watercolor. The understanding of light on a painted surface and the response of painted colors to colored light is part of the knowledge gained in the nineteenth century. This layering technique and the translucent qualities of paint respond more favorably to artificial light as well.

Panoramas and Dioramas

The *panorama* was invented in 1787 by Robert Barker, a Scottish artist. A large and highly realistic painting, it was designed originally to be placed around the interior of a circular building. Panoramas typically depicted great landscapes or cityscapes in striking detail and realism. They were curiously photographic in nature, arriving decades before photography itself. The more effectively realistic *diorama* appeared in 1822 in Paris, a creation of Louis J. M. Daguerre and Charles Bouton. The diorama used transparencies and layers of painted surfaces for even more realistic imagery than the panorama. The diorama either moved itself or occasionally moved its viewers around for a real sensation of movement of place. These were complex scenic devices that became popular in their own right as entertainment.

The panorama and diorama launched scenic artists into a totally new phase of their craft, one that was tremendously popular in the nineteenth century. The panorama scarcely could have been adapted to a stage because of the specific placement of the viewer. However, the diorama was ideally suited for the theatre, and it became a great entertainment. By 1820, the Grieves had perfected a more dynamic diorama for the Covent Garden pantomimes. Their work consisted of a long painting wrapped around rollers and unrolled so that its image appeared to move from one place to another much as De Loutherbourg had done with his Eidophusikon. The audience was taken on a journey by the device of a diorama. The Grieve's device worked splendidly, was enthusiastically reviewed, and assured the diorama a secure place on the English stage for decades. From this point on, no theatre owner would dare present the holiday pantomimes without a diorama.

The nineteenth century was a period of British colonization, great exploration, and scientific inquiry. The dioramas played a significant role in reporting back to the English public what the world looked like. They were remarkably realistic paintings of tropical scenes, playing the same popular role that newsreels did a century later and National Geographic television specials do now. The diorama brought the savage and wondrous world to the public, thanks completely to the skill and imagination of the scenic artist. A diorama's subject matter varied from newsworthy to merely geographical in interest, but it always was extremely realistic. The dioramas also made their creators, the scenic artists, famous. People went to the theatre strictly for the visual delight of the diorama, and that work was always attributed to the scenic artist. The scenic artist generally was the sole researcher, designer, and executant (with assistants) of the dioramas.

Dioramas were popular for years, staying part of English theatre until at least 1977 (Rosenfeld, 1981)! Dioramas depicted news events, such as Napoleon's conquest of Egypt or the battle at Moscow. Warfare was popular, particularly naval battles, which were virtually restaged complete with explosions, burning ships, storms, and daring rescues. Travel was another common theme for the diorama. There are references to travel-oriented dioramas to Niagara Falls; up the Nile; to Belgium, France, and Ireland by sea; from Constantinople to St. Petersburg; on polar expeditions; into Africa; and to the top of glacial mountains. The Grieves produced a sensational moving diorama that took the audience on a balloon journey from London to Paris, including the ascent of the craft, aerial views of the entire journey, and a descent into the Tuileries gardens.

The dioramas included many of the techniques explored by De Loutherbourg's Eidophusikon in the previous century. Transparent and translucent materials for greater atmospheric accuracy, cutout two-dimensional miniatures to enhance depth, backlighting, colored lighting, even fog and mists were now in use. All these devices were in the hands of the scenic artist for use in depicting the known world as realistically as possible.

Phantasmagoria and Optical Illusion

Phantasmagoria were displayed first in 1798 in Paris. These were akin to magic lanterns and the forerunners of today's scenic projectors. They consisted of a rolling lantern and a transparency, usually a painted glass, that was projected onto a thin screen from behind. The projector was moveable so that the image could shrink or loom large during the display as needed. Images could be made to move by combining slides, and a system of dissolve from one to another was created with two projectors and a synchronized shutter. The eerie images must have dazzled audiences of the time, as the specterlike pictures shown in a very dark theatre had a somewhat lifelike quality. They were revolutionary for the time, although limited in their theatrical use, as they required near-total darkness to be visible. These phantasmagoria were another theatrical entertainment totally dependent on the scenic artist. The slides were carefully painted miniature panoramas and necessitated particularly skilled theatrical artists to paint them.

Scenic Studios and Working Conditions in the Nineteenth Century

Studios solely for the scenic arts were built during the nineteenth century, first in Paris, then later throughout Europe, and eventually in America. Some were very large, open studios with dozens of individuals at work preparing and painting scenery. These studios probably would look familiar to us, because the basic, essential tools have changed very little. Some studios were small adjuncts to a theatre building that serviced the theatre itself. In some instances, scenic artists simply worked on stage at night after a performance. What is different from our time to the recent past is the sheer quantity of scenic artists and assistants employed, for the theatre was far greater in the nineteenth century. Scenic studios today tend to be adjuncts to the carpentry shop and staffed by a much smaller team of painters than in the past.

In the nineteenth century, the scenic artist also was what we know today as the scenic designer. But these artists worked much differently than today's designers. A nineteenth century scenic artist was expected to imagine and create delightful illustrations for the background of a play's performance. Little thought was given to the unified expression of a play's meaning through the scenery in the way it is understood today. It was common practice that several scenic artists would work on one play, each creating in their own style without regard the overall style. The scenic artist was to provide wonderment and delight in a painted medium, often one piece at a time. The scenic artist was expected to be thoroughly knowledgeable of architecture, history, mythology, and the exotic, to be better prepared to decorate a play. The scenic artist was a walking encyclopedia of history and styles who could call on that knowledge to create stunning dramatic images meant to be viewed under peculiar lighting. This is not so far off from a description of a truly talented scenic artist of today, but in the nineteenth century scenic painters were given free rein to create the scenery at will, based on some rough sketches. A nineteenth century theatrical production might feature several large scenic pieces, each from a different artist. The variety itself may have been desirable to the audiences of the time.

England in the Nineteenth Century

Perhaps in no other place and time in history has the scenic artist gained such status as in the English theatre of the nineteenth century. Scores of brilliantly talented artists were known exclusively for their work in the theatre. They were placed prominently in the advertising of plays and reviewed along with the actors. These scenic artists were attached to specific theatres, sometimes for decades, and their departure could mean financial disaster for the unfortunate manager. Theatre had become an extensive entertainment business in England, and the scenery or visual aspects of any performance were a very important selling point.

The English Romantic Style

The romantic scenic style of the English theatre generally overtook Italian Baroque scenic style in worldwide acceptance. Romanticism began in the late eighteenth century and was to flower during the nineteenth century, particularly in England; and it was a crucial step toward the realistic movement of the latter nineteenth century, because many precepts of Romanticism were to be useful in realistic style. Romantic style embraced historical accuracy, topographical interest, and more sensitively reflected England itself. The interest in travel and exploration was reflected in the romantic depiction of heroic efforts on the fringes of civilization. Romanticism created a more palatable heroic figure for English audiences of the time than the abstract classical heroes of the Baroque. Scenery was perhaps more interesting to the viewer at large when it portrayed real places in an engaging way.

The sheer vigor of the popular theatre in London gave fuel to the popularity of scenic spectacle. Theatre was the primary source for entertainment. There was no competition from other media, so theatre was news teller, storyteller, travel partner, entertainer, and magician. The nineteenth century mind sought the distant, exotic, dramatic, and curious. The theatre and its scenic artists brought all that to the stage, from natural disasters to war to many brilliant plays themselves.

The Victorian Style—Romantic Realism and Spectacle

The middle and latter nineteenth century, known as the Victorian Age, saw subtle shifting in the overall romantic spirit. The pursuit of historical accuracy in stage productions grew considerably. Scenic artists were prevailed on to reproduce known places with accuracy and detail. It was by no means the realism we know from the turn of the century, but a curious blend of the real and the romantic. Stages were infused with even greater atmospheric spectacle, as moonlight, storms, wind, fire, rain, turbulent cloudy skies, and other meteorological phenomena became commonplace as a means to express the mood of a play as well as to accurately depict realistic imagery. The Victorian stage saw its first attempt at literal place description in the form of a box setting in 1832. This led to a continuing style of seemingly real dramatic settings. Scenic artists and producers went to increasingly great lengths to mimic the recognizable for the stage. This formula proved to be as popular as the more generic settings of the past.

The emphasis was on spectacle through all styles of the nineteenth century in England. Romanticism brought rugged, tempestuous landscapes, full of lifelike atmosphere. The popular panoramas brought the remote parts of the world to the stage with convincing illusion. The interest in history and historically accurate productions, particularly of Shakespeare, allowed for considerable application of research and knowledge to the stage scenery. Whatever the role of the design itself, it is clear that Victorian romantic scenic artistry was at a level of remarkable expertise and had fully displaced the Italian Baroque format and style. The technological advances of the late Georgian and early Romantic eras brought many more tools to the scenic artists' disposal. The theatre was still the realm of the painter, but the science of perspective had now given way to a more complex marriage of color, light, motion, and painting technique. The few that could successfully control all of these elements were highly regarded artists for their time. They ensured that scenery itself was a primary attraction of the theatre.

English Scenic Artists and Theatres

Philip De Loutherbourg, without question, was the first leading scenic artist of the Romantic era and one of the first star scenic artists of the English stage. His influence reverberates through the entire nineteenth century because of the techniques and effects he devised, both on stage and with his Eidophusikon. De Loutherbourg was an accomplished easel painter, too, and another profound contribution to the English theatre was his popularizing the English landscape style. These contributions, both artistic and technical, became standard practice for scenic artists that followed him. The numbers of steadily working scenic artists grew with the theatre in this century in England. With its commercial success came increasing demand for scenic artists and these unique skills.

De Loutherbourg died in 1812. Shortly before his death, two of the four major theatres in London burned again, Covent Garden in 1808 and Drury Lane in 1809. The rebuilt theatres competed with each other for audiences, and both relied on scenic spectacle as a drawing card. Both theatres entered into a prolonged period of great scenic art, employing the finest scenic artists of the era.

Covent Garden was the leading London theatre in the nineteenth century. The scenic artists for Covent Garden, for the first half of the century, came principally from the Grieve family. John Henderson Grieve (1770–1845) began work in 1806, his sons Thomas in 1817 and William in 1819. The Grieves became the leading scenic artists at Covent Garden by the 1820s. The family split up in 1829, when William went to the King's Theatre and Thomas followed soon after. J. H. Grieve stayed at Covent Garden as the principal scenic artist until 1843, with only a four-year hiatus elsewhere. The staff at Covent Garden numbered eleven full-time scenic artists in this era, with additional painters brought in as needed. The Grieve family elevated Covent Garden to a high standard of quality in scenic artistry as well as earning the artists and the theatre excellent reviews from journalists and writers of the time. Covent Garden reached its status as the preeminent theatre of London at that time, chiefly due to their work. The Grieves created settings for melodrama, pantomimes, and operas. In 1820, they introduced the panorama to Covent Garden, further increasing the popularity of the theatre and their own good name. J. H. Grieve is reported to have introduced a paint technique of layering transparent glazes, as in watercolor, providing far superior depth and richness over the solid colors used before this.

The Drury Lane Theatre was nearly as active as Covent Garden, although it emphasized melodrama and Shakespeare over the spectacles at Covent Garden. It employed nine full-time scenic artists by its reopening after the 1809 fire. These included William Capon and Thomas Greenwood. However, hiring David Roberts and Clarkson Stanfield in 1822 brought even greater attention to Drury Lane and its scenic artists. The work of these two together began to rival that of the Grieves. A description of a diorama for the melodrama *Zoroaster* in 1824 describes a 482-foot-long moving backdrop, depicting several periods of the day. The drop included a desert with Arab tents at twilight, a caravan of merchants crossing the desert in the morning, the sphinx and the pyramids, the ruins of the temple at Apollinopolis Magna, the Colossus of Rhodes, the bay of Naples by sunset, Vesuvius by moonlight, the effects of an eruption with obscure skies suddenly dispersing to present an allegorical vista, a momentary glimpse of Home Sweet Home, the falls of Tivoli, and the Hanging Gardens and the city of Babylon

(Rosenfeld, 1981). The spectacle also included other scenery such as interiors of the tomb of Cheops, the palace of Gebir at Memphis, a temple of light, and the abode of Isis. The entire production was painted by Roberts and Stanfield with Gaetano Marinari and six assistants. The design of the diorama, however, was entirely the work of Clarkson Stanfield.

The scenic artists at Drury Lane and Covent Garden often were in direct competition, due to the management electing to offer identical plays or spectacles in the same season. Contemporary critics and audiences had the benefit of seeing the finest scenic artists of all time in a constant whirl of bravura and one-upmanship. The great scenic artists would take research voyages to sketch foreign landscapes in preparation for the next great work. Great coronation dramas—in which actual coronation scenes were recreated, fully depicting all the famous cathedrals of England and France—were very popular and a great test of the architectural skills of a scenic artist. Scenic painters commonly were known for superiority in either architecture or landscape painting. William Capon, Gaetano Marinari, and Clarkson Stanfield all were considered exquisite architectural painters, although Stanfield often is described as the best of the group.

Clarkson Stanfield was perhaps the finest English scenic artist since the great De Loutherbourg. His panoramas and dioramas were considered stunning examples of landscape painting. He remained at Drury Lane throughout his entire career. David Roberts had left by 1827 to work with J. H. Grieve at Covent Garden. Stanfield's work did not suffer in the least from the end of this partnership; perhaps his greatness stood out even more boldly. A contemporary description of a single wing of his scenic painting is revealing:

> "part of a fisherman's cottage, and there was a group of oars, masts, tackle, baskets and blocks, beautifully painted, and in the same delightfully chaste manner. What first struck me was the absence of that offensive strong yellow which is so common in the work of scene painters. At the bottom of the wing, on the left hand side, a small portion of the priming of the canvas was bare and I saw how carefully the drawing of all the objects had been made out upon it. The details of the baskets were expressed in the most charming way, and so clear and firm that the markings still showed through, after a couch [glaze] of semi-opaque colour had been passed

over them. I observed also that all the positive shadows were put on them with transparent colours, while the great masses of half-tint were laid on with half-opaque tints, and the lights of course, solid and firm." (Rosenfeld, 1981)

This quotation was from the account of a scenic artist who was well trained in the technique of the profession. Clearly, Stanfield relied on the newer transparent wash effects that J. H. Grieve also was using.

Clarkson Stanfield was honored with a silver wine cooler from the owners of the Drury Lane for "his genius and skill in the scenic department" in 1826. He retired from the theatre in 1834 with few exceptional commissions after that date. He died in 1867.

Scenic Studios in Nineteenth Century England

The Grieves and Clarkson Stanfield were the most renowned scenic artists of the nineteenth-century English theatre. It is no accident that they were regularly employed at the largest of London theatres, Covent Garden and Drury Lane. Together these two theatres probably employed twenty full-time painters each season, with an additional large number of assistants. London alone housed an additional dozen or so major theatres, which would employ another fifty painters and dozens of assistants. Often the work was done in a room attached to the theatre itself, the scene-painting room. David Roberts, a painter who started at Drury Lane with Clarkson Stanfield, complained of working conditions at the Edinburgh Pantheon. He was forced to work on stage late at night, when the theatre was closed, because there was no special room for painting scenery. Scenic shops did not appear to have the presence in England as they had in France. Roberts was the subject of a biography in 1866 (Rosenfeld, 1981) in which his financial success was traced. Roberts was paid weekly £1 10s in his early days to £2 at the Edinburgh Royal, but he had to pay his own color boy from that. At the Drury Lane, he reached a peak of £10 for two to six hours of work a day. An engagement in Dublin earned him £100 for fourteen views (backdrops) for a pantomime, which he executed in fourteen days. The Grieves were well paid at Covent Garden, well enough that J. H. Grieve eventually set up his own studio and the scenery was transferred to the theatre by wagon.

English painters generally worked in the eastern technique with the drop stretched on a frame. Alternately, a drop could be hung from a batten and attached at the foot to a roller. It would then be rolled up as sections were completed and dried. A watercolor of Michel Angelo Rooker at work in the 1790s shows an artist alone at work at a paint frame that slips into the floor. The room is well lighted and tall but not terribly deep. Paint frames are on both long walls, no more than sixteen feet apart. Paint and glue are stored in clay pots, some of which are kept on a rolling cart near the painter's side. Rooker uses a small brush and a hand rest and wears a hat while working.

France in the Nineteenth Century

After the brilliant work of Servandoni, the traumas of the French Revolution and the reign of Napoleon made for a difficult transition for theatre into the nineteenth century. The Royal Academy of Music and Dance did survive, except for the "Royal" part, which was dropped for obvious reasons. France was stylistically somewhere between the Italian Baroque and English Romanticism as the theatre came back to life after the rocky opening of the century. It had its own landscape school of fine arts painting, as we certainly see through the work of Watteau and Boucher, both of whom also did theatrical work for the Paris Opéra. That style was delicate and whimsical in relation to the stormy drama of the English school.

French Scenic Style

M. J. Moynet wrote in 1873 (Moynet, 1976): "For forty years, scenic painting has been improving. In recent times, introduction of English scenic decoration momentarily threatened an invasion of bad taste, but the good sense of our artists has turned to profit the methods used by our neighbors exclusively to obtain exaggerated effects. The Italians, who for a long time were our masters and the principal designers of Europe, are remarkable in their great speed of execution and in their perfect knowledge of the mechanical processes. But today, they would have to make a huge effort to recover their old supremacy."

In a typically diplomatic French manner, Moynet is saying that the other great countries are not so good, so France must be great. He does not reveal directly what is the French style, but we can observe it just by looking at the records of stage pictures of that time. France never really abandoned the Italian Baroque approach nor did it embrace English Romanticism. Clearly, the emotional and melodramatic qualities of the English styles are what he meant by "bad taste." The French painters of the era seemed content with a reserved classicism, which was consistent with the prevailing Beaux-Arts style (Colorplate 4).

France had, and still has, spectacular theatres, built by a generous and appreciative government. The French system allowed for the state and the academy to establish a serious classical theatre and tolerate the popular boulevard theatres that catered to working-class tastes. Theatre is still going strong in France. A striking railway worker in the crisis of late 1995 said (*New York Times*, December 11, 1995) that the state could not dare cut his wages or benefits; how could he still go to the theatre? The opera was ever popular in Paris, particularly in the stunning new Paris Opéra of Charles Garnier, one of the most beautiful theatres in all the world.

France clung to the techniques of the Italian stage far into the nineteenth century. The system of substage chariots with wings attached to them by poles was found in many of the major theatres. France adopted changes in lighting technology as well as advanced stage machinery, but the painting styles changed much more slowly. The English romantic style so abhorred by Monsieur Moynet was not embraced. The stage designs of the time generally are careful architectural vistas with gorgeous landscapes. All are still reliant on the careful Italian technique of symmetrical deployment on the stage.

France applied sensational technology as it came along. Moynet's illustrations for *L'Africaine* at the Paris Opéra in 1875 show an amazing use of complex stage machinery to create a huge moving ship deck in calm and stormy seas. Apparently, the hated atmospheric effects of English romanticism somehow crept into the French theatre.

French Scene Shops and Scenic Artists

Scenic artists worked either at the theatre itself or in a scenic studio on the fringes of town. The first independent scenic studio in Paris opened in 1822, under the direction of Charles Ciceri, who had worked as a scenic artist for the Paris Opéra. Parisian painters more than likely went to work in the low-rent suburbs surrounding the city, where huge warehouselike

structures could be built for relatively low cost. In these buildings, the drops were stretched out on the floor in the continental method, which required considerable space. The scenic artist worked with long-handled brushes and walked directly on the painting. The major theatres like the Paris Opéra had their own shops and carted the scenery back and forth much as they still do for the Metropolitan Opera in New York City and many, many other large urban theatres. Independent scenic shops like Rubé and Chaperon were in operation at that time as well. Contemporary illustrations show these shops to be remarkably familiar. The Rubé and Chaperon shop in Belleville (Moynet, 1976) was a vast, open room, easily 60' × 100' in size. At least six painters would work on a single drop. Three other painters might work on flats leaning against the walls or down on the floor. Another scenic artist could be engaged in the layout for another drop. Three more assistants might be snapping a line at the top of the first drop. Off to a side would sit the painter's model of the scenery, as a guide. Simple wooden galleries hung from the rafters about 20 feet overhead so the drop could be checked.

The staff of a nineteenth century scene shop could be quite large. Gustave Coquiot (1910) stated that up to thirty or forty people were employed for painting scenery. These included not only master painters (Coquiot was trained at the Académie des Beaux Arts) but assistant painters, color grinders, color mixers, and fire tenders for the glue pots. Painters worked with dry pigment mixed with the colorless glue as a binder. Working down appears to have been vastly preferred over working up. Moynet (1976) claimed working up was done only in the case of "absolute necessity" and not possible at all for landscapes. That must have ruled out a lot of French scenery! The scenic artist worked from a huge palette about 3' × 4' with twenty or so pots of color around three sides of the portable palette.

Several individuals were recognized as outstanding artists of the nineteenth century in France, but none of them appear to have reached the heights of the great Servandoni. An Italian, Degotti, headed the academy in the first decades of the century and was succeeded by Pierre Luc Charles Cicèri (1782–1868). Both of them trained an important new generation of painters, who took over their place for the better part of the rest of the century. Cicèri's pupils Charles Polycarpe Séchan, Jules Pierre Michel Diéterle, Leon Feuchères, Edouard Désiré Joseph Despléchin, and

Charles Antoine Cambon continued in the more romantic landscape style that their teacher had begun. Cicèri had broken away from the more formal, classical style of his predecessor, Degotti, and began to embrace the landscape style more closely identified with the English artists.

Moynet described the design and execution process for us. After a play was accepted for production, the scenic designer and the machinist met with the director to determine what would be built and what would be used from stock for the play. Then, he said, "the painter . . . concerns himself with designs for the new settings" (Moynet, 1976). The new design was shown by a painted model to director, actors, ballet master, author, and painters. All had their say and the model might have been thoroughly torn up in the process. The painters gave measurements for the flats and drops to the machinist. The scenery then was built and painted. In the case of the Paris Opéra, the completed setting was taken to the stage in the middle of the night, when the theatre was available, and set up. The painter and master lighting technician worked together to determine the lighting when the setting was in place. The scenery then was returned to the studio and the final shading completed.

The Scenic Arts in the United States

The Beginning Years

Theatre grew hesitantly in America throughout the seventeenth century. The Puritanical spirit at the foundation of the country generally resisted the urge to put on plays, let alone decorate them. The first theatre building in America was constructed in 1718 in Williamsburg, Virginia. There is no record from it of scenic decoration. New York City had its first playhouse in 1732 and Philadelphia in 1752. Boston, the center of Puritanism, did not see even a play until 1792.

The early playhouses were simple buildings unable to support the scenic conventions current in Europe at that time. Not until 1785 do we hear of any substantial scenic accompaniment to plays, this happening first in New York. John Henry and Lewis Hallam's productions at the John Street Theatre in New York in February 1787 may best reflect the state of scenery at that time. A notice in the *New York Advertiser* stated, "Tho' we do not look for a theatre here conducted in so regular a manner as

those in Europe, or the decorations so expensive and elegant, yet a proper respect to the audience, and decent and proper scenery, is and ought to be expected . . . frequently where the author intended a handsom street or a beautiful landscape, we only see a dirty piece of canvas . . . nor is it uncommon to see the back of a stage represent a street, while the side scenes represent a wood" (Hughes, 1951).

In the first phase of scenic development, stage scenery was physically brought to America. Lewis Hallam imported scenery from London, probably used scenery, to build a stock from which he would assemble a set. He chose the work of the best scenic artists of Drury Lane and Covent Garden, but the condition of the scenery probably had deteriorated by the time it arrived. American audiences became familiar with the work of French and English scenic artists such as Charles Cicèri (who emigrated to the United States), John Inigo Richards, and Nicholas Thomas Dall through this system. Sign painters, ship painters, house painters, and similar craftsmen were employed to touch up the work or add more pieces to the set. Little scenic construction or invention took place during this early period, certainly nothing on the scale of the European theatre.

The Freelance American Scenic Artist of the Nineteenth Century

Native scenic artists emerged in force during the nineteenth century in America. The huge success of the theatre as a business during the course of this century fueled the demand for scenery as the country grew westward. Theatre was good business, and eventually awareness grew that scenery made the theatre even more appealing; hence, more successful. Theatres were built in cities across the country as a sort of great civilizing force. Cities put up theatre houses in short order, much as the Roman civilization made a theatre the cornerstone of many cities it built. Often these theatres or opera houses required intricate painted interior decoration as well as actual scenery for the stage. This construction boom created a need for scenic artists. Scenic artists would immigrate from Europe, which provided the first direct exposure to contemporary painting techniques and styles. Many famous European actors found great profit in tours of America and created a direct conduit for the theatrical styles to migrate from Europe, particularly England, to the United States and Canada. These forces and the great popularity of dioramas eventually made scenic artistry a vigorous commercial enterprise.

Scenic artists in America came to have many outlets for their work. Nearly every city in America had an opera house or theatre for entertainment. Of course, the major cities like New York, Philadelphia, Boston, and Baltimore had many theatres operating successfully. Museums often were theatres in their own right, like the museums P. T. Barnum established in New York, based more on sensationalism than science. Cycloramas, dioramas, and panoramas—all were popular entertainment in nineteenth century American life and relied completely on skilled scenic artistry. Even the Masonic Temples and their practice of Scottish Rites demanded large amounts of fantastic scenic invention made by scenic artists.

Scenic Artists at Work for Actor-Managers

The actor-manager arose as a pivotal figure in America, seeming to produce plays for profit, plays that required scenery. Independent actor-managers served as today's producers, as the theatre grew into a healthy business across America. The actor-managers were familiar names from the American stage like Edwin Booth, Joseph Jefferson, and Edwin Forrest. The actor-manager might be permanently installed in a theatre in a major city or the head of a touring ensemble bringing shows to smaller towns. In either case, these enterprising businessmen discovered a market for a new product, the theatre. Some actor-managers put a greater emphasis on the quality of production than had been seen in the past, initiating the need for high-quality original scenery; and audiences witnessed an improving stage picture. The actor-manager generally maintained a company of actors and a scenic artist, or more, to paint and maintain the scenic decoration. Harry Isherwood was a scenic artist recorded as painting for Joseph Jefferson from 1830–1845. Jefferson, who was a member of David Garrick's troupe in London, was the son of Thomas Jefferson. Joseph Jefferson was an early pioneer in theatre outside of the East Coast cities. He brought theatre to the West and Southwest as America expanded. Isherwood's work has not survived, but he is one of the few individuals to be credited with having a career solely as a scenic artist during this time.

Another such artist was Russell Smith, a landscape painter brought to the theatre by a Pittsburgh producer in 1833. Smith worked until 1884 and recorded his thoughts in his unpublished "Autobiographical Recollections," one of the very few documents describing scenic artists in America in the nineteenth century. Russell Smith revealed that it was common practice for scenic artists of the time to copy readily available engravings, down to the cross-hatching, for stage pictures. He described a popular impression of the uneven state of the craft: "I was often made conscious that scene painting in the eyes of many who ought to know better is but a coarse kind of daubing, indeed an inferior trade: and no doubt much of it deserves no higher position with its want of nature and extreme exaggeration of colors" (Larson, 1989). Russell Smith was a perfectionist who created original work as a designer and scenic artist, which in itself tells us something of the state of the art at the time he was working. Smith described much stage painting of his contemporaries as unoriginal and derivative. The influence of the producer put pressure on the scenic artist to work quickly and cheaply. Originality and quality went unrewarded by the producers according to Russell Smith.

Russell Smith's career spanned a crucial period in American scenic painting. When Smith began scenic art in the 1830s, the theatre was relatively new to the country. The theatre grew considerably and, along with it, the demand for stage scenery. It was a time of hectic activity and expansion. The realization that the theatre was highly profitable put a new sort of pressure on the scenic artist by the time of Smith's retirement in the 1880s. By then, the theatre was an established entertainment industry. Actor-managers were being replaced by more powerful producers, seeking higher profit margins. The complaints, that Smith revealed in his autobiography, of poor materials and artisanship in the field as a result of greedy and uncaring producers would be echoed more loudly by the turn of the century, as the theatre in America faced the crisis of labor organization.

The best-known and best-documented freelance scenic artist of the nineteenth century in America easily may have been Charles W. Witham (1842–1926). Witham's life span went from the end of the era of the actor-manager through the powerful producing syndicates at the turn of the century and well into the birth of the craft unions and the development of the scenic designer. Witham's work reflects the dominant styles of scenic painting at that time.

He began in Boston in the 1860s, painting for the actor-manager Edwin Forrest. In that decade he moved to New York to work for the Booth Theatre. He stayed in New York until shortly before his 1909 retirement in Boston. Witham was trained as an artist and made a living as a landscape painter before moving to the theatre. His stage work indicates a great awareness of architectural history, particularly in the Shakespearean revivals of the 1870s staged by Augustin Daly. The preoccupation in historicism was a dominant feature in the design and painting of Witham for Daly. Witham would incorporate familiar paintings as the basis for stage pictures of his Shakespearean designs, creating massive living tableaus for the stage. Witham also brought an early sense of realism through his depiction of New York City locales for a series of comedies about the various immigrants of the city. Witham brought scenic advances to the Booth Theatre as well. He eliminated the English-style wing and groove system and removed the raked deck, creating a flat stage floor on which scenery could be placed freely.

The Diorama in America

The diorama played a large role in the United States, as it did in Europe. Diorama displays were common by the 1840s in America, particularly as a device to describe the wild western frontier to the larger eastern cities. An immense and popular work by John Banvard was set up in St. Louis in 1846. Described as the "biggest painting in the world," it was a moving painted strip of canvas that presented a journey down the Mississippi from the confluence of the Mississippi and the Missouri to the Delta. It was accompanied by a lecture, given by the artist, describing his own journey making the sketches for the painting. Dioramas described the far-flung corners of the country to eager audiences but rarely made it to the stage as a part of the action of a play.

Cycloramas emerged later in the century. They were similar to the dioramas in Europe, remarkably lifelike assemblages of paintings and three-dimensional decoration. Cycloramas were static paintings that covered all or a major part of the inside of a building. The special buildings were circular, allowing for a 360° surround painting. The roofs of the buildings had skylights so the interior lighting could be controlled to some degree. Spectators stood in the middle of the painting to view the cyclorama.

The cyclorama combined realistic painting with real objects like trees, rocks, carts, models, and statues for remarkably realistic effects. The Civil War became a very popular topic of these cycloramas, as famous battles were described in full detail complete with severed limbs of dead soldiers. One of the largest Civil War cycloramas has been restored and reopened to the public. Located in Grant Park in Atlanta, it is one of the few remnants of this American scenic phenomenon.

Fraternal Organizations

It was reported that, in 1896, America had some three hundred fraternal organizations, or secret societies, with six million members. Some of these organizations, such as the Scottish Rites of Freemasonry, used scenery extensively in their rituals. Initiation ceremonies in particular required elaborate allegorical presentations, which required very elaborate scenery and costuming. Masonic Temples spread across the country much like theatres, and nearly every city had at least one temple or lodge. The scenic demands were nearly as great as in a new theatre, and the scenery itself was very lavish. The nineteenth century fascination with archeology and the life of ancient civilizations certainly contributed important imagery to these rites. In any case, it provided further opportunities for the growth of the scenic artist as an important member of any community.

In America, the scenic artists of the nineteenth century never achieved the fame that their British, Italian, and French counterparts had in Europe. Production values were lower in America than in Europe, with the exception of a few remarkable producers, like Forrest, the Booths, and Daly. Theatre buildings were generally less elaborate in America than Europe, with a few exceptions, until the end of the nineteenth century. Scenic art was practiced by a number of talented individuals across the country, but for every good painter, there were several mediocre ones willing to work for less money.

However, the need for scenery was large and growing. The expansion of the theatre as a business; the growth of cities and population at a tremendous rate; the popularity of cycloramas, panoramas, and museums; and the popularity of fraternal organization—all relied on scenic decoration. The growth of the business of the theatre was crucial to the next phase of development. As the theatre grew, more producers entered the field for the pursuit of profit over art, which forced an obvious reaction to building and painting scenery—at least, obvious to anyone who has tried to do a big budget show for less money. Producers cut corners to save money, and scenery was one of the first targets for savings. Economic reality forced scenic artists to band together in commercial ventures, called *scenic studios,* to provide good scenery at a lower cost, keeping a large part of the market. Out of this need came an American phenomenon, the scenic studio.

The American Scenic Studio

If the scenic artist was generally an anonymous figure in the American theatre scene in this century, the scenic studio was to become better known than any individual within it. In England and France, individual artists in the theatre became popular and recognized. In America, the scenic studio became the workshop where relatively unknown artists churned out yards of scenic decoration for a rapidly growing business. The studios consolidated the finest scenic artists into centralized locations and raised the overall level of quality in American scenic painting. The studios provided a large enough work force that an apprentice system would emerge to provide the labor to assist the master painters. Eventually, the scenic artists working in the studios would become powerful enough to join together in a labor union and create the rules for working conditions that we have inherited. America certainly did not invent the scenic studio; they were quite common in France, Germany, and Italy. But, in America, studios grew so quickly in response to the exploding population of the country and the need for entertainment that they became an industry in their own right by the turn of the century (Figure 13.1).

Armbruster Scenic Studio

Scenic studios profited from the new railroad network developing in America. A theatre in Menomonie, Wisconsin, could order its scenery from Minneapolis, Minnesota, with ease. The theatre could avoid the cost of having a scenic shop, and the scenic studio could profit from the business. The Armbruster Scenic Studios was the first studio to establish a mail-order business. Mathais Armbruster was a immigrant German scenic artist, who worked in Cincinnati as an art-glass painter. After working as a portrait artist after the end of the Civil War, he opened a scenic studio in Columbus, Ohio,

in 1875. Armbruster Studios were contracted by a traveling minstrel show to supply backdrops and, as both Al G. Field's Minstrels and Armbruster grew, by 1904, the studio came to be the second largest scenic studio in the country, a remarkable feat considering the location. From Ohio, Armbruster provided scenic decoration for theatres, vaudeville, schools, Masonic Temples, and the Broadway stage. Most of the work was ordered from a catalogue, and the designs were essentially generic. Armbruster proved that a scenic studio in nearly any location could be a profitable venture. The studio operated until 1958.

The Armbruster Studios established the profitability of a scenic studio that could work inexpensively at a distance from the client. This format was to be widely copied in the United States at that time and provide employment to hundreds of scenic artists, assistants, and sales representatives.

Scenic Studios in New York City

New York City was clearly the capital of the American theatre by the latter half of the nineteenth century. The growth of the theatre syndicates cemented that even further. In 1896, a syndicate of producers formed in New York controlled nearly all the theatres in the United States. They controlled bookings, actors, managers, and the profits. The actor-manager was very nearly completely squeezed out of business. The business of making and painting scenery centralized itself in New York City, where the producers were and the business was to be had. New York had the greatest concentration of scenic artists in the country. At least thirty major scenic artists were working in New York at the time, many of them in their own studios. This included Sidney Chidley, Homer F. Emens, George Gros, Lee Lash, Harley Merry, Russell Smith, Charles W. Witham, and Robert Marston (Larson, 1989). This small group represented the past, Smith and Witham, and the future, as Chidley, Emens, and Merry would be instrumental in the formation of a union.

Robert Marston was an English scenic artist who came to America with the tour of a European actor and stayed in New York for the rest of his career. He was interviewed at length in 1894, producing a rather dismal view of the state of scenic art at that time ("Art in the Theatre," 1894). Marston described a very different scene than the one in his home country when Clarkson Stanfield was awarded a silver wine cooler! He blamed the economy and greedy producers: "First and foremost is cost, artistic quality is second. Get the artists to do it cheapest. The materials are bought wholesale, to the disadvantage of the competing artist. Cheap colours are used instead of the more expensive ones. Certain colours have qualities for which there are no substitutes and no matter how skilled the hand that uses them, the work will be inferior." Marston found weakness in the studios themselves. These were run by unscrupulous owners, who reused stencils, patterns, and designs in any combination they saw fit, if only to make the job cheaper. Marston found no pride in the work or originality from the studios. He stated, "The result of all this is that the best artistic talent in America will either leave the scenic profession or the country." Marston also described terrible working conditions, including poorly lit paint frames and paint bridges sixty-five feet in the air with no safety considerations.

Edward G. Unitt and Homer Emens, both interviewed about a decade later, related that the conditions had improved but that the role of the scenic artist was still impoverished ("Stage Scenery and the Men Who Paint It," 1908). Unitt explained, "The scene painter is not part of a theatrical staff. He is an employee of a firm. He is required to produce as rapidly as possible the scenery for perhaps twenty plays. The greatest number of these will be failures and others must be ready to take their place. This means a large plant and more rapid work. He has absolutely no opportunity toward individuality and naturally does not take the same interest as he did in that atmosphere engendered when he was a member of the staff of a theatre."

Figure 13.1 Artists, from left to right, Joe Folta, Art Rovik, Calvin Robert Brown, Frank Stengel, an unknown artist, Jack Westrom, and Bob Verne, working on the paint bridges at the Twin City Scenic's Studio, Minneapolis, Minnesota (photo courtesy of C. Lance Brockman).

Homer Emens was more specific as to the actual work of a scenic artist:

> The scene painter often does not see a play at all. The stage manager brings him a plot. That is all he knows. He carries out what he is expected to do, the scenery is finished and perhaps he never sees it afterwards. Frequently a scene will consist of forty pieces, all being painted at once and the scene painter must carry the tone in his mind for each of these pieces in order to preserve the unity of the scene. Or perhaps there are several plays underway at the same time, each relating to different country and different periods. These, in all their details, must be kept distinct in mind. In fact a scene painter must be a cyclopedia of architectural styles. Persia, Greece, Rome, Ireland and Siberia, Italian gardens and Western plains must all be at his command. He must know periods and epochs. He must be an authority on matters of appropriate decoration and ornamentation for there is no time for research and deliberation.

Scenic studios were staffed by four types of personnel: owners, scenic artists, assistant scenic artists, and paint boys (Wischmeier, 1978). The owner often had been scenic artists but concentrated on the financial and contracting end of the business. These owners occasionally might paint, but the majority of the work was done by the scenic artists they employed. The scenic artists designed the setting, made a model of it, and painted what they designed. Sometimes, several scenic artists would work on the settings for a single, large production, sharing the designing duties by act or by scene. The scenic assistants prepared the drops, mixed paints, did large initial washes, cartooned the drops, and assisted the scenic artist. The last group, the paint boys, did the washing, brush cleaning, transported drawings around the city, and helped wherever possible. These were low-paid positions, but they were an effective way to gain an apprenticeship.

Scenic Studios Outside New York

Chicago was a railroad hub and became the center of the scenic industry outside of New York City. Major studios like Sosman and Landis, Silko Scenery, and Daniel's Scenic Studio were located in Chicago by the turn of the century. They provided the scenery for theatres, schools, lodges, and opera houses just like Armbuster in Columbus. Many jobs were available in the area. Sosman and Landis itself employed twelve to twenty full-time scenic artists, and the Chi-

cago Grand Opera had five scenic artists on staff directed by Peter Dunigan (Wischmeier, 1978).

Many other cities had large scenic studios by the turn of the century, including Kansas City Scenic, Toomey and Volland in St. Louis, and the Twin Cities Scenic Studio in Minneapolis (Brockman, 1987). The Twin Cities Scenic Studio has been superbly catalogued and documented by C. Lance Brockman and The University of Minnesota Museum of Art. Brockman's book provides us with an excellent insight into the workings of a scenic studio of the time. Twin Cities began as part of the Bijou Opera House in Minneapolis in 1890. The studio moved to a free-standing location in 1905, as business was booming. The new shop had fourteen moveable paint frames with narrow bridges between them. Scenic artists worked with a full palette of dry pigments that they combined with water or denatured alcohol for a small amount of pastelike paint, called pulp, as they went along. The paint shop had a full carpentry shop attached to it as well as a drapery shop that was a large part of their business. The scenic artists worked with the assistants as described previously, letting the assistants and paint boys prepare the drops for final painting. It would take a scenic artist no more than one or two days to fully complete all but the most complicated drops (Figure 13.2).

The Unionization of Scenic Artists

The force of scenic artists was great enough that, between 1892 and 1918, they would form the powerful union that today still determines the working conditions, pay scale, and benefits for all member painters in the country.

In July 1892, the American Society of Scenic Painters registered its existence in New York. It was an alliance of New York–based scenic artists. Little is known about the effect of this group, but in April, 1896, the group was renamed The Protective Alliance of Scenic Painters and became a national organization with corresponding secretaries in San Francisco, Cincinnati, Boston, Milwaukee, Chicago, and Philadelphia. The union was dedicated to working in harmony with the National Alliance of Stage Employees (later renamed the International Alliance of Theatrical Stage Employees, or I.A.T.S.E.). That in itself caused several members to break off into The Scenic Art League, to distance themselves from the actual labor union that was the National Alli-

Figure 13.2
English town perspective,
Twin City Scenic Collection
(used with the permission of
the Performing Arts Archives,
University of Minnesota Libraries, St. Paul, MN).

ance of Stage Employees. The idea of labor interven-
tion was distasteful and the goal of the league was
to protect "the dignity of scenic art as a profession"
(Wischmeier, 1978).

In 1912, the alliance re-formed into the United
Scenic Artists' Association. Its clear goal was the betterment of working conditions, wages, and job security within the New York City scenic studios. United
Scenic Artists' Association represented over 600 scenic artists working for some twenty-two scenic studios in the metropolitan New York area. In 1918,
the association staged a lengthy strike against the
studios, forcing the studios to hire "regular artists"
to paint the scenery for the upcoming Broadway season. The strike failed its stated goals of specific pay
scales and hourly restrictions, but it gained the estab-
lishment of an arbitration committee recognized by
the studio owners.

Prior to the strike itself, the association gained
an autonomous subcharter within the Brotherhood
of Painters, Decorators and Paperhangers union.
The name of the association was changed to the
United Scenic Artists of America (U.S.A.A.). Only
recently was the name shortened to the United Scenic Artists. U.S.A. has established itself as the sole
union voice for stage designers, costume designers,

lighting designers, scenic artists, art directors, mural
artists, and allied crafts in the United States. It has
successfully set the standard for working conditions
and wages in the profession. One must remember
that the union, which today is often called the
designer's union, began as a collection of scenic artists seeking a better way of life in the work they
love.

American Scenic Style

Nineteenth century scenic styles in America were
unique derivations from the European masters. Scenic artists from Europe brought with them the
Romantic, Baroque, or classical landscapes that they
knew from their homes, but the styles seemed to
change when they landed on the American shore.
Theatres in America were different from the European theatres. There was no historical theatrical
background to draw on in the construction or rigging of theatres. They tended to be simpler structures
with less complex stage machinery. The Italian
Baroque style rarely was seen on the stages of the
American theatre. The Romantic English landscape
was adapted to the American image. The more rugged American landscape, particularly in the West,

was idealized by native scenic artists throughout the century. The highly generalized stock settings of scenic studios, distributed to most theatres who could not afford a full complement of scenery for each new production, set an overall tone in America that scenery indeed was generic. An all-purpose landscape, European city, prison, palace, village, mountain pass, and forest were common sets available to theatres and opera houses. Often, a theatre might boast a single new drop, oleo, or act curtain as an enticement to patrons. The oleo was a versatile drop for any sort of entertainment, such as a song, a pantomime, a lecture, or a skit. The oleo drop often hung in the *in-one* position, subdividing the stage into a shallower depth that was more appropriate for a brief interlude. The act curtain or drop curtain functioned as today's main drape, the decorative divider wall between audience and stage. Often, it was the most elaborate piece a theatre owned and was painted to harmonize with the interior decorations of the theatre itself (Brockman, 1987).

Stylistic and technological inventions were reserved mostly for the New York City theatres or found in the complex dioramas or cycloramas. The new interest in historicism of the London theatre was imported with the Shakespearean revivals of Charles Kean and later Augustin Daly. However, fully mounted productions in that style remained in New York. The tours that many European acting companies took across America had to rely on simplified versions of the original scenery so that the production easily could be adapted to the many diverse theatres it would find on tour.

The new pursuit of realism, with roomlike box settings and fully dimensional architecture was seen on the New York stage in the 1880s. David Belasco is best known for his ultrarealistic melodramas of the turn of the century. He and his chief scenic artist, George Gros, created meticulously detailed interiors, realistic exteriors, and stunning atmospheric effects. Belasco and Gros produced some of the most memorable scenic inventions of the American theatre and certainly some of the finest realistic scenery of the theatre worldwide up to their time. But Belasco and Gros's memorable scenic achievements usually were for less than memorable plays, and ironically, their work was timed for the eve of the revolution that would displace them. As Czar Nicholas II and Louis XVI may be remembered chiefly as unlucky monarchs who were swept away because they could not decipher the powerful mood of their unhappy subjects, David Belasco's studiously perfect realism also became a victim of dramatically bad timing. His laborious scenic and lighting techniques were seen by the avant-garde as the embodiment of every ill of the stage and were severely ridiculed by history.

Realism was but a passing style like Romanticism and the Italian styles we had seen for so long. The twentieth century would bring the scenic designer an entirely new aesthetic for the world of the theatre. As movies replaced theatre's popularity, an international aesthetic weighed in against painted scenery, scenic studios began to shrink, and scenic artists began to disappear. The modern theatre saw traditional painting in a new, harshly critical light. The golden age of scenic painting of the nineteenth century rapidly turned to a much more fragmented twentieth century, as theatre styles changed radically and eventually the theatre lost popularity to movies and television.

THE TWENTIETH CENTURY

The twentieth century is called the *century of revolution* by theatre historians. It is the time when all theatrical arts were remade into completely new forms from the conventions that evolved from the Renaissance. The visual world of theatre profoundly changed at the turn of the century. Radical visionaries, such as Adolphe Appia and Edward Gordon Craig, proclaimed illusionistic painted scenery of the past to be inadequate, worthless. They, and others, saw the stage stripped bare of the painted, two-dimensional artifice of the past. The stage was to become the world of the sculptor, a molded, plastic topography ruled no longer by artists as Clarkson Stanfield and George Gros. The stage now was the realm of the scenic designer, an artist invented for the occasion, a hero to lead the theatre out of the cluttered attic of nineteenth century romanticism into the crystalline visions of a "real" artist.

Appia and Craig had reason to despise painted scenery. Most of it was probably mediocrity itself. The scenery they despised represented an entire style of theatrical performance, including the self-indulgent, declamatory actor milking Shakespeare for all his worth or the inept company of actors unable to pay any attention to each other on stage for fear of missing the chance to please an adoring audience.

Appia and Craig sought a unified, passionate performance style that spoke directly to the soul of the audience. The theatre they envisioned sought truth, meaning, poetry, and relevance. They worshipped the text and music of the theatre and felt, particularly Appia, that the scenery should only evoke imagery not dictate it, for the betterment of drama. Their solution was radical and uncompromising. No illusionistic painting was permitted in their brave new world. The new stage was truthful, a real space for the actor to live in. The scenery could not conflict or compete with the actor's voice, movement, and presence.

Appia and Craig did not remove nineteenth century scenic painting from the theatre by themselves. They were part of a larger philosophical movement that advocated scientific inquiry into the human condition and respected the artist's power of imagination. The theatre was a part of an international artistic revolution, including painting, music, architecture, literature, and dance; in short, all the elements of theatre. It was inevitable that the theatre would change to reflect the lives and spirits of the audiences that attended it, not just entertain these people with diversions. The revolution allowed scenic design to mature into a unique art form and to integrate new technology into theatrical production. The nineteenth century scenic artist was the victim of this revolution, that is certain. The stature, skills, and techniques of scenic artists have atrophied since 1900. The nature of the profession of scenic artistry has changed with the theatre; the scope of the job is far broader than ever. Perhaps the skills of the Bibienas, De Loutherbourg, Servandoni, and Stanfield no longer are relevant. However, we have seen architecture turn its back to the Renaissance during this century and later return to "rediscover" classicism in the postmodern age. The so-called antique skills of the scenic artist should not be forgotten.

Technology and Scenic Art

In the twentieth century, technology had a far greater impact on the scenic artist than in any previous time. The process of painting is much as it has been for centuries, but the materials available to the scenic artist are radically different now from the beginning of the century. Electric lighting in the theatre forced scenic artists to adapt their painting techniques to new effects and increased visibility. The impact of photography as a means of perception and image reproduction has affected the sort of painting a scenic artist might be called upon to execute. Digital imaging and Xerography have put powerful new tools in the hands of the scenic designer, even replacing the scenic artist through projected images, photographic collages, and mechanically painted scenic units.

Paint and Painting Tools

Much of the discussion of Chapter Five is the history of this century's tools for the scenic artist. It is worthwhile to review how many of the tools common to us now are new.

Paint itself has changed tremendously in the last hundred years. For centuries, scenic artists used ground dry pigments as the base for paint. They mixed the pigment with heated animal glue, water, and denatured alcohol to make a batch of paint as they went. Maintaining the glue pot was a primary chore of a paint boy or assistant scenic artist. The process is time-consuming and the product is rather perishable. Painting in warm climates is terrific for drop drying, but encourages odd growths in the paint bucket left too long in the sun. Paint mixed from pigment is a little finicky, as it needs continual stirring to prevent settling. The glue to pigment to water ratios are delicate. Too little glue (binder), and the paint will flake off; too much, and the paint is difficult to use or the finish will crack.

Scenic paint was made available in premixed form by the 1940s. American scenic paint manufacturers like Iddings and Gothic took the standard pigments and mixed them with casein as a binder, producing the thick, pastelike paint common today. This has simplified the painting job to a great degree. The several hours of preparing dry pigment into paint for a drop now is a relatively simple task.

Aniline dyes were widely used during most of the twentieth century but are found less commonly now, due to concerns about their toxicity and the availability of modern highly-saturated paints. These dyes are chemically created powdered color. They were mixed in small amounts with water and denatured alcohol to create watercolorlike dye. The vibrancy of the color, even when significantly diluted, made aniline dyes well-suited for loose, watercolor painting techniques, washes, scrim work, working whenever transparency was desired, and wonderful cast shadows.

Highly-saturated acrylic-based paints are now common and widely available. Their ease of use and cleanup make them very attractive to the scenic artist. Acrylics are flexible enough for painting on traditional scenic materials like canvas and are excellent paints over properly treated wood, metal, and compound textures.

Many tools common to the scenic artist are new to this century. Brushes have changed little, except perhaps that good brushes are harder to find and very expensive when available. Paint spraying tools were made possible with finer metal-working techniques, which allowed mass production of the small parts required for a sprayer. Sprayers are common now in hand-pump, compressed air, and airless varieties, all of which were unknown to the scenic artist of the nineteenth century.

Stage Lighting

The electrification of stage lighting greatly affected the way the work of the scenic artist was seen on the stage. Most scenic artists of the time preferred gaslight over electric. The gaslight was a softer, dimmer light than electric. Homer Emens had this reaction to electric light: "Nor do we owe much that is good to electric light. Nothing is better than gas for stage lighting, it is softer. It contributes more to the atmosphere of the stage than electric light. The real advantage of electric light is that it is more readily handled and since it is found in every village, one-night stands have all the effects of light that city stages can have" ("Stage Scenery and the Men Who Paint It," 1908).

Electric light had so many advantages for play production that its presence was unavoidable. Once adapted for the stage, there was no turning back. Electric lighting facilitated translucency effects and it also made possible radical color shifts on the scenery on stage. New scenic designers of the early twentieth century, particularly Joseph Urban, quickly grasped the profound shift in the relationship of painting and the new flexible lighting that would illuminate it. Urban employed a "broken color" system that allowed a painted drop, for example, to respond to different colors of light with subtlety. Instead of red light making a drop turn all red, the broken color system layered

underpainting of one overall palette with overpainting of another. The color actually broke through in places and the underpainted colors, perhaps cool tones, responded to cooler light. The upper layers of color were geared to the warmer lights of amber and red. In this way drops could be painted to respond atmospherically to the changing light (Brockman, 1997).

Xerography and Digital Imaging

The ability to copy and create images electronically or digitally has been the most radical influence of technology on the scenic artist in the late twentieth century. Photography altered audiences' and artists' sense of perception in the nineteenth century by creating the definitive "realistic" image. Film turned the photograph into a moving image, and the movie industry made that into an entertainment form. The presence of all of these challenged the stage picture and the scenic artist's ability to portray reality. It was inevitable that the photographic image would work its way onto the stage as a tool for the scenic designer.

The result for the scenic artist is an increased amount of copy work as a painter. Designers use the literal qualities of a photograph and the starkness of black and white photography as an important part of modern stage design. This requires that the scenic artist paint mechanically or have a machine print the image to be used, applied like wallpaper to the scenery. The quality of half-tone images that we see in newspapers is one that a scenic designer may often employ in a design. To reproduce that quality the scenic artist must carefully reproduce stage versions of the dot screens used to dither the black and white dots of the image.

A scenic designer can effortlessly photocopy, in color or black and white, nearly any image and incorporate it into a stage design. The proliferation of "borrowed" images, collage designs, and outright copying has placed further pressures on scenic artists. Often, scenic designers will do the photocopying and the assemblage of the copied pieces as a substitute for traditional paint elevations. The scenic artist is invited to sort out the details of copying the style.

By the 1980s, mechanical painting machines were available to make full stage drops. These machines took the paint elevations of a scenic designer and converted the images into digital information through a high-resolution scanner. The digital information of the paint elevation on tape controls an enormous painting machine. These machines are large enough to paint goods measuring 28' × 60' and can paint onto a variety of materials including muslin, vinyl, and Plexiglas. Paint is applied by a four-color gun that moves over the material. The paint used is not scenic paint, but a solvent-based paint more appropriate for use in the delicate paint guns. The quality of the painting is not unlike that of an ink jet color printer, which may be appropriate for stage use, particularly under certain stylistic conditions. Depending on the material that was painted, the painting may be modified by a scenic artist after it has left the machine. Certainly the image quality will improve in the future and the undeniable economic benefits of these automated painting devices will draw considerable business away from scenic artists.

This painting machine is an expensive process at the moment but not totally cost-prohibitive. It is certain to become increasingly competitive with the cost of using human scenic artists. This poses interesting questions as to the value of handmade painted imagery and the role of the scenic artist. For those of us who appreciate the living quality of the painter's craft and the simple expression of the artist's gesture, such a machine may seem abhorrent at first. The argument in favor of such a machine is very persuasive, and the presence of such devices, as with electric lighting, is not likely to disappear.

The Twentieth Century Scenic Artist

The development of the scenic designer in the twentieth century is one of the best documented stories in all theatre history. It bears no new examination on these pages other than to accept the existence of the scenic designer and to remind the reader that the scenic designer came from the ranks of the scenic artists. How, then, has the role of the scenic artist changed?

Scenic Studios

By the turn of the century, the scenic studio was a strong presence in the major theatre countries of the world—Austria, England, France, and Germany—as it was in the United States. In Europe, the studio had the effect of standardization of scenery, just as it had

in America. Fewer and fewer theatres could maintain full-time scenic shops of their own, so the studio fulfilled the need for scenery. The theatre was a growing business in Europe, too, so the quantity of scenery generated around the turn of the century was quite great. Studios increased efficiency and profits but discouraged the individual star painter.

Scenic painting was learned only by apprenticeship. The skills were handed down from one generation to the next in a very closed society of artists. The increasing business of the theatre put tremendous pressure on this society simply to produce. The generation of scenic artists at the turn of the century were not only painters but businessmen as well. Their concerns were with running the studios, acquiring work, and finishing on schedule. Artistic integrity was beginning to slip from the profession.

The studios isolated the scenic artist from the world. This isolation may be seen no place more profoundly than in Paris, where the art of painting had been embroiled in revolution from the beginning of the impressionist movement in the 1860s. The radical and famous new styles of painting, publicly displayed at length, had little or no effect on the scenic artists of the time. The closed world of the scenic artist did not embrace any sense of the change in artistic direction.

Perhaps the existence of the studios and the popularity of the theatre made this change impossible. Studios responded to the growing demand for scenic decoration by creating more and more scenery. Ready-made scenery was common in Europe by 1900, as in the United States. The weight of effort to create drops, keep scenery available, and stay competitive with other studios did not foster an atmosphere of experimentation and change. The success of business consumed the possibility of variation from accepted traditional forms.

The Scenic Designer

The scenic artist had been creator and executor of the stage picture for four hundred years of development. The revolution of the twentieth century would tear those two roles apart from one another, putting the scenic artist in the supporting role of executant. The scenic designer would determine the style; the scenic artist would make it happen. This new relationship finally would alter the scenic studio's relationship to current artistic trends by bringing a new artist, the scenic designer, into the studio.

New Forms of Stage Scenery

A modern revolution in theatre began in Europe and spread to England, Scandinavia, Eastern Europe, Russia, and the United States. By the early twentieth century, theatre had been thoroughly changed in its literature, acting styles, directing, and designing. The first visible change was a naturalistic stage picture of the world as it truly is, in great detail. The naturalistic style first brought to the stage by André Antoine's Théâtre Libre in Paris was famously characterized as if it were a "slice of life" placed on the stage.

Naturalism and realism gave way quickly to symbolism, exoticism, expressionism, idealism and many forms of nonrealistic stage design. The two primary elements of stage design from the Renaissance to the end of the nineteenth century, painted scenes and illusionistic scenes, suddenly disappeared. Scenic designers worked three-dimensionally as well as two-dimensionally from this point forward. The scenic artist was faced with very new forms and challenges to work with. Sculpting and texturing became new skills for the scenic artists. Painting styles changed with every new design and scenic designer. The fundamental shift for the scenic artist from creator to replicator had a profound impact on the job. The scenic artist became stylistically anonymous, transparent. This artist's job was to replicate the style of the scenic designer and rarely would one work with the same designer for extended periods.

The ability to emulate the style of another is perhaps the greatest asset of a modern scenic artist. The chameleonlike skill of shifting from one designer's taut, detailed style to another's loose cartoonish style is a common demand on the painter of today. The scenic artist has been removed from top billing to a secondary role, yet the work is as difficult as ever, if not more so. The work of the great early scenic designers of the twentieth century was realized by scenic artists who had to learn new skills to achieve the work. Robert Edmund Jones's dense atmospheric settings would only be illustrations in a book if Robert Bergman had not attempted pouring paint right from the bucket. Even Leon Bakst and Pablo Picasso, two of the most painterly scenic designers of the twentieth century, had their work done by another: Vladimir Polunin.

Scenic Artists and Scenic Designers in America

In this century, theatre in the United States reached its height in popularity and impact. New York City remained the center of theatre in America. Most of the significant scenic studios in the United States were in the metropolitan New York area for most of this century. Many still are, and most of the members of United Scenic Artists are New York City residents.

The union that began around 1896 had grown to have nearly 900 members by 1941 in the New York City area alone (Larson, 1989). Of those members, 213 were scenic artists, almost one and a half times the number of scenic designers. Close to thirty scenic studios were operating in the New York area at that time.

Scenic designers and scenic artists in America comprised both Americans and Europeans. Many scenic artists came from Europe during the first half of the century, as theatre boomed and well-paying jobs were available. One of the earliest scenic designers of the modern era, Joseph Urban, brought an entire team of scenic artists from Vienna with him to America. That team brought the continental style of painting with them and introduced it to New York at the beginning of contemporary design. The team eventually created Triangle Studios, one of the largest and most respected scenic studios in America.

The first professional American scenic designers, such as Jones, Lee Simonson, Jo Mielziner, and Donald Oenslager, relied on their own expressive style of painting in their designs. Painting was still a dominant force in design, but it was a simpler and more personal style. The challenge to the scenic artist was to recreate the work of the scenic designer accurately and sensitively with ultimate regard for the style. Such painters as Robert Bergman and Raymond Sovey of Lee Lash Studios incorporated the continental style of Triangle Studios with the personal styles of the new designers and invented unorthodox techniques to get the job done. This newest generation of scenic artists was willing to use any tool or technique to achieve what the designer intended. Here, the break from the old system, where designer and painter were one person, is most distinct. The scenic designer is free to imagine anything appropriate to the stage picture he or she seeks. The scenic artist becomes the magician who can solve the riddle of how to achieve the design.

The Impact of the Film Industry

It is ironic that movies have also preserved nineteenth century illusionistic painting. The irony is doubled when one realizes that the presence of the movies had such a profoundly negative effect on the theatre's business after the 1930s. Certainly, the film industry attracted scenic artists in great numbers, as film established itself as a major industry during the early part of the twentieth century. In the early days, most film scenery was like old-fashioned theatrical scenery with painted dimension and shadows. The camera lens was fooled more easily than the eye.

Modern filmmaking relies heavily on illusionistic painting, although usually in miniature. Most special effects scenes are shot in layers that are assembled in postproduction. Exaggerated, remote, dangerous, or physically impossible backgrounds normally are created by skilled matte artists and layered onto film behind the actors during post-production after the action is shot. Film production relies more and more heavily on successful illusionistic painting for backgrounds because they are cost-effective and visually perfect. Most audiences are unaware that nearly all stunt shots take place in front of paintings.

The Current Scene

United Scenic Artists merged its locals (New York, Chicago, Florida, and Los Angeles) into one single union during the early 1990s. The membership of the union has grown with the adoption of the two-track examination process. Major scenic studios have emerged in Florida and Nevada to support the explosion of entertainment theme parks and casinos. Broadway theatre has undergone a significant upsurge of popularity through the megamusical format of such works as *The Phantom of the Opera* and *Sunset Boulevard*, both of which rely extensively on what might appear to be nineteenth-century styles of scenic grandeur. The film industry continues to rely on skilled muralists, matte painters, and digital art-

ists to create in two dimensions what is too expensive or too dangerous to film on location. There is no doubt that the art of scenic painting continues throughout the world and that talented painters, who command the art of illusion, will continue to be in demand.

CONCLUSION

The craft of scenic artistry came from distant beginnings in the Greek and Roman theatre. During the Italian Renaissance, scenic designing first was scientifically explored and practiced by some of the greatest talents and minds of the time, particularly Aleotti, Serlio, and Torelli. Italy thoroughly dominated the field of stage painting, creating a systematic approach to decorating the stage that was copied worldwide, often under the supervision of Italian artists. The Bibiena family of scenic artists were at the apex of the Italian style for over one hundred fifty years, several decades into the nineteenth century. The Italians created a stunning world of illusion and motion.

Gradually, the rigid Italian format was replaced by a less symmetrical array of scenic units on the stage, particularly in England. Painting techniques changed in the English style also, as a more romantic and atmospheric landscape filled the stage. The French painter Servandoni and the English painter De Loutherbourg explored evocative lighting effects, transparency, and more subtle means of moving scenery combined with masterful illusionistic painting techniques. Their innovations were fully exploited worldwide during the nineteenth century by such as J. H. Grieve and Clarkson Stanfield in England and Charles Cicèri in France, who became some of the most famous scenic artists in history. The illusionism they and others practiced made the theatre extremely popular and gave rise to other entertainment, panoramas and dioramas, based totally on scenic spectacle.

These arts were imported to the United States at the beginning of the nineteenth century. By the end of the century, America had developed its own scenic artists and an important scenic studio system to produce high volumes of scenery for a growing theatre business. Scenic studios became a major force in Europe as well as America by 1900 and have remained so ever since.

The twentieth century completely changed the role of the scenic artist, as the new figure of the scenic designer emerged. The film industry also eroded the importance of theatre in society, and scenic artists drifted to films as an outlet for their skills. With the shrinking of theatrical production and the radical change in theatrical production styles from the nineteenth century to the twentieth century, scenic artistry began to lose grasp of the older techniques of illusion and perspective. Some of these skills are now so far out of favor and practice that few scenic artists or designers fully understand the rules of perspective.

Scenic artists rose in recognition to become famous in the eyes of the public during the nineteenth century. The modern theatre world turned so rapidly from the techniques scenic artists had practiced for three hundred years that those who had been famous in the nineteenth century became the subject of ridicule by modern scenic designers. The modern scenic artist generally is much more anonymous than his or her predecessors. However, the reliance on scenic artists in theatre and film continues and is likely to continue for centuries to come. There are magical things that only a brush, paint, and talent can describe.

Reading and Resources

This chapter identifies useful addresses, resource books, and Web sites for scenic artists.

HEALTH AND SAFETY PUBLICATIONS

ACTS Facts Newsletter
Monthly newsletter of ACTS (Arts, Crafts and Theatre Safety)
Attn: M. Rossol
181 Thompson Street, #23
New York, NY 10012
(212) 777-0062

Artists Beware
Michael McCann
Watson-Guptill, 1979
ISBN 0-8230-0295-0

The Artist's Complete Health and Safety Guide
Monona Rossol
New York: Allworth Press, 1994
ISBN 1-880559-18-8

The MSDS Pocket Dictionary
(Updated yearly)
Schenectady, NY: Genium Publishing
1145 Catalyn Street
Schenectady, NY 12303-1836
(518) 377-8854

Stage Fright: Health and Safety in the Theatre
Monona Rossol
New York: Allworth Press, 1991
ISBN 0-9607118-3-X

Ventilation: A Practical Guide
Nancy Clark, Thomas Cutter, and Jean-Ann McGrane
New York: Center for Occupational Safety, 1984
ISBN 0-918875-00-5

Government Safety Standards Resources

For extra help in complying with the Hazard Communication Standard (federal "Right to Know"), the following publications are available from:

Occupational Safety and Health Administration (OSHA)
Publication Office
Room N-3101
200 Constitution Avenue, N.W.
Washington, DC 20210
(202) 219-4667
http://www.osha.gov/

OSHA distributes these booklets free of charge:

Chemical Hazard Communication; OSHA 3084
A booklet describing overall OSHA compliance.

Hazard Communication Guidelines for Compliance; OSHA 3117
Hazard Communication Guidelines for Compliance; OSHA 3111
Two booklets specifically written for employers describing OSHA compliance.

Hazard Communication: A Compliance Kit; OSHA 3104
GPO order no. 929-022-00000-9
A step-by-step compliance.
This OSHA kit is sold for $18 through the address below:
Superintendent of Documents
U.S. Government Printing Office
Washington, DC, 20210
(202) 783-3238

OSHA Handbook for Small Businesses
U.S. Department of Labor, 1993
OSHA 2209 (revised)
(GPO order no. 029-016-001-441)
A handbook for general OSHA compliance for small businesses. Enclose a check for $4 made out to Superintendent of Documents at:
U.S. Government Printing Office
Washington, DC, 20210

National Institute for Occupational Safety and Health (NIOSH)
A division of the Center for Disease Control (CDC) and an excellent on-line source for chemical hazard information.
http://www.cdc.gov.niosh/

International Chemical Safety Cards (ICSC)
These cards give comprehensive containment, hazard, and handling information for thousands of chemicals and products.
http://www.cdc.gov.niosh/ipcs/icstart.html#international

First determine if you are regulated under state or federal OSHA rules. State regulated people should contact their state OSHA for publications and compliance materials. Those under the federal law should have a copy of the sections of the Code of Federal Regulations (CFR) that applies to their work. These are 29 CFR 1900-1910 (General Industry Standards) and 29 CFR 1926 (Construction Standards). Call your local OSHA office for information on obtaining copies.

Data Sheets

United Scenic Artists, Local 829 (IBPAT). The publications are free to all Local 829 members. Others may order them at $.25/page to cover copy and mailing costs. Contact:

M. Rossol
181 Thompson Street #23
New York, NY 10012-2586
(212) 777-0062

- A Hazard Communication Program—6 pages
  A fill-in-the-blanks program for employers.
- A Respiratory Protection Program—18 pages
  A fill-in-the-blanks program for employers.
- Americans with Disabilities in the Scenic Arts—5 pages
  ADA and EEOC regulations that apply to scenic work.
- Assessing Locations Hazards for Scenic Artists—6 pages
  Hazards in old buildings used for scenic studios.
- Carbon Monoxide Detectors—4 pages
  How to use CO detectors in shops where internal combustion engines and other CO sources are present.
- Hazard Communication Training Outline—6 pages
- Heat Exposure—1 page
  Dealing with shops in the summer.
- Reproductive Hazards—4 pages
  Chemicals used in scenic work that may affect reproduction and/or the fetus.
- Solvents—9 pages
  General discussion of the hazards of solvents and a chart listing technical data on over 50 common solvents.
- Threshold Limit Values—2 pages
  A simple way to understand and use this MSDS term.

- Understanding MSDSs—4 pages
  Definitions of the most common terms found on material safety data sheets.
- Urethane Resin Systems—3 pages
  Hazards and precautions for use of these systems.
- Using Artist's Paints—5 pages
  Hazards and precautions for safe use of these paints.
- Ventilation for Theaters and Shops—6 pages
  The types of ventilation discussed.

THEATRE REFERENCE PUBLICATIONS

Backstage Handbook:
  An Illustrated Almanac of Technical Information
Paul Carter
New York: Broadway Press, 1994
ISBN 0-91-174729-X

Designing and Drawing for the Theatre
Lynn Pecktal
New York: McGraw-Hill, Inc., 1995
ISBN 0-07-557232-X

Materials of the Scene: An Introduction to Technical Theatre
Welby B. Wolf
New York: Harper and Row, 1977
ISBN 0-06-047184-0

Scene Design and Stage Lighting, Sixth Edition
W. Oren Parker, Harvey K. Smith, and R. Craig Wolf
Fort Worth, TX: Holt, Rinehart, and Winston, 1990
ISBN 0-03-020761-4

Scenery for the Theatre
Harold Burris-Meyer and Edward Cole
Boston: Little, Brown, 1938
Library of Congress no. 72-154968

Scenography and Stage Technology
Willard Bellman
New York: Crowell, 1977
ISBN 0-690-00872-4

An Introduction to Scenic Design
A. S. Gillette
New York: Harper and Row, 1967
Library of Congress no. 67-11649

GENERAL SCENIC ARTISTRY REFERENCE PUBLICATIONS

Designing and Painting for the Theatre
Lynn Pecktal
New York: Holt, Rinehart, Winston, 1975
ISBN 0-03011901-4

Notes on Scene Painting
Bradford Ashworth and Donald Oenslager
New Haven, CT: Whitlock's, 1952, 1956

Secrets of Scene Painting and Stage Effects
Van Dyke Brown
London: Routledge and Sons, 1921

Scene Painting Tools and Techniques
Daniel Veaner
Englewood Cliffs, NJ: Prentice-Hall, 1987
ISBN 0-13-79-1658-2

Theatrical Scene Painting: A Lesson Guide
William H. Pinnell
Carbondale: Southern Illinois University Press, 1987
ISBN 0-80-931332-4

The Twin Cities Scenic Collection
University Art Museum
Minneapolis: University of Minnesota, 1987
ISBN 0-938713-01-9

PERSPECTIVE DRAWING REFERENCE PUBLICATIONS

Linear Perspective: Its History, Directions for Construction, and Aspects in the Environment and in the Fine Arts
Willy A. Bartschi
New York: Van Nostrand Reinhold, 1981
ISBN 0-442-24344-8

Perspective
Jose Maria Parramon
Tucson, AZ: H. P. Books, 1982
ISBN 0-8956-082-1

Perspective for Artists
Rex Vicat Cole
New York: Dover Publications, 1965
ISBN 0-486-22487-2

Perspective Drawing for the Theatre
Harry Morgan
New York: Drama Book Specialists, 1979
ISBN: 0-910-482-87-X

DRAFTING REFERENCE PUBLICATIONS

Basic Drafting
John Feirer and John Lindbeck
Peoria, IL: Chas. A. Bennett, 1978
ISBN 87002-273-3

Drafting for the Theatre
Dennis Dorn and Mark Shanda
Carbondale: Southern Illinois Press, 1990
ISBN 0-8093-1508-4

A Manual of Engineering Drawing
Thomas E. French and Charles J. Vierck
New York: McGraw Hill, 1953

DRAWING AND PAINTING REFERENCE PUBLICATIONS

The Figure in Motion
Thomas Easley
New York: Watson-Guptill, 1986
ISBN 0-8230-1618-8

The Natural Way to Draw
Kimon Nicolaïdes
Boston: Houghton Mifflin, 1941
ISBN 0-395-20548-4

The Seeing Hand: Treasury of Master Drawings
Colin T. Eisler
New York: Harper and Row, 1975
ISBN 0-06-011143-7

COLOR REFERENCE PUBLICATIONS

The Art of Color
Johannes Itten
New York: Van Nostrand Reinhold, 1973
ISBN 0-04-4224037-6

Color
Paul Zelanski and Mary Pat Fisher
Englewood Cliffs, NJ: Prentice Hall, 1984
ISBN 013-151259-5

Colour: Why the World Isn't Gray
Hazel Rossotti
New York: Penguin, 1983
ISBN 0-1-402201-4

Theory and Use of Color
Luigina De Grandis
New York: Abrams, 1986
ISBN 0-8109-2317-3

PAINTING TECHNIQUE REFERENCE PUBLICATIONS

Airbrush: The Complete Studio Handbook
Radu Vero
New York: Watson-Guptill, 1983
ISBN 0-8230-00166

The Big Book of Oil Painting
Jose Maria Parramon
New York: Watson-Guptill, 1985
ISBN 0-8230-00495-3

Gold Leaf Techniques
Raymond J. Leblanc
Cincinnati, OH: Signs of the Times Publishing, 1980
ISBN 0-911380-50-7

The Illuminated Landscape
Peter Poskas
New York: Watson-Guptill, 1987
ISBN 0-8230-2533-0

Lettering Tips
Bill Gray
New York, London: W. W. Norton, 1996
ISBN 0-3-937300-50

Sign Painting Techniques
Ralph Gregory
Cincinnati, OH: Signs of the Times Publishing, 1973
ISBN 0-9113-8029-9

Sign Work: A Craftsman's Manual
Bill Stewart
London: Collins Professional and
    Technical Publishing, 1984
ISBN 0-00-383068-3

DECORATIVE PAINTING REFERENCE PUBLICATIONS

The Art of Decorative Stenciling
Adele Bishop and Cile Lord
New York: Viking Press, 1976
ISBN 0-67013458-9

The Art of Marbling
Stuart Spencer
London: MacDonald and Company, 1988
ISBN 0-517-57-120-X

The Art of the Painted Finish for Furniture and Decoration
Isabel O'Neil
New York: Morrow, 1971
Library of Congress no. 70-151928

The Art of Woodgraining
Stuart Spencer
London: MacDonald and Company, 1989
ISBN 0-356-17536-7

Decorating with Paint
Jocasta Innes
Avenal, NJ: Random House, 1997
ISBN 0-517-57229-X

International Book of Woods
Martyn Bramwell
New York: Crescent, 1976
ISBN 0517-44384-8

New Paint Magic
Jocasta Innes
Avenal, NJ: Random House, 1997
ISBN 0-517-19285-3

Parry's Graining and Marbling
John P. Parry, B. Rhodes, and J. Windsor
London: Collins Professional and Technica
    Publishing, 1949
ISBN 0-00-383131-0

Professional Painted Finishes
Ina Marx, Allen Marx, and Robert Marx
New York: Watson-Guptill, 1991
ISBN 0-8230-4418-1

Trompe l'Oeil Painted Architecture
Miriam Milman
New York: Skira/Rizzoli, 1986
ISBN 0-8478-0713-4

Trompe l'Oeil Painting
Miriam Milman
Geneva: Skira, 1982
ISBN 0-3333415-38

Wood and Woodgrains
Phil Brodatz
New York: Dover, 1971
ISBN 0-486-22424-4

ARTIST'S MATERIAL REFERENCE PUBLICATIONS

The Artist's Handbook
Ray Smith
New York: Alfred A. Knopf, 1987
ISBN 0-394-55585-6

The Artist's Handbook of Materials and Techniques
Ralph Mayer
Updated by Steven Sheehan
New York: Viking, 1991
ISBN 0-6-7083701-6

The Materials and Techniques of Painting
Kurt Wehlte
New York: Van Nostrand Reinhold, 1975
ISBN 0-442-29162-0

*Henley's Twentieth Century Book of
    Formulas, Processes and Trade Secrets*
Norman W. Henley
London: Norman W. Henley Publishing, 1937
ISBN 0-87781-0281-1

PICTORIAL REFERENCE PUBLICATIONS

An Age of Barns
Eric Sloane
New York: Funk and Wagnalls, 1967
ISBN 345-24680-2-595

Architecture of the Western World
Michael Reaburn
London: Orbis, 1980
ISBN 0-8478-0435-6

The Artistic Anatomy of Trees
Rex Vicat Cole
New York: Dover, 1965
ISBN 0-356017536-7

Decorators Supply Corporation
3610 South Morgan Street
Chicago, IL 60609
(312) 847-6300
Plaster Ornaments; Catalogue no. 130
Capitols and Brackets; Catalogue no. 127
Mantels; Catalogue no. 131

A Dictionary of Architecture
Nikolaus Pevsner, John Fleming, and Hugh Honour
London: Allen Lane, 1975
ISBN 0-87951-040-4

Early American Stencils on Walls and Furniture
Janet Waring
New York: Dover, 1973
ISBN 0-486-21906-2

Florid Victorian Ornament
Karl Klimsch
New York: Dover, 1977
ISBN 0-486-23490-8

The Glory of the English House
Lionel Esher
Boston: Bulfinch, 1991
ISBN 0-8212-1851-4

Handbook of Ornament
Franz Sales Meyer
New York: Dover, 1957
ISBN 486-29392-6

Handbook of Painted Decoration
Yannick Guégan and Roger Le Puil
New York: W. W. Norton, 1996
ISBN 0-393-730018

Historic Ornament
C. B. Griesbach
New York: Dover, 1975
ISBN 0-486-23215-8

Illustrated Dictionary of Historic Architecture
Cyril M. Harris
New York: McGraw-Hill, 1975
ISBN 0-070-26756-1

Lettering in Architecture
Alan Bartram
New York: Whitney Library of Design, 1976
ISBN 0-8230-7340-8

Miniature Rooms: The Thorne Rooms at the Art Institute of Chicago
The Art Institute of Chicago
New York: Abbeville, 1983
ISBN 0-89659-408-4

Period Details: A Sourcebook for House Restoration
Martin Miller and Judith Miller
New York: Crown, 1987
ISBN 0-51788013-X

Pugin's Gothic Ornament
Augustus C. Pugin
New York: Dover, 1987
ISBN 0-486-25500-X

The Styles of Ornament
Alexander Speltz
New York: Dover, 1959
ISBN 486-20557-6

Surfaces
Judy A. Juracek
New York and London: W. W. Norton, 1996
ISBN 0-393-73007-7

Wallpaper: A History
Francoise Teynac, Pierre Nolot, and Jean-Denis Vivien
New York: Rizzoli, 1982
ISBN 0-8478-0434-8

Wallpapers of France, 1800–1850
Odile Nouvel
New York: Rizzoli, 1981
ISBN 0-302-00547-1

INSPIRATION AND CATS

Concerning the Spiritual in Art
Wassily Kandinsky
New York: Dover, 1977
ISBN 0-486-23411-8

Why Cats Paint: A Theory of Feline Aesthetics
Heather Busch and Burton Silver
Berkeley, CA: Ten Speed Press, 1994
ISBN 0-89815-612-2

THEATRICAL MATERIAL REFERENCE PUBLICATIONS AND RESOURCES

The New York Theatrical Sourcebook
(Updated Yearly)
New York: Broadway Press
ISBN 0-911747-16-8

TCI Buyers Guide
A publication of *Theatre Crafts International Magazine*
New York: Intertec, 1996
32 West 18th Street
New York, NY 10011-4612
(212) 229-2965
Fax: (212) 229-2084

Musson Equipment Manufacturers
http://www.musson.com/manufact.htm
Maintains a Web site of theatrical suppliers' links.

PAINTING TOOLS AND MATERIALS RESOURCES

Bamboo Suppliers

Bamboo and Rattan Works, Inc.
470 Oberlin Avenue
South Lakewood, NJ 08701
(908) 370-0220

Scenic Brushes Suppliers

A. Haussmann International Corporation
132 Ninth Street
San Francisco, CA 94103
(415) 431-1336
Fax: (415) 863-0959

Epstein Sons, Inc.
809 Ninth Avenue
New York, NY 10019
(212) 265-3960
Fax: (212) 765-8841

Gothic Coatings, Inc.
P.O. Box 268
Glen Cove, NY 11542
(516) 759-3300

Janovic/Plaza
30-35 Thomson Avenue
Long Island City, NY 11101
(718) 786-4444
Fax: (718) 361-7288
http://www.janovic.com/products.htm

Mann Brothers
757 North La Brea Avenue
Los Angeles, CA 90038
(213) 936-5168
(800) 245-MANN
Fax: (213) 936-1980

Pearl Paint
308 Canal Street
New York, NY 10013
(212) 431-7932
(800) 221-6845
Fax: (212) 431-6798

Rosco Laboratories, Inc. (East Coast Office)
52 Harbor View Avenue
Stamford, CT 06902
(203) 708-8900
(800) ROSCO-NY
Fax: (203) 708-8919
http://www.rosco.com/

Rosco Laboratories, Inc. (West Coast Office)
1135 N. Highland Drive
Hollywood, CA 90038
(213) 462-2233
(800) ROSCO-LA
Fax: (213) 426-3338
http://www.rosco.com/

Rose Brand (East Coast Office)
517 West 35th Street
New York, NY 10001
(212) 594-7424
(800) 223-1624
Fax: (212) 629-4826
http://www.rosebrand.com/

Rose Brand (West Coast Office)
10856 Vanowen Street
North Hollywood, CA 91605
(818) 505-6290
(800) 360-5056
http://www.rosebrand.com/

Wolf Paints (Division of Janovic/Plaza)
771 Ninth Avenue
New York, NY 10019
(212) 245-3241
Fax: (212) 974-0591

Flame Retardant Services and Suppliers

BMI Supply (New York Office)
28 Logan Avenue
Glens Falls, NY 12801
(518) 793-6706
(800) 836-0524
Fax: 518-793-6181

BMI Supply (South Carolina Office)
60 Air View Drive
Greenville, SC 29607
(864) 288-8983
(800) 670-4264
Fax: (864) 288-0841

Bonomo's Grace Ltd.
8 Ivy Court
Reisterstown, MD 21136
(410) 526-6283
(800) 289-1420
Fax: (410) 526-4889
110313.220@compuserve.com

DuPont Co.
1007 Market Street
Wilmington, DE 19898
(800) 755-9762

Spartan Flame Retardants, Inc.
345 E. Terracotta Avenue
Crystal Lake, IL 60014
(815) 242-2265
(800) 435-5700
Fax: (815) 459-8560

Refer to Rosco Laboratories and
   Rose Brand from Scenic Brushes
   Suppliers section.

World Wide Coatings
P.O. Box 27638
Tucson, AZ 85726
(800) 626-7983
Fax: (520) 885-0906

Zeller International Ltd.
Main Street, Box Z
Downsville, NY 13755
Orders: (800) 722-8739
Technical: (607) 363-7792
Fax: (607) 363-2071

Garden Sprayer Manufacturers and Suppliers

Chapin Manufacturing
(800) 444-3140

H. D. Hudson Manufacturing Co.
500 North Michigan Avenue
Chicago, IL 60611
(312) 644-2830
Fax: (312) 644-7989
http://www.hdhudson.com

Pneumatic Spray Gun Manufacturers and Suppliers

Binks Manufacturing Co.
9201 Belmount Street
Franklin Park, IL 60131
(312) 671-3000

De Vilbiss Co.
300 Philips Avenue
Toledo, OH 43612
(419) 474-5411

Theatrical Paints, Dyes, and Finishes Suppliers

Refer to A. Haussmann International and Epstein
   Sons, Inc. from Scenic Brushes Suppliers section.

Golden Artist Colors, Inc.
188 Bell Road
New Berlin, NY 13411
(607) 847-6154
(800) 959-6543
Fax: (607) 847-6767
http://www.goldenpaints.com

Refer to Gothic Coatings, Janovic/Plaza,
   Mann Brothers, Pearl Paint, Rosco Laboratories,
   and Rose Brand from Scenic Brushes Suppliers section.

Sculptural Arts Coatings, Inc.
901-B Norwalk Street
Greensboro, NC 27407
(910) 229-7579
(800) 743-0379
Fax: (910) 229-1359

Refer to Wolf Paints from Scenic Brushes Suppliers section.

The Paint/Coatings Net
http://www.horizonweb.com/pcn/pcnmain.htm

Aniline Dyes
Manufacturers and Suppliers

Alcone Co., Inc.
4-49 49th Avenue
Long Island City, NY 11101
(718) 361-8373
Fax: (718) 729-8296

Aljo Mfg. Co., Inc.
81-83 Franklin Street
New York, NY 10013
(212) 226-2878 and (212) 966-4046
Fax: (212) 274-9616

Refer to A. Haussmann International,
  Epstein Sons, Inc., Gothic Coatings, Janovic/Plaza,
  and Mann Brothers from Scenic Brushes Suppliers
  section.

Tricon Colors, Inc.
16 Leliarts Lane
Elmwood Park, NJ 07407
(201) 794-3800 and (201) 797-4664

Bronzing Powders
Manufacturers and Suppliers

Crescent Bronze Powders
3400 N. Avondale Avenue
Chicago, IL 60618
(312) 539-2441
(800) 445-6810
Fax: (312) 539-1131

Refer to A. Haussmann International, Alcone Co.,
  Epstein Sons, Gothic Coatings, Janovic/Plaza,
  and Mann Brothers from previous sections.

Adhesives and Textures
Manufacturers and Suppliers

Cementex Latex Corp.
121 Varick Street
New York, NY 10013
(212) 741-1770
(800) 782-9056
Fax: (212) 627-2770

Refer to Gothic Coatings from Scenic Brushes
  Suppliers section.

Industrial Adhesives
6516 Massachusetts Avenue
Indianapolis, IN 46218
(317) 541-1100

Spectra Dynamics (Phlexglue)
415 Marble N.W.
Albuquerque, NM 87102
(505) 843-7202

Plastic Coatings Corporation
4904 Texas Valley Road
Scotts Depot, WV 25560
(304) 755-9151

Refer to Rosco Laboratories from
  Scenic Brushes Suppliers section.

3M Company
3M Center
St. Paul, MN 55144
(612) 737-6501
(800) 364-3577
Fax: (800) 713-6329
http://www.mmm.com/

Schools, Unions, and Organizations

Cobalt Studios
P.O. Box 79
White Lake, NY 12786
(914) 583-7025
cobalt@catskill.com

United Scenic Artists (U.S.A.)
16 West 61st Street, 11th Floor
New York, NY 10023
(212) 581-0300
usa829@aol.com
http://frontpage1.shadow.net/usa829fl/
Chicago Office: (312) 857-0829
Los Angeles Office: (213) 965-0957
Miami Office: (305) 596-4772

United States Institute of Theatre Technology (U.S.I.T.T.)
6443 Ridings Road
Syracuse, NY 13206
(800) 93-USITT
http://www.ffa.ucalgary.ca/usitt/

International Alliance of Theatrical Stage Employees (I.A.T.S.E.)
Suite 601 1515 Broadway
New York, NY 10036
(212) 730-1770
http://www.iatse.lm.com/

Bibliography

"Art in the Theatre: The Decline of Scenic Art in America." *Magazine of Art* (April 1894).

Ashworth, Bradford. *Notes on Scene Painting.* New Haven, CT: Whitlock's, 1952, 1956.

Association of Theatrical Artists and Craftspeople. *The New York Source Book.* New York: Source Book Press, 1997.

Auletti, Toni. "The Use of a Computer Painting Machine for Theatrical Applications." Masters thesis, University of Michigan, 1995.

Bablet, Denis. *Esthétique Générale du Décor de Théâtre de 1870 à 1914.* Paris: Centre National de la Recherche Scientifique, 1975.

Brockman, Lance. "Revisiting the Twin Cities Scenic Collection." *Theatre Design and Technology* (Winter 1997).

————. *Theatre of the Fraternity.* Jackson: University Press of Mississippi, 1996.

————. *The Twin Cities Scenic Collection.* Minneapolis: University Art Museum, University of Minnesota, 1987.

Burris-Meyer, Harold, and Edward Cole. *Scenery for the Theatre.* Boston: Little, Brown and Co., 1938.

Cambell, Lily B. *Scenes and Machines on the English Stage.* Cambridge: Cambridge University Press, 1923.

Cole, Rex Vicat. *Perspective for the Artist.* New York: Dover Publications, Inc., 1976.

Coquiot, Gustave. *Nouveau Manuel Complet de Peintres-Decorateurs de Théâtre.* Paris: Roret, 1910.

Decugis, Nicole, and Suzanne Reymond. *Le Décor de Théâtre en France du Moyen Age à 1925.* Paris: Compagnie Française des Arts Graphiques, 1953.

De Grandis, Luigina. *Theory and Use of Color.* New York: Harry N. Abrams, Inc., 1984.

Edgerton, Samuel Y., Jr. *The Renaissance Rediscovery of Linear Perspective.* New York: Harper and Row, 1975.

Fontanesi, Francesco. *Illustrazioni Teatrali.* 1812.

Galli Bibiena, Ferdinando. *L'architettura,* trans. Dunbar H. Ogden. Berkeley: University of California Press, 1978.

————. *Direzioni,* trans. Dunbar H. Ogden. Berkeley: University of California Press, 1978.

Gregory, Ralph. *Sign Painting Techniques.* Cincinnati: Signs of the Times Publishing Co., 1973.

Hughes, Glenn. *A History of the American Theatre 1700–1950.* London: Samuel French, 1951.

Itten, Johannes. *The Art of Color.* New York: Reinhold Publishing Corporation, 1961.

Joseph, Stephen. *Scene Painting and Design.* London: Pitman and Sons, 1964.

Lancaster, Henry Carrington, trans. *Mémoire de Mahelot, Laurent et d'autres décorateurs de l'Hôtel de Bourgogne.* Paris: Champion, 1920.

Larson, Orville K. *Scene Design in the American Theatre from 1915 to 1960.* Fayetteville: University of Arkansas Press, 1989.

Lucie-Smith, Edward. *Dictionary of Art Terms.* London: Thames and Hudson, 1984.

Mancini, Franco. *Scenographia Italiano del Rinascimento al'eta Romantica.* Rome: Fratelli Fabbri Editori, 1966.

Mayer, Ralph. *The Artist's Handbook of Materials and Techniques.* New York: Viking Press, 1940.

McCann, Michael. *Artist Beware.* New York: Watson-Guptill, 1979.

Moynet, Jean. *French Theatrical Production in the Nineteenth Century,* trans. Allan Jackson. Binghamton, NY: Center for Modern Theatre Research, 1976.

Nicoll, Allardyce. *The Development of the Theatre.* New York: Harcourt, Brace and World, 1966.

Ogden, Dunbar H. *The Italian Baroque Stage.* Berkeley: University of California Press, 1978.

Orsini, Baldassare. *Geometria,* trans. Dunbar H. Ogden. Berkeley: University of California Press, 1978.

————. *Le Scene,* trans. Dunbar H. Ogden. Berkeley: University of California Press, 1978.

Pecktal, Lynn. *Designing and Painting for the Theatre.* New York: Holt, Rinehart, Winston, 1975.

Polakov, Lester. *We Live to Paint Again.* New York: Logbooks Press, 1993

Polunin, Vladimir. *The Continental Method of Scene Painting.* London: Dance Books Ltd., [1927] 1980.

Pozzo, Andrea. *Prospettiva*, trans. Dunbar H. Ogden. Berkeley: University of California Press, 1978.

Rose, A. *Scenes for Scene Painters*. London: George Routledge and Sons, 1925.

Rosenfeld, Sybil. *Georgian Scene Painters and Scene Painting*. Cambridge: Cambridge University Press, 1981.

———. *A Short History of Scene Design in Great Britain*. Totowa, NJ: Rowman and Littlefield, 1973.

Rossol, Monona. *The Artist's Complete Health and Safety Guide*. New York: Allworth Press, 1994.

———. *Stage Fright*. New York: ACTS, 1987.

Scholz, János, ed. *Baroque and Romantic Stage Design*. New York: E. P. Dutton and Co., 1962.

Simonson, Lee. *The Stage Is Set*. New York: Theatre Arts Books, 1970.

———, ed. *Theatre Art*. New York: W. W. Norton and Co., 1934.

Smith, Ray. *The Artist's Handbook*. New York: Alfred A. Knopf, 1987.

Southern, Richard. *Changeable Scenery*. London: Faber and Faber, 1951.

———. *The Seven Ages of Theatre*. New York: Hill and Wang, 1971.

"Stage Scenery and the Men Who Paint It." *Theatre Magazine* 16 (August 1908).

TCI. *Buyers Guide*. New York: Intertec Publishing, 1997.

Troili, Giulio. *Paradossi*, trans. Dunbar H. Ogden. Berkeley: University of California Press, 1978.

Vitruvius. *The Ten Books on Architecture*, trans. Morris Hickey Morgan. New York: Dover, 1960.

Wagman, Howard M. "Bristle and Its Importance to the American Paint Brush Industry." Masters thesis, Graduate Division of the Wharton School, University of Pennsylvania, 1952.

Wischmeier, Randolph Jay. "A History of the United Scenic Artists, Local Union 829 and Local Union 350," Masters thesis, University of Texas–Austin, 1978.

Wolcott, John R. "The Scene Painter's Palette: 1750-1835." *Theatre Journal* 33, no.4 (December 1981).

Index